EMPRESS MARIE THERESE AND MUSIC AT THE VIENNESE COURT, 1792–1807

This is the first study of the musical achievements of Empress Marie Therese, one of the most important patrons in the Vienna of Haydn and Beethoven. Building on extensive archival research, including many documents published here for the first time, John A. Rice describes Marie Therese's activities as commissioner, collector, and performer of music, and explores the rich and diverse musical culture that she fostered at court. This book, which will be of interest to musicologists, historians of artistic patronage and taste, and students of women and music, elucidates this remarkable woman's relations with a host of professional musicians, including Haydn, and argues that she played a significant and hitherto unsuspected role in the inception of one of the era's greatest masterpieces, Beethoven's *Fidelio*.

JOHN A. RICE is a musical historian who has taught and published widely. In addition to many journal articles on eighteenth-century music he has published two books, *W. A. Mozart: La clemenza di Tito* (Cambridge, 1991) and *Antonio Salieri and Viennese Opera* (Chicago, 1998), recipient of the American Musicological Society's Kinkeldey Award.

Marie Therese at the harp, with her father King Ferdinand IV of Naples, her mother
Queen Maria Carolina, and two of her siblings. Detail of a painting of the Neapolitan
royal family by Angelica Kauffmann.

EMPRESS MARIE THERESE AND MUSIC AT THE VIENNESE COURT, 1792–1807

JOHN A. RICE

CAMBRIDGE
UNIVERSITY PRESS

PUBLISHED BY THE PRESS SYNDICATE OF THE UNIVERSITY OF CAMBRIDGE
The Pitt Building, Trumpington Street, Cambridge CB2 1RP, United Kingdom

CAMBRIDGE UNIVERSITY PRESS
The Edinburgh Building, Cambridge, CB2 2RU, UK
40 West 20th Street, New York, NY 10011–4211, USA
477 Williamstown Road, Port Melbourne, VIC 3207, Australia
Ruiz de Alarcón 13, 28014 Madrid, Spain
Dock House, The Waterfront, Cape Town 8001, South Africa

http://www.cambridge.org

© John A. Rice 2003

First published 2003

Printed in the United Kingdom at the University Press, Cambridge

Typeface Adobe Garamond 11/12.5 pt.   *System* LATEX 2$_\varepsilon$ [TB]

A catalogue record for this book is available from the British Library

ISBN 0 521 82512 1 hardback

For my father
Eugene F. Rice Jr.

Contents

Acknowledgments

I presented parts of this book as papers at congresses of the International Musicological Society in London (1997) and Louvain (2002), at the conferences "L'Opéra-comique à l'époque de Boieldieu" (Rouen, 2001), "Simon Mayr und Wien" (Ingolstadt, 2001), and "Domenico Cimarosa: un napoletano in Europa" (Aversa, 2001), and at colloquia at Rice University (1997) and the University of Southern California (2002). I am most grateful to those who organized the conferences and colloquia for inviting me to participate and to those who attended the talks for their comments and questions.

Studies of musical patronage, especially when they have as their central figures musicians as energetic, cosmopolitan, and adventurous as Empress Marie Therese, cross many lines separating more frequently cultivated fields of scholarship, such as those involving single composers and genres. One of the chief pleasures of writing this book was the contact into which it brought me with a large number of scholars, including several outside of musicology, who generously shared their expertise and specialized knowledge with someone they may legitimately have felt was trespassing on their turf. I have thanked many of them in footnotes. But many others contributed to this book, including Evan Baker, Dwight Blazin, Peter Branscombe, Walther Brauneis, Annedore Brock, Bruce Alan Brown, David Charlton, Malcolm S. Cole, Franz Eichenseher, Cliff Eisen, Christine Getz, Alvar Gonzalez-Palacios, Géza Hajós, Kathleen Kuzmick Hansell, Ernst Hintermaier, Leopold Kantner, Thomas Leibnitz, Bruce C. MacIntyre, Jeremiah W. McGrann, Paolo Mechelli, Robert Münster, Rupert Ridgewell, Ronald T. Shaheen, Tomislav Volek, and Neal Zaslaw. To all of them I express heartfelt gratitude.

The staffs of the Haus-, Hof- und Staatsarchiv and the Wiener Stadtbibliothek were as expert and helpful as they have always been. In the Musiksammlung of the Österreichische Nationalbibliothek the former director Günter Brosche gave me access to manuscript inventories of the

Kaisersammlung, while Ingeborg Birkin-Feichtinger provided useful information and advice on numerous occasions. Otto Biba, director of the archive of the Gesellschaft der Musikfreunde, shared with me his knowledge of Viennese musical culture and helped me identify items from the Kaisersammlung that form part of his collection. Martin Czernin, archivist of the Schottenstift, made available to me the autographs of church music written by Joseph Eybler for the empress and a quiet place to study them.

The British Library, the Boston Public Library, the New York Public Library, the Pierpont Morgan Library, and the libraries of Rice University, the University of Texas, the University of Minnesota, the University of California at Los Angeles, the University of California at Berkeley, the University of Southern California, the University of Iowa, and Harvard University have generously allowed me to use their collections. The Rochester Public Library in Rochester, Minnesota provided me with both a pleasant place to work and – by way of its efficient inter-library loan service – scholarly books from around the country.

Michael Lorenz and Dorothea Link read an early version of the typescript and gave me much helpful advice. Dr. Lorenz in addition checked my transcriptions of Viennese documents against the originals and answered many queries involving Viennese culture and language. Rita Steblin took time out of her busy schedule of research and teaching in Vienna to inspect and in some cases transcribe documents and musical manuscripts. Lorenzo della Chà read and corrected my transcriptions of documents in Italian.

Two of the composers whose music Marie Therese especially loved are the subject of research by scholars who helped me greatly. Charles H. Sherman, having devoted much of his life to the music of Michael Haydn, gave me the benefit of his vast knowledge of documents related to Haydn's life and of sources for his music. Wolfram Enßlin, who recently finished a dissertation on Ferdinando Paer, sent me copies of parts of the dissertation and of several librettos set by Paer and answered numerous queries.

Eva Badura-Skoda chaired the sessions at the congresses of the International Musicological Society in 1997 and 2002 in which I discussed Marie Therese's musical activities. She followed the project during the intervening years, equally generous in her musicological guidance and her Viennese hospitality.

For more than a decade Dexter Edge has shared with me his knowledge of eighteenth-century musical sources and concert life, and his enthusiasm and intellectual vigor have repeatedly energized my own research. As this book neared completion, he read the typescript (some parts of it in more than one draft) and commented on it with a thoroughness and insightfulness that allowed me to improve it greatly.

My wife Mariza and my daughter Lydia have put up gracefully with my fascination with Marie Thérèse, and even (I hope) shared it a little.

Rochester, Minnesota
October 2002

Illustrations

Tables

Musical examples

Abbreviations

A-Wgm	Vienna, Gesellschaft der Musikfreunde, Archiv
A-Wn	Vienna, Österreichische Nationalbibliothek, Musiksammlung
A-Ws	Vienna, Schottenstift, Archiv
A-Wth	Vienna, Österreichisches Theatermuseum
AmZ	*Allgemeine musikalische Zeitung*
CaM	*Catalogo alter Musickalien*, inventory of the Kaisersammlung in A-Wn (see chapter 1)
D-Bds	Berlin, Deutsche Staatsbibliothek
H-Bn	Budapest, National Széchényi Library
Herrmann	Hildegard Herrmann, *Thematisches Verzeichnis der Werke von Joseph Eybler*, Munich, 1976
HHStA, Fa	Vienna, Haus-, Hof- und Staatsarchiv, Familienarchiv HKF Handarchiv Kaiser Franz Sb Sammelbände
HSS	*Hof- und Staats-Schematismus der röm. kaiserl. auch kaiserl. königl. und erzherzoglichen Haupt- und Residenz-Stadt Wien*, Vienna, 1795–1805
I-Fc	Florence, Conservatorio Luigi Cherubini
KK	*Kathalog der Kirchenmusickalien*, inventory of Marie Therese's church music in HHStA (see appendix 1)
MT	Marie Therese
Poštolka	Milan Poštolka, "Thematisches Verzeichnis der Sinfonien Pavel Vranickys," *Miscellanea musicologica* 20 (1967), 101–27
Robinson	Michael F. Robinson, *Giovanni Paisiello: A Thematic Catalogue of His Works*, 2 vols., Stuyvesant, NY, 1991
Schröder	Dorothea Schröder, *Die geistliche Vokalkompositionen Johann Georg Albrechtsbergers*, 2 vols., Hamburg, 1987
Sherman	Charles H. Sherman and T. Donley Thomas, *Johann Michael Haydn (1737–1806): A Chronological Thematic Catalogue of His Works*, Stuyvesant, NY, 1993

Two intertwining family trees:
The Habsburg-Lorraines of Austria and the
Bourbons of Spain and Naples

This very selective genealogy indicates relations between, and is largely limited to, members of the Habsburg-Lorraine and Bourbon families mentioned in this book.

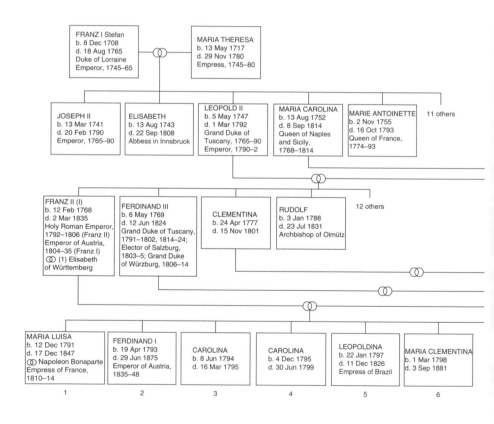

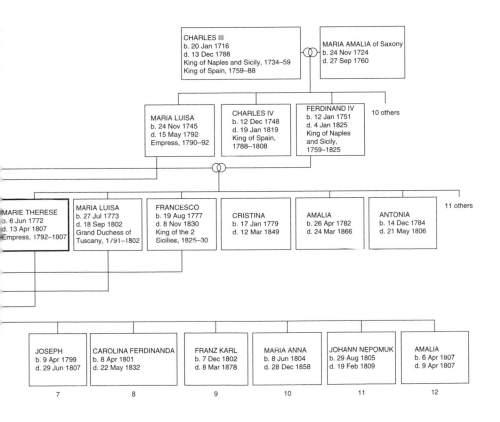

CHARLES III
b. 20 Jan 1716
d. 13 Dec 1788
King of Naples and Sicily, 1734–59
King of Spain, 1759–88

MARIA AMALIA of Saxony
b. 24 Nov 1724
d. 27 Sep 1760

MARIA LUISA
b. 24 Nov 1745
d. 15 May 1792
Empress, 1790–92

CHARLES IV
b. 12 Dec 1748
d. 19 Jan 1819
King of Spain,
1788–1808

FERDINAND IV
b. 12 Jan 1751
d. 4 Jan 1825
King of Naples
and Sicily,
1759–1825

10 others

MARIE THERESE
b. 6 Jun 1772
d. 13 Apr 1807
Empress, 1792–1807

MARIA LUISA
b. 27 Jul 1773
d. 18 Sep 1802
Grand Duchess of
Tuscany, 1791–1802

FRANCESCO
b. 19 Aug 1777
d. 8 Nov 1830
King of the 2
Sicilies, 1825–30

CRISTINA
b. 17 Jan 1779
d. 12 Mar 1849

AMALIA
b. 26 Apr 1782
d. 24 Mar 1866

ANTONIA
b. 14 Dec 1784
d. 21 May 1806

11 others

JOSEPH
b. 9 Apr 1799
d. 29 Jun 1807

CAROLINA FERDINANDA
b. 8 Apr 1801
d. 22 May 1832

FRANZ KARL
b. 7 Dec 1802
d. 8 Mar 1878

MARIA ANNA
b. 8 Jun 1804
d. 28 Dec 1858

JOHANN NEPOMUK
b. 29 Aug 1805
d. 19 Feb 1809

AMALIA
b. 6 Apr 1807
d. 9 Apr 1807

7   8   9   10   11   12

A note about quotations and transcriptions of documents

When quoting from texts in languages other than English I have used my own translations, except where specifically indicated. When the source for a quotation is an unpublished document or a printed text that might not be readily available to readers with access to a good scholarly library and inter-library loan services, I have generally given the original in a footnote. One exception to this policy involves the words of Marie Therese herself, which I have always quoted in the original language (when this has been accessible to me) as well as in English translation.

In quotations that include references to keyboard instruments with strings, I have left the notoriously ambiguous words *cembalo*, *clavecin*, and *Klavier* untranslated.

In transcriptions of documents I have kept editorial interventions to a minimum and have made no attempt to bring capitalization, punctuation, and spelling into agreement with current practice.

Introduction

Yesterday morning at 10 was the rehearsal of the mass. At first a little bashfully, but with gradually rising courage, the empress sang all her solos, but especially the *Et incarnatus est de spiritu sancto ex Maria virgine* (all of which she did quite pleasantly) and the *Benedictus*, very accurately and charmingly. But what gave me most pleasure was her satisfaction with my composition. Again and again: "Bravo!" "Schön!" And her highest expression was: "Haydn! Superb!"

Don't be angry! But I have fallen in love with my most gracious empress. She is also a beautiful, warm-hearted woman.[1]

Thus in 1801 Michael Haydn wrote to his wife of a rehearsal of a mass commissioned by Empress Marie Therese.[2] Second wife of Emperor Franz II from 1790 and empress from 1792 to her death in 1807, from complications arising from the birth of her twelfth child, Marie Therese devoted much of her short life to music. She played the piano and sang, organized and participated in many private concerts, compiled a large music library, and befriended and supported professional musicians. With these activities, which brought her into fruitful contact with some of Europe's finest composers and performers, she helped shape Viennese musical life during the period when Michael Haydn's older brother was writing his last works and Beethoven his first masterpieces, winning for herself a place among the leading musical patrons of the age.

As eldest daughter of King Ferdinand IV and Queen Maria Carolina of Naples, Marie Therese grew up at the Neapolitan court, where she was given thorough musical training. Her keyboard teacher Vincenzo Orgitano wrote a vast amount of music for her, mostly sonatas that she played on a piano built by the celebrated Johann Andreas Stein of Augsburg.[3] In

---

[1] Michael Haydn to his wife, Vienna, 24 September 1801, in Hans Jancik, *Michael Haydn: Ein vergessener Meister*, Vienna, 1952, 239.

[2] I adopt this version of her name (French, but without the accents), frequently used by historians to distinguish her from her more famous grandmother, the Maria Theresa who ruled from 1740 to 1780.

[3] On Orgitano, his keyboard music for MT, and its place in the musical life of the Neapolitan court see Hanns-Bertold Dietz, "Instrumental Music at the Court of Ferdinand IV of Naples and Sicily

correspondence about Marie Therese's future marriage to her cousin Franz, Maria Carolina sent Emperor Leopold II, Franz's father, a description of her daughter that mentioned her musical abilities: "Elle sait la musique bien, le clavecin, le chant, un peu de harpe; elle danse bien."[4] A painting of the Neapolitan royal family by Angelica Kauffmann shows her as a teenager at the harp (frontispiece).

Marie Therese's musical taste was shaped by two primary influences. On the one hand she absorbed the language and aesthetic values of Neapolitan music, with its emphasis on vocal melody and improvised embellishment and its allegiance to the castrated male voice. On the other hand her mother, an archduchess of Austria and daughter of Maria Theresa, inculcated in her a love for and knowledge of the Viennese musical tradition, with its emphasis on craftsmanship, harmonic sophistication, and richness of instrumental color. In Vienna she gave expression to both sides of her musical personality, and in her patronage and performance she championed the synthesis of these traditions. Several of the composers she favored, including Johann Simon Mayr, Ferdinando Paer, and Peter Winter, successfully straddled the musical cultures of Italy and Germany.

These same composers were among the most popular in Vienna during her reign, partly because she helped to mold Viennese taste through her influence on the repertory in the court theaters. But long before her arrival, Vienna had been a musical melting pot, out of which came composers who could "bind all the power of German music to the sweet Italian style," as one critic wrote of Antonio Salieri.[5] The empress owed some of her success as a patron to the fact that her hybrid musical taste to a large extent embodied that of many of her Viennese subjects.

Partly in reaction to the dark times in which she reigned – wars with France and increasing political repression in Austria – Marie Therese often withdrew from Viennese society to the palaces of Schönbrunn and Laxenburg. There she immersed herself in music and other arts and entertainments, amusing herself and her rapidly growing brood and giving her husband respites from the cares of government with plays, games, and fancy-dress balls. Her music-making, under these circumstances, followed two separate paths. In a series of private concerts in which neither her

---

and the Works of Vincenzo Orgitano," *International Journal of Musicology* 1 (1992), 99–126. On MT's ownership of a Stein piano see John A. Rice, "Stein's 'Favorite Instrument': A Vis-à-vis Piano-Harpsichord in Naples," *Journal of the American Musical Instrument Society* 21 (1995), 34, 56.
[4] Maria Carolina to Leopold, 21 April 1790, HHStA, Fa, Sb, Kart. 19.
[5] "Salieri, der die ganze Kraft der deutschen Musik mit der süsseren italiänischen zu verbinden weiss" (*Musikalisches Wochenblatt* [Berlin], 1791, p. 15).

husband nor her children participated, her performances increased in seriousness and scope. But much of the music she commissioned for occasions outside her private concerts is characterized by a childlike playfulness, and can be best understood as a musical counterpart to the games she organized at Schönbrunn and Laxenburg.

For her private concerts Marie Therese formed a coterie of amateur and professional musicians, ranging from chamber servants to virtuosos, instrumental as well as vocal, German as well as Italian. With orchestra, chorus, and vocal soloists she performed music by many celebrated composers. She explored a remarkably large repertory: excerpts from operas and oratorios, complete operas, oratorios, secular cantatas, masses, concertos, symphonies, and chamber music. In its frequency her music-making resembled the chamber-music sessions of her uncle, Emperor Joseph II. But in variety of repertory and size of musical forces she went well beyond Joseph, who often performed excerpts from opera and oratorio from the score with just three or four musicians clustered around a keyboard.[6]

Baroness Alexandrine du Montet, whose husband served as chamberlain to Emperor Franz, wrote in her memoirs that Marie Therese was "capricious, her activities trivial, and her games often very common."[7] This side of her personality expressed itself rarely in her private concerts, whose repertory could hardly be called superficial or common, but does help to explain some of the music that she performed on other occasions, such as her elaborate celebrations of Franz's nameday and birthday. Several of these works contain quodlibets, playfully combining excerpts from popular operas and other vocal music. Others, breaking down the distinction between music-making and children's play, make use of Berchtesgadner Instrumente, toy instruments of the kind made in the Bavarian Alps.

But the birthday and nameday celebrations also featured music of impressive grandeur and seriousness, including the two masses that Michael Haydn wrote for the empress. Haydn's *Missa S. Theresiae* and *Missa S. Francisci* represented a new kind of concerted mass that has attracted surprisingly little attention from scholars and performers: a cycle including not only the Ordinary but also a gradual, an offertory, and a Te Deum. Marie Therese cultivated the plenary mass with great energy; her library contained about sixteen such works.

The empress commissioned much of the music she performed in private concerts and on Franz's nameday and birthday. She asked many leading

---

[6] John A. Rice, *Antonio Salieri and Viennese Opera*, Chicago, 1998, 23.
[7] Alexandrine du Montet, *Souvenirs de la Baronne du Montet, 1785–1866*, Paris, 1904, 6.

composers, not only in Vienna but in Germany, France, and Italy, to write music, including Johann Georg Albrechtsberger, Beethoven (*Die Geschöpfe des Prometheus* and possibly the Septet, Op. 20, "most humbly dedicated to Her Majesty the Empress"), Luigi Cherubini, Joseph Eybler, Joseph Haydn (the Te Deum in C), Michael Haydn, Mayr, Paer, Giovanni Paisiello, Anton Reicha, Salieri, Joseph Weigl, Winter, Paul Wranitzky, and Niccolò Zingarelli. Not all of them fulfilled her commissions, but most did. Marie Therese's contacts with librettists occasionally led to new works for the public theaters of Vienna. Her request to Giovanni de Gamerra for "a grand opera seria" resulted in Paer's *Achille*; her repeated declarations to Joseph Sonnleithner that "no opera text had ever given her so much pleasure" as Jean-Nicolas Bouilly's *Léonore* resulted in Beethoven's *Fidelio*.

In studying Marie Therese's musical activities we can draw on a wealth of musical and documentary evidence. Most of her music library survives, though little in the musicological literature would lead one to suspect its size and significance, or even its existence. Many of the letters written to her by the musicians and poets she patronized are preserved in Vienna. She recorded in a diary the names of the musicians who performed with her, the pieces they executed, and the rewards she gave librettists, composers, and performers. Involved not only in the performance but also in the inception, commissioning, and shaping of musical works, she preserved manuscript librettos, ballet scenarios, and outlines (some in her own hand) of theatrical works not yet set to music.

At Marie Therese's death most of her collection of music became part of the "Kaisersammlung," Emperor Franz's music library, now split between the Österreichische Nationalbibliothek and the Gesellschaft der Musikfreunde; the rest, consisting of liturgical music, went to the Hofkapelle, the court chapel, most of whose library has also been incorporated into the Nationalbibliothek. An inventory of the church music, hitherto unpublished, is presented here in appendix 1. Franz contributed to the Kaisersammlung before, during, and after his marriage to Marie Therese. But I hope to demonstrate in chapter 1 that a very large part of the Kaisersammlung belonged to her and that her personal library can be identified with some confidence and precision within the larger collection. Is it wise to begin a book with what is essentially a bibliographical essay? I would argue that we cannot begin to understand Marie Therese unless we know of her activities as a collector of music; and we cannot fully understand her activities as a collector without knowing what she collected and where her music is now.

Marie Therese's musical diary, preserved in the Haus-, Hof- und Staatsarchiv in Vienna, documents the private concerts she organized and in which she took part between 1801 and 1803. It is the single most important record of her musical activities. Although displayed in 1982 in an exhibition celebrating the 250th anniversary of Joseph Haydn's birth and discussed in its catalogue,[8] the diary has never been published and remains little known. Demonstrating the empress's musical ambition and energy, the high quality of the musicians with whom she performed, and the sophistication of her musical interests, it is a valuable source of information not only about music at court but about Viennese musical life in general at the beginning of the nineteenth century. Appendix 2 is an annotated edition of the diary.

Also in the Haus-, Hof- und Staatsarchiv are many of the letters, mostly unknown to musical scholarship, that the empress received from musicians and poets concerning works commissioned by her, and from others who informed her about musical events far from Vienna and helped her obtain music. From Salzburg her brother-in-law Ferdinand, whose passion for collecting music equalled hers, asked for copies of music in her library and offered her copies of his latest acquisitions. From Paris the Marchese di Gallo, the Neapolitan ambassador, sent operas by Cherubini, Winter, and many others, and reported Cherubini's reluctance to write anything for her; and Paisiello promised to set to music librettos she had sent him (promises he did not keep). From Venice Giuseppe Carpani sent operas that had recently been performed and cantatas for which he supplied the text, and wrote of his collaboration with Weigl and Zingarelli on works commissioned by her. From Naples her sisters Cristina and Amalia sent a never-ending chronicle of theatrical events, an occasional score, and requests for music from Vienna. Among the most useful letters are the thirty-four that Paer wrote between 1803 and 1807 while serving as Kapellmeister at the court of Dresden. Paer's letters, which frequently refer to the music he wrote for Marie Therese and to the process of bringing it to performance, are presented in appendix 3.

Very few of the empress's letters to composers have apparently survived. That makes the correspondence between Paisiello and her, even if it did not result in any new works, particularly interesting and valuable. Three letters from Marie Therese to Paisiello and one from him to her are transcribed in appendix 4.

---

[8] *Joseph Haydn in seiner Zeit*, exhibition catalogue, Eisenstadt, 1982, 492, 496.

Marie Therese's theatrical papers, also in the Haus-, Hof- und Staatsarchiv, include a wide variety of documents related to plays, operas, ballets, and various combinations of music, dance, and spoken theater. She wrote out in her own hand sketches for possible theatrical productions. Librettists submitted detailed plans for future works, indicating the number and organization of acts, the number and voice-type of characters, and the locations and types of arias and ensembles. Entire librettos were elegantly written out in manuscript, some of which were never apparently set to music. Some of the documents concern the Last Judgment, a subject that held Marie Therese's interest for several years and on which she urged Joseph Haydn to compose a sequel to *Die Schöpfung* and *Die Jahreszeiten*. Others (in appendix 5) concern *Il conte Clò*, a comic cantata by Paer to which he referred often in his letters and of which the autograph score, formerly in the empress's library, is now in the Nationalbibliothek.

Marie Therese's musical library, diary, correspondence, and theatrical papers illuminate one another. The diary, for example, helps us decide what music belonged to her. Her library, once we have reconstructed its contents, allows us to understand references to particular works in the letters. Together, these sources offer insights into the process by which she brought new music to performance, her relations with poets and musicians, and her musical taste.

This book is the first to attempt a comprehensive survey of Marie Therese's activities as musician and patron and of the musical culture at court that this remarkable woman fostered and enjoyed. Because many of the archival and musical documents on which it is based are themselves little known, and because of the interdependence of these documents, I have devoted a large part of the study to their transcription and explication. The preliminary nature of this inquiry has kept me from interpreting the empress's activities within a single theoretical framework and from exploring in depth their manifold implications for gender studies, economics, sociology, and cultural politics. Yet a number of important themes do emerge from the following pages, all of which are related to a question that will occur to anyone who reads this book: Why have historians of music largely ignored Marie Therese and the vibrant musical culture she supported?

One reason why Marie Therese occupies such a marginal place in the historiographical tradition is that scholars have tended to view artistic patronage after the French Revolution with less interest than earlier patronage. Many patrons of the Renaissance, the Baroque, and the Ancien Régime have appeared to historians of music and the visual arts as heroic figures, as worthy of research as the musicians and artists who depended on them.[9] Most of these patrons belonged to absolutist courts, to the nobility, or to the Catholic Church – institutions greatly weakened in wealth, prestige, and power by the Revolution and its aftermath. As nineteenth-century artists freed themselves from a system of patronage rooted in the feudal past, preferring one in which they could sell their work, one piece at a time, to whoever could pay for it, patrons became mere purchasers of art. But not Marie Therese, who could still ask a celebrated composer to write an opera for her, on a libretto chosen by her, without offering any payment: "The kindness with which I have no doubt you will satisfy my request will be most delightful and pleasing to me, and will give you a new claim on my admiration and benevolence, of which I am now pleased to assure you." As addressed to Paisiello in 1802 such a statement must have sounded distinctly old-fashioned. "Benevolence" meant a reward, of course; and Marie Therese was a generous dispenser of the exquisite gifts – the snuffboxes, watches, writing sets, and diamond rings – characteristic of the world of artistic patronage through which the child Mozart had so profitably travelled during the 1760s. But Paisiello would have probably required a more definitive offer before agreeing to write an opera for the empress, whose patronage was an anachronism that may have left her contemporaries, and some historians as well, puzzled about what to make of her.

Many of the composers Marie Therese patronized have been studied almost as little as she herself. Scholars interested in music in Vienna at the end of the eighteenth century and the beginning of the nineteenth have naturally directed most of their attention to Joseph Haydn and Beethoven, and to the aristocratic and predominantly male circles that supported them. It is not surprising that the system of patronage within which Weigl, Wranitzky, and Eybler – to name three of the composers most closely associated with the empress – worked is largely unexamined.

Although historians have usually mentioned Marie Therese in connection with those occasions when her musical interests brought her into contact with Haydn and Beethoven, they have tended to pass over such contacts quickly. Students of *Fidelio* have failed to follow up on Sonnleithner's statements concerning the empress's role in the conception of the opera. They have found it difficult to accept the idea that Beethoven – the prototype of the new kind of independent artist – could have allowed an empress's tastes to shape one of his most important works, and have preferred to cite reasons

[9] See, among other important studies, Alan Yorke-Long, *Music at Court: Four Eighteenth-Century Studies*, London, 1954, and Francis Haskell, *Patrons and Painters*, 2nd ed., New Haven, 1980.

why Beethoven himself might have been attracted to the story on which it is based.[10] One recent study of Beethoven's place in Viennese musical patronage at the turn of the century, by the sociologist Tia DeNora, does not mention Marie Therese at all.[11]

A considerable cultural distance separated the court of Franz and Marie Therese from the highest ranks of the Viennese nobility.[12] DeNora has argued that the high aristocracy projected its identity and distinguished itself from the middle classes and lower levels of the nobility with a self-conscious promotion of greatness in music at the expense of music it perceived as merely entertaining or pleasing. Her argument suggests the possibility that music played a similar role in defining differences between the nobility and the court.

Haydn and Beethoven benefitted from the empress's patronage, but their relations with her were not as warm or as productive as those she maintained with many other musicians. Did Haydn and Beethoven fear that a close association with Marie Therese might endanger aristocratic ties that not only brought them financial gain but enhanced their reputations as great masters? If they had come more noticeably into her orbit, would they have become less attractive to a nobility that prided itself on its cultural independence from the court?

I believe the musical cultures of the court and the nobility were more similar than they might appear in a musicological literature that has focussed so doggedly on Haydn and Beethoven. Members of the high nobility patronized and otherwise encouraged many other composers, including some of Marie Therese's favorites. Indeed, the musical tastes and practices of the court sometimes coincided with those of the aristocracy so closely that they became rivals for the same musical talent and resources.

A related issue is Marie Therese's status as an outsider (and, from a Viennese perspective, as an Italian, despite the fact that she, like her husband, was a grandchild of Maria Theresa) in the cultural politics of the capital during a period of increasing nationalism. When German opera

---

[10] For example, according to William Kinderman (*Beethoven*, Berkeley, 1995, 102–3), in composing *Fidelio*, "Beethoven was captivated by the great, over-reaching themes of freedom and tyranny, life and death." For more detailed discussions of the libretto's appeal to the composer see Maynard Solomon, *Beethoven*, New York, 1977, 198–200, and Barry Cooper, *Beethoven*, Oxford, 2000, 137–8. None of these writers mentions Sonnleithner's claims in regard to MT.

[11] Tia DeNora, *Beethoven and the Construction of Genius: Musical Politics in Vienna, 1792–1803*, Berkeley, 1995. Table 2, "Key Viennese Music Patrons in the 1790s and 1800s," does not include MT.

[12] On the often strained relations between the court and the aristocracy during MT's reign see Annedore Brock, *Das Haus der Laune im Laxenburger Park bei Wien*, Frankfurt, 1996, 250–82.

was reintroduced to the court theaters in 1795 the libretto for the inaugural *Singspiel*, Wranitzky's *Die gute Mutter*, was dedicated to the empress in a prefatory letter (transcribed in chapter 7): "Your Majesty most graciously demonstrates at every opportunity how much you wish for German diligence, German art, and German merit to be recognized, encouraged, and rewarded." A document whose aim was to emphasize Marie Therese's "Germanness" managed, through exaggeration, to remind readers that she was in fact a Neapolitan princess.

A looming presence during the whole period of Marie Therese's reign, without which the nationalism expressed in the preface to *Die gute Mutter* would have been unthinkable, was the long series of wars with France. If the musical culture that Marie Therese promoted at court represented at some level an escape from military preoccupations, at other levels post-revolutionary France and its wars fascinated her. She owned a collection of French revolutionary currency; worse, she owned a tricolor freedom cap, a symbol of the Revolution that scandalized the official who, after her death, compiled the inventory of her effects. He listed the cap under a special rubric – "Things that no one will treasure" – and, as if that disapproval were not strong enough, added after the entry, with surprising vehemence and impudence: "Since moreover the spirit of this decoration has brought so much unhappiness to all mankind, only Beelzebub in Hell will be able to treasure this souvenir."[13]

War and music went hand in hand for Marie Therese, whose library contained a large assortment of programmatic works on military themes. Among her several battle symphonies was Wranitzky's *Grande Sinfonie caractéristique pour la paix avec la Republique Françoise*, which she included in one of her private concerts despite her husband's having forbidden it to be performed in public. *L'uniforme*, an opera that Weigl wrote for her and in which she created the principal female role, contains two spectacular battle scenes.

Marie Therese took advantage of the peaceful interlude that followed the Treaty of Lunéville (1801) to collect music from Paris on a grand scale. Here again her tastes paralleled those of Viennese theatergoers, who welcomed the *opéras-comiques* that suddenly flooded Viennese theaters at exactly this time. Her patronage brought her into competition with Napoleon, whose musical tastes, especially in Italian opera, resembled hers.[14] Paisiello, responding to her request for a new opera, wrote from

---

[13] Quoted in Brock, *Das Haus der Laune*, 259.
[14] Théo Fleischman, *Napoléon et la musique*, Brussels, 1965.

Paris that he could not fulfill her commission for the time being because he was working on an opera, *Proserpine*, for the First Consul. The empress had to be satisfied with music written by Paisiello for Napoleon's chapel.

War and Napoleon finally caught up with Marie Therese. Forced to flee Vienna before the advancing French army in November 1805, she expressed in letters to her mother the misery she felt when faced with the realities of war. Napoleon's military victories at Austerlitz and Jena presaged a musical victory over Marie Therese in the form of an agreement with the Saxon court (December 1806) that brought Paer to Paris and ended his close and productive relations with her. But by then she had only a few months to live.

The same nationalism that Marie Therese had to answer to in Vienna, that led a court official to express horror at her freedom cap, has also influenced thinking in musicology. The mixture of cultures that she embodied may fascinate us today; but during much of the last two hundred years it may have disturbed or even repelled some historians. Neither purely Viennese nor purely Neapolitan, she has attracted the sustained attention of no musical scholar writing in either German or Italian.

Marie Therese's activities as musician and patron (and her neglect by musicologists) need to be considered in light of the constraints that limited the actions of any woman of her time and place, even one at the highest levels of power and wealth. Some of these constraints were self-imposed, at least in part. When she spoke with Michael Haydn about the *Missa S. Theresiae*, she referred to her own abilities with a modesty that she probably felt suited her status as a woman: "You haven't made the soprano part too difficult for me? I'm singing it myself."[15] Scholars have tended to take such statements at face value. All assessments of her musical abilities in the following pages, by her and others, need to be evaluated in the context of a culture that generally did not expect or reward virtuosity in female amateurs.

As a woman, the empress had to deal with the tendency of her contemporaries to interpret her relations with male musicians as amorous and therefore immoral. Even her mother recoiled at her fondness for the great *musico* Luigi Marchesi, while tongues wagged all over Vienna when she was seen walking arm in arm in the gardens of Schönbrunn with the tenor Giuseppe Simoni. Rumors of sexual impropriety could easily have dampened the pleasure she took from music; they could even have kept musicians

---

[15] "Sie haben mir doch die Sopranstimme nicht zu schwer gesetzt? ich singe sie selbst" ([Georg Schinn and Franz Joseph Otter], *Biographische Skizze von Michael Haydn*, Salzburg, 1808, 30).

away from her private concerts. (Marchesi, for example, left Vienna shortly after Queen Maria Carolina criticized her daughter's relations with him.)

Such rumors probably helped inspire Marie Therese's interest in musical dramas, including rescue operas, that celebrate conjugal devotion. In Weigl's *L'uniforme* she portrayed Giannina, who disguises herself as a soldier in order to rescue her fiancé from prison. Her scenario for a ballet on the story of Alcestis pays tribute to a wife who dies so that her husband might live. She asked Paer to compose an opera, *Le mine di Polonia*, in which a husband tries to rescue his wife, imprisoned for resisting the advances of a tyrant. In her diary she twice misspelled the title of Mozart's last comic opera – "Così fan tutti" – as if in quiet protest against its denigration of female constancy.

During the years of Marie Therese's most energetic activities as musician and patron (1800–6) she gave birth to four children. This naturally brings up the question of how much her pregnancies and childbirths affected her music-making. The question invites two different kinds of answers.

On the one hand, the amount of time that Marie Therese's pregnancies and childbirths took away from music was surprisingly small. From her diary we know that she participated in the performance of masses by Joseph and Michael Haydn on 5 December 1802. Two days later she gave birth to a son, Franz Karl. A month after that she was back with her musicians, taking part in a concert of excerpts from Italian operas and singing a duet from Haydn's *Die Schöpfung* with Carl Weinmüller, one of Vienna's leading basses.

On the other hand, giving birth threatened the empress's life repeatedly, as the death in childbirth of her husband's first wife must have always reminded her. That threat influenced her music-making, in which one can find evidence of a preoccupation with death that might otherwise seem odd in one so young. She collected a large number of requiems and performed several of them during the period covered by her diary. Her fascination with the idea of an oratorio about the Last Judgment caused her to sketch out, in her own hand, plans for oratorios in Italian and German that begin with the death of a young woman, mourned by her husband and children. A young mother's death is also a central element of the scenario for the ballet *Alceste*. Did the empress, frequently subjected to the mortal dangers of childbirth, see herself in these virtuous but tragic women?

The secrecy within which Marie Therese hid many of her musical activities may also reflect her gender. She sometimes had a composer approached by a third party so that he would not know her identity. Some of those who knew of her commissions alluded to them with a vagueness that probably

resulted from her desire for secrecy. Carpani, in his epistolary biography
of Haydn, never mentioned the empress in discussing the translation of
the text of *Die Schöpfung* that she had asked him to make; he referred
enigmatically to another work commissioned by her, Paer's *La lanterna
magica*, as having been written "for the entertainment of a ruling house."[16]

Because of the secrecy that surrounded Marie Therese's musical activities,
we have to rely on indirect evidence of various kinds to document her role
in the inception of several important works. Such evidence has sometimes
been misconstrued or ignored, often resulting in the attribution to various
men of Marie Therese's ideas and of actions she took or may have taken.
A partially autograph manuscript of Michael Haydn's *Missa S. Francisci*,
which we know with certainty she commissioned, contains an inscription
in which the commissioner's gender has been switched: "Made according to
the command of the emperor of Austria." Documents related to Cherubini's
Faniska attribute to Emperor Franz and to Baron Peter Braun, impresario of
the Viennese court theaters, a project almost certainly conceived by Marie
Therese. It was only when censors forbade *Fidelio* from being performed
that Sonnleithner revealed he had written the libretto in response to the
empress's expressions of admiration for Bouilly's *Léonore*. If the censors had
not tried to ban the opera, her role in its inception would have remained
entirely secret.

Almost as secret, until now, was the existence of the empress's music
library – hidden, in part, by the term "Kaisersammlung." No one seems
to have considered the possibility that the "Emperor's Collection" could
have been largely assembled by an empress. But that is the subject of
chapter 1.

[16] Giuseppe Carpani, *Le Haydine, ovvero Lettere sulla vita e le opere del celebre maestro Giuseppe Haydn*, Padua, 1823, 115, 190.

The empress as collector of music

In the two centuries since her death Marie Therese's vast music library has been dispersed and more or less forgotten. But enough information about it survives for us to determine what music she owned and how she got much of it, and to identify, in the three libraries to which most of the music eventually went, most of her manuscripts and prints.

The empress directed in her will (not as precisely as one might wish) that her husband Franz choose what he wanted from her collection of music and that what he left was to be divided between the Hofkapelle and Eybler:

F. *Disposition of all games, works, painting materials, music.*

First, whatever of these things His Majesty the emperor wishes to keep for himself or his children, he should have first choice...

Fifth, the church music, which is not here, and which can be used, goes to the Chapel.

Sixth, the rest of the church music goes to Eibler, as does all the rest of the music.[1]

Next to the first of these stipulations Franz wrote: "I have kept the music for myself, in so far as it does not belong in the chapel, to which it is being transferred."[2]

A list of liturgical music that Franz sent to the Hofkapelle, dated December 1807 and entitled *Kathalog der Kirchenmusickalien*, contains detailed and accurate information about this part of Marie Therese's library.[3] Most of the Hofkapelle's music (including the empress's church music) has been

---

[1] "F. *Disposition über alle Spiele, Arbeiten, Mahlersachen, Musikalien.* 1.^{tens} Was Se. Majestät der Kaiser von allen diesen Sachen für Sich oder für die jungen Herrschaften behalten wollen, sollen Höchst Selbe am ersten aussuchen.... 5.^{tens} Die Kirchenmusikalien, was nicht hier, und was zu brauchen ist, erhält die Kapelle. 6^{tens} Das übrige der Kirchenmusikalien erhält Eibler, wie auch alle übrigen Musikalien" (Testament Ihrer Majestät der Höchstseeligen Kaiserin und Königin Maria Theresia, nach den Vermächtnissen geordnet, HHStA, Fa, HKF, Kart. 10, Beylage 2, fol. 5r–v).

[2] "Die Musikalien habe ich für mich behalten in so weit sie nicht in die Kapelle gehörten wohin sie abgegeben werden."

[3] I learned of the existence of this inventory from Brock, *Das Haus der Laune*, 253–4.

transferred to the Musiksammlung of the Österreichische Nationalbibliothek, where many of the manuscripts formerly in the Hofkapelle are identified with call numbers with the prefix HK; others carry call numbers widely scattered between Mus. Hs. 15000 and Mus. Hs. 19500.[4]

More difficult to identify than Marie Therese's church music is the much larger part of her library that became Franz's property. Of this music too an inventory survives, but because this inventory was later expanded to cover the contents of the collection into which her library was incorporated, its significance in relation to her collection in particular has hitherto gone unrecognized. In order to establish that this inventory does indeed document the contents of her music library, we must first follow the history of the collection that absorbed her library in 1807. That history, as Ernst Fritz Schmid, one of the scholars involved in its rediscovery and exploration, has noted, comes close to sounding like a fairy tale.[5]

Sometime between 1846 and 1879 the massive collection of music that had belonged to Emperor Franz was discovered in thirty-six trunks in a closet in the Hofburg. Emperor Franz Joseph took little interest in his grandfather's music. In 1879 he donated it to the Steiermärkischer Musikverein in Graz, but not before inviting Carl Ferdinand Pohl, archivist of the Gesellschaft der Musikfreunde in Vienna, to pick whatever material he wished for the Gesellschaft's library. Thus the so-called Kaisersammlung was split in two: much the larger part went to Graz, where it was soon forgotten; a smaller part (but including many works of Joseph Haydn and Mozart) stayed in Vienna.

Schmid rediscovered the larger part of the Kaisersammlung in 1933. The Austrian government bought the collection, and since 1936 it has constituted an important part of the music collection of the Nationalbibliothek. This library also owns an inventory entitled *Catalogo alter Musickalien u. gehört in das privat Musikalien Archiv S. Maj. des Kaisers* (henceforth abbreviated *CaM*), which was probably compiled over several

---

[4]   On the transfers of music from the Hofkapelle to the Nationalbibliothek see Günter Brosche, "Das Hofmusikarchiv," in *Musica Imperialis: 500 Jahre Hofmusikkapelle in Wien, 1498–1998*, exhibition catalogue, Tutzing, 1998, 117–24; and Günter Brosche, "Besondere Neuerwerbungen der Musiksammlung der Österreichischen Nationalbibliothek in den Jahren 1998 und 1999," *Studien zur Musikwissenschaft* 48 (2002), 489–91. The provenance of manuscripts with call numbers between Mus. Hs. 15000 and Mus. Hs. 19500 can be identified with the help of an inventory entitled *Erwerbungs-Nachweis* (A-Wn, Mus. Hs. 2485, INV. III/Tabulae 2).

[5]   Ernst Fritz Schmid, "Die Privatmusikaliensammlung des Kaisers Franz II. und ihre Wiederentdeckung in Graz im Jahre 1933," *Österreichische Musikzeitschrift* 25 (1970), 596–9. See also Dexter Edge, *Mozart's Viennese Copyists*, Ph.D. dissertation, University of Southern California, 2001, 2090–5. I am grateful to Dexter Edge for telling me about the Kaisersammlung in 1991 and for giving me, since then, much useful information about it.

years, ending around 1815, though it contains annotations made much later.[6]

The librarians of the Gesellschaft der Musikfreunde and the Nationalbibliothek catalogued their respective shares of the Kaisersammlung differently. Working in a period in which music librarianship did not always aspire to rigorous scholarly standards, the Gesellschaft's staff catalogued its part of the collection piecemeal, without any consistent effort to identify the provenance of individual works. Fortunately, however, it preserved a list that Pohl had made of the music he transferred from the Kaisersammlung in 1879; I shall refer to it as "Pohl's list."[7] Corroborating evidence of the transfers is in *CaM*, where someone has written "Wien" next to the items that Pohl brought to the Gesellschaft. A few minutes' walk from the Gesellschaft, and about half a century later, the Nationalbibliothek catalogued its share of the Kaisersammlung as a block soon after it acquired it. The library assigned to the manuscripts all the call numbers from Suppl. mus. 9861 to Suppl. mus. 13017 (the classification "Suppl. mus." has more recently been changed to "Mus. Hs." but the numbers have remained unchanged) and to the prints all the call numbers from MS 27001 to MS 27480 (this "MS" being an unfortunate abbreviation for "Musiksammlung").[8]

Table 1.1 shows how Marie Therese's music was dispersed, the collections through which it has passed, and its present location in three Viennese libraries. (The special case of Eybler's autographs will be discussed later in this chapter.)

THE KAISERSAMMLUNG

The scholarly integrity with which the Nationalbibliothek catalogued its part of the Kaisersammlung and the survival of *CaM* and Pohl's list allow us to reconstruct the contents of a collection that documents in extraordinary detail the musical tastes and activities of the imperial court during the late

---

[6] A-Wn, call number INV. I / Kaisersammlung Graz 1, cited in Warren Kirkendale, *Fugue and Fugato in Rococo and Classical Chamber Music*, Durham, NC, 1979, 41 and 277. My thanks to Dexter Edge for directing me to this inventory. It does not include the few works from the Kaisersammlung known to have been composed after about 1814, leading me to conclude that its compilation ended around 1815.

[7] *Verzeichniss der mit Allerhöchster Genehmigung an das Archiv der Gesellschaft d. Musikfreunde in Wien abgegebenen Musikalien a. d. Sammlung weiland S. Mj. d. Kaisers Franz I*. My thanks to Otto Biba, director of the archive of the Gesellschaft der Musikfreunde, for showing me this document and helping me interpret it, and for other help in identifying works from the Kaisersammlung in the Gesellschaft.

[8] I am grateful to Günter Brosche for telling me of the handwritten inventories and showing me how they could be used to reconstruct the Musiksammlung's part of the Kaisersammlung.

Table 1.1 *Dispersal of Marie Therese's music library and present location of its contents*

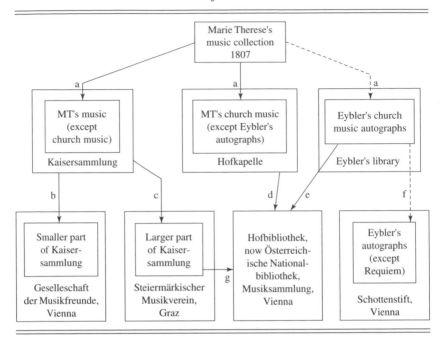

───────► Documented transfers

- - - - - -► Undocumented transfers

[a] Transferred by terms of Marie Therese's will
[b] Transferred by Pohl in 1879
[c] Transferred by order of Emperor Franz Joseph in 1879
[d] Transferred in several stages between 1825 and 2000
[e] Eybler's Requiem donated by the composer in 1831
[f] Transferred to Schottenstift at Eybler's death in 1846?
[g] Transferred in 1936

eighteenth and early nineteenth centuries. No one has ever fully described the Kaisersammlung in print. I will not attempt to do so here, but will give only a general idea of its contents and then focus on the part of it that belonged to Marie Therese.

The Kaisersammlung contained several thousand items in manuscript and several hundred items in print (the totals vary according to whether one counts individually works published or otherwise arranged in groups, and whether one counts a score and a set of parts as one item or two). It included operas, oratorios, cantatas, operatic extracts, songs, ballets, symphonies, concertos, keyboard music, chamber music, and dance music. Some of the orchestral music and vocal music with orchestral accompaniment was preserved in parts, some in full score, some in both parts and score, and some in reductions for keyboard.

The vast majority of complete, large-scale vocal works were operas, oratorios, and secular cantatas in Italian. The collection also included smaller numbers of German and French operas, some of the latter in German or Italian translation. In addition to the complete works it contained many individual vocal pieces in Italian: excerpts from operas and oratorios, *ariette*, *canzonette*, *divertimenti vocali*, *romanze*, and so forth.

Instrumental music was dominated by ballroom dances, sonatas and sets of variations for keyboard, and chamber music for strings. Much of this chamber music – by a wide variety of composers active in many parts of Europe – is in the form of manuscript parts inscribed with the initials N. H., frequently followed by a date.[9] N. H. has not yet been identified. Whoever made or commissioned these copies apparently wanted to own an encyclopedic collection of chamber music of the second half of the eighteenth century.

Many of the manuscripts from the Kaisersammlung other than those marked N. H. are dated or preserve datable music; the vast majority of dated and datable pieces were written or copied before Marie Therese's death in 1807. She could have collected any of this music, some before she came to Vienna in 1790, some after. But Franz and his first wife Elisabeth of Württemberg also contributed music to the collection before 1807. Is it possible to distinguish Marie Therese's personal music library from the larger collection of Franz and his family?

MUSIC OF EMPEROR FRANZ AND TWO ELISABETHS

Before trying to define Marie Therese's part of the Kaisersammlung, let us first identify some manuscripts and prints that we have reason to believe were bought by or presented to people other than her.

Emperor Franz played the violin. Marie Therese called him "my beloved fiddler."[10] Writing to her when she was ill, he promised to "practice fiddling,

---

[9] The chamber music collection with the initials N. H. is discussed in Kirkendale, *Fugue and Fugato*, 41. Much of the music to which Kirkendale refers elsewhere in the book is preserved in manuscript copies from the Kaisersammlung marked N. H., as documented in his appendix 1. For facsimiles of the hand of the copyist who produced these manuscripts see Warren Kirkendale, *Fuge und Fugato in der Kammermusik des Rokoko und der Klassik*, Tutzing, 1966, plate IX, and Warren Kirkendale, "More Slow Introductions by W. A. Mozart to Fugues by J. S. Bach?" *Journal of the American Musicological Society* 17 (1964), 43–65.

[10] "Mit dem Gedanken an meinem geliebten Geiger" (MT to Franz, 16 November 1803, HHStA, Fa, Sb, Kart. 39, Briefe I. M. der K. Maria Theresia a. S. M. K. Franz I. 1803, fol. 1r–v).

the better to be able to serve" her when she recovered.[11] His ownership of two violins, a viola, and a cello suggests that he participated in the performance of string quartets.[12] This is confirmed, though unfortunately without supporting documentation, by a nineteenth-century German writer:

> Emperor Franz was one of the last of the "musical princes" of the previous century who not only had music performed but also – and by preference – played themselves; and the emperor played the best and most elegant music, namely quartet music. His string quartet accompanied him on journeys and military campaigns, for without the quartet he was never truly happy. It is said that during the Battle of Leipzig he had to do without his quartet for three days. Then, when he entered Leipzig in triumph, he said: "Tonight we wish to reconvene our quartet." And so it happened.[13]

Like his uncle Joseph, Franz was fond of contrapuntal artifice. "His Majesty loves fugues, properly worked out, but not too long," wrote Count Moritz Dietrichstein in 1823.[14]

Elisabeth of Württemberg, who arrived in Vienna in 1782, married Franz in 1788, and died in 1790, played the piano. Emperor Joseph wrote to Franz's father Leopold in 1782, shortly after the marriage was arranged: "She has a predilection for music and a fairly good ear, but her voice amounts to nothing at all; she plays the piano a little."[15] In Vienna she studied piano with Georg Summer (Mozart having been disappointed in his hope of being appointed to the position) and singing with Vincenzo Righini.[16]

Franz's musical purchases, well documented for the period between 1785 and 1790, probably reflect Elisabeth's tastes as well his own. In January 1790, only a month before Elisabeth's death, he bought a piano from the great Viennese builder Anton Walter.[17] He paid Sigismund Rummel,

---

[11] Quoted in translation (used here) in Walter Langsam, *Francis the Good*, New York, 1949, 162.

[12] *Joseph Haydn in seiner Zeit*, 491.

[13] Wilhelm Heinrich Riehl, *Musikalische Charakterköpfe*, 7th ed., 2 vols., Stuttgart, 1899, II, 218 (cited in Kirkendale, *Fugue and Fugato*, 184). Franz's quartet consisted at one time of the emperor, Count Wrbna, Lieutenant Field Marshal Kutschera, and Eybler (Eduard Hanslick, *Geschichte des Concertwesens in Wien*, 2 vols., Vienna, 1869, I, 51). At another time, according to Riehl, Franz Krommer was a member.

[14] Quoted in translation in Kirkendale, *Fugue and Fugato*, 4. On Emperor Joseph's predilection for fugues see Kirkendale, 4, 11, 14.

[15] Quoted in translation (used here) in Langsam, *Francis the Good*, 77.

[16] That Elizabeth studied with Righini we know from the title page of a manuscript of *L'incontro inaspettato* (A-Wn, KT 220) that describes the composer as "Maestro di Musica all'attual Servizio di S: A. S: La Principessa Elisabetta di Wirtemberg." My thanks to Dorothea Link for telling me of this inscription and giving me a copy of it.

[17] HHStA, Fa, HKF, Kart. 3: "Quittung Für fünfzig fünf dugaten die ich endes gefertigter von Ihro Königlichen Hoheit dem durchlauchtigst Erzherzog für ein Pianoforte erhalten habe. Wien den 9ten Januar 1790. Anton Walter mp. Orgel und Instrumentmach."

"K. K. Hoforgel- und Instrumentmacher," for frequent tuning and Summer for keyboard lessons.[18] He bought large amounts of printed keyboard music, including sonatas by Muzio Clementi, Joseph Haydn, Leopold Kozeluch, Ignaz Pleyel, Johann Samuel Schroeter, and Franz Xaver Sterkel.[19] In 1788 the copyist Lorenz Lausch sold him vocal scores of Salieri's *Il talismano* and of two arias by Angelo Tarchi added to Vicente Martín y Soler's *L'arbore di Diana* for the benefit of the newly arrived *prima donna* Adriana Ferrarese.[20] In 1789 he bought from the copyist Wenzel Sukowaty another vocal score of *Il talismano*, vocal scores of Paisiello's *Il re Teodoro*, Christoph Gluck's *Die Pilgrime von Mekka*, Salieri's *Il ricco d'un giorno*, and Weigl's *Il pazzo per forza*, and transcriptions for string quartet of Martín's *Una cosa rara* and *L'arbore di Diana*.[21] He also bought dance music from both Lausch and Sukowaty.[22]

The musical practices of Franz and Elisabeth and the archduke's music buying suggest that they owned some of the Kaisersammlung's printed keyboard music, some of its vocal scores of Viennese comic operas, and its transcriptions of *Una cosa rara* and *L'arbore di Diana*.[23] And since Franz bought string-quartet versions of these operas, he probably bought – and owned – some of the other operatic transcriptions for string quartet from the Kaisersammlung (Mus. Hs. 12522–51). Franz the fiddler, the player of string quartets, probably collected the chamber music marked N. H., which included many string quartets. Many of these works contain fugues, which would have appealed to his taste for counterpoint.[24]

---

[18] For example, in HHStA, Fa, HKF, Kart. 3: "Bey Seyner Kög. Hocheit Erzherzog Frantz ist im Monad April, das *pianovorte* fünf Mall gestimed worden ... Sigismund Rummel, 30 April 1790." This tuning must have been for Franz himself, since Elisabeth had already died and Marie Therese had not yet arrived in Vienna.

[19] See, for example, receipts from Artaria dated 8 October 1785 (HHStA, Fa, HKF, Kart. 1) and 10 June 1789 (HKF, Kart. 3), and from Christoph Torricella dated 22 October 1785 (in HKF, Kart. 1).

[20] Receipt dated 21 November 1788 in HHStA, Fa, HKF, Kart. 2. On Tarchi's arias see Mary Hunter, *The Culture of Opera Buffa in Mozart's Vienna*, Princeton, N.J., 1999, 252–6.

[21] Undated receipt signed by Sukowaty filed among papers from 1789, in HHStA, Fa, HKF, Kart. 3.

[22] In 1788 he paid Lausch 6 Gulden for copies of minuets and German dances (HHStA, Fa, HKF, Kart. 2). From Sukowaty he bought manuscripts of German dances in 1790 and 1791, including two sets by Joseph Heidenreich (HKF, Kart. 4).

[23] The Kaisersammlung had vocal scores of Tarchi's insertion arias for *L'arbore di Diana* (Mus. Hs. 10771–2), *Il talismano* (Mus. Hs. 10076), *Il re Teodoro* (Mus. Hs. 10060), *Il ricco d'un giorno* (Mus. Hs. 10074), and *Il pazzo per forza* (Mus. Hs. 10084). CaM and Pohl's list document the Kaisersammlung as the provenance of vocal scores of *Die Pilgrime von Mekka* and *Il talismano* in A-Wgm. These vocal scores, and the transcriptions for string quartet of *Una cosa rara* and *L'arbore di Diana* (Mus. Hs. 12529 and 12530), are almost certainly among the items that Franz bought in the 1780s.

[24] Kirkendale, *Fugue and Fugato*, 41, emphasizes the importance of the Kaisersammlung as a repository of fugal chamber music of the second half of the eighteenth century. Kirkendale's appendix 1

Not that Franz bought music only for himself and Elisabeth. The eldest son of Emperor Leopold II, he grew up in Florence, where his father ruled as grand duke of Tuscany from 1765 to 1790. He satisfied the hunger of his family in Italy (especially his brother Ferdinand, later one of Marie Therese's musical collaborators) for new music by sending it from Vienna.[25] On 6 November 1789 Elisabeth wrote to Franz that she had received a request from Ferdinand "for various pieces of music that he says are available at Artaria," and that she would have the music obtained.[26] Franz bought full scores of operas, including Salieri's *Axur*, *Il pastor fido*, and *La cifra*, and Cimarosa's *I due baroni di Rocca Azzurra*, probably with the intention of sending them to Florence. The Kaisersammlung contained scores of none of these operas; and in the case of *Axur*, we know that Elisabeth sent Salieri's opera to Ferdinand.[27] In exchange for such shipments she and Franz received from Florence olive oil, chocolate, and hams.

Several manuscripts from the Kaisersammlung have book plates identifying them as belonging to an Archduchess Elisabeth. Most are Italian operas composed between 1760 and 1780 and performed in Vienna during that period, but they also include two volumes of keyboard music (including chamber music and concertos) by Christoph Georg Wagenseil and other musicians active in and around Vienna during the third quarter of the eighteenth century. Although it is possible that the archduchess who owned this music was Franz's first wife, its early dates (relative to her arrival in Vienna in 1782) make it more likely that it belonged to another, older Elisabeth: the sister of Joseph II.[28] The emperor may have inherited these scores when

documents the Kaisersammlung as the provenance of much chamber music with fugues, most of it in manuscripts marked N. H. Although much of this music was written during Joseph's reign, most of the manuscripts are dated 1786 and later. Since 1786 is only one year after Franz began collecting music on a large scale (as documented by receipts in HHStA, Fa, HKF), he is more likely than his uncle to have been the principal collector of chamber music marked N. H.

25 Cölestin Wolfsgruber, *Franz I. Kaiser von Oesterreich*, 2 vols., Vienna, 1899, II, 125. HHStA, Fa, HKF, Kart. 3 includes a list of music sent to an unnamed archduchess in Florence.

26 "Briefe an Erzherzog Franz (nachmals K. Franz II.) von seiner ersten Gemahlin Elisabeth, 1785–1789," ed. H. Weyda, *Archiv für Österreichische Geschichte* 44 (1870), 250.

27 Receipts in HKF, Kart. 3 record the purchase from Sukowaty of all four operas for 36 Gulden (8 ducats) each. The receipt for *Axur* is dated 6 August 1789; the other three are undated but filed under 1790. Elisabeth wrote to Franz on 3 September 1789, less than a month after his purchase of the full score of *Axur*: "Votre frère Ferdinand m'a aussi écrit, il me remercie pour l'opéra Axur que je lui ai envoyé" ("Briefe an Erzherzog Franz," 189).

28 On the manuscripts with keyboard music (Mus. Hs. 11084 and 11085) see A. Peter Brown, *Joseph Haydn's Keyboard Music*, Bloomington, Ind., 1986, 173, 176, which assumes the Elisabeth in question was Franz's aunt; Dexter Edge, who has studied the manuscript in detail, agrees (personal communication). Archduchess Elisabeth's operatic scores from the Kaisersammlung include Pasquale Anfossi's *Metilda ritrovata* (now in A-Wgm) and the following operas in A-Wn: Alessandro Felici's *L'amor soldato*, Baldassare Galuppi's *Il marchese villano* and *Le nozze*, Giuseppe Gazzaniga's

his aunt Elisabeth died in 1808. The *ex libris*, in any case, means that most full scores of operas composed before 1780 came to the Kaisersammlung from a collection other than Marie Therese's.

MARIE THERESE'S "PRECIOUS ARCHIVE"

Several kinds of evidence allow us to proceed further in defining Marie Therese's personal collection. Many manuscripts contain dedications to her. Several cantatas celebrate her or members of the Neapolitan royal family to which she belonged. Some works are referred to in letters addressed to her as having been written for, requested by, or sent to her. She probably owned many of the works whose performance she documented in her diary. Her records of the presents she gave to composers in reward for works written for her constitute strong evidence that she owned these works. Her collection of manuscript plays, librettos, and ballet scenarios contains several items that can be connected with music in whose inception she played a role, and which she consequently probably owned. Musicians sometimes wrote, either in autobiographical statements or in their autograph scores, that they composed particular pieces for her.

Among the works dedicated to Marie Therese is a large group of instrumental pieces by Orgitano, her music teacher in Naples, who wrote these pieces, mostly piano sonatas (with or without the accompaniment of violin or violin and cello), especially for her. She probably brought them to Vienna when she married Franz in 1790; most of them survive only here.[29] Johann Plunder, an official in the Imperial-Royal Ministry of War, dedicated to her a vocal score of the celebrated aria "Ombra adorata," composed by the singer Girolamo Crescentini for performance in Zingarelli's *Giulietta e Romeo* (Mus. Hs. 10846). From Eybler she accepted a collection of minuets and German dances for piano (Herrmann 208, Mus. Hs. 12961); from Ferdinand Kauer *XII. Neue Ungarische Tänze für das Fortepiano gewiedmet Ihro Königlichen Majestät Maria Theresia* (Mus. Hs. 13003); from Ignaz Schweigl *Sechs Variazioni Concertant per Septetto... Seiner Majestet der Kaiserin in aller Dieffester Ehrfurcht gewidmet* (Mus. Hs. 11398). Georg Joseph Vogler dedicated to the empress his *L'Inno di Metastasio moriente*,

---

L'isola d'Alcina, Christoph Gluck's *La corona* and *Il parnaso confuso*, Pietro Alessandro Guglielmi's *La sposa fedele*, Niccolò Piccinni's *La buona figliuola*, *La buona figliuola maritata*, and *Le contadine bizzarre*, Antonio Sacchini's *Il finto pazzo per amore*, Salieri's *Il barone di Rocca Antica*, *La fiera di Venezia*, *La locandiera*, and *La secchia rapita*, Giuseppe Scarlatti's *Issipile*, Tommaso Traetta's *Armida* and *Ifigenia in Tauride*, Wagenseil's *Demetrio*, and *Talestri* by Maria Antonia Walpurgis of Bavaria.

[29] Dietz, "Instrumental Music," includes a catalogue of extant instrumental music composed by Orgitano in MT's service from 1782 to 1790.

a tiny but harmonically eventful work for soprano and chorus (Mus. Hs. 9939).

Similar to dedications, but not quite the same, are statements on title pages that music was written at the empress's command. According to the title page of Theodor Schacht's scena "Che risolvo, che fo" (Mus. Hs. 10745) he composed it "per ordine di Sua Maestà l'Imperatrice Romana e d'Austria...in Vienna nel Febraio 1806." The current location of the Kaisersammlung's copy of Kauer's massive military symphony *Das Aufgeboth* (*CaM*, p. 14) is unknown; but a copy in the Wiener Stadt-bibliothek, entitled *Darstellung der Geschichte des Wiener Aufgeboths, nach der Angabe Ihro k. k. Majestät Maria Theresia*, suggests she owned the manuscript that became part of the Kaisersammlung.[30]

Marie Therese's birthday and nameday gave musicians opportunity to express their gratitude and eagerness for patronage. Weigl collaborated with Weinmüller, a frequent participant in her concerts, in presenting her with an undated vocal trio "Zur Allerhöchst glorreichen Namensfeyer S. M. der Keyserin Königen etz. unserer allergnädigsten Monarchin" (Mus. Hs. 10920), while Wilhelm Rong celebrated her twenty-fourth birthday in 1796 with a short dramatic work, *Volks-Freude* (Mus. Hs. 10204). Weigl celebrated not only her name and birth but also those of her mother. For Maria Carolina he wrote the cantata *Per la nascita della S. M. la regina delle due Sicilie* (Mus. Hs. 10148) and *L'amor filiale, cantata per l'arrivo di Sua Maestà la regina di Napoli* (Mus. Hs. 10146–7; the Nationalbibliothek has assigned two consecutive call numbers to *L'amor filiale* and many other works from the Kaisersammlung, indicating that they are preserved in parts – the second number – as well as score). Other cantatas can be directly connected with the Neapolitan royal family: Francesco Piticchio's *I voti della nazione napoletana*, performed in celebration of a visit to Vienna of the king and queen of Naples in 1790 (Mus. Hs. 10142), and Cimarosa's *Cantata in occasione del ritorno di Ferdinando IV* (1800, Mus. Hs. 10109). All this music probably belonged to Marie Therese.

Even more important for Marie Therese than these occasions were Emperor Franz's birthday (12 February) and nameday (4 October), which she celebrated with much musical ado. The composers who supplied works for these festivities frequently mentioned in their manuscripts the date of performance, allowing us to assign to the empress's library several more pieces of whose ownership we might otherwise have been in doubt. For

---

[30] Cited in R. M. Longyear, "Ferdinand Kauer's Percussion Enterprises," *Galpin Society Journal* 27 (1974), 4.

example, Wranitzky's divertissement *Die Binder* (Mus. Hs. 11003) announces on its title page that it was performed on 12 February 1801, while his "Ball," a collection of dances (Mus. Hs. 11017), is dated 4 October 1801.

Marie Therese the letter-writer enlisted her correspondents in collecting music. From Count Ludwig Cobenzl, the Austrian ambassador in Paris, we learn how such an arrangement might begin. In response to what was apparently an indiscriminate request for music, he urged the empress to be more specific:

As for the music in score that Y. M. desires, because you already have a big and beautiful collection I would object to sending you things you already have or can easily obtain for yourself in Vienna, [which is what might happen] if I pick things at random. I have consequently felt obliged, for the time being, to limit myself to sending you, Madam, a list of what I have found, all ready to be sent. Y. M. need only indicate to me what pieces you do not yet have, and I will purchase them. After Y. M. has obtained in this way everything good that is available at the moment, I will be on the look-out for what is newly available, in order to acquire everything that is good enough to deserve to be sent to you.[31]

Shortly thereafter Cobenzl acted as intermediary in Marie Therese's efforts (to be discussed in chapter 8) to persuade Paisiello to write an opera for her; but for help collecting Parisian music she turned from Cobenzl to Gallo, the Neapolitan ambassador, who soon became her main agent in the French capital. In his letters he mentioned several shipments of music, including scores of Henri-Montan Berton's *Le Concert interrompu*, François-Adrien Boieldieu's *Ma tante Aurore*, Cherubini's *Anacréon* and *La Prisonnière*, Jean-François Lesueur's *Ossian, ou Les Bardes*, Etienne-Nicolas Méhul's *Johanna* and *Une Folie*, and Paisiello's *Proserpine*. The Kaisersammlung contained copies of most of these operas, which Gallo's letters and bills of lading allow us to identify as having belonged to Marie Therese.

Giuseppe Carpani was Marie Therese's most important supplier of new Italian music. A poet, librettist, and writer on music, Carpani helped to introduce *opéra-comique* to Italy during the 1780s and 1790s by translating

[31] "Quant a la Musique en partition que V. M. desire, Comme Elle en a deja une grande et belle Collection je m'opposerois a Lui envoyer des choses qu'Elle tient deja ou qu'Elle peut facilement Se procurer a Vienne si j'en prenois au hazard. J'ai cru par consequent devoir me borner cette fois cy a Vous envoyer Madame une Note de ce que j'ai trouvé tout prêt a etre expedié. Il dependra de V. M. de me marquer les pieces qu'Elle n'a point, et j'en ferai l'acquisition. Après que V. M. aura obtenu ainsi tout ce qu'on a de bon dans ce moment cy je serai a l'affut de ce qui sortira de nouveau pour faire l'acquisition de tout ce qui sera assez bon pour meriter de Vous etre envoyé" (Count Cobenzl to MT, Paris, 3 February 1802, HHStA, Fa, Sb, Kart. 62, Verschiedene an Kaiserin Marie Therese 1802, fol. 204r–206v).

and arranging several French operas for performance at Monza, the summer residence of the Habsburg Archduke Ferdinand, governor of Lombardy.[32] Carpani's theatrical tastes were French, but not his politics. On the French occupation of Lombardy he remained faithful to the Habsburgs. He moved to Vienna, where he came into contact with Marie Therese and began to receive commissions from her, such as that for an Italian translation of *Die Schöpfung* used in a manuscript piano-vocal score from the Kaisersammlung, "umigliata e dedicata a S. M. l'Imperatrice Maria Teresa" (Mus. Hs. 9882).[33] From 1801 to 1805 Carpani lived in Venice (which had become part of the Austrian monarchy under terms of the Treaty of Campo Formio in 1797), serving as theatrical censor and the empress's musical agent. He wrote often to her and sent much music.[34] Almost all the scores he named in his letters can be identified with items from the Kaisersammlung; his references serve as evidence that Marie Therese owned them.[35] Fully aware of the ultimate destination of the music he sent, he referred to Valentino Fioravanti's comic opera *Il credentesi filosofo* as "most beautiful music, which I will have copied if Your Majesty does not have it in her precious archive."[36]

With her sisters in Naples Marie Therese engaged in a lively musical exchange. She sent Viennese music to Naples, often in response to specific requests from her sisters, while they sent Neapolitan scores to her. Antonia (known as Totò) wrote in 1802 that she was sending a copy of Giuseppe Millico's serious opera *Ipermestra;*[37] that accounts for the score from the Kaisersammlung (Mus. Hs. 9966). A request from Amalia shows that she

---

[32] On Carpani see Helmut C. Jacobs, *Literatur, Musik und Gesellschaft in Italien und Österreich in der Epoche Napoleons und der Restauration: Studien zu Giuseppe Carpani (1751–1825)*, Frankfurt, 1988, 214–43. Carpani's adaptations of *opéras-comiques* are the subject of a paper by Emilio Sala read at the conference "L'Opéra-comique à l'époque de Boieldieu" (Rouen, 15–17 March 2001).

[33] That Carpani translated the text of *Die Schöpfung* at MT's request is confirmed by a letter from Georg August Griesinger to Breitkopf & Härtel of 3 April 1801, in *"Eben komme ich von Haydn . . .": Georg August Griesingers Korrespondenz mit Joseph Haydns Verleger Breitkopf & Härtel, 1799–1819*, ed. Otto Biba, Zurich, 1987, 67. MT's commission resulted in two versions of the translation: one in prose, of which she owned a manuscript copy dated 1798 (HHStA, Fa, Sb, Kart. 66, fol. 411–22), and the singing version in the manuscript dedicated to MT and the piano-vocal score published by Artaria in 1801.

[34] Carpani's letters to MT are transcribed in Jacobs, *Carpani*.

[35] Works from the Kaisersammlung that Carpani mentioned include Weigl's oratorio *La passione di Gesù Cristo* (Mus. Hs. 9919–21), Stefano Pavesi's comic opera *L'amante anonimo* (Mus. Hs. 10061) and cantata *Il giudizio di Febo* (Mus. Hs. 10141), Ignazio Gerace's cantata *L'incontro* (Mus. Hs. 10121), Zingarelli's serious opera *Ines de Castro* (Mus. Hs. 10018), two numbers from Zingarelli's *Edipo* (Mus. Hs. 10834 and 10851), and the pasticcio *Pilade ed Oreste* (Mus. Hs. 10019).

[36] Carpani to MT, 5 May 1804, in Jacobs, *Carpani*, 242.

[37] Totò to MT, undated but filed in HHStA, Fa, Sb, Kart. 62, Briefe der Geschwister der Kaiserin 1802, fol. 228r.

and her sisters depended on the empress's musical expertise as much as on her generosity:

Since you have the goodness to ask us for our commissions, I ask you for the music of the ballet of *D. Giovanni Tenorio* of Gluck, if it is to be found in Vienna, for I have been told that it is superb, and know of no one to turn to in order to obtain it better than you, dear sister, who are so knowledgeable in this art, and who show us so much affection.[38]

Several composers sent scores directly to the empress. In an undated letter (written between 1805 and 1807; Fig. 1.1) Winter wrote: "In the accompanying package I most respectfully lay at Your Majesty's feet scores of the operas *Zaira* and *Calipso*, also a Missa Pastoralis and a Missa Solemnis, with the most humble prayer that they be accepted with a sign of Your Majesty's most gracious satisfaction."[39] The copies of *La grotta di Calipso* and *Zaira* from the Kaisersammlung (Mus. Hs. 10013 and 10090, 10016–17) must have belonged to Marie Therese.

Paer's letters are particularly important as a source of information about the empress's library. A native of Parma, he made his debut as a theatrical composer in 1791 and within two years began accepting commissions from Italy's leading opera houses. In 1798 he was called to Vienna, where he lived for the next four years, directing some of his earlier operas, composing new ones, and participating as a singer in private concerts, including the empress's. In 1802 he was named Kapellmeister at the court of Dresden.[40] But he stayed in touch with Marie Therese by post.

Paer referred to several pieces commissioned by the empress, such as the cantatas *Il conte Clò* and *La lanterna magica*, and to others of which she arranged performances, such as the oratorio *Il trionfo della chiesa*; copies of these works were among the many by Paer in the Kaisersammlung. He

---

38 "Come Vous avez la bonté de nous demander nos commissions, je Vous prie si on la trouve a Vienne, la Musique du ballet de *D. Giovanni Tenorio* par Gluck car on me dit qu'elle est superbe, et je ne scait pas a qui mieux me diriger pour l'avoir qu'a Vous Chere Soeur qui estes si scientifique dans cette art, et qui nous montrez tant d'amitié" (Amalia to MT, Naples, 5 June 1804, HHStA, Fa, Sb, Kart. 63, Briefe der Geschwister der Kaiserin, fol. 172v).

39 "Euer Majestät lege ich die im Anschluße mitfolgende Partituren der Oper *Zaira*, und *Calipso*, dann eine *Missa Pastorale*, und *Missa Solemne*, mit der unterthänigsten Bitte ehrfurchtvollest zu Füssen, selbe mit dem Zeichen allergnädigsten Wohlgefallens aufzunehmen" (HHStA, Fa, Sb. Kart. 65, Private an Kaiserin Marie Therese, fol. 41r). *Zaira* was first performed in January 1805 and the Pastoral Mass was written in 1805.

40 The most complete account of Paer's life and works, including a thematic catalogue of the operas, is Wolfram Enßlin, *Die Opern Ferdinando Paërs (1771–1839)*, dissertation, University of Saarbrücken, 2001. On Paer in Dresden see Richard Engländer, "Ferdinando Paer als sächsischer Hofkapellmeister," *Neues Archiv für Sächsische Geschichte und Altertumskunde* 50 (1919), 204–24, and Agatha Kobuch, "Ferdinando Paer in Dresden," *Die Dresdner Oper im 19. Jahrhundert*, ed. Michael Heinemann and Hans John, Laaber, 1995, 35–41.

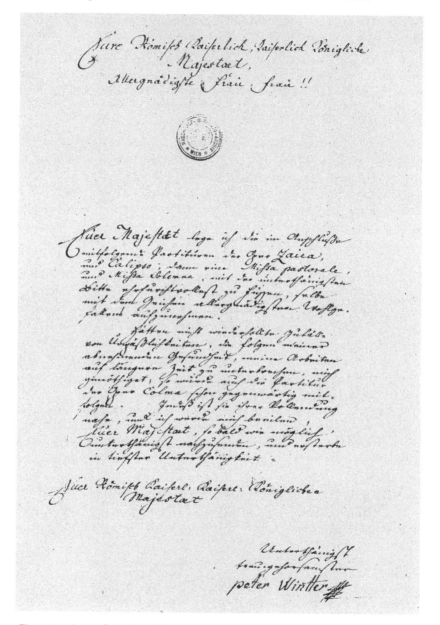

Figure 1.1 Letter from Peter Winter to the empress, written between 1805 and 1807, announcing his shipment of two operas and two masses and promising the completion of an opera commissioned by her, *Colma*.

seems to have had an understanding with her that he would send her a copy of each opera he wrote, whether for Dresden, Rome, or Bologna. He mentioned several times the shipment of scores to Vienna, once even explaining his acceptance of a commission from a public theater as an opportunity to enhance the variety of music he sent: "When the opera seria for the opening of the new theater in Bologna came my way I accepted, if for no other reason than to be able to present Your Majesty with a second score in a different genre."[41] He composed four operas during the period in which he corresponded with the empress: *Sargino* (Dresden, 1803), *Leonora* (Dresden, 1804), *Una in bene e una in male* (Rome, 1805), and *Sofonisba* (Bologna, 1805; revised for Dresden, 1806). The copies of these works from the Kaisersammlung almost certainly belonged to Marie Therese.

The empress's musical diary shows that from 1801 to 1803 her concerts were dominated by excerpts from Italian operas but also included performances of complete operas, oratorios, cantatas, liturgical works, and instrumental music. The Kaisersammlung contained copies of the vast majority of the pieces she performed, with the conspicuous exception of two categories of works. Her performances of liturgical music made use of materials that, as mentioned earlier, she bequeathed to the Hofkapelle. And several concerts organized by her brother-in-law Ferdinand probably used material from his library rather than hers, as we will see in chapter 2.

A concert in which Marie Therese participated on 15 November 1801 may serve as an example of the close connections between her music-making and the contents of the Kaisersammlung. The program was as follows:

Trio from Giuseppe Sarti's *Armida e Rinaldo*
Unidentified aria by Domenico Cimarosa
Duet from Mayr's *Adelaide di Guesclino* ("Ti lascio, mia vita")
Aria composed by Weigl for the Viennese production of Mayr's *Lodoiska*
 ("Coraggio, Boleslao")
Finale of act 1 of *Adelaide*
Chorus from Weigl's cantata *Il miglior dono*
Trio from *Il miglior dono*
Aria with chorus from *Il miglior dono*
Quintet from *Il miglior dono*
Aria from *Il miglior dono*
Duet from *Die Schöpfung* ("Holde Gattin")
Polonaise from Mayr's *Lodoiska* ("Pietoso a' miei lamenti" or "Contento il
 cor nel seno")
Finale from *Il miglior dono*

---

[41] Paer to MT, Parma, 5 March 1805. All letters by Paer cited in this book are transcribed in appendix 3.

The Kaisersammlung could have supplied scores, mostly with sets of parts, for the entire concert. It contained full scores of *Armida e Rinaldo* and *Adelaide di Guesclino*; and full scores of and parts for *Die Schöpfung*, *Il miglior dono*, "Ti lascio, mia vita," "Coraggio, Boleslao," the first-act finale of *Adelaide*, "Pietoso a' miei lamenti," "Contento il cor," and many arias by Cimarosa. These materials must have belonged to Marie Therese; so did most if not all the scores and sets of parts from the Kaisersammlung containing music whose performance is documented in the diary.

The diary also demonstrates Marie Therese's preference for certain composers. She performed with great frequency music by Cimarosa, Mayr, Paer, Weigl, and Paul Wranitzky. Most of the music by these composers from the Kaisersammlung probably came from her library. In the cases of Weigl and Wranitzky we have corroborating evidence that she owned their music. Weigl mentioned in his two autobiographical sketches that he wrote many pieces – the operas *L'uniforme* and *Il principe invisibile*, the oratorios *La passione di Gesù Cristo* and *La risurrezione*, the cantata *Il miglior dono*, and several other cantatas and small ballets – for the empress.[42] An early biographical sketch of Wranitzky states that in addition to his published compositions he also wrote "many works not yet communicated to the public, which, in accordance with the highest commission he ever received, he composed for the personal use and private pleasure of Empress Maria Theresia."[43] This does not prove that the unpublished works by Wranitzky from the Kaisersammlung belonged to her, but it makes her ownership of them very likely.

In recording her gifts to composers Marie Therese usually wrote down more details about the presents than about the pieces whose completion she was rewarding. But it is sometimes possible to identify these pieces with works from the Kaisersammlung. The "two cantatas" that earned Anton Cartellieri a gold snuffbox worth 300 Gulden and 500 Gulden in cash on 28 March 1804 must have been the oratorios *Per celebrare la festività del Santissimo Natale* (Mus. Hs. 9892–3) and *Per celebrare la festività della Purificazione di Maria Vergine* (Mus. Hs. 9891).[44] The "Terzett" for which the empress rewarded Eybler with a silver coffee service on 8 June

[42] "Zwei Selbstbiographien von Joseph Weigl," ed. Rudolph Angermüller, *Deutsches Jahrbuch der Musikwissenschaft* 16 (1971), 52, 57.

[43] "...nebst vielen andern dem Publicum noch nicht mitgetheilten Arbeiten, die er, dem ihm geschehenen höchsten Auftrage gemäß, für die Kaiserin Maria Theresia zu ihrem eigenen Gebrauche, und Privatvergnügen verfaßt hatte" (*Oesterreichische National-Encyklopädie*, 6 vols., Vienna, 1835–7, VI, 190–1).

[44] "Dem Kapellmeister Cardelieri für 2 Cantaten / Eine goldene Dose von 300 fl. / 500 fl im Geld" (HHStA, Fa, HKF, Kart. 24, diary, fol. 207r).

1803 was probably "Sposa d'Emireno tu sei" (Herrmann 155, Mus. Hs. 10359–60).[45]

The papers preserved in the Haus-, Hof- und Staatsarchiv that document Marie Therese's theatrical activities include many manuscript librettos, ballet scenarios, and proposals for theatrical works that can be identified with works from the Kaisersammlung.[46] Particularly useful are archival documents that establish links between the empress and works not mentioned in her diary. A manuscript copy of Luigi Prividali's libretto for Paer's cantata *Arianna consolata* begins with a dedicatory poem "alla Sacra Maestà di Maria Teresa Imperatrice e Regina."[47] Although we do not know when, or even if she performed *Arianna*, this manuscript suggests strongly that she commissioned it and that the score and parts from the Kaisersammlung (Mus. Hs. 10134–5) belonged to her.[48] Similarly, her manuscript copy of an anonymous libretto entitled *Parodia della Ginevra di Scozia* suggests that she owned the musical setting of that libretto (Mus. Hs. 10097–9).

By taking into account the empress's choice of repertory, her practice of commissioning works for performance on 12 February and 4 October, her habit (amply documented in the *Kathalog der Kirchenmusickalien*) of collecting not only full scores but also sets of orchestral parts, dedications and letters addressed to her, presents she gave, and the evidence of her theatrical *Nachlass*, and by eliminating those parts of the Kaisersammlung apparently assembled by Emperor Franz and his aunt Elisabeth, we arrive at a picture of the empress's music library whose general outlines are clear. She collected most of the Kaisersammlung's operas, oratorios, and cantatas in full score and parts composed after 1780. She also owned most if not all the excerpts of Italian operas and oratorios in full score and parts, and most of the music by composers of whose work she was obviously fond, such as Weigl, Eybler, and Wranitzky.

Instrumental music by other composers presents more difficulties. The largest corpus of instrumental music that we can ascribe with certainty to the empress's library is Orgitano's. But since she was a pianist, we might expect her to have owned a large part of the Kaisersammlung's holdings in

---

[45] "Juny [1803] / Dem 8. Dem Eibler für ein Terzett / Ein Dejeuné von Silber für Caffee auf 1 Person von 120 fl." (ibid., fol. 167r).

[46] MT's theatrical papers are preserved in HHStA, Fa, Sb, Kart. 65, 66, and 66a.

[47] HHStA, Fa, Sb, Kart. 66a.

[48] *Arianna* was probably performed in 1803, the date of publication of the libretto, which does not, however, contain any indication of the occasion of the performance. In a letter of 7 November 1803 Marie Therese's brother-in-law Ferdinand, grand duke of Tuscany, mentioned that she had sent him a copy of *Arianna* (ibid., Kart. 62, Erzherzog Ferdinand v. Toskana an Kais. Marie Therese, 1803, fol. 27r).

late eighteenth-century keyboard music, despite the evidence preserved in Franz's papers that he bought some of that music.

Also subject to conflicting claims is the dance music: many minuets, German dances, Ländler, and other social dances, some in manuscript orchestral parts and some in piano reductions, both manuscript and printed. Marie Therese loved to dance. As a newlywed she participated enthusiastically in several balls given during a visit to Hungary in 1790, including a "very gay" one she referred to in her diary: "I danced four *colonnes*, three *quadrilles allemandes*, and the *galopade*."[49] Did her passion for dancing lead her to collect most of the dance music from the Kaisersammlung?

Franz's musical purchases can account for only a tiny part of this dance music. Yet few of the dances contain evidence that links them with Marie Therese; nor do documents about her dancing and her organizing of balls refer to music with enough specificity to allow us to identify dances as having been written for, played by, or otherwise used by her.

Much of the dance music is dated, and almost all the dated works were written, performed, copied, or published during Marie Therese's residence in Vienna. This would suggest, but of course does not prove, that she collected much of it. Dedications to her of dance music by Eybler and Kauer were mentioned earlier as evidence that these works were part of her library. She surely also owned the *12 Menuetti in k: k: großen Redouten Saal per Clavi Cembalo gewidmet Auf den Glorreichsten Nahmenstag S*ʳ *Majestätt unserer Allergnädigsten Kayserin* by Adalbert Gyrowetz (Mus. Hs. 12964). But her ownership of these manuscripts does not necessarily mean that she was involved in the obsessive collecting of dance music that would have been necessary to compile the vast quantities of it that became part of the Kaisersammlung.

Evidence of a very unusual sort might seem to offer information about Marie Therese as collector of dance music. The Haus der Laune, an elaborate garden folly at Laxenburg to whose conception and design she contributed (it will be discussed in more detail in chapter 6) contained a music room whose walls were covered with musical title pages and scores. One of several illustrations of the musical wallpaper depicts about twenty title pages, some fully, some partially legible (Fig. 1.2). Four of these refer to dances: "Minueten in...", "Deutsche aus dem...", "Minuet," and "Contra und Deutsche." From the fact that 20 percent of the legible title pages refer to dance music we might be tempted to conclude that dance music played a

---

[49] "Au Ball, qui fut bien gay. Je dansa 4 Colonnes 3 Quadrilles Allemands et la Gallopade" (*Journal du voyage de Hongroie [179]0 IX*ᵇᵉʳ, HHStA, Fa, HKF, Kart. 24, fol. 21r, 12 November).

Figure 1.2 Watercolor illustrating a wall panel in the music room of the Haus der Laune at Laxenburg.

proportionately large role in the empress's collecting. Unfortunately, however, we do not know if this watercolor accurately represents the wall or if the choice of music on the wall accurately reflects the contents of her music library.

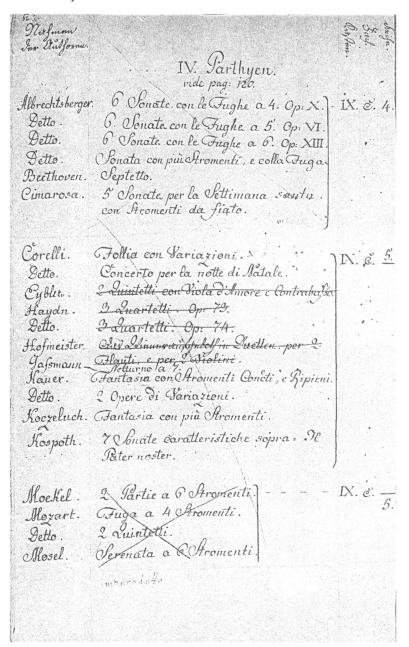

Figure 1.3 Page 62 from the original inventory of *Catalogo alter Musickalien*, with entries for several works mentioned in this book: Albrechtsberger's *Sonata con più stromenti*

A NEWLY IDENTIFIED INVENTORY OF THE EMPRESS'S COLLECTION

We are now in a position to apply our knowledge of Marie Therese's collection, however incomplete, to the identification of an inventory that records it much more fully.

CaM was compiled in at least two stages, which can be distinguished with the help of the table of contents at the beginning of the inventory. This table begins with the statement "The whole collection consists of: I. Vocal Music, and II. Instrumental Music, together with an Appendix."[50] It goes on to summarize the contents of pp. 9–108. This means that the material listed on pp. 9–108 consisted, at the time the table was made, of a "whole collection." Henceforth I will refer to the inventory on pp. 9–108 as the "original inventory." The rest of *CaM* (pp. 109–43) represents an addendum to and, to some extent, a reorganization of the original inventory. As part of that reorganization, several sections of the original inventory were crossed out with pencil, and page numbers were added directing users to those parts of the addendum that supersede parts of the original inventory.

On p. 62, for example (Fig. 1.3), under the rubric *Parthyen* the original inventory lists miscellaneous orchestral and chamber music. The diagonal lines in pencil and the inscription "vide pag: 120" indicate that most of this material was, at some time after the completion of the original inventory, recatalogued on p. 120. I say "most" because at some point between the compilation of the original inventory and the recataloguing some music was apparently discarded or lost. The entry on p. 62 for Cimarosa's *5 sonate per la settimana santa con stromenti da fiato* refers tantalizingly to a work otherwise unknown and presumably lost. The entry for Beethoven's Septet, Op. 20 (to be discussed in chapter 10) refers to a source (almost certainly a manuscript) that seems to have disappeared.

---

[50] "Die ganze Sammlung zerfällt in I. Vocal Musick. II. Instrumental Musick. nebst einen Anhang."

←

(written for Marie Therese in November 1801 and played in her concerts of 1 April and 18 July 1802), Beethoven's Septet (dedicated to Marie Therese), Cimarosa's *5 sonate per la settimana santa con stromenti da fiato*, Corelli's *Follia con Variazioni* (an orchestral arrangement by Eybler, played on 18 July 1802), two quintets by Eybler with viola d'amore and double bass (one of which was performed on 3 October 1802), Gassmann's *Notturno a 7* (apparently added, out of alphabetic order, after the original inventory was complete, and probably not part of Marie Therese's library), three works by Kauer that require various arrays of unconventional instruments, and Kozeluch's Fantasy for piano and orchestra in F minor.

Despite the cancellations, the original inventory can still be read. The "whole collection" it records corresponds closely to what we have assigned to Marie Therese's collection on the basis of other evidence. The correspondence is so close, indeed, that the original inventory appears to be nothing less than a catalogue of that part of the empress's music inherited by Franz. Almost all the music in the original inventory that I have been able to identify and date was composed before Marie Therese's death in April 1807. The only exception of which I am aware, Gasparo Spontini's *La vestale* (first performed in December 1807), was probably added to the inventory after it was complete.[51] Largely absent from the original inventory is the music we assigned to Franz on the basis of what we know of his musical tastes and activities, including the vast quantities of chamber music inscribed with the initials N. H. (most of which is listed on pp. 121–9; some rare exceptions again appear to have been inserted after the original inventory was complete.[52]) Absent too are the operatic scores collected by Archduchess Elisabeth (listed on pp. 139–40). The only items in the original inventory for which there is strong evidence of Franz's ownership are several keyboard sonatas and operatic vocal scores. But these represent a very small fraction of the sonatas and vocal scores in the original inventory, some of which, as mentioned earlier, contain dedications to Marie Therese. If Franz bought sonatas and vocal scores for his first wife, he could easily have given them to his piano-playing, opera-loving second wife. These scores do not significantly weaken the probability that the collection listed on pp. 9–108 of *CaM*, with the exception of a few works inserted into the inventory after it was complete, belonged to Marie Therese. Throughout the rest of this book I will assume that everything listed in the original inventory was part of the empress's music library, except (as in the case of *La vestale*) when there is strong evidence to the contrary.

CaM is closely related to the *Kathalog der Kirchenmusickalien*. A single scribe appears to have written out both inventories, using the same kind of paper.[53] Since the *Kathalog der Kirchenmusickalien* was compiled in connection with the settlement of Marie Therese's estate in 1807, it is likely that the original inventory in *CaM* was compiled at the same time and for the same reason. But while court officials filed the catalogue of

---

[51] *La vestale* was entered at the bottom of p. 12. But the pen used to make this entry seems to have differed from the one used immediately above it, and the curly brackets indicating the location of the other manuscripts on the page do not extend down to *La vestale*.

[52] Gassmann's *Notturno a 7* (*CaM*, p. 62; see Fig. 1.3) and Wranitzky's *Divertimenti a 7* (*CaM*, p. 63), for example, were both squeezed into spaces made available by the cancellation of entries made earlier. The entry for Gassmann's *Notturno*, moreover, is out of alphabetic order.

[53] Watermark: A RITSCHEL.

church music in the family archive, where it was never altered, the original inventory of *CaM* served as the nucleus of a catalogue of Franz's even larger collection of music, and its function as a record of Marie Therese's music library was soon forgotten.

ITALIAN OPERA

Marie Therese's collection of Italian operas in full score, as recorded on pp. 9–11 and 13–18 of *CaM*, consisted of about eighty-five works: about fifty-four serious or heroicomic, about thirty-one comic. (The totals are approximate because some of the works I have counted as secular cantatas and *drammi sacri* could legitimately be called operas, and some of the works counted as heroicomic operas could be called comic, and vice versa.) Most of the Italian operas were written between 1780 and 1805 by that epoch's best composers, both German and Italian, including Mozart (represented by *Idomeneo* and *La clemenza di Tito*: Mus. Hs. 9969–70 and 9971–2), Paisiello, Sarti, and Winter.

Despite the catholicity of taste that this variety suggests, the empress was clearly drawn to two operatic composers whose popularity was at its zenith in the first decade of the nineteenth century. Mayr and Paer wrote the most operas in the collection (see Tables 1.2 and 1.3). The large number of Paer's works resulted in part from his sending Marie Therese copies of his operas written between 1803 and 1807.

Many of the scores of operas performed in public before entering the empress's collection carry on their title pages information about their first production. In the score of Mayr's *Ginevra di Scozia*, for example, we read that the opera was performed "in occasione dell'apertura del nuovo Ces. Reg. Teatro di Trieste la primavera del anno 1801." And the title page of Cimarosa's *Artemisia* describes it as "opera postuma rappresentata nel Carnovale 1801 nel nob.^{mo} Teatro La Fenice dopo la morte dell'autore" (Mus. Hs. 9945). Such inscriptions suggest that these scores preserve versions of the operas close to those of the original production. Even if some of the scores were actually copied in Vienna (as in the case of *Ginevra di Scozia*[54]), many others are clearly of Italian origin, and were probably made at the time of the operas' first production or shortly thereafter by copyists associated with the theaters where the operas were performed. Thanks to Carpani and her other Italian correspondents, Marie Therese could study

---

[54] In a paper given at the conference "Simon Mayr und Wien" (Ingolstadt, October 2001), Daniel Brandenburg reported that the score of *Ginevra di Scozia* from the Kaisersammlung is the work of Viennese copyists.

Table 1.2 *Operas by Mayr in Marie Therese's library*

Title	Page no. in *CaM*	Call no. A-Wn, Mus. Hs.
Adelaide di Guesclino	9	9954
L'amor coniugale	9	9955
Elisa	13	9956–7
Ercole in Lidia	9	9958
Le finte rivali	14	10037–8
Ginevra di Scozia	14	9959–60
Lubino e Carlotta	14	10035–6
I misteri eleusini	14	9961–2
Gli sciti	13	9963–4
Telemaco	9	9965

In this table and those that follow, unless otherwise indicated, a single call number refers to a score; two consecutive call numbers refer to a score and a set of parts.

Table 1.3 *Operas by Paer in Marie Therese's library*

Title	Page no. in *CaM*	Call no. A-Wn, Mus. Hs.
Achille	14	9974–5
I fuorusciti di Firenze	15	10044–5
Ginevra degli Amieri	10	9978
Leonora	14	9976–7
Numa Pompilio	15	9979–80
Sargino	15	10050–1
Sofonisba	15	9981–2
La sonnambula	15	9983–4
La testa riscaldata	14	10052–3
Una in bene e una in male	15	10054–5

and perform operas soon after their first appearance in some of Italy's leading theaters.

ORATORIO AND *DRAMMA SACRO*

Marie Therese accumulated full scores of about forty-three oratorios and *drammi sacri* – the latter essentially serious operas in Italian on Old Testament subjects – by a wide range of composers, from Handel to Paer, from Guglielmi to Haydn. She commissioned several oratorios. From Carpani's letters we know that she oversaw his collaboration with Weigl on *La passione di Gesù Cristo* (Mus. Hs. 9919–21). She gave Weigl an enormous reward for the oratorio on 28 March 1804: twelve place settings of silverware worth 600 Gulden and 2,000 Gulden in cash.[55] Paer's letters reveal that she organized a public performance of *Il trionfo della chiesa*. She added to her collection oratorios by composers in whom she otherwise showed little interest. When her brother-in-law Ferdinand offered her a copy of Luigi Gatti's *Oratorio per il giorno dell'Epifania di Gesù Cristo*, of which he had just heard the premiere in Salzburg, she quickly accepted.[56]

Her extensive holdings of oratorios by Haydn reflected her special interest in this part of his output. She participated in performances of *Die Schöpfung*, *Die Jahreszeiten*, and *Die sieben letzten Worte*, of which she owned full scores and sets of parts (*CaM*, p. 19).[57] She owned no copy of *Il ritorno di Tobia*, but not for lack of trying. In 1797 she applied to the Tonkünstler-Sozietät, which had presented the premiere of *Tobia* in 1775 and revived it in 1784, for a copy of Haydn's Italian oratorio. The directorate claimed, much to the dismay of its secretary Paul Wranitzky, that the performing materials had been discarded.[58]

Marie Therese also owned sacred vocal music by several members of the Bach family, including a manuscript score of J. S. Bach's *St. Matthew Passion* (*CaM*, p. 12) and C. P. E. Bach's *Die Auferstehung und Himmelfahrt Jesu* in score and parts (*CaM*, p. 18).

SECULAR CANTATAS

The term "secular cantata" is a convenient label for a large number of vocal works in German and Italian owned by Marie Therese, generally composed to mark specific occasions, and often performed in concert rather than fully staged. Most secular cantatas are shorter than operas; several distinguish themselves from operas in consisting of loosely linked chains of musical numbers or scenes without much dramatic coherence; many of them make some reference to the occasion for which they were composed. Such works are sometimes called cantatas in the original sources,

---

[55] HHStA, Fa, HKF, Kart. 24, diary, fol. 207r.

[56] For Ferdinand's letters concerning Gatti's oratorio see chapter 2.

[57] Full scores with parts for all three oratorios were transferred from the Kaisersammlung to A-Wgm by Pohl, according to *CaM* and Pohl's list. Although the catalogue of A-Wgm does not allow us to identify these materials with absolute certainty, Otto Biba, in the course of a conversation on 28 June 2000, expressed his belief that the score of *Die Schöpfung* with the call number III 7938 / Q 832 (3 volumes) and the score of *Die Worte des Heilands am Kreuze* (III 3429 / Q 849) came from the Kaisersammlung.

[58] Carl Ferdinand Pohl, *Denkschrift aus Anlass des Hundertjährigen Bestehens der Tonkünstler-Societät*, Vienna, 1871, 45. That claim has proved false. Some performing materials for *Tobia* do indeed survive among the papers of the Tonkünstler-Sozietät in the Wiener Stadtbibliothek; see Dexter Edge, "Recent Discoveries in Viennese Copies of Mozart Concertos," *Mozart's Piano Concertos: Text, Context, Interpretation*, ed. Neal Zaslaw, Ann Arbor, Michigan, 1996, 54, 63, and Edge, *Mozart's Viennese Copyists*, 505, 1159–61.

Table 1.4 *Secular cantatas by Weigl in Marie Therese's library*

Title	Generic designation(s)	Page no. in *CaM*	Call no. A-Wn, Mus. Hs.
L'amor filiale	cantata	17	10146–7
La festa di Carolina negli Elisi	cantata	17	10152–3
Flora e Minerva	cantata	11	
Der gute Wille	accademia e cantata, ländliche musikalische Unterhaltung	19	10213–14
Il miglior dono	cantata	17	10150–1
Le pazzie musicali	cantata	17	10082–3
Per la nascita di S. M. la regina delle due Sicilie	cantata	17	10148–9
Il riposo dell'Europa	concerto allegorico	7	10154–5
Il sacrifizio interrotto	cantata, concerto pastorale	44	10156–7

but sometimes "accademia per musica," "divertimento," "accademia e cantata," "operetta," or even "opera comica." Different sources for a cantata often differ in their generic terms for it.

We have already seen that several cantatas in the Kaisersammlung were dedicated to the empress or other members of the Neapolitan royal family. Others, commissioned by her, celebrated Franz's birthday or nameday. She depended largely on Weigl and Paer for such occasional works (Tables 1.4 and 1.5). Between 1801 and 1803 she programmed four of Weigl's cantatas, *L'amor filiale*, *La festa di Carolina*, *Il miglior dono*, and *Le pazzie musicali*, in her private concerts.

While some of the cantatas are quite short (for example, *La festa di Carolina* is in two brief parts), others are as long as full-length operas. One of the grandest of all is *Arianna consolata*. The score of this sprawling work, which features a large cast of characters from Greek mythology, is bound in no fewer than nine volumes.

EXCERPTS FROM ITALIAN OPERAS AND *DRAMMI SACRI*

About five hundred excerpts from Italian operas and *drammi sacri* – arias, ensembles, and choruses – in manuscript scores and parts constituted one of the largest and most important parts of Marie Therese's music library. Her

Table 1.5 *Secular cantatas by Paer in Marie Therese's library*

Title	Generic designation(s)	Page no. in *CaM*	Call no. A-Wn, Mus. Hs.
L'amor timido	cantata a voce sola	44	10133
Arianna consolata	accademia per musica, divertimento	15	10134–5
I bisogni sollevati	concerto drammatico	14	10136–9
Il conte Clò	cantata, opera comica	14	10042–3
Eloisa ed Abeilardo agli Elisi	cantata a due voci	10	10140
La lanterna magica	cantata comica, divertimento	100	10046–7
Operetta cinese	operetta, divertimento	100	10048–9

practice, well documented in the diary, of constructing musical programs out of excerpts from operas and oratorios required a carefully organized collection of arias and ensembles. Composers well represented among the complete operas and oratorios were also well represented here, with some exceptions. On the one hand, she had so many operas and cantatas by Paer in score and parts that she found it unnecessary to collect excerpts. On the other hand, her collection included few complete scores of such major composers as Cimarosa and Pietro Alessandro Guglielmi, but many excerpts from their operas.

The case of Cimarosa can serve as an example of how Marie Therese, despite owning very few complete works of a composer, had access to a wide variety of his theatrical music. She had only one complete opera by Cimarosa in full score: the posthumously performed *Artemisia*. But her collection of extracts from ten operas and one *dramma sacro*, in score and parts, was large and varied, extending from relatively early works such as *L'italiana in Londra* to *Artemisia*, including comic operas as well as serious ones, and covering the full spectrum of musical numbers from arias to finales (Table 1.6).

Her diary documents performances of excerpts from seven works by Cimarosa: *Artemisia*, *L'impresario in angustie*, *Il matrimonio segreto*, *Gli Orazi e i Curiazi*, *Penelope*, *Il sacrificio d'Abramo*, and *Le trame deluse*. She owned excerpts from all these works.

CHURCH MUSIC

The *Kathalog der Kirchenmusickalien* tells us that Marie Therese owned at least 208 pieces of church music. To these we can add several works not

Table 1.6 *Extracts from operas and one* dramma sacro *of Cimarosa in Marie Therese's library (full scores and/or orchestral parts)*

Title of opera	Extract	Page no. in *CaM*	Call no. A-Wn, Mus. Hs.
Artemisia	introduzione (parts)	20	10287
	recit. and trio (parts), "Tremante, confusa"	25	10302
	scena and aria with chorus (parts), "Ah, che la morte"	36	10321–2
	aria (parts), "Sol dal primo amato oggetto"	36	10323
L'impegno superato	aria, "Vado smarrito e solo"	31	10325–6
L'impresario in angustie	aria, "Vado in giro"	31	10327–8
L'italiana in Londra	duet (score), "Caro amico"	29	10304
	aria (score), "Straniera abbandonata"	36	10329
Il matrimonio segreto	trio, "Le faccio un inchino"	23	10290–1
L'Olimpiade	rondò, "Nel lasciarti, o prence"	31	10332–3
	aria, "Se cerca, se dice"	31	10334–5
	aria (score), "Superbo di me stesso"	36	?
Gli Orazi e i Curiazi	finale of act 2 (sotterraneo)	20	10285–6
	trio, "Quando nel campo"	23	10292–3
	trio, "Germe d'illustri eroi"	23	10294–5
	duet, "Se torni vincitor"	26	10306–7
	duet (score), "Quando nel campo" (first part of trio)	29	10308
	aria, "Se alla patria"	31	10336–7
Oreste	aria (score), "Cara, nel pianto mio"	36	10338
Penelope	trio, "Perché eguale all'amor mio	24	10296–7
	recit. and trio, "Questi Ulisse il padre mio"	24	10298–9
	duet, "Non ho più costanza"	26	10311–12
	duet, "Da questo lido sgombri"	26	10313–14
	duet, "Va, non ti temo o barbaro"	26	10315–16
	scena ed aria, "Barbari, alfin cadeste" (sotterraneo)	31	10339–40
	aria, "Ah serena, oh madre, il ciglio"	31	10341–2
	aria, "Vado, vado ma dove"	31	10343–4
	march and cavatina, "Pur ti riveggo, amate spiagge"	31	10345–6
Il sacrificio d'Abramo	trio, "Volgi o Dio"	23	10300–1
	duet, "Consola il tuo dolore"	26	10309–10
Le trame deluse	quintet, "Che tremore nelle vene"	22	10288–9
	duet (score), "Vanne, o cara"	29	10317
	duet (score), "Vanne, o cara"	29	10318
unidentified opera	recit. and aria (parts), "Ah parlate"	36	10348

transferred to the Hofkapelle after her death: Eybler's autographs (to be discussed below) and two masses that must have been considered unsuitable for performance in the court chapel. Wranitzky's mass with children's instruments that Marie Therese performed on 28 February 1802 and the comic "Schulmeister-Messe" wrongly attributed in *CaM* to Michael Haydn entered the Kaisersammlung instead.[59]

The empress's church music consisted largely of masses, requiems, Te Deums, offertories, and graduals: precisely the kind of sacred music she performed in her concerts. I will argue in chapter 5 that in many cases a gradual, an offertory, a Te Deum, and a setting of the Ordinary constitute a single composite work. Marie Therese's interest in building musical spans longer than that of the Ordinary helps to explain her love of requiems, for which of course plenary settings were customary. Her collection included many requiems: three by the Neapolitan Francesco Durante, two by Michael Haydn (the C minor Requiem of 1771 and another in Bb, commissioned by Marie Therese but left unfinished at the composer's death), and one each by Carl'Antonio Campion, Eybler (commissioned by the empress), Florian Gassmann, Filippo Gherardeschi, Johann Hasse, Giuseppe Moneta, Mozart, Orgitano, Salvador Pazzaglia, Georg Reutter, and Winter.

The empress's church music reflected Austrian traditions more closely than most other parts of her music library. It included music of major Austrian composers – Michael Haydn, Reutter, and Gassmann – otherwise largely absent from her collecting and performances.

The sacred collection contained more music composed before 1780 than the rest of the library. For all her musical experience and sophistication, Marie Therese was a child of her time in her lack of interest in dramatic music more than about twenty years old. She limited her performances of opera and oratorio, with few exceptions, to works written after 1780. But like many of her contemporaries she enjoyed older church music. She owned sacred music by Italian composers represented little or not at all in the rest of her collection, such as Leonardo Leo, Giovanni Battista Pergolesi, and Niccolò Jommelli. She must have known they wrote operas – Jommelli celebrated her baptism in 1772 with a *festa teatrale*, *Cerere placata* – but

---

[59] Wranitzky's mass with children's instruments (*CaM*, p. 100) is in A-Wn, Mus. Hs. 10235; Pohl transferred the "Schulmeister-Messe" (*CaM*, p. 99) to A-Wgm. Michael Haydn denied authorship of the latter in a letter to Franz Xaver Göggl, Kapellmeister in Linz: "Ich zweifle sehr, ob die bekannte komische Schulmeister-Messe vom Mozart sey; von mir ist sie gewiß nicht; denn ich habe es niemals in Gebrauch gehabt, ernsthafte oder andächtige Texte lächerlich machen zu wollen. Mir scheint es eine Posse von Brixi zu seyn" (quoted in Jancik, *Michael Haydn*, 260; my thanks to Charles Sherman and Otto Biba for this citation).

she owned no operas by Pergolesi or Leo and only one by Jommelli (*Ezio*, Mus. Hs. 9952). Her fascination with requiems caused her to think of music older than most of what she performed. When she met Michael Haydn in 1801, the music she mentioned was thirty years old: "Oh, I know some of your compositions, and especially your *Requiem*, very well, and love them."[60]

Yet even her collection of church music favored the performance of contemporary works. She owned sets of parts for much of her more modern music, while most of the older works were represented by scores only. And in collecting music of living composers, such as Albrechtsberger and the Haydn brothers, she preferred recent compositions. Of her twelve sacred works by Albrechtsberger, who began composing for the church in the 1750s, at least eight were written after 1793.

Marie Therese rarely let politics get in the way of acquisitions of music; her collection of liturgical works included some that Paisiello wrote for Napoleon's chapel between 1802 and 1804. Gallo sent two motets with an amusing comment on Napoleon's churchgoing:

In the meantime I do not want to delay sending you two beautiful compositions of Paesiello, made for the chapel of the First Consul for the recent holidays. These pieces pleased very much, and since church music was not cultivated here, now its novelty has created a furor, like all novelties in Paris. Your Imperial Majesty will find them most beautiful, and moreover very easy to perform, and short; for although the First Consul is pleased to hear Mass, and to kneel, yet he does not have the patience to remain a while, and wishes that this ceremony finish as soon as possible. I hope Your Majesty will be happy with them; and be certain that I will pay all the attention necessary to send you everything in this genre that may be of interest to you.[61]

Marie Therese ended up with three of Paisiello's Napoleonic motets: "Splendete o coeli," "Absit sonitus," and "Non est in vita."

---

[60] "O ich kenne einige ihrer Compositionen, besonders ihr *Requiem*, recht gut, und liebe sie" (*Biographische Skizze von Michael Haydn*, 29).

[61] "Intanto non voglio tardare di mandarle due bellissime musiche di Paesiello fatte per la cappella del Pr. Console in queste feste. Queste musiche hanno piaciuto assai, e siccome qui le musiche di chiesa erano fuori di esercizio, ora la novità ha fatto furore; come tutte le novità fanno in Parigi. V. M. I. le troverà belle assai, ed inoltre molto facili ad eseguirsi, e corte; giacchè sebbene il Pr. Console si contenta di sentir la Messa, e di stare in ginocchio; pure non ha pazienza di starci un pezzo, e vole che questa cerimonia si sbrighi più presto che sia possibile. Spero che V. M. ne sarà contenta: e sia pur sicura che io avrò tutta l'attenzione che devo per mandarle tutto quello che la può interessare in questo genere" (Gallo to MT, 8 January 1803, HHStA, Fa, Sb, Kart. 62, Verschiedene an Kaiserin Marie Therese 1803, fol. 147v–148r).

Table 1.7 *Eybler's autograph scores of church music written for Marie Therese*

Title	Call number (A-Ws, unless otherwise indicated)
Te Deum Laudamus / Missa [added later: Sti. Wolfgangi]. / Graduale ["Nocte surgentes"]. Offertorium ["Fremit mare"]. 180[0]	567 (436)
Partitura / Te Deum / [added later: Stae Theresiae] / Missa, Offertorium ["Levavi in montes"], e Graduale ["Magnificate Dominum"] / 1802 / Del Sig. Gius. Eybler	570 (439)
2 Psalmi / Laudate pueri / De profundis	548 (417)
Requiem / Libera / De profundis. / Del Sig.ᵉ Eybler / 803	A-Wn, Mus. Hs. 16591
Te Deum / Missa [added later: Sti Michaelis] / Graduale ["Cantate Domino"] et / Offertorium ["Ad te levavi"] / 1804	566 (435)
Missa [added later:] in B. Sti Francisci / Graduale ["Exaltate Dominum"] / ed Offertorium ["Lux est orta"] / a 2 Cori. / 1806	699 (708)

A few important church music manuscripts that Marie Therese almost certainly owned (listed in Table 1.7) are not cited in the *Kathalog der Kirchenmusickalien*, were never part of the Kaisersammlung, and (with one exception) are not preserved in the Nationalbibliothek or the Gesellschaft der Musikfreunde. She bequeathed church music "which can be used" to the Hofkapelle; "the rest of the church music goes to Eibler." Eybler seems to have taken advantage of these vague instructions to reclaim the autograph scores of works he had written for her.

Eybler's own collection of music went to the library of the Schottenstift, the Viennese monastery where he served as Kapellmeister for many years. Among his autograph scores in the Schottenstift are several works he wrote for Marie Therese. Most of these are bound in pale blue covers with white labels glued to the front, identical to the covers on many of the scores in the Nationalbibliothek that belonged to her. This suggests that she owned these autographs. Eybler apparently removed them from her library before the church music inventory of 1807.

One liturgical work written by Eybler for Marie Therese of which the Nationalbibliothek rather than the Schottenstift owns the autograph score is the Requiem (Mus. Hs. 16591). According to an inscription on its cover, Eybler donated the autograph in 1831 to the court library, which subsequently became the Nationalbibliothek. Bound in pale blue with a white label on the front, this score too probably belonged to Marie Therese.

The original inventory in *CaM* clarifies Marie Therese's activities as a collector of instrumental music, for which there is less evidence of other kinds than in the case of vocal music. She seems to have accumulated instrumental music with as much avidity as operas, oratorios, cantatas, and church music.

In view of her long experience as a pianist, it is not surprising that she owned a great deal of keyboard music other than that of her former teacher Orgitano. She collected many solo sonatas, sets of variations, sonatas with violin accompaniment, piano trios, quartets, other chamber music with piano, concertos, and keyboard reductions of operas and ballets (*CaM*, pp. 71–89). Her collection of keyboard music by Mozart, much of it printed, ranged from concertos to solo sonatas (Table 1.8); it shows that she made an effort to include in her library the very finest recently composed instrumental music.

Most of the overtures and symphonies performed in Marie Therese's concerts probably came from her large collection of orchestral music in parts. She owned many concert symphonies, opera overtures, concertos for a wide variety of solo instruments, and programmatic works on military themes (*CaM*, pp. 57–61). Her favorite symphonists were Paul Wranitzky (she owned sixteen of his symphonies, *CaM*, p. 58) and Joseph Haydn (fifteen symphonies, *CaM*, p. 57); that is consistent with the frequent performances of symphonies by Wranitzky and Haydn recorded in her diary. The original inventory does not identify individual symphonies, but since this part of the inventory was reorganized and the works listed there were listed again in more detail later in *CaM*, we know the identity of most of the symphonies by Wranitzky (Table 1.9).

Although the empress's papers contain little evidence about how much of the dance music from the Kaisersammlung came from her, the original inventory in *CaM* (in which dance music is listed on pages 65–71 and 90–7) leaves little doubt that she owned most of it. In addition to hundreds of dances by musicians who specialized in the composition of ballroom music, such as Joseph Bock, Joseph Heidenreich, and Stanislaus

Table 1.8 *Keyboard music in Marie Therese's library by (or attributed to) Mozart*

This table includes concertos and chamber music but not keyboard arrangements of orchestral or orchestrally accompanied vocal music. The titles given in *CaM* do not allow us to identify some of these items; contributing to the difficulty of identification is that Pohl transferred most of Mozart's music from the Kaisersammlung to A-Wgm, where the provenance of many items in its vast Mozart holdings is now hard to trace. Because the nine concertos listed in detail in the addendum to *CaM* (pp. 109–110) are almost certainly the same nine concertos listed very briefly on p. 59 of the original inventory ("Mozart. Concerto per 2 Cembali / Detto. 8 Concerti per Cembalo"), I have taken the titles of the concertos from the addendum.

Titles as recorded in *CaM*	Page nos. in *CaM*	Köchel numbers
Concerto in C	59, 109	467 or 503
– in B	59, 109	450, 456, or 595
– in B	59, 109	450, 456, or 595
– in D	59, 109	451 or 537
– in D minore	59, 109	466
Concerto grande in D	59, 110	451 or 537
– per 2 Cembali in Es	59, 110	365
Concerto in Es	59, 110	449 or 482
– per 2 Cembali in F	59, 110	242
Trio per C[embalo]. Violino e Basso. Op. 16	75	564
Sonata I per C e Violino. nb Violino manca	75	301
3 Son. per C. S[olo]. Op. 6	75	330, 331, 332
Rondo per C. S.	75	485, 494, or 511
Son. in Es per Cem. e Violino	75	481
Son. in B per C. e Violino. Op. 40	75	570
3 Son. per C. con Violino. Op. 30	75	303, 305, 306
6 Son. per C. con Violino. Op. 2	75	296, 376, 377, 378, 379, 380
Quartetto in Es. Op. 13. nb in dupplo	75	493
Son. per 2 Cembali con Accomp. di 2 Violini, Viola, e Basso. Op. 34	75	448?
Quintetto in B per C. 2 Violini, Viola, e Violoncello	75	595-Anh. B
Quintetto in Es per C. Oboe, Clarinetto, Corno, e Fagotto	75	452
L'Istesso ridotto in un Quartetto per C. Violino, Viola, e Violoncello. Op. 29	75	452-Anh. B
Quintetto in G per C. 2 Vio. Viola, e Violoncello	75	453-Anh. B
Son. III per C. con Violino	75	303
Son. IV per C. con Violino	75	304

(*cont.*)

Table 1.8 (*cont.*)

Titles as recorded in *CaM*	Page nos. in *CaM*	Köchel numbers
3 Son. per C. S.	75	284, 333, 454, or 309, 310, 311
17 [sets of variations for keyboard, probably including some with violin accompaniment]	80	
Fuga per 2 Cembali	84	426
Fantasia con Son. per C. S. Op. 11	84	457, 475

Table 1.9 *Symphonies by Paul Wranitzky in Marie Therese's library*

Title, Poštolka number (P), and source	Page nos. in *CaM*	Call no.
Symphony in C, P. 5, *bei Gelegenheit der Erhebung Franzens zum deutschen Kaiser*, printed parts, Offenbach, [1792]	58, 119	A-Wgm, XIII 27101
Symphony in C, P. 8, *A Magyar Nemzet Öröme*, printed parts, Offenbach, [1790]	58, 119	A-Wgm, XIII 8587
Symphony in C minor, P. 12, *Grande Sinfonie caractéristique pour la paix avec la Republique Françoise*, printed parts, Augsburg, [1797]	58, 119	A-Wgm, XIII 18959
Symphony in D, P. 18, *bei Gelegenheit der hohen Vermählung Sr. K. K. Hoheit, des Erzherzogs Joseph*, printed parts, Offenbach, [1799]	58, 119	A-Wgm, XIII 27100; A-Wn, MS 27429
Symphony in D, P. 20, orchestra includes Turkish instruments, ms. parts	58, 120	A-Wn, Mus. Hs. 11052
Symphony in D, P. 23, *bey Gelegenheit der Vermählungs-Feyer des Herrn Grafen Nicolas Esterhazy*; orchestra includes Papageno-pipes; printed parts, Offenbach, [1793]	58, 119	A-Wn, MS 27430
Symphony in D, La chasse, P. 25, printed parts, Offenbach, [ca. 1799–1800]	58, 119	A-Wn, MS 27428
Quodlibet Symphony in D, P. 27, orchestra includes piano	58, 120	A-Wn, Mus. Hs. 11086–7

(*cont.*)

Table 1.9 (*cont.*)

Title, Poštolka number (P), and source	Page nos. in *CaM*	Call no.
Symphony in G, P. 38, orchestra includes glockenspiel and Papageno-pipes, parts	58, 119	A-Wn, Mus. Hs. 11053
Symphony in G minor, P. 42, orchestra includes piano	58, 120	A-Wn, Mus. Hs. 11088–9
Synf. per i Violini molto difficile	58, 120	?
Synfonia strepitosa	58, 120	?
Synfonia grande con Eccho	58, 120	?
Three other unidentified symphonies	58	?

von Ossowsky, she also owned most of Mozart's Viennese production, in both piano arrangements and orchestral parts, of minuets, German dances, Ländler, and contredanses.

CHAPTER 2

Marie Therese's musicians

The instrumentalists and singers who made music with the empress included some of Europe's most celebrated professional musicians and Vienna's most admired amateurs. Some of them performed with her only occasionally, others more or less regularly. To these and to herself she referred, only partly in jest, as "i fedeli credenti" (the faithful believers).[1]

GRAND DUKE FERDINAND IN EXILE

Marie Therese's brother-in-law and cousin Ferdinand, a baritone and pianist, sang with her often during the period covered by her diary.[2] As second son of Grand Duke Pietro Leopoldo of Tuscany – later Emperor Leopold II – he received much the same musical training as his older brother Franz; he shared a love of music not only with Franz but also with a much younger brother, the Archduke Rudolph who would later be Beethoven's pupil and patron. We have seen in chapter 1 that as a teenager Ferdinand was already collecting music, asking Franz and his first wife Elisabeth to send scores from Vienna to Florence. Shortly after Leopold succeeded his brother Joseph to the throne of the Austrian monarchy in 1790, he abdicated Tuscany to Ferdinand. But the young grand duke was destined for a fifteen-year game of musical thrones, swept from one minor capital to another by the powerful military and diplomatic forces of the Napoleonic era.[3]

---

[1] See MT's sketch for the cantata *Il conte Clò* in Appendix 5A. Paer used a similar phrase: "I give myself the courage to place myself at Your Imperial Feet and to declare myself forever and ever one of *Suoi Fedeli Credenti* (Paer to MT, Rome, 3 November 1804).

[2] Ferdinand was Marie Therese's brother-in-law by way of both her husband Franz and her sister Maria Luisa: he was Franz's brother and Maria Luisa's husband.

[3] On Ferdinand's life see Anton Chroust, *Lebensläufe aus Franken*, 6 vols., Würzburg, 1930, IV, 142–72; and Franz Pesendorfer, *Ein Kampf um die Toskana: Großherzog Ferdinand III, 1790–1824*, Vienna, 1984.

In the face of a French invasion of Tuscany in 1799 Ferdinand fled to Vienna with his family and personal possessions that included a music library and a collection of prints.[4] The unemployed grand duke devoted much of his time to music. He sang bass and baritone parts with Marie Therese very frequently during 1802, in concerts at her residence and his. Only three years older than she, he fully matched her enthusiasm and energy, her passion for collecting and performing contemporary music, and her musical taste. He probably shared with her not only decisions about what music to perform but also responsibility for providing performance materials. That would help explain why several works they performed, especially in concerts at his residence, were not in her library: the scores and parts probably belonged to him.[5]

The grand duke's collection, which appears to have been even bigger than Marie Therese's, later became part of the library of the Conservatorio Luigi Cherubini in Florence, making it a crucial repository of late eighteenth- and early nineteenth-century music. Among the Conservatorio's manuscripts are performing materials for most of the works sung by Marie Therese and Ferdinand in their concerts, including some works absent from her library.[6]

In 1803 Ferdinand's music-making with Marie Therese was interrupted by an agreement between Austria and France that made him electoral prince of Salzburg. He left Vienna in April 1803 and soon began a correspondence with his sister-in-law that gives us an idea of what musical conversations between them in Vienna might have been like.

Just a few weeks after his arrival in Salzburg Ferdinand wrote: "Music still languishes here, and I have hardly touched the cembalo because, between audiences, papers, and unpacking, I have so much to do."[7] But that did not keep him from quickly organizing, like Marie Therese, a group of musicians with whom to give private concerts. He wrote five days later: "This evening I'll try out my musicians. They wanted to do *La Creazione*, but I disagreed, saying that instead they should each choose a piece by which I could get to

---

[4] Chroust, *Lebensläufe* IV, 144, citing *Vertrauliche Briefe des Freiherrn von Thugut*, ed. Alfred Vivenot, 2 vols., Vienna, 1872, II, 167.
[5] See, for example, the contents of the concert of 7 March 1802.
[6] On the Conservatorio's holdings see R. Gandolfi, C. Cordara, and A. Bonaventura, *Catalogo delle opere musicali... Biblioteca del Conservatorio di Musica a Firenze*, Parma, 1929, reprint Bologna, 1977. Two manuscript inventories in the Archivio di Stato, Florence, record part of the contents of Ferdinand's library: I.R.C. 5429 ("Catalogo delle Opere ridotte Sinfonie &ra") and I.R.C. 5430 ("Catalogo della Musica da Chiesa"). I am grateful to Robert Weaver for telling me of these catalogues.
[7] "Qui la Musica ancora languisce, ed io appena ho toccato ancora il Cembalo perchè ho sempre da fare tra Udienze fogli, e spacchettamenti" (Ferdinand to MT, Salzburg, 7 May 1803, HHStA, Fa, Sb, Kart. 62, Erzherzog Ferdinand v. Toskana... an Kais. Marie Therese, 1803, fol. 5r).

know them. I will tell you what happens another day."[8] Three days later he reported:

I had music performed, and truly it wasn't bad, the things they did being well executed although a little old-fashioned in taste. The concertmaster, the leader of the second violins, and a double bass are really excellent; the tenor and the bass – who is still young – have good voices; I don't remember the pieces well, but they were short. Today they will do another, and I want to surprise them by giving them that symphony that can break one's neck, just to see what happens.[9]

In another letter we can almost see Ferdinand rummaging through his library, looking for a missing part and finding one that did not belong there:

Dearest sister, having found in my music collection a bassoon part from *Griselda*, I write to you because if it's yours I can send it to you. Also, in the music of *Arianna consolata* that you were so kind to send me, the whole of Arianna's part is missing in Act [number missing]. So I ask you please to send it to me. At the moment *Il trionfo della chiesa* is being copied for you, but it's going slowly because the copyists here are not bolts of lightning as they are in Vienna, and they are very lazy.[10]

A letter that Ferdinand wrote a few weeks later shows how he and the empress helped each other build up their libraries by trading copies:

With the first diligence you will receive the first act of Pär's *La risurrezione*; the second act is still being copied. You will also receive Kreutzer's *La Lodoiska*, but I don't know if you will like it. To tell you the truth, I have never looked at it. I ask you to send me the aria and the new quartet written for Brocchi in *L'amor marinaro*, as well as the aria written last year for Saal to sing in that opera. I also

---

8 "Questa sera dò una provata ai miei Musici. Volevano far la Creazione, ma io hò protestato, ed hò detto, che piuttosto ogni uno si scelga un pezzo in cui farsi conoscere, la Relazione ve la manderò un altro giorno" (Ferdinand to MT, Salzburg, 12 May 1803, ibid., fol. 7r).

9 "Feci fare musica, e veramente non vi è male, essendo bene eseguito quello che hanno fatto, benchè di un gusto un poco antico. Il primo Violino, ed il primo dei secondi, ed un Contrabbasso sono veramente bravi; il Tenore, ed il Basso che è ancora giovine hanno buona voce; i pezzi non me li ricordo bene ma fu breve. Oggi ne fanno un altra e li voglio dare all'improvviso quella tale Sinfonia da rompere il Collo per vedere che cosa succede" (Ferdinand to MT, Salzburg, 15 May 1803, ibid., fol. 9r).

10 "Carissima Sorella. Avendo trovata frà la mia Musica una parte di Fagotti della Griselda ve lo scrivo, perché se mai fosse vostra ve la possa rimandare. Poi in quella Musica dell'Arianna consolata che mi avete favorita manca tutta la parte d'Arianna nel Atto [number omitted] vi prego dunque di farmela avere. Attualmente si va copiando il Trionfo della Chiesa per voi, ma adagio perché quà i Copisti non sono fulmini come a Vienna e sono molto agiati" (Ferdinand to MT, Salzburg, 7 November 1803, ibid., fol. 27r.).
    MT owned the three works to which Ferdinand referred, in score and parts: several excerpts from Piccinni's *Griselda* (Mus. Hs. 10654–61), Paer's cantata *Arianna consolata* (Mus. Hs. 10134–5), and Paer's oratorio *Il trionfo della chiesa* (Mus. Hs. 9932–3). This last, on a libretto by Pietro Bagnoli, had been commissioned by Ferdinand, who gave MT a copy, perhaps in exchange for the copy of *Arianna consolata* that she had sent him.

ask you to send me the most recent mass and Te Deum written by Eybler for Laxenburg two years ago, I believe. In the last few days we have performed Mayr's *Gli sciti*, and I discovered that my score is missing, in Act 2, the gatherings 9, 10, and 11 of the *Sotterraneo*, which are precisely those belonging to that beautiful scene you like so much. If they remained with you, you would have duplicates, since it was you who gave me this music. The parts are all right, so I would ask you to please send them [i.e. the missing sections of the score] to me, otherwise I will have them recopied here.[11]

In Salzburg Ferdinand came into frequent contact with Michael Haydn, who had served the prince-archbishops of Salzburg as Konzertmeister from 1763 and as organist from 1783 (he succeeded Mozart in the latter post). Indeed it was because of Ferdinand's anticipated arrival in Salzburg that Haydn turned down an offer to replace his brother Joseph as music director to the second Prince Nicolaus Esterházy. Writing to Michael on 22 January 1803, Joseph Haydn compared Ferdinand to his own employer: "Both patrons are great, but the Grand Duke's love for and understanding of music surpass that of my Prince."[12]

Ferdinand formed a fine collection of Michael Haydn's music, now in Florence. In doing so he was faced with an occasional problem in textual criticism, as when he discovered that the first of the two masses Haydn wrote for Marie Therese, the *Missa S. Theresiae*, existed in two different versions (Sherman 796 and 797): "In the mass that the Haydn from here

---

[11] "Colla prima diligenza riceverete il primo Atto della Risurrezione di Pär, il secondo si sta scrivendo. Riceverete ancora la Lodoiska di Kreutzer ma non sò se vi piacerà. Io veramente non l'hò esaminata mai. Vi prego di mandarmi l'Aria, ed il Quartetto nuovo scritto per Brocchi nell'Amor marinaro come anche l'aria che fù scritta l'anno passato per la Saal in quest'Opera. Vi prego ancora di mandarmi l'ultima Messa e Te Deum fatto dall'Eybler per Laxemburg credo due anni sono. Abbiamo fatto questi giorni gli Sciti di Mayer, ed ho trovata la mia partitura mancante nel 2do Atto dei quinterni 9 10 11 del Sotterraneo che sono appunto quelli della bella Scena che a voi tanto piace. Se mai vi fossero rimasti a voi vi sarebbero doppi giacché foste voi che mi daste questa Musica. Le parti cavate stanno bene allora vi pregherei di mandarmeli altrimenti li farò supplire qui" (Ferdinand to MT, Salzburg, 28 November 1803, ibid., fol. 31r–v).
"Pär's *La risurrezione*" was *Il trionfo della chiesa*, the full title of which, according to the libretto published in Vienna (1803), is *Il trionfo della chiesa nella resurrezione di N. S. G. C.* MT must have returned Rodolphe Kreutzer's *Lodoiska*; her library contained no copy of it. The veteran comic bass Giambattista Brocchi made his Viennese debut in March 1803. In a revival of Weigl's *L'amor marinaro* later that year he portrayed the music teacher Cisolfaut. The soprano Therese Saal took the role of Lucilla in the same production. The "most recent mass and Te Deum" by Eybler were the *Missa S. Theresiae* in B♭ (Herrmann 29) and the version for single choir of the Te Deum in B♭ (Herrmann 120), composed in 1802 and performed by MT on 21 September of that year. She also performed several times the *sotterraneo* from Mayr's *I sciti*, of which she owned a score and parts (Mus. Hs. 9963–4).
[12] Rough draft transcribed in *Joseph Haydn: Gesammelte Briefe und Aufzeichnungen*, ed. Dénes Bartha, Kassel, 1965, 419, quoted in translation (used here) in Karl Geiringer, *Haydn: A Creative Life in Music*, 3rd ed., Berkeley, 1982, 180.

wrote for you, which you had the goodness to give me, there is a fugue completely different from the one in the score that Haydn gave me."[13] The fugues in question are two settings of "In gloria Dei Patris" at the end of the Gloria. One is to be found in the set of parts for the *Missa S. Theresiae* in Florence, the other in an autograph score in the same library.[14] Ferdinand presumably received the parts from Marie Therese, the autograph score from Haydn himself.

While amassing manuscripts of Michael Haydn, Ferdinand helped Marie Therese build up her collection as well. Of Haydn's great Mass in C for double chorus ("Missa hispanica") he wrote excitedly on 7 February 1804: "I have dug up here a mass of Michele Haydn a 2 cori. First I will try it, and if I find it nice, I will write to you so that you may decide if you want it or not."[15] But it was not until 1805, when Franz and Marie Therese visited Salzburg, that Ferdinand showed her the "Missa hispanica." "It pleased her so much that she wished to own it."[16] Her wish was granted (see appendix 1).

Among the manuscripts in Florence that almost certainly belonged to Ferdinand is the autograph of an oratorio by Luigi Gatti, who had served as Hofkapellmeister at Salzburg since 1783, *Oratorio per il giorno dell' Epifania*.[17] In Ferdinand's letters we can follow Gatti's work from before its premiere in Salzburg to its being copied and sent to Marie Therese.

On 29 December 1804 Ferdinand wrote:

Since you were good enough to ask me about new music, I ask you to please send me Salieri's new Te Deum and Mass, and the opera *I riti d'Efeso* of Farinelli.

---

[13] "Nella Messa che scrisse il Haydn di qui per voi che aveste la bontà di darmi vi è una Fuga affatto differente da quella che è nella Partitura che me ne ha data il Haydn medesimo" (Ferdinand to MT, Salzburg, 12 May 1804, HHStA, Fa, Sb, Kart. 63, fol. 11).

[14] Both sources have the same call number: F.P. Ch. 318.

[15] "Ho scavato qui una Messa di Michele Haydn a 2 Cori, prima la proverò, e se mai la troverò bella, ve lo scriverò perche possiate decidervi se la volete o no" (Ferdinand to MT, Salzburg, 7 February 1804, ibid., fol. 1v).

[16] The report of the imperial visit to Salzburg in *AmZ* 7 (1804–5), cols. 625–8, describes a concert given by Ferdinand at which a mass by Gatti was performed. It continues: "Dann legten Seine Durchlaucht die zweychörige Messe Michael Haydn's auf, die dieser vormals nach Spanien verfertigte, und die der Kaiserin noch nicht bekannt war. Sie gefiel ihr so, daß sie sie zu besitzen wünschte." Although the first sentence has been interpreted (for example, in Gerhard Croll and Kurt Vössing, *Johann Michael Haydn: Sein Leben, sein Schaffen, seine Zeit*, Vienna, 1987, 147) to mean that the "Missa hispanica" was performed before the imperial couple, the verb *auflegen* (considered in light of our knowledge of the empress's highly developed musicianship) suggests another possible interpretation: that Ferdinand "laid out" the score or parts for Marie Therese's inspection.

[17] I-Fc, F.P. T 115.

Abate Gatti has composed an oratorio for Epiphany, which I have not yet heard. I am curious to see how it turns out. When it is performed I will tell you about it."[18]

He fulfilled his promise on 20 January 1805: "Abate Gatti's oratorio was a great success. The music is very difficult to play and to sing, and if it has a defect, it is that it is too heavily orchestrated, and covers the voices; but it pleased everyone. Tell me if you would like it, and I will have it copied immediately."[19]

Marie Therese must have accepted Ferdinand's offer, for he wrote less than a month later: "Abate Gatti's oratorio will be copied right away, and since you have the kindness to offer it, I ask you to please send me Farinelli's *farsa, Odoardo e Carlotta*."[20] On 24 April he told her he had already shipped the oratorio: "With last week's diligence I sent the score of Abate Gatti's new oratorio. I beg your pardon if the gatherings are of different sizes. It is not my fault because I could do nothing less than leave the supervising of the copying to the composer himself, so that it would be accurate. I hope you will like it."[21] The score from Marie Therese's library (Mus. Hs. 9896), in which some gatherings are almost two centimeters longer than others, must be the one sent by Ferdinand.

The Treaty of Pressburg, concluded at the end of 1805, formalized the defeat of the Austro-Russian alliance at Austerlitz. It ended Ferdinand's rule in Salzburg and set him up in yet another tiny principality. He became grand duke of Würzburg, which he entered in May 1806, taking up residence in the great palace whose ceilings glowed with Tiepolo's frescos. There he continued to collect and to perform music until 1814, when, the tide of war having turned against the French, he found Tuscany restored to him. He

---

[18] "Giacchè avete la bontà di domandarmi delle nuove Musiche vi prego di mandarmi il nuovo Te Deum e Messa di Salieri, e l'Opera de' *Riti d'Efeso* di Farinelli. L'abate Gatti ha composto un Oratorio per l'Epifania che non ho ancora sentito. Sono curioso di vederne l'esito. Quando sarà stato eseguito ve ne darò conto" (Ferdinand to MT, Salzburg, 29 December 1804, HHStA, Fa, Sb, Kart. 63, fol. 23).

[19] "L'oratorio dell'Abate Gatti è riescito molto bene, la musica è molto difficile a cantarsi, ed a suonarsi, e se ha un diffetto, si è che è troppo istrumentata, e copre le voci ma ha piaciuto universalmente. Se mai la desiderate ditemelo che la farò subito copiare" (Ferdinand to MT, Salzburg, 20 January 1805, HHStA, Fa, Sb., Kart. 65, Erz. Ferdinand von Toskana an Kaiserin Marie Therese, fol. 1r).

[20] "Si copierà subito l'oratorio dell'Abate Gatti, e giacchè avete la bontà di offerirmela vi prego di mandarmi la farsa di Farinelli *Odoardo, e Carlotta*" (Ferdinand to MT, Salzburg, 16 February 1805, ibid., fol. 3r). This passage confirms that MT owned the copy of *Odoardo e Carlotta* from the Kaisersammlung (Mus. Hs. 10022).

[21] "Colla diligenza della settimana passata vi ho mandato lo spartito del nuovo oratorio dell'Abate Gatti vi dimando perdono se i quinterni sono così differenti di grandezza, non è colpa mia non avendo potuto fare a meno di lasciare la cura della copiatura all'autore medesimo perchè fosse esatta. Spero che vi piacerà" (Ferdinand to MT, Salzburg, 24 April 1805, ibid., fol. 5r).

made his triumphal entry into Florence on 17 September 1814, bringing with him a music library to which he had added throughout his years of wandering.[22]

One of the most important of the empress's musicians rarely appears in her diary as a performer. Joseph Weigl, son of a cellist in the Burgtheater orchestra, Salieri's student and protégé, served as assistant music director of the Italian opera during the 1780s, in which capacity he helped run rehearsals for *Figaro* and *Don Giovanni*; after Mozart led the first three performances from the keyboard, Weigl took over those duties as well. He replaced Salieri as music director in 1791 and during the following decade wrote several *opere buffe*, the most successful of which was *L'amor marinaro*. He won even more applause in the early nineteenth century with a series of *Singspiele*, including the celebrated *Die Schweizerfamilie* (1809).

Weigl seems to have come into Marie Therese's orbit when she commissioned him to write *L'uniforme* in 1800. "I had the good fortune of receiving the all-highest satisfaction," he wrote in the second of his autobiographical sketches, "and from that time I had to conduct from the *Klavier* at all her private music-making (*Kammermusiken*)."[23] That he also supervised the copying of parts for her is suggested by a remark Carpani made when sending her the first act of a *pasticcio*, *Pilade e Oreste*, in 1803: "The slowness of these copyists [in Venice] discouraged me from having the whole first act copied here, and I have written to maestro Weigl everything necessary for it to be done there."[24] The empress's diary contains many references to presents for Weigl, usually half-yearly payments of 300 Gulden, along with snuffboxes and other valuable objects. Since she recorded few payments to him for specific pieces of music, she probably intended her gifts as rewards for his compositions as well as for his conducting and accompanying.

Another musician whose many gifts from the empress suggest that he occupied an important place in her music-making was Paul Wranitzky (not to be confused with his brother Anton, another musician active in Vienna who seems to have had nothing to do with Marie Therese). A violinist and a prolific composer of symphonies, chamber music, ballets, and *Singspiele* (the best known of which was *Oberon, König der Elfen* of 1790), Wranitzky served as concertmaster in the Kärntnertortheater and

[22] Chroust, *Lebensläufe* IV, 171.   [23] Weigl, "Zwei Selbstbiographien," 57.
[24] Carpani to MT, 9 March 1803, in Jacobs, *Carpani*, 220–1, quoted at greater length in chapter 8.

Burgtheater for several years. He maintained friendly relations with Haydn and Beethoven, both of whom valued his abilities as leader. So did Marie Therese. Paer mentioned Wranitzky's duties in instructions for the performance of the cantata *Il conte Clò*: "I leave the execution, but even more the correction of any wrong notes, if there is occasion for it, in the hands of the worthy director of the orchestra Sig. Vraniski."[25]

At least three other musicians shared with Weigl and Wranitzky responsibility for leading Marie Therese's performances. In May 1801 she gave "the younger Weigl" – presumably Joseph's younger brother Thaddäus – a coffee service as reward for having accompanied three times.[26] In November 1802 she presented Eybler with a writing set and a silver candlestick "for directing concerts five times."[27] In November 1805 she gave a certain Scheidl a gold snuffbox "for directing during the previous year."[28]

Eybler's contact with Marie Therese was probably even closer and more frequent than Weigl's or Wranitzky's because unlike them he had a post within the imperial household. Together with the composer and pianist Leopold Kozeluch and the harpist Josepha Müllner (to be introduced below), Eybler gave music lessons to Marie Therese's children. He himself had attended the choir school of St. Stephen's Cathedral and had studied composition with Albrechtsberger. During the 1780s he served musical apprenticeships with Haydn (to whom he was distantly related) and Mozart (supervising rehearsals for *Così fan tutte*). Eybler's close ties with Mozart led Constanze Mozart to ask him to complete the Requiem that her husband had left unfinished at his death. After orchestrating five movements he gave up, and the job was completed by Franz Xaver Süssmayr, another of Mozart's protégés. Eybler served as Kapellmeister of the Schottenstift from 1794. To the responsibilities of that position and of teaching the imperial children he added in 1804 those of deputy Hofkapellmeister under Salieri, whom he succeeded twenty years later, thus reaching the pinnacle of the Viennese musical establishment.

PROFESSIONAL SINGERS

The male singers who performed with Marie Therese were mostly professionals, the females mostly amateurs. Related to this discrepancy was the

---

[25] *Annotazioni* for the performance of *Il conte Clò*, transcribed in Appendix 5D.

[26] HHStA, Fa, HKF, Kart. 24, diary, fol. 112r.

[27] "November 1802 / Dem 29. Dem Eibler für 5 mahl dirigiren bey Musik" (ibid., fol. 142v).

[28] "November [1805] / Dem 6. . . . Dem Scheidl für das Jahr dirigiren" (ibid., fol. 222v). This was probably Joseph Scheidl (1751–1819), a violinist in the Hofkapelle who served as concertmaster in Tonkünstler Sozietät concerts from 1796 to 1811 (Pohl, *Tonkünstler-Societät*, 96, 104).

empress's practice of drawing on the Hofkapelle for some of her singers; the vocalists of the Hofkapelle consisted only of men (many of them active or re-tired opera singers) and boys. Whether her dependence on the Hofkapelle for singers was a cause or an effect of the predominance of professional singers among Marie Therese's male collaborators I do not know. One pos-sible reason why she rarely invited professional women to sing with her was that she might have feared that sopranos more brilliant and confident than she would overshadow or even intimidate her. During an audience with Therese Rosenbaum, a soprano in the court theaters whose ability to sing high coloratura made her successful as Queen of the Night, the em-press said: "You sing confoundedly high, I am often frightened when you sing so high, and almost tremble."[29] Although she occasionally summoned Rosenbaum to perform on festive occasions at court, it is not surprising that her diary documents not a single private concert in which Rosenbaum participated.

On assuming charge of the court theaters in 1794, Baron Braun reshaped the operatic troupe from one capable of performing only in Italian to one that, from May 1795, presented operas in both Italian and German.[30] He brought Italian *musici* to Vienna on short-term contracts to participate in the performance of *opera seria*. In forming a bilingual troupe that included, temporarily, some of the greatest male sopranos of the age, Braun assembled in Vienna most of the professional singers who were to perform with the empress.

By 1797 many of these singers were present, working closely with one another in the court theaters. A performance on 24 July 1797 of Paisiello's *Il barbiere di Siviglia* in German translation included in its cast five men who would sing with Marie Therese: Carl Weinmüller, Ignaz Saal, Johann Michael Vogl, Philipp Korner, and Jakob Wallascheck.[31] Two days later, in the first Viennese performance of Mayr's *Un pazzo ne fa cento*, another of the empress's future collaborators, Giuseppe Simoni, sang a leading role. With the arrival of Luigi Marchesi in Vienna for a limited engagement in 1798, another of Marie Therese's musicians came on the scene. The Viennese premiere of Mayr's *Lodoiska* on 31 May 1798 brought four of the empress's

---

[29] "Verflucht hoch singen sie, ich habe manchmal Furcht, wenn sie hoch singen und zittere fast" (quoted in the diary of Therese Rosenbaum's husband, Joseph Carl Rosenbaum, 2 July 1800, in Rosenbaum, "Die Tagebücher von Joseph Carl Rosenbaum, 1770–1829," ed. Else Radant, *Haydn Jahrbuch* 5 (1968), whole issue, 84 [translation, used here, in "The Diaries of Joseph Carl Rosenbaum, 1770–1829," *Haydn Yearbook* 5 (1968), 83]).

[30] Rice, *Salieri*, 532–6. MT's role in the return of German opera to the court theaters will be discussed in chapter 7.

[31] A-Wth, *Theaterzettel*.

singers together: Marchesi, Simoni, Saal, and Vogl.[32] The presence of Saal and Vogl, who also sang *Singspiel*, in the cast of an *opera seria* illustrates the bilingualism that many of Marie Therese's singers shared with her and that made them particularly valuable to her. Korner and Wallaschek, too, occasionally sang in Italian opera.

What, if anything, did Marie Therese do to persuade Marchesi to return later to Vienna, and the other professional singers with whom she wanted to collaborate to stay there? Between 1795 and 1800 many of these singers joined the Hofkapelle: Saal was appointed in 1795, Korner in 1797, Simoni and Weinmüller in 1798.[33] We will see that Marie Therese played a role in Simoni's induction into the Hofkapelle, thereby encouraging him to stay in Vienna and to accept her invitations to join her private music-making. Some of the other men who sang with her may have received similar favors. But since we have no evidence that they sang privately with her before they joined the Hofkapelle, it is also possible that in choosing vocal collaborators the empress simply turned to the Hofkapelle as a convenient source of talent.

The most celebrated of the virtuosos who performed with Marie Therese was also the only male soprano who participated in her concerts during the period covered by the diary: Marchesi, near the end of a career that had taken him from La Scala to St. Petersburg and London.[34] During the summer of 1798 he appeared in the court theaters in two *opere serie*: Zingarelli's *Pirro* and Mayr's *Lodoiska* (he had participated in the Italian premieres of both). It was probably his success in these operas that caused the court, almost certainly at the empress's instigation, to grant him the unusual title of "K. K. Hofkammer Sänger."[35] Marchesi may have thought at first he had received a largely honorary position, like those of which many eighteenth-century singers boasted in librettos by referring to themselves as "virtuoso di camera" of one ruler or "nel servizio" of another. But he was to discover that Marie Therese's Hofkammersänger had his work cut out for him.

Marchesi returned to Vienna at least twice, for engagements in the court theaters that Baron Braun probably arranged in consultation with

[32] A-Wth, *Theaterzettel*.

[33] Ludwig Köchel, *Die kaiserliche Hof-Musikkapelle in Wien von 1543 bis 1867*, Vienna, 1869, repr. Hildesheim, 1976, 92–3. My thanks to Dexter Edge for reminding me of this source and for sending me a copy of parts of it.

[34] On Marchesi's career and vocal technique see John A. Rice, "Sense, Sensibility, and Opera Seria: An Epistolary Debate," *Studi musicali* 15 (1986), 110–15.

[35] A *Theaterzettel* dated 1 August 1798 calls Marchesi "k. k. Hofkammer Sänger" (A-Wth). A later poster, announcing his appearance in Paer's cantata *Per il santo sepolcro* on 3 and 4 April 1803, calls him a member of the Hofkapelle, but that identification is almost certainly mistaken. Köchel, *Die kaiserliche Hof-Musikkapelle in Wien*, does not list Marchesi among members of the Hofkapelle.

the empress. He divided his time between the Kärntnertortheater and her apartments. On 27 October 1801 he appeared in Mayr's *Ginevra di Scozia* (in the role of Ariodante that he had created earlier that year in Trieste). Performances continued intermittently until March 1802.[36] Meanwhile, from November 1801 to July 1802 he sang very often in the empress's concerts.

During this period of frequent music-making relations between the *musico* and the empress became close, alarming her mother, who was also in Vienna at the time. Queen Maria Carolina considered her daughter's behavior inexcusable, and said so at length to her friend and confidant the Marchese di Gallo, Neapolitan ambassador to France (and Marie Therese's supplier of music from Paris). Oddly, she did not allude to Marchesi's being a eunuch:

My daughter is behaving very, very badly: without heart, without soul, without care. To all her other shortcomings and follies she has added her very, but very obvious infatuation with the old singer Marchesi. She has all of Vienna talking. With this impetuosity of mood, and her headstrong and intemperate disposition, she does unbelievable things: she dances the galop and the waltz with him; she thinks of nothing except him and of what concerns him; she goes to her ladies-in-waiting so as to be with him without limitations; in short, incredible things. She has persuaded her good husband that she must conduct herself this way so as to defy the public and demonstrate her innocence. But if the good emperor ever opens his eyes, the explosion will be terrible.[37]

Marchesi left Vienna in July 1802, carrying with him rich presents from the empress: Gluck's *Orfeo* bound in red satin, a silver breakfast service with Wedgwood cameos, and a watch decorated with pearls and diamonds on a golden chain with clasps set with diamonds.[38] Less than a year later he returned to perform with the Tonkünstler-Sozietät in Paer's *Per il santo sepolcro*.[39] Given the empress's influence over repertory in Tonkünstler concerts (to be discussed in chapter 7) and her fondness for Paer's music, we can be reasonably sure that she helped arrange this concert and Marchesi's participation in it. Of course she took advantage of his presence in Vienna to perform privately with him during March and April 1803.

[36] A-Wth, *Theaterzettel*.

[37] Maria Carolina to Gallo, Vienna, 6 March 1802, *Correspondance inédite de Marie-Caroline reine de Naples et de Sicile avec le Marquis de Gallo*, ed. M. H. Weil and C. di Somma Circello, 2 vols., Paris, 1911, II, 297.

[38] HHStA, Fa, HKF, Kart. 24, diary, fol. 133v.

[39] Although Mary Sue Morrow (*Concert Life in Haydn's Vienna: Aspects of a Developing Musical and Social Institution*, Stuyvesant, NY, 1989, 318–19), following the *Theaterzettel* in A-Wth, gives only a German title (*Das heilige Grab*), the same poster states that the cantata would be sung in Italian. We know the Italian title from the printed libretto (Vienna, 1802).

One of Marchesi's principal duties in the empress's concerts was to sing with her duets from serious operas, many of which he had sung in Italy. Together they explored a wide range of duets for two sopranos, most of them love duets. Singing them with Marchesi may have served Marie Therese as a means to express her intense affection for the aging *musico*.

Girolamo Crescentini, another great *musico*, took Marchesi's place in Marie Therese's music-making at some time after the period covered by the diary. Anton Reicha, who lived in Vienna from 1802 to 1808, mentioned only one singer in writing of the empress: "She received me with exceptional kindness, invited me to see her and to take part in her private concerts, in which Crescentini almost always sang."[40] The soprano also served as a musical courier. Paer, writing from Parma, used "l'amico Crescentini" to convey to the empress both his regret at not being at her side and the score of his latest opera.[41]

Of a performance of *Die Zauberflöte* in Salzburg in 1804 Ferdinand wrote: "The Sarastro isn't Weinmüller, but he isn't bad."[42] Carl Weinmüller, one of the most constant of the empress's "faithful believers," was a leading member of the court opera troupe from his debut as Lax in the premiere of Johann Schenk's *Der Dorfbarbier* in 1796.[43] During his many years in Vienna he set a standard of excellence difficult to match, participating in the performance of many German operas, both serious and comic, original *Singspiele* and translations of Italian and French operas. About half a century after Weinmüller's death Constant von Wurzbach paid tribute to a singer very fondly and vividly remembered:

His voice, capable of every gradation and perfectly trained – a truly masculine, powerful, and brilliant bass – extended from D below the bass clef to tenor F in a silvery pure tone, with which he united the most distinct enunciation and a tender style of performance that went straight to the heart; and he knew how to meld acting and singing into a complete, artistic whole. Among his most brilliant roles were Thoas [in Gluck's *Iphigénie en Tauride*], Leporello, Sarastro, Figaro, Don Alfonso, Richard Boll [in Weigl's *Die Schweizerfamilie*], [Thomas] the gardener in [Weigl's] *Das Waisenhaus*, Rocco in *Fidelio*, Zamosky in [Cherubini's] *Faniska*, the captain in [Cherubini's] *Der Wasserträger*, Kalaf, Osmin [in Mozart's *Die Entführung*], Axur; in short all the serious and comic roles offered by a repertory then chiefly dominated by Gyrowetz and Weigl. Weinmüller was not only a

[40] *Notes sur Antoine Reicha*, ed. Jiří Vysloužil, Brno, 1970, 24.
[41] Paer to MT, 5 March 1805.
[42] "Il Sarastro non è Weinmüller, ma però non è cattivo" (Ferdinand to MT, Salzburg, 7 February 1804, HHStA, Fa, Sb, Kart. 62, fol. 1).
[43] A-Wth, *Theaterzettel*. He had appeared earlier as a guest artist, in Dittersdorf's *Der Apotheker und der Doktor*.

great operatic singer but a no less perfect singer of church music, and in the Tuba mirum of Mozart's Requiem, as in Haydn's oratorios, he could not easily find his equal.[44]

Between 1801 and 1803 Weinmüller's exceptional versatility allowed him to take part in at least thirty-six of Marie Therese's concerts. His performances must have given her and her musicians much pleasure and contributed to some of the concerts' most memorable moments. These performances, in turn, helped shape his later public repertory. During the period in which Weinmüller sang with Marie Therese, Saal, who created the bass role in *Die Schöpfung*, sang it in public concerts so effectively that no one thought of giving it to anyone else. But in 1805 Weinmüller took over the role, which he had sung several times with the empress in private. From then on, until 1814, he owned the part.[45]

The tenor Simoni was born in Bohemia in 1764 (his name may have originally been Joseph Simon).[46] He sang *opera seria* in Italy during the 1780s and early 1790s but never reached the top rank of heroic tenors. Having made his Viennese debut in 1796, he sang in serious operas and, more frequently, portrayed serious and *mezzo-carattere* characters in comic and heroicomic operas.[47] In 1801, taking advantage of his ability to sing in German, he moved to Emanuel Schikaneder's newly opened Theater an der Wien, where he helped introduce the Viennese to post-revolutionary *opéra-comique* in German translation, singing such roles as the heroic Floreski in Cherubini's *Lodoiska*.[48]

Ernst Moritz Arndt, visiting Vienna in 1798, wrote: "Among the Germans Herr Simoni is also a good singer; but one must listen only, for acting that is clumsier or more stilted cannot be imagined." That did not keep him from being an effective church singer. A memorandum compiled by the police in 1810 mentioned Marie Therese's role in Simoni's appointment to the Hofkapelle in 1798: "Through his good conduct and the grace of Her Majesty the late empress he was subsequently engaged in the Hofkapelle."[49] He spent the rest of his career in Vienna, first dividing

---

[44] Constant Wurzbach, *Biographisches Lexikon des Kaiserthums Oesterreich*, 60 vols., Vienna, 1856–91, LIV, 54–6.

[45] Pohl, *Tonkünstler-Societät*, 66–9.

[46] In the libretto recording one of his earliest appearances in Italy (in Salvatore Rispoli's *Nitteti*, Turin, 1783) he is referred to as "Giuseppe Simon boemo." His birthdate is from an annotation to Johann Friedrich Reichardt, *Vertraute Briefe*, ed. Gustav Gugitz, 2 vols., Munich, 1915, I, 140.

[47] Rice, *Salieri*, 573.

[48] See the portait of Simoni as Floreski in Cherubini's *Lodoiska* in Rice, *Salieri*, 574, where I misattributed the opera to Mayr; Simoni sang Boleslao in Mayr's *Lodoiska* in Vienna in 1798.

[49] Quoted in the annotations to Reichardt, *Vertraute Briefe* I, 140.

his time between the chapel and the stage, and later devoting himself to the performance of sacred music.

From March 1802 Simoni sang often with Marie Therese, who valued not only his long, first-hand experience with a genre she loved – *opera seria* – but also his ability to sing in German. As with another singer of *opera seria*, Marchesi, the empress found herself attracted to Simoni the man as well as the musician, and again she scandalized her Viennese subjects, one of whom wrote in her memoirs: "The Viennese spoke of their empress with little discretion, and took offence when she was seen on Simoni's arm in the allées of Schönbrunn."[50] Paer's letters reveal the practical side of her relations with Simoni, who served as a kind of musical secretary, relaying Paer's messages to her and hers to him.

AMATEUR SINGERS

The many amateur singers who performed with Marie Therese ranged from chamber servants whose musical abilities were probably modest to musicians of professional quality who sang in Vienna's most sophisticated musical circles.

The empress's amateur sopranos included a woman named Altamonte, probably to be identified with Katherina Altamonte, lady-in-waiting to Archduchess Maria Clementina,[51] and with the "Fräulein Altamonte" whom Johann Ferdinand von Schönfeld called "a true musical genius":

Her truly Italian style of singing is beautiful, full of expression, flexibility, and correct technique. In the *adagio* she has outstanding strength, and in recitative she is extraordinarily powerful, which makes her one of our best amateurs. In addition she reads so well that she can accompany a full score at sight. With a full ensemble she sings masterfully; but when she performs at the keyboard, and accompanies herself, her song is even more delightful, because she has more opportunity for her own *tempi rubati*. Expressive songs she sings not only with great judgment but with enthusiastic feeling.[52]

This passage brings up several qualities that Marie Therese valued in her vocal soloists, professional as well as amateur: an ability to sing in Italian, a flexibility that allowed them to sing with the accompaniment of ensembles both large and small, and an ability to read music at sight with ease. This last was particularly important, given the vastness of their repertory and

---

[50] Countess Lulu Thürheim, *Mein Leben*, ed. René van Rhyn, 2 vols., Munich, 1913, I, 126.

[51] *Joseph Haydn in seiner Zeit*, 469.

[52] Johann Ferdinand von Schönfeld, *Jahrbuch der Tonkunst in Wien und Prag*, Prague, 1796, reprinted, with notes by Otto Biba, Munich, 1976, 4–5.

their tendency (to judge from the many very clean manuscript parts from her music library) to perform without correcting or otherwise marking up their parts.

Another important member of Marie Therese's circle of female amateurs was Christine Frank, née Gerhardi. Active in Viennese concert life from 1797 to 1803, she took part in the first performance of Haydn's *Die Schöpfung* at the Palais Schwarzenberg. She specialized in the performance of excerpts from *opera seria*, as, for example, in a benefit concert in the Grosser Redoutensaal conducted by Haydn (30 January 1801) that included music from Sebastiano Nasolini's *Merope* and Cimarosa's *Gli Orazi e i Curiazi*.[53] Of her performance in this concert Joseph Carl Rosenbaum, husband of the aforementioned soprano Therese Rosenbaum and a well-informed lover of vocal music, wrote that she "sang with much art and expression, much in the manner of Crescentini."[54] Joseph Sonnleithner remembered her as

an excellent singer, but [she] remained a dilettante and sang chiefly in concerts for charitable purposes (which she herself arranged), or for the benefit of eminent artists... She was at the time the most famous amateur singer in Vienna, and inasmuch as Haydn knew her well there is no doubt but that he had her in mind when he composed *The Creation*... All reports agree that she met Beethoven often at Frank's and that he frequently accompanied her singing on the pianoforte.[55]

Frank's knowledge of the Italian serious style and her familiarity with Haydn's great German oratorio must have endeared her to the empress, and so also her interest in musical fundraising, an activity to which Marie Therese too gave much effort, as we will see in chapter 7.

Among the other amateurs who sang with Marie Therese was the lawyer Mathias Rathmayer, a tenor who brought to their music-making many of the same talents for which Schönfeld praised Altamonte. He sang frequently in performances of Haydn's oratorios for the Tonkünstler-Sozietät, winning Schönfeld's approval for his "very beautiful and exceptionally strong tenor voice, a very sensitive and accurate ear, and such extraordinary skill in reading music that he is able to perform at sight with ease."[56] He must have been able to sing as effectively in Italian as in German, to judge from the vast amount of Italian operatic music he performed with Marie Therese.

53 Morrow, *Concert Life*, 307; see chapter 7.
54 Quoted in translation (used here) in H. C. Robbins Landon, *Haydn: Chronicle and Works*, 5 vols., London, 1976–80, V, 24.
55 Quoted in translation (used here) in Alexander Wheelock Thayer, *Life of Beethoven*, ed. Elliot Forbes, Princeton, NJ, 1967, 232–3.
56 Schönfeld, *Jahrbuch der Tonkunst*, 51. In *HSS*, 1804, Rathmayer is listed among "Hof- und Gerichts-Advokaten" (p. 262) and also as "Prof. des Österreich. Privatrechts am k. k. Theresianum" (p. 294).

He sang with her as often as Weinmüller, and over the entire period covered by the diary.

One important professional musician appeared as an amateur in Marie Therese's concerts. Paer sang with her several times, sharing a tenor voice that he may never have displayed in public; he also sang in the musical salons of Prince Joseph Lobkowitz and Count Moritz Fries.[57]

AN INSTRUMENTAL VIRTUOSO

Although some of Vienna's leading instrumentalists made occasional appearances in Marie Therese's concerts, only one of them returned so frequently that she can be said to have belonged to the "faithful believers." Josepha Müllner, born in Vienna in 1768, was Vienna's leading harpist.[58] Emperor Joseph II, recognizing her exceptional talent, gave her a pedal harp of great beauty and sent her on an educational trip to Italy, where she won enthusiastic applause. Later she toured Germany, playing her own compositions and delighting audiences with improvisations.

Back in Vienna, Müllner appeared frequently as soloist in the court theaters; according to the account book for the theatrical year 1801–2 payments to her for "extra-Dienste" amounted to the substantial sum of 637 Gulden.[59] She taught the daughters of Franz and Marie Therese to play the harp and received the title (similar to Marchesi's) of "Imperial Chamber Virtuoso." It was probably in this capacity that she participated several times in the empress's concerts and composed, at her request, the opera *Der heimliche Band* (1799). Marie Therese collected many works with important harp solos, most if not all of which were probably intended for Müllner.[60]

CHORUS

Much of Marie Therese's music-making – her performances not only of liturgical music and oratorios but also of opera – required chorus. Late eighteenth- and early nineteenth-century composers of opera in Italian

[57] Morrow, *Concert Life*, 392–7.
[58] This account is based on Gerlinde Haas, " 'Wunschtraum und Wirklichkeit': Korrigierende Notizen zu Leben und Werk der Josepha Müllner-Gollenhofer," *Studien zur Musikwissenschaft* 44 (1995), 289–302, and Wurzbach, *Lexikon*.
[59] HHStA, Hoftheater, Sonderreihe 34, p. 112. My thanks to Theodore Albrecht for this information.
[60] There are harp solos in *Der heimliche Band* (Mus. Hs. 10197); Kauer's *Der Einsiedler* (Mus. Hs. 10189), *Sei variazioni* for orchestra (Mus. Hs. 11380), and *Fantasia fürs ganze Orchester* (Mus. Hs. 11378); Salieri's *Gesù al Limbo* (Mus. Hs. 9915–16); Weigl's *L'uniforme*, *La festa di Carolina negli Elisi* (Mus. Hs. 10088–9), and Concertino for harp and winds (*CaM*, p. 60); and Wranitzky's *Das Picknick der Götter* (Mus. Hs. 11005–7).

incorporated chorus into their dramas with increasing frequency. Many arias and ensembles from the operas of Paer, Mayr, and their contemporaries include chorus; the empress and her musicians performed such numbers often.

We know little about the size of the empress's chorus and its personnel, both of which may have changed frequently. Of the size we can get some indication from the number of choral parts preserved among the manuscripts from her library. While not all the parts for every work have survived, in some cases the parts are numbered, and these numbers give us a good idea of how many parts originally existed. For example, the surviving choral parts for Weigl's cantata *La festa di Carolina negli Elisi* consist of the following:

> Soprano: No. 2, 3, 4
> Alto: No. 1, 2, 3, 4
> Tenor: No. 1, 2, 4
> Bass: No. 1, 3, 4

This suggests that there were four parts each for soprano, alto, tenor, and bass; when the cantata was first performed in 1801 to celebrate the nameday of Queen Maria Carolina, the chorus probably consisted of at least sixteen voices. I say "at least" because vocal soloists, including Marie Therese, may have sometimes participated in choruses: the *parti cantanti* for the soloists in *La festa di Carolina* contain music for choruses as well as solos. Furthermore, two choristers could have sometimes sung from one part.

On less festive occasions the choir was probably smaller. The "grosser Chor" by Eybler performed on 18 July 1802 was almost certainly "Es töne dann in rascher Saiten Sturme," the only known source for which is Marie Therese's set of parts (Mus. Hs. 10893). The choral parts consist of two each for soprano, alto, tenor, and bass.

Who sang in Marie Therese's chorus? On at least one occasion the entire Hofkapelle. The *cantatina* that Seyfried wrote to celebrate Franz's nameday in 1805 was sung, according to the composer, by "the seminary boys and all the members of the Hofkapelle."[61] The emperor had founded the Imperial-Royal Seminary two years earlier. Its responsibilities included the education of choirboys of the court chapel; Franz Schubert attended lessons there

---

[61] "Die Convictes-Knaben, und sämmtliche Hofcapellisten" (Ignaz von Seyfried, *Scizze meines Lebens. Theilnehmenden Freunden zum Andenken geweiht*, manuscript I.N. 36561 in the library of the Universität für Musik, Vienna, p. 17). I am grateful to Rita Steblin for telling me of Seyfried's unpublished autobiography and for transcribing his account (of which longer excerpts will be quoted in chapters 3, 5, and 6) of the rehearsal and performance of the *Serenata con una cantatina*.

from 1808 to 1813.[62] The boys who sang in Seyfried's *cantatina* probably included the choirboys who regularly sang with the Hofkapelle; on this occasion they were perhaps reinforced by other boys from the school. Since so many of the Hofkapelle's tenors and basses sang regularly in Marie Therese's concerts, it is not surprising that she gathered the whole group of them when their singing could be admired not only by her but by Franz.

Choirboys performed for Marie Therese on other special occasions as well. Her record of the presents she gave after the celebration of Franz's nameday in 1797 mentions a payment of 18 Gulden to each of the *Sängerknaben* who took part.[63] Paer, in instructions for the performance of *Il conte Clò*, wrote: "The part of Ascanio, which amounts to only a couple of words, is for a boy from the chorus."[64] But the frequency and length of the empress's private concerts make it unlikely that choirboys participated in these on a regular basis.

ORCHESTRA

Marie Therese, her vocal and instrumental soloists, and her chorus were accompanied by an orchestra the identity of whose members is unknown, but whose size we can estimate by the number of orchestral parts from her library for works she performed. Typical in this respect is a set of parts for a duet for two sopranos from Cimarosa's *Il sacrificio d'Abramo*, "Consola il tuo dolore" (probably the duet from that *dramma sacro* she and Marchesi sang on 24 January 1802). It contains (in addition to the vocal parts) two parts for first violin, two for second violin, and single parts for viola, basso, oboe 1 and oboe 2, and horn 1 and horn 2. Assuming two string players read from each part and one cellist and one bassist played from the basso part, we arrive at an orchestra of sixteen, including twelve strings. Doubled parts for strings were common in the empress's church music as well: the *Kathalog der Kirchenmusickalien* frequently mentions "parti cavate in dupplo."

While an orchestra of about sixteen may have represented the norm for Marie Therese's music-making, she was sometimes satisfied with smaller ensembles; at other times she gathered an orchestra of over twenty. Eybler, in writing of preparations for a performance of two scenes from Giovanni de Gamerra's libretto *Caio Coriolano* that he had set to music (Herrmann 151–2, Mus. Hs. 10357–8 and 10361–2; Fig. 2.1), told her he had "had

---

[62] *Schubert: Die Dokumente seines Lebens*, ed. Otto Erich Deutsch, Kassel, 1964, 7. My thanks to Rita Steblin for this reference.

[63] HHStA, Fa, HKF, Kart. 24, diary, fol. 113v. [64] Paer's *Annotazioni*, transcribed in appendix 5.

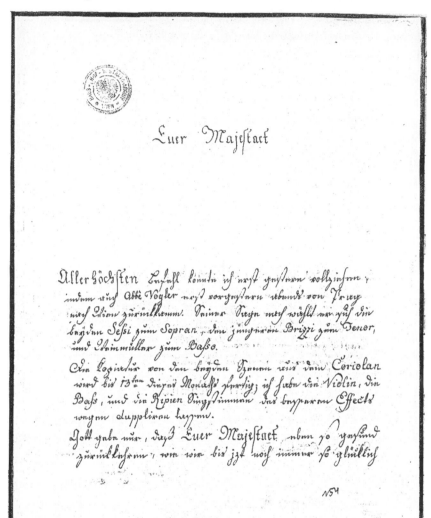

Figure 2.1 Letter from Joseph Eybler to Marie Therese, 6 November 1804, discussing arrangements for a concert in which Georg Vogler was to participate and informing her that the parts for two scenes from *Coriolano* (on a libretto by De Gamerra) would be copied by 13 November.

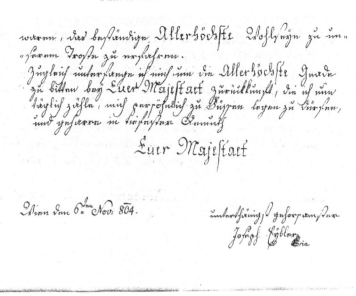

Figure 2.1 (*cont.*)

the violin, the bass, and the choral parts doubled for better effect."[65] That implies that such doubling was not done as a matter of course. Performing materials for Cimarosa's trio "Perché eguale all'amor mio" from *Penelope*, probably performed on 27 December 1801, contain only one part each for first violin, second violin, viola, and basso. Together with single parts for pairs of oboes, clarinets, and horns, that set allows for a performance by an orchestra of only fourteen. For some performances of instrumental music, however, the empress may have assembled an orchestra with a considerably larger group of strings. A programmatic symphony in G minor by Wranitzky played in her concert of 22 January 1802 (discussed in chapter 4) is preserved in parts (Mus. Hs. 11089) that allow for a performance by twenty-two strings: three parts for first violin, three for second violin, two for viola, and three basso parts.

Marie Therese had at her disposal many wind and brass players, whom she sometimes brought together in orchestras that must have made a brilliant and colorful sound. Her concert on 18 July 1802 ended with what she referred to as "Die Follia di Spagna mit allen Instrumenten von

[65] "Die Kopiatur von den beyden Szenen aus dem Coriolan wird bis 13ten dieses Monaths fertig; ich habe die Violin, die Bass, und die Ripien Singstimmen des besseren Effects wegen duppliren lassen" (Eybler to MT, 6 November 1804, HHStA, Fa, Sb, Kart. 63, fol. 154r).

Eybler." Eybler is not known to have composed such a work.[66] But she owned, under the title *Follia a più strumenti*, an anonymous orchestral transcription of the variations on La Follia from Corelli's violin sonatas, Op. 5 (*CaM*, p. 62; see Fig. 1.3), which the diary allows us to attribute to Eybler. The orchestral parts call for (in addition to strings) pairs of flutes, oboes, clarinets, bassoons, horns, trumpets, and timpani.[67] An even larger orchestra was required by Wranitzky for his *Quodlibet aus verschiedenen Opern* (Mus. Hs. 10233), in which the forces used in Eybler's transcription of *La follia* were augmented by piccolo, two basset horns, three trombones, bass drum, military drum, and cymbals. Wranitzky called for this variety of instruments in order to reproduce the original scoring of the operatic excerpts from which he created this potpourri, to be discussed in chapter 6. For the most part he used various groups of winds, brass, and percussion in turn, rather than en masse, which helps to explain why, to judge from the surviving string parts – two each for first violin, second violin, viola, and basso – sixteen strings at most participated in the performance of the quodlibet.

Of the quality of Marie Therese's orchestra we know from her own words that some of the players were very good. In asking Paisiello to set to music De Gamerra's libretto *La corona del merito* she gave him only a few bits of musical guidance, including the following: "If you wish to introduce a concertante instrument into some arias or other pieces, keep in mind that we have an excellent cello, oboe, and clarinet."[68]

---

[66] No orchestral variations on La Follia by Eybler are listed in Herrmann.
[67] A-Wgm, XIII 29392.   [68] MT to Paisiello, 18 July 1802; transcribed in appendix 4.

CHAPTER 3

The empress as soprano

Although Marie Therese played "un peu de harpe" (in her mother's words) and the many sonatas Orgitano wrote for her in Naples suggest she was a capable pianist, her diary contains no evidence that she played the harp during her private concerts and records only one instance of her playing keyboard (to be discussed in chapter 4). She probably played the piano more frequently than the diary might suggest. According to Reicha, she "was not only passionately fond of music but also an excellent musician: she sang, played the piano, and realized figured-bass accompaniment."[1] But clearly she devoted most of her musical energy to singing.

The empress sight-read well, but her voice was not exceptionally powerful, agile, or extensive in compass. Joseph Haydn, who conducted private performances of *Die Schöpfung* and *Die Jahreszeiten* in which she sang on 24 and 25 May 1801, concluded that she had "much taste and expressivity, but a weak voice."[2] Paer wrote to her in 1804 of his music-making with Queen Maria Luisa of Etruria (the kingdom with which Napoleon had replaced the grand duchy of Tuscany), whose skill he tactfully compared with that of his Viennese patron: the queen had "a strong, clear voice, but to be honest... neither the musical knowledge nor the sight-reading ability of Your Majesty."[3] That seems to acknowledge tacitly some degree of weakness and lack of clarity in Marie Therese's voice. Michael Haydn, writing to his wife of a rehearsal of the *Missa S. Theresiae* (quoted in the Introduction to this study), mentioned the empress's initial bashfulness and said she sang "pleasantly," "accurately," and "charmingly" – a group of adverbs as revealing for what it omits as for what it includes.

---

[1] *Notes sur Antoine Reicha*, 24.

[2] As reported by Griesinger to Breitkopf & Härtel, Vienna, 27 May 1801; in *Griesingers Korrespondenz*, 75–6. This performance of *Die Schöpfung* is not mentioned in A. Peter Brown, *Performing Haydn's The Creation: Reconstructing the Earliest Renditions*, Bloomington, Ind., 1986 (Table 1: Viennese Performances of *The Creation* to Early 1810).

[3] Paer to MT, Rome, 3 November 1804.

Seyfried left a similar picture of the empress's self-deprecation and fine musicianship, which compensated for her less than outstanding vocal power and agility. The rehearsal of music he had written for Franz's nameday in 1805 required secrecy, so that the emperor would not learn of his wife's plans:

We were all already assembled and waiting, hidden in the shrubbery, for the moment the Master (as the monarch was simply referred to by everyone) would go away, when finally the empress, holding her vocal part in her hand, came down the steps of the palace toward us. Responding to my respectful bows with a friendly nod, she approached me and addressed me with the following words: "You must have patience with me; stage fright bothers me a great deal, and especially today I am not in good voice." Reuter Stauff could not have been prouder when his emperor smiled on him than I will be, until my dying day, of this apology that so thoughtfully honored the artist, although it put me in a state of embarrassment that almost robbed me of speech. The apology was, in fact, completely unnecessary. The gracious, all-too-anxious sovereign did indeed sing a little weakly, but with perfect correctness, deep feeling, and true expression.[4]

Marie Therese the soprano participated in musical performances in several different ways. In concerts of operatic extracts she occasionally sang arias but more often took part in ensembles. In the less frequent concerts devoted to the performance of single works, she sang entire roles, sometimes leading roles. She rarely mentioned in her diary the names of soloists in church music. But since she sang the soprano solo in Michael Haydn's *Missa S. Theresiae*, she probably sang solos in many of the masses and other liturgical works that she programmed between 1801 and 1803.

It is perhaps a sign of the empress's modesty and shyness that in the many private concerts whose programs consisted of excerpts from operas or oratorios she sang no more than a handful of arias. As a music lover she used her concerts as an opportunity to hear professional virtuosos sing arias; as a performer, she much preferred ensembles. She participated in

---

[4] "Wir waren schon alle versammelt; und harrten, in den Gebüschen verborgen, nur des Augenblicks, daß der *Herr* (so wurde der Monarch von allen kurzweg titulirt) sich entfernt haben würde, als endlich die Kaiserinn, Ihren Singpart in den Händen haltend, über die Schloßtreppe zu uns herabkam, meine ehrfurchtsvolle Verneigung durch freundliches Kopfnicken erwiedernd, sich mir nährte, und mit folgenden Worten mich anredete 'Sie müssen schon etwas Nachsicht mit mir haben; ich bin sehr von Furcht befangen, u. auch heute gerade nicht gut bey Stimme.' – Unmöglich konnte *Reuter Stauff* stolzer darauf gewesen seyn, daß ihn sein Kaiser anlachte, als ich es bis zu meinem letzten Athemzuge auf diese, den Künstler so sinnig ehrende Entschuldigung, seyn werde, wiewohl sie mich damals in eine die Sprache beynahe raubende Verlegenheit setzte, auch in so ferner in der That ganz überflüßig war, als die gütige, allzubesorgte Fürstinn zwar etwas schwach, aber nichtsdesto weniger vollkommen richtig, mit innigem Gefühl, u. wahren Ausdruck sang" (Seyfried, *Scizze meines Lebens*, 17–18). I have been unable to identify Reuter Stauff.

a wide variety of ensembles, from duets to finales, representing dramatic situations ranging from slapstick comedy that must have tempted her into a good deal of acting (the finale of the first act of *Così fan tutte*) to high tragedy (the finales of the first act of *La clemenza di Tito* and of the second act of Cimarosa's *Gli Orazi e i Curiazi*). In the period covered by her diary she performed trios eighteen times (some of them more than once), quartets fifteen times, quintets six times, and finales eighteen times. But she was particularly fond of duets, which she sang twenty-six times. Although she occasionally sang duets from comic operas, she preferred those from serious operas: Mayr's *Adelaide di Guesclino*, *Ginevra di Scozia*, *Lodoiska*, and *Telemaco*, Paer's *Achille* and *Numa Pompilio*, Paisiello's *Antigono* and *Elfrida*, Salieri's *Annibale in Capua*, Sarti's *Giulio Sabino*, Tarchi's *Alessandro* and *Ezio*, and Zingarelli's *Il conte di Saldagna* and *Pirro*.

The empress twice sang "Per pietà, deh non lasciarmi," from *Ginevra di Scozia*. In one of those performances her partner was Marchesi, who created the role of Ariodante in the premiere of Mayr's opera in Trieste in 1801 and sang it repeatedly in the Kärntnertortheater in 1802 and 1803. Marchesi was near the end of his theatrical career when Mayr wrote *Ginevra di Scozia*. The composer took care not to overtax him; nor did he allow the *prima donna* who created the role of Ginevra, Teresa Bertinotti Radicati, to put him in the shade. Ginevra's part in "Per pietà, deh non lasciarmi" is not overtly virtuosic. Neither especially high nor difficult, it does not require acrobatics or great power. Thus it suited Marie Therese, who must have delighted in this opportunity to blend her voice with that of one of Europe's most famous singers. Of exceptional beauty is the passage that begins with the words "Che palpiti atroci," where, after agitated dialogue, the lovers express their agony in the sweetest parallel thirds (Ex. 3.1). The empress, whose concerts included several ensembles from *Così fan tutte*, was in a good position to appreciate Mayr's allusion (at the second statement of "penar") to Mozart's "Soave sia il vento."

Another duet that must have given the empress much pleasure was "Holde Gattin," sung by Adam and Eve in the third part of Haydn's *Die Schöpfung*. She sang it several times with Weinmüller in performances of the complete oratorio and in concerts consisting of excerpts from several works.

MARIE THERESE AS GIANNINA IN WEIGL'S *L'UNIFORME*

The empress's diary does not always tell who took part in her performances of operas, oratorios, and cantatas; and even when it names singers, it never

Ex 3.1 Mayr, *Ginevra di Scozia*, "Per pietà, deh non lasciarmi," mm. 75–97

mentions their roles. But other evidence sometimes allows us to be relatively
certain of her participation and of what character she portrayed. Weigl
wrote the role of Giannina in *L'uniforme* (the opera's principal female part:
Paulina in the later German version of the opera) for her, and she created the

role at Schönbrunn in 1800.[5] We can be fairly sure she also sang Giannina in the performance of *L'uniforme* on 20 December 1801. Giannina's music suggests something of the quality and tessitura of the empress's voice and how they shaped her portrayal of a major character in a full-length opera.

Carpani's libretto, though Italian in form as well as language, carries the unmistakable imprint of *opéra-comique*: not surprising in view of his experience in the adaptation of *opéras-comiques*. Like several post-revolutionary French operas, *L'uniforme* is based on an apparently true story. Carpani derived his libretto from an episode in the War of the Polish Succession (1733–5), according to his preface: "The action takes place in the village of Forni and its vicinity. The event from which it is drawn is believed to have happened around 1733, during the war in Italy between the Spanish and the Empire" [i.e. the Austrian Monarchy].[6]

The villagers Giannina and Bastiano love one another, but their wish to wed is frustrated by Giannina's father, who wants her to marry a soldier. Giannina suggests that Bastiano put on an old Austrian uniform belonging to her uncle and pretend to her father that he has joined the army. The plan goes wrong when the Austrian army enters the village and an officer arrests Bastiano on suspicion of spying for the Spanish.

In an effort to mollify the Austrian officer, Giannina offers him a basket of strawberries, of which she sings in her aria "Queste fragole dolci odorose." One of the highpoints of Giannina's role, the aria features a cello solo as intricate as the one in Mozart's "Batti, batti, bel Masetto." Marie Therese must have enjoyed the effect of her voice in combination with a single cello. "Queste fragole" is one of the first of several arias and other solos written for her in which a cello accompanies the vocal line.

The aria begins with a naive gavotte tune played by the cello and repeated by Giannina (Ex. 3.2). The bass, pizzicato, provides the simplest and lightest possible harmonic support, while the violins and violas quietly undulate. The range of the opening melody is limited to an octave and a fourth, from E above middle C up to A above the staff; most of the melodic motion is conjunct or triadic. (In the rest of the aria Giannina never goes above A and only once ventures a half-step below E.)

Michael Haydn, in his report of the rehearsal of the *Missa S. Theresiae*, wrote that Marie Therese sang her solos "at first a little bashfully, but with

---

[5] Weigl, "Zwei Selbstbiographien," 57.
[6] "L'azione succede nel villaggio di Forni, e nelle vicinanze. Il fatto da cui è tratta, si suppone accaduto circa il 1733, durante la guerra d'Italia fra gli spagnuoli, e gl'Imperiali" (*L'uniforme*, opera comica in tre atti da rappresentarsi nel Teatro Elettorale di Sassonia, Dresden, 1805). I have been unable to find a libretto, printed or manuscript, that can be connected with the first production of *L'uniforme* at Schönbrunn in 1800.

Ex 3.2 Weigl, *L'uniforme*, "Queste fragole dolci odorose," mm. 10–28

gradually rising courage." Weigl crafted "Queste fragole" as if in anticipa-
tion of the same emotional transformation. The opening melody almost
demanded to be sung "a little bashfully"; yet the empress's "gradually rising
courage" allowed her to end the melody with a run of sixteenth-notes and to
attack the modulation that follows, which offered not only tonal instability
but the potentially distracting return of the cello, first in dialogue with the
voice and then in increasingly ornate patterns of arpeggiation. Giannina's
reference to the field of battle encouraged Weigl to ask even more of the
empress. He embellished the arrival of the new key with awkward leaps (a
seventh down, a tenth up) and a series of new rhythmic ideas in the vocal
line that required precision and confidence.

During the next few scenes Giannina evolves from a timid young girl into
a heroic woman who, like Beethoven's Leonore, disguises herself as a man
in order to free from prison the man she loves. Believing that Bastiano has
been sentenced to death, she puts on a soldier's coat and hat and persuades
Bastiano's guards to let her see the prisoner. Once inside she gives Bastiano
her soldier's outfit and urges him to escape:

> Son tua se vinci,
> E se muori, la vita
> Peso è per me: m'uccidano gloriosa.
> Comunque sia la morte,
> Se per lo sposo muor, muore una sposa.

I am yours if you triumph. If you die, life would be a burden for me: I would die
gloriously. Whatever death is, if one dies for one's husband, one dies as a wife.

Bastiano escapes. Alone and imprisoned, but thinking only of Bastiano's
safety, Giannina sings "È partito…a mezza scala." The aria, marked
"Agitato," begins with a series of short, breathless phrases that need to
be more gasped than sung, accompanied by an obsessively repeated motive
in the first violins and by offbeat chords in the other strings (Ex. 3.3).

As Giannina thinks of the possibility of Bastiano being arrested again,
she steers the melodic line toward the parallel minor but then sidesteps
the minor mode in favor of a more pathetic shift to the flat mediant. In
a moment of silence, sustained by a fermata, she falls to her knees. The
arrival of B♭ major coincides with the aria's first lyrical melody, to which
Giannina prays fervently for Bastiano's delivery.

Through most of the aria Giannina stays within a vocal range even more
restricted than in "Queste fragole." But Weigl coaxed more from her for
dramatic purposes. Before Bastiano's escape Giannina asks him to call out
"Giannina addio" from outside the prison, to let her know that he has gotten

Ex 3.3 Weigl, *L'uniforme*, "È partito . . . a mezza scala," mm. 1–19

Ex 3.3 (*cont.*)

away safely. When she hears those words in the distance, she expresses her overwhelming joy by going finally beyond A, up to B.

While the "Strawberry Aria" required little in the way of acting, the prison scene would fail without it, even in a concert performance. That Weigl wrote such a scene for Marie Therese is a tribute not only to her musicianship but to her ability as an actress.

EMBELLISHMENTS AND OTHER ALTERATIONS IN WEIGL'S *LA FESTA DI CAROLINA NEGLI ELISI*

Many of the sets of parts in Marie Therese's library include *parti cantanti*: parts for singers (both soloists and choristers), normally consisting of a single vocal line and bass. The *parti cantanti* sometimes contain the names of singers who performed them or for whom they were written. Those for Weigl's cantata *La festa di Carolina negli Elisi* indicate that solo parts were written for or sung by Marie Therese herself (in the role of Cornelia), Marchesi (Augusto), Fräulein v. Bock[7] (Artemisia), Rathmayer (Orfeo), and Weinmüller (Ercole); Mercurio's part has no name. These singers presumably created their roles when the cantata was first performed on Maria Carolina's nameday, 4 November 1801.[8] In her diary Marie Therese left no information about who sang in performances of Weigl's cantata on 11 and 17 November, but since we know from the diary that both Rathmayer and Weinmüller were active in her music-making at that time, they almost certainly continued to sing in *La festa di Carolina* along with the empress.

---

[7] Probably Theresia Bockh von Polloch, chamber servant to Archduchess Maria Luisa from about 1795.

[8] The manuscript score from MT's library is dated 29 October 1801. The opening chorus makes a clear reference to the day for which Weigl composed this cantata: "Di Carolina / Somma Eroina / Se fra i mortali / Oggi si celebra / Il fausto giorno..." *La festa di Carolina negli Elisi* was probably inspired by Paer's enormously popular cantata *Eloisa ed Abeilardo agli Elisi*, of which MT owned a manuscript score.

Ex 3.4 Weigl, *La festa di Carolina negli Elisi*, "Di labbro in labbro," mm. 29–32

Extensive alterations to Cornelia's vocal line are written in pencil in the *parte cantante*. They offer a glimpse at how the empress actually sang Weigl's music. Whether she or Weigl (presumably in consultation with her) made these changes is unknown. But the hand of an amateur can perhaps be sensed in two cadenzas that consist of single measures with more beats than in the other parts. If the empress wrote out these cadenzas herself, she apparently did so with confidence that her fellow musicians would wait for her to finish her solos, despite the extra beats.

The alterations in Cornelia's part fall into two categories. Some served to ornament the vocal line, others to make a passage easier to sing by removing leaps and notes above G. Sometimes a single change served both purposes. The embellishments are mostly conjunct runs, often seasoned with chromatic notes. In Cornelia's aria "Di labbro in labbro" (in which Marie Therese was again accompanied by a solo cello) a leap of a seventh was replaced with a scalar ascent and repeated notes at the end of the phrase gave way to a chromatic appoggiatura (Ex. 3.4). A fermata over a rest invited an improvisatory flourish (notated in a five-beat measure) with the same combination of conjunct sixteenth notes and mild chromaticism (Ex. 3.5). Cornelia's second aria, "Deh rendi, o ciel pietoso," is a relatively early example of a musical type that was to be a standard feature of nineteenth-century Italian opera: Weigl called it a *preghiera*. Here again the vocal line was altered to eliminate a leap and to introduce a chromatic appoggiatura at the end of a phrase (Ex. 3.6). A cadenza that Weigl wrote into the original vocal line was changed to avoid a high A♭ and to add a touch of chromaticism (again with an extra beat; Ex. 3.7).

Ex 3.5 Weigl, *La festa di Carolina*, "Di labbro in labbro" mm. 42–4

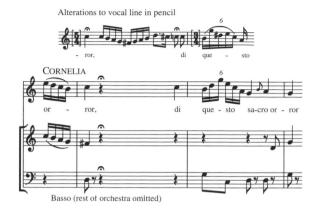

Basso (rest of orchestra omitted)

Ex 3.6 Weigl, *La festa di Carolina*, "Deh rendi, o ciel pietoso," mm. 32–5

Basso (rest of orchestra omitted)

Ex 3.7 Weigl, *La festa di Carolina*, "Deh rendi, o ciel pietoso," mm. 46–7

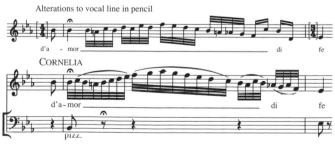

Basso (rest of orchestra omitted)

LITURGICAL MUSIC

For a clear sense of Marie Therese's qualities as a singer of sacred music, the best place to begin is a mass commissioned by her, written for her, and named in her honor: Michael Haydn's *Missa S. Theresiae*. In writing of the rehearsal of the mass, Haydn praised her performance of the soprano solos, singling out "Et incarnatus est" in the Credo and the Benedictus.

In both these solos Marie Therese gained special prominence by interacting not with the other soloists but with the chorus. In the Credo, the chorus, entering at "Crucifixus," provides the dramatic contrast that one expects at this moment with a sudden shift to the minor mode, *forte*, and a unison texture, all of which retrospectively emphasize the sweetness and gentleness of the soprano solo (whose accompaniment includes the empress's beloved solo cello). The chorus plays a more unusual role in the Benedictus, a movement that exemplifies the outstanding musical quality that the empress could inspire in the composers who wrote for her. While the soprano sings her solo, the chorus sings a kind of back-up, marked "tutti sempre p" on a different text, "Hosanna in excelsis," which according to the liturgy should be sung before and after the Benedictus, not during it (Ex. 3.8).

Both solos respect the limits of Marie Therese's voice. They have few melismas and no difficult intervals. The vocal compass extends no higher than G. In "Et incarnatus" the lowest note (used several times) is F above middle C; although the Benedictus asks the soprano to descend to D above middle C, most of the part stays in the octave between G in the treble staff and the G above.

Another soprano solo in a work commissioned by Marie Therese closely resembles in style and spirit those in the *Missa S. Theresiae*. Her musicians performed Eybler's Requiem on 2 April 1803. Although I know of no evidence that Eybler wrote the soprano solo for her or that she sang it, the music strongly suggests that she helped to shape it. The Recordare begins with a long and beautiful soprano solo that seems to express not only religious ardor but the gratitude and love that so many musicians felt for the empress. Entwined with a concertante part for English horn (in the absence of which Eybler allowed for a performance by clarinet), the vocal line unfolds within a range even smaller than in Michael Haydn's solos, from E♭ above middle C up to G♭ (Ex. 3.9).

Marie Therese's performances of church music were not limited to lyrical solos of the type found in the *Missa S. Theresiae* and Eybler's Requiem. Occasionally she sang something more dramatic and exciting.

Ex 3.8 Michael Haydn, *Missa S. Theresiae*, Benedictus, mm. 19–55

Ex 3.8 (*cont.*)

Ex 3.8 (*cont.*)

She commissioned the *Missa S. Francisci* from Michael Haydn in April 1803 for performance on Franz's nameday, 4 October. Haydn, who did not come to Vienna to conduct this mass, reported that it was performed under Eybler's direction "in the presence of Their Majesties" – a phrase implying that Marie Therese did not actually take part in the

Ex 3.9 Eybler, Requiem, Recordare, mm. 1–51

Ex 3.9 (*cont.*)

Ex 3.9 (*cont.*)

performance.[9] Yet it is hard to believe that Haydn did not tailor the soprano solo for his imperial patron. The splendid, aria-like "Christe eleison" with which the part begins resembles many of her other church-music solos in featuring interaction between soprano solo and chorus, but differs from the solos described above in its combination of fast tempo and minor mode, with tumultuous passage work in the strings and a vocal melody full of leaps and short stretches of ornate coloratura (Ex. 3.10).

Even in this "Christe," however, Marie Therese's vocal profile is apparent. The tempo, tonality, and vocal style invite comparison with another soprano solo, in the Kyrie of Joseph Haydn's *Missa in angustiis* of 1798 ("Nelsonmesse," for which the empress owned a set of parts). Both solos are in fast tempo, D minor, and triple meter, and feature alternation between solo and tutti; but the similarities end there. Michael's soprano sings complete phrases, ending with full cadences; the solo passages never overlap with the chorus. Joseph's alternation of solo and tutti is much more varied and unpredictable, with frequent overlap, requiring of the singer more concentration and confidence. Joseph's tessitura is higher than Michael's, whose soprano reaches several times up to G but never goes above it; Joseph's sings A several times, and once ascends to B♭. That climactic

---

[9] The contents of a letter from Michael Haydn to a Dr. Stifft (possibly Baron Stifft, Emperor Franz's personal physician), Salzburg, 29 October 1803, are summarized in Croll and Vössing, *Johann Michael Haydn*, 142–3. My thanks to Gerhard Croll for information about this letter, which he transcribed in an antiquarian bookstore in Vienna before it disappeared into private hands.

Ex 3.10 Michael Haydn, *Missa S. Francisci*, Kyrie, mm. 40–68

Ex 3.10 (*cont.*)

ascent is accompanied by full orchestra and unison chorus, demanding a voice of considerable power, while Michael's soprano is accompanied throughout by strings alone. Joseph's soprano must also be flexible: capable of spinning strands of coloratura much longer than those in Michael's solo.

The similarities between the "Christe" of the *Missa S. Francisci* and the Kyrie of the "Nelsonmesse" lead me to suspect that Michael Haydn, who must have known his brother's D minor mass by the time he wrote his, set out to recreate something of its effect, with music that would take Marie Therese to the limits of her abilities but not beyond them.

CHAPTER 4

Private concerts

Most of the concerts in which Marie Therese participated between 1801 and 1803 took place in one or another of her apartments (in her diary she wrote only "bey mir") or in Ferdinand's residence. According to a nineteenth-century biographical sketch of Weigl, on these occasions "all courtly ostentation was shunned: the most informal atmosphere prevailed and the empress herself appeared in simple house clothes."[1] The same account states that "only a few favored persons were invited," but leaves unclear whether they came to listen or to perform. In any case the empress and her musicians performed mainly for their own enjoyment; the audience for a particular piece probably consisted mostly of the assembled musicians who were not performing at that moment. On 27 December 1801, when she made music with nine other soloists, chorus, and orchestra, she and Marchesi sang a duet from Sarti's *Giulio Sabino* before an audience that probably consisted of the eight idle soloists and the chorus. The performances that Haydn directed of *Die Schöpfung* and *Die Jahreszeiten*, in which she sang the solo soprano part, were attended only by members of her family.[2] Should one apply the word "concert" to such private events? In doing so, I have followed the empress herself, who used the word *Ackademie* in referring to her music-making on 27 December 1801 and on many other occasions.

These concerts were not only musical but social occasions, and the line between musical and other kinds of human interaction was a thin one, frequently crossed. At a performance of Weigl's *La festa di Carolina* in 1801 the composer was distracted by Elisabeth Bertier, who, as chamber servant to Archduchess Leopoldina, was probably singing in the chorus: "I felt myself attracted to her... In a word, H. M., who thought about me as

---

[1] Wurzbach, *Lexikon* LIII, 283.
[2] Griesinger to Breitkopf & Härtel, Vienna, 27 May 1801, in *Griesingers Korrespondenz*, 75–6.

if she were my mother, condescended in the most flattering terms to bless our marriage."[3]

Considered together, the length and frequency of Marie Therese's concerts are astonishing. During one particularly busy period, between January and April 1802, she participated in thirty-nine concerts: an average of ten per month, most of them consisting of over ten vocal and instrumental numbers. Since both she and Ferdinand were singers, it is not surprising that their repertory was mostly vocal. They performed opera, oratorio, and liturgical music, but rarely combined them in a single concert.

EXCERPTS FROM OPERAS, ORATORIOS, AND *DRAMMI SACRI*

Contemporary Italian music dominated the operatic programs, which usually consisted of two parts mirroring the structural elements of a two-act opera. The first half began with an operatic overture, continued with arias and ensembles, and concluded with an operatic finale. In the second half, more arias and ensembles were followed by a second finale. The empress avoided mixing not only sacred and secular but also comic and serious. Operatic concerts featured excerpts from serious or comic opera, but rarely both.

On 28 March 1802 an opera buffa program took place in Ferdinand's apartment. After the overture to Paer's *L'oro fa tutto*, the first half continued with a quartet and a trio by Portugal, a duet and an aria by Paer, a finale and a trio by Paisiello, and a trio by Martín y Soler; it concluded with a finale from Weigl's *L'amor marinaro*. Ferdinand sang in most of these excerpts. Marie Therese took over at the beginning of the second half, participating in the performance of a trio by Weigl, a duet by Cimarosa, and a quartet by Paisiello, and bringing the concert to an end with a finale from Cimarosa's *Le trame deluse*. The second half also included performances by Weinmüller and Marchesi of arias from comic operas. (Marchesi of course specialized in the portrayal of young heroes in serious operas, but like many *musici* he had begun his career singing female roles in comic opera. His portrayal of such characters in concert was not as outlandish as it may seem.)

---

[3] Weigl, "Zwei Selbstbiographien," 57. Those "flattering terms" included a generous wedding present: a silver and porcelain coffee service for six in a mahogany case (HHStA, Fa, HKF, Kart. 24, diary, fol. 143v). Eybler too married into the imperial household. His wedding in 1806 to Theresia Müller, one of MT's chamber servants, drew a comment from Paer that suggests something of the closeness of the empress's musical circle: "I was amused and surprised at the same time by the marriage of our Ebler. I have no doubt that through their good will they will perhaps be happy (and I wish them that with all my heart); but from their personalities it seems to me that Lent is being joined with Famine. Forgive me, Your Majesty, for putting it this way" (Paer to MT, 6 June 1806).

Other concerts were just as heavily dominated by *opera seria*. Mayr spent several months in Vienna during fall 1802 and winter 1803 and presented a new opera in the court theaters, *Ercole in Lidia*; that visit was reflected in the music performed by Marie Therese on 26 April 1803. Although it is not divided into two parts in her diary, the program contained a finale about halfway through that probably functioned as the end of the first part. The overture to *Ercole* preceded a duet from Paer's *Numa Pompilio*, an aria from Zingarelli's *Ifigenia in Aulide*, a quartet from *Numa*, a *rondò* from Tarchi's *Alessandro nell'Indie*, and the finale from the first act of *Ercole*. The second part began with a trio from *Ercole* and continued with a *rondò* from Mayr's *Gli sciti*, a duet by Zingarelli, an aria from *Ercole*, a duet from Paisiello's *Elfrida*, and a finale from *Gli sciti*.

Marie Therese's sense of genre allowed a good deal of flexibility in her design of concert programs. She must have understood *Die Zauberflöte* and Winter's *Das unterbrochene Opferfest* as closely akin to Italian serious opera, despite their being in German and their comic elements.[4] A concert on 22 November 1801 consisted mostly of excerpts from *opere serie*, but it also included a trio and the first-act finale from *Das unterbrochene Opferfest*, and an aria – probably "In diesen heil'gen Hallen" – from *Die Zauberflöte*.

The empress's diary records one concert dominated by oratorio and *dramma sacro* as fully as others were dominated by comic or serious opera, on 24 January 1802. Like the operatic programs it fell into two halves; and like the concert of 22 November 1801 it brought together German and Italian texts. The first half began with the overture to Zingarelli's *Gerusalemme distrutta* and ended with the final chorus from the second part of *Die Schöpfung*, "Vollendet ist das große Werk." The second half began with a sextet from Guglielmi's *Gionata Maccabeo* and ended with the chorus from the end of the first part of *Die Schöpfung*, "Die Himmel erzählen die Ehre Gottes." In between Marie Therese and Ferdinand took part in the performance of excerpts from the works already mentioned as well as Guglielmi's *La morte di Oloferne* and *Debora e Sisara*, Cimarosa's *Abramo*, and Dittersdorf's *Giobbe*.

SCENE COMPLEXES AND THE *SOTTERRANEO*

One of the most characteristic features of Italian serious opera around 1800 was the scene complex that brought together solos, ensembles, and

---

[4] On Winter's opera see Malcolm S. Cole, "Peter Winter's *Das unterbrochene Opferfest*: Fact, Fantasy, and Performance Practice in Post-Josephinian Vienna," *Music in Performance and Society: Essays in Honor of Roland Jackson*, ed. Malcolm S. Cole and John Koegel, Warren, Mich., 1997, 291–324.

orchestrally accompanied recitative, often using chorus as a unifying or framing device. Like finales, many scene complexes were internally coherent units, self-contained musically as well as dramatically; thus they served as an excellent medium through which to present operatic music in concert. Although Marie Therese referred to the extracts from serious operas in her concerts as arias, duets, trios, and so forth, many of these were in fact scene complexes of considerable length and dramatic interest.

A good example is "Germe d'illustri eroi," from act 1 of Cimarosa's *Gli Orazi e i Curiazi* (Venice, Carnival 1797), of which Marie Therese owned score and parts. She took part in a performance of it on 4 April 1802, calling it in her diary "A trio with choruses from *Orazi* by Cimarosa, sung by me, Marchesi, and Ratmayer." Far more than a trio, "Germe d'illustri eroi" is a spectacular scene, about ten minutes in length, that introduces in quick succession the opera's three leading characters: Marco Orazio (tenor), created by Matteo Babini, Curiazio (soprano), created by Crescentini, and Orazia (soprano), created by Giuseppa Grassini. With Rathmayer singing Marco Orazio and Marchesi Curiazio, Marie Therese had the thrill of recreating with two of the finest singers in Vienna one of the most famous scenes in contemporary opera.

"Germe d'illustri eroi" begins with an orchestral introduction in brilliant, trumpet-dominated C major. The Orazi, a Roman clan (male chorus), call forth the principals one after the other. First they summon their finest young warrior, Orazio, who announces himself in a short orchestrally accompanied recitative. The Orazi now encourage Curiazio to approach: he has come with his family (the Curiazi of the neighboring town of Alba, with whom the Orazi have long been in conflict) to celebrate his marriage to his beloved Orazia, Marco Orazio's sister. Curiazio enters, declaring, in a tender passage in G, that he has put fighting aside in favor of "Puro amor, cara pace, e dolce ardore." After an orchestral modulation back to C major, the chorus enters again, with music very close to what it sang to Orazio (thus fulfilling its unifying function); but it addresses Orazia. She appears, lovingly addressing her fiancé in recitative. With all three principals on stage, the action stops. Marco Orazio, Curiazio, and Orazia reflect on this blissful moment in a gorgeous, hymn-like passage in F major, "Oh dolce e caro istante" (Ex. 4.1), before the scene concludes with a rousing fast movement.

Some of the grandest scene complexes are set in dungeons or other underground chambers. The *sotterraneo*, or *scena sotterranea*, frequently represents a dramatic climax in operas of the late eighteenth and early nineteenth centuries: a scene to which composers devoted special attention, and for which they developed a special musical vocabulary of darkness, mystery,

Ex 4.1 Cimarosa, *Gli Orazi e i Curiazi*, "Germe d'illustri eroi," mm. 112–19

Orchestral accompaniment omitted

and horror.[5] Marie Therese shared with many of her contemporaries a fond-ness for the *sotterraneo*: she participated in the performance of underground scenes from *Gli Orazi e i Curiazi* and Mayr's *Gli sciti*. The latter, which she may have performed as many as six times, was one of her favorites.[6] Ferdinand, in a letter quoted in chapter 2, called Mayr's *sotterraneo* "that beautiful scene you like so much."[7]

Twice, on 22 November 1801 and on 25 July 1802, Marie Therese participated in performances of the finale of act 2 of *Gli Orazi*. This splendid scene, about twenty-two minutes in length, can serve as an example of the *sotterraneo* and can help explain why Marie Therese found such scenes so attractive. The libretto describes the setting:

An intensely dark and deep cavern carved in the cliffs of the Aventine, into which one descends by various rocky stairways, which meander down from the highest

[5] Helga Lühning, "Florestans Kerker in Rampenlicht: Zur Tradition des Sotterraneo," *Beethoven: Zwischen Revolution und Restauration*, ed. Helga Lühning and Sieghard Brandenburg, Bonn, 1989, 137–204.

[6] In her diary MT recorded three performances of a quartet from *Gli Sciti* in which the performers included chorus; on three other occasions her musicians performed a quartet from *Gli Sciti*, but without chorus. Since the only quartet in the opera is in the *sotterraneo*, and the chorus participates only in the last part of this scene (see Uta Schaumberg, *Die opere serie Giovanni Simone Mayrs*, 2 vols., Munich, 2001, II, 59), the *sotterraneo* (or some part of it) may have been performed in all six of these concerts.

[7] MT's predilection for this *sotterraneo* is confirmed by Mayr himself, who wrote of *Gli sciti* in an autobiographical sketch: "Ne fu apprezzato particolarmente il quartetto del secondo atto dalla fu Imperatrice Maria Teresa seconda consorte del regnante Imp. Francesco" (quoted in Ludwig Schiedermair, *Beiträge zur Geschichte der Oper um die Wende des 18. und 19. Jahrh.*, 2 vols., Leipzig, 1907–10, I, 172).

part of the scenery to the walls of the cavern below. At the moment indicated the splendid temple of Apollo, at the back of the stage, will be opened, from which the oracle's responses will issue forth.

Like many *sotterranei*, this one begins with a long instrumental introduction in slow tempo and minor mode (Ex. 4.2). Tonally unstable, the introduction presents a series of short melodic fragments. A lyrical tune begins to emerge only once, in the clarinet, at the establishment of the relative major at m. 20; but it soon breaks off. Frequent alternations of loud and soft, dissonant intervals, and syncopations contribute to this musical evocation of horror.

Also typical of *sotterranei* is the initial appearance of a single character who describes and responds to the scene with a series of exclamations in orchestrally accompanied recitative. Here that character is Curiazio:

> Qual densa notte! Qual silenzio! Quale
> Spaventevol, funesto,
> A fati sacro, orrido albergo è questo!
> Numi! Qui non penetra
> Sottil raggio di luce
> Che in questi alpestri sassi
> Additi un' orma a miei tremanti passi.[8]

What impenetrable night! What silence! What a dreadful, horrifying place this is, sacred to the fates. Gods! Here the faintest ray of light does not penetrate, which might point the way, among these mountainous rocks, for my trembling footsteps.

Orazia enters; her recitative adds further details to the dungeon-like picture painted by Curiazio and helps us interpret the orchestral images that accompany her words:

> Guidami amor, scendiam ... il cor m'investe
> Profondo orror ... Che fia? Qui non s'ascolta
> Che il cader raro e lento
> D'umide stille ... e il basso mormorio
> Dell'aer grave e del cadente rio.

Love, be my guide; let us descend ... my heart is filled with deepest horror ... What is happening? Here one hears nothing but drops of water, infrequently and slowly falling ... and the low murmuring of the stagnant air and the flowing stream.

Orazio's entrance is preceded by fast music in the major mode – completely different from everything heard so far – that expresses his bravado

---

[8] These and the following verses are quoted in Lühning, "Florestans Kerker im Rampenlicht," 169, where motivic relations between the orchestral introduction and the recitative are pointed out.

Ex 4.2 Cimarosa, *Gli Orazi e i Curiazi*, Finale of act 2 (sotterraneo), mm. 1–38

Ex 4.2 (*cont.*)

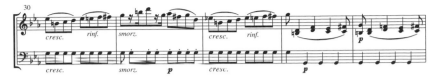

and fearlessness. In response to his taunts, Curiazio declares his willingness to face the oracle of Apollo, who is to tell the assembled families whether they must fight to the death. To slow music in E♭ ("Regni silenzio") the soloists and chorus call for silence as they await the oracle's pronouncement. This ensemble is remarkably similar in its dramaturgy and music to "Silenzio facciasi," the a cappella quartet in Salieri's *Palmira regina di Persia* (Vienna, 1795).

Curiazio embarks on his second big accompanied recitative, a prayer to the oracle: "Voce augusta del Ciel." This serves as a prelude to what appears at first to be an aria, "A versar l'amato sangue." But Curiazio's lyrical outpouring is interrupted by an earthquake as the chorus exclaims "Trema il suol, l'antro si scuote." The oracle orders the rival clans to fight. They respond eagerly: "Dunque al campo." The finale approaches its climax with an intensely dramatic juxtaposition of martial fervor and private agony. As if returning to the aria that was earlier interrupted, Curiazio describes the pain of his dilemma – he is about to fight his beloved's brother – in a gavotte tune of the kind frequently used in the concluding fast section of the two-tempo *rondò*. In a *rondò* the gavotte tune is usually sung at least twice, and here too Curiazio repeats his plaintive "Ah! chi vide mai di questa" amid the chorus's call to arms.

Cimarosa's *sotterraneo* brings together a wide variety of musical elements: orchestral tone-painting, accompanied recitatives, ariosos, lyrical passages that resemble parts of arias, ensembles, and choruses. The important role that Curiazio plays helps to hold the scene together. From his opening monologue to his passionate declaration in gavotte rhythms near the end of the scene, Curiazio dominates the *sotterraneo*, so much so that it might be called a scena for the *primo uomo* in which the other soloists and the chorus serve as *pertichini*. But an equally important source of dramatic coherence is the scenery itself, and the atmosphere of darkness and mystery that prevails throughout this and other *sotterranei*: scenes that aroused in Marie Therese and her contemporaries both horror and pleasure.

CHORUSES

While Marie Therese's choristers often played a subsidiary role in arias, ensembles, and scene complexes dominated by soloists, occasionally they took center stage in the performance of excerpts from larger works. They sang two choruses from *Die Schöpfung*, three from Handel's *Judas Maccabaeus*, and one from Sarti's *Alessandro e Timoteo*.

The empress's concerts twice included choral depictions of storms. Her choir sang "Onnipotente Dio" from Dittersdorf's *Giobbe* on 24 January 1802 and less than two and a half months later, on 4 April, "Qual nuovo terrore" from Mozart's *Idomeneo* (where the storm brings forth a sea monster). Both choruses are addressed to the god who has sent the storm: in Dittersdorf's, Jehovah tests Job's faith by destroying his possessions; in Mozart's, Neptune keeps Idomeneus from sending his son away so as to avoid sacrificing him. Job's family and friends and the people of Crete plead for mercy, while the orchestra depicts the storm in all its violence with a combination of musical devices that one would expect to find in such a situation: fast tempo, minor mode, tonal instability, tremolo, syncopation, sudden contrasts in dynamics, and rushing scales.

That Marie Therese should find storm choruses appealing is consistent with another aspect of her musical taste: her interest in the requiem. The Dies irae often drew from composers choral music as stormy as "Onnipotente Dio" and "Qual nuovo terrore."

CONCERTS DEVOTED TO SINGLE OPERAS, CANTATAS, AND ORATORIOS

Marie Therese sometimes devoted entire programs to the performance of single works, including full-length operas. She did not use the word *Ackademie* in referring to such occasions. Did she stage these operas, with costumes and scenery? Probably not. In asking Paisiello to compose *La corona del merito*, she wrote "this opera must be suited to the chamber, and not to the theater." Weigl, remembering the premiere of *L'uniforme*, said explicitly that it was "given as a concert at Schönbrunn."[9] If the empress did not give a fully staged production of an opera that she had actually commissioned and in which she sang a major role, it is hard to believe she staged other operas that she performed in private.

When the works to which she devoted entire concerts were relatively short cantatas (such as Weigl's *La festa di Carolina*), we can assume that she and her musicians performed the entire work. But one wonders if they really had the time and musical resources to present complete performances of operas as elaborate and difficult as *Don Giovanni*, *Das unterbrochene Opferfest*, and Cherubini's *Elisa*. The concerts that Marie Therese devoted to these operas probably consisted of a large number of excerpts from them.[10] She never, in the period covered by her diary, devoted a whole program to any opera more than once. But in scheduling oratorios and cantatas she quite frequently returned to works performed earlier.[11]

Several of the operas and oratorios whose performance constituted entire concerts, such as *L'uniforme* and *Die Schöpfung*, existed in Italian and German versions (*Elisa*, of course, was originally in French), and it is not always possible to tell in what language the empress performed them. In view of her love of Italian opera and oratorio, however, it is interesting to note that only three of these works were first performed in Italy – Mayr's *Lubino e Carlotta* and *I misteri eleusini* and Vincenzo Pucitta's *Teresa e Wilk* – and that most of them, when performed in public in Vienna during the early nineteenth century, were sung in German. Most of the amateurs who performed with Marie Therese were presumably Austrian, and some of them probably knew little or no Italian. One of her key professional collaborators, Weinmüller, sang Italian rarely in public. She may have felt that concerts devoted to single works would go more smoothly, and would give her Austrian musicians more pleasure, if sung in German.

CHURCH MUSIC

The several masses, including at least two requiems, that Marie Therese commissioned between 1800 and 1806 were presumably intended in the

---

[9] Weigl, "Zwei Selbstbiographien," 57.

[10] The other operas that MT listed as having been performed by themselves were Eybler's *Das Zauberschwert*, Mayr's *Lubino e Carlotta* and *I misteri eleusini*, Paer's *Numa Pompilio*, Vincenzo Pucitta's *Teresa e Wilk*, Weigl's *L'uniforme* and *I solitari*, and Winter's *Marie von Montalban*.

[11] Among the oratorios to which MT devoted entire concerts were *Die Hirten an der Krippe* (probably by Eybler, although MT attributed it to Paer), Haydn's *Die Schöpfung*, Paer's *La passione*, and Paisiello's *La passione*. Among the cantatas (in addition to Weigl's *La festa di Carolina*, performed at least three times) were Weigl's *Le pazzie musicali* and *L'amor filiale*, and Winter's *Das Friedensfest*.

first place for performance in a liturgical context. But more significant from an historical point of view was her performance of sacred music in concert. Although Latin-texted motets (often settings of psalms) had been frequently performed in the Concert Spirituel in Paris since its founding in 1725, in eighteenth- and early nineteenth-century Vienna liturgical texts seem to have been rarely sung in public or private concerts. In Marie Therese's concerts, however, masses, requiems, and Te Deums represented an important part of the repertory. She participated in the process by which works conceived for performance within Catholic services gradually came to be viewed as suitable for performance in concert.

The empress's private concerts included works she had commissioned for special occasions. Michael Haydn's *Missa S. Theresiae*, having been sung in celebration of Franz's nameday on 4 October 1801, was performed again in Marie Therese's apartment on 19 November, along with the gradual "Petite et accipietis" and the Te Deum in D that Haydn had also written for the nameday festivities. The empress's musicians sang Eybler's Requiem on 2 April 1803, when she rewarded him with a watch decorated with diamonds and pearls on a golden chain and 600 Gulden in cash.[12] It was also performed in the Hofkapelle on the anniversary of the death of Emperor Leopold II (1 March), the occasion for which Marie Therese commissioned it. That performance may have taken place in 1803 (a month before her private one) or two years later.[13] Other concerts of liturgical music probably served as rehearsals for the singing of the same music in liturgical contexts. I will argue in chapter 5 that private performances of Eybler's *Missa S. Theresiae* on 21 September and 3 October 1802 were rehearsals for the performance in celebration of Franz's nameday on 4 October.

---

[12] "Dem 2. [April 1803] Dem Eibler für sein Requiem. Eine Frantzblaue Repetiruhr mit kleinen Brillianten und Perlen an einer goldenen Ketten mit Schnallen von Brillianten. 600 fl. im Geld" (HHStA, Fa, HKF, Kart. 24, diary, fol. 161r).

[13] In a review of the printed score of Eybler's Requiem, Friedrich Rochlitz reported: "E's *Requiem* ist ursprünglich zur Feyer des Todtenamtes für Kaiser Leopold II. geschrieben" (*AmZ* 28 [1826], col. 307). Eybler responded to Rochlitz's statement in a letter of 15 July 1826 (transcribed and reproduced in facsimile in Johanna Senigl, "Neues zu Joseph Eybler," *De editione musices: Festschrift Gerhard Croll zum 65. Geburtstag*, ed. Wolfgang Gratzer and Andrea Lindmayr, Laaber, 1992, 329–37), stating "daß ich dieses *Requiem* im Jahre 1803 auf allerhöchsten Befehl der Kaiserinn *Maria Theresia* schrieb, also 11 Jahre nach Kaiser *Leopold II* Tod." That statement suggests that MT commissioned the Requiem to commemorate the eleventh anniversary of Leopold's death, on 1 March 1803. But in 1805 a report from Vienna in the *AmZ* included Eybler's Requiem "among our musical novelties," and mentioned a performance in the Hofkapelle that took place, apparently, earlier that year: "Wien den 15ten May [1805]. Unter unsern musikalischen Neuigkeiten nimmt ein Requiem zur Todesfeyer des Kaisers Leopold II. den vorzüglichsten Platz ein. Es ist von dem Vice-Hofkapellmeister Eybler, und wurde am Sterbetage des Kaisers in der Hofkapelle ganz vortrefflich aufgeführt" (*AmZ* 7 [1804–5], col. 591).

Concerts reflected the closing of theaters during Lent by favoring church over theatrical music at that time of year. In 1802, when Lent began on 3 March, Marie Therese gave concerts of sacred music on 4 and 5 March: Campion's Requiem, masses by Michael Haydn and Reutter, Jommelli's celebrated offertory "Confirma hoc Deus," an offertory by Eybler (probably "Laudate pueri"), and responsories by David Perez. In the following weeks she performed requiems by Michael Haydn and Mozart, a mass by Gyrowetz, and a Te Deum by Reutter. There is no reason to think that any of these performances were liturgical in function, except in so far as they marked the penitential season. The observation of Lent culminated in 1802 during Holy Week with the performance of Passion oratorios: settings of *La passione* by Paisiello and Paer, and, on Holy Saturday, Joseph Haydn's *Die sieben letzten Worte*. Marie Therese celebrated Easter (18 April) with a performance of *Die Schöpfung*.

INSTRUMENTAL MUSIC

Marie Therese did not always identify in her diary the overtures with which some of her concerts began; sometimes she listed the composer only. But when she named an operatic source, we can see that she and Ferdinand observed in their choice of overture the distinction between comic and serious that shaped the rest of the program. The *opera seria* concert on 10 January 1802 began with the overture to Paer's *Achille*; the *opera buffa* concert on 7 March 1802 with the overture to Weigl's *L'amor marinaro*.

Among concert symphonies Marie Therese favored programmatic works, showing the same interest in musical pictorialism as in her performances of storm choruses by Dittersdorf and Mozart. The "Sinfonie mit der Jagd" (with the hunt) by Wranitzky that her musicians performed on 22 January 1802 must have been the programmatic symphony in G minor from her library whose second movement is entitled "eine Jagd." It contains not only a hunt but yet another storm. The first movement, entitled "Donnerwetter," includes a detailed commentary:

The storm begins in the distance . . . The inhabitants' terror . . . The storm gets closer . . . Sighing of the wind . . . Lightning . . . Loud thunder . . . It strikes . . . The rain . . . The thunder rolls . . .[14]

---

[14] "Das Wetter beginnt von ferne . . . Furcht der Einwohner . . . Das Wetter nähret sich . . . Saufen der Winde . . . Das Blitzen . . . Es donnert stark . . . Es schlägt ein . . . Der Regen . . . Der Donner rollt . . ." (A-Wn, Mus. Hs. 11088, "Donnerwetter")

The empress also programmed Wranitzky's "Sinfonia strepitosa," and his symphonic depiction of the French Revolution, to be discussed in chapter 6.

Several symphonies from Marie Therese's library, including Wranitzky's Quodlibet Symphony (discussed below) and his Symphony in G minor depicting the hunt and the storm, contain unusual obbligato keyboard parts. Other orchestral works that call for keyboard are the Fantasy in F minor for piano and orchestra by Leopold Kozeluch (Mus. Hs. 11388); Kauer's *Fantasia fürs ganze Orchester*, *Sei variazioni*, and *Variazioni a più strumenti* (Mus. Hs. 11382–3); and the *Serenata grande con cembalo concertato* by Wenzel Pichl (Mus. Hs. 11389). The presence of these unpublished works in Marie Therese's library and the fact that both she and Ferdinand played the piano suggest that Wranitzky, Kozeluch, Kauer, and Pichl wrote them for the empress or her brother-in-law to perform.

Marie Therese certainly played the keyboard in one orchestral work that combines, like Wranitzky's Symphony in G minor and Quodlibet Symphony, an important keyboard part with programmatic elements. On 21 March 1802, in the middle of a concert consisting entirely of music by Weigl, she displayed her abilities in "a concerto on the *Clawier* representing the passions, played by me." This was the Concertino in D that Weigl wrote, according to the autograph (A-Wn, Mus. Hs. 19398), in 1801, shortly before the empress played it. Along the lines of Dittersdorf's symphony *Il combattimento delle passioni umane*, the Concertino depicts human emotions in a series of six movements, some of which present a single emotion and others two contrasting passions: "L'orgoglio" (pride), "Amore ed odio" (love and hate), "L'indifferenza e la pazzia" (indifference and madness), "La malinconia" (melancholy), "L'allegria" (joy), and "La gara degl'instrumenti" (the competition of the instruments). Although Marie Therese referred to the Concertino as "Ein Concert auf das Clawier," it is not really a keyboard concerto: it gave many of her players a chance to display their virtuosity in solos for bassoon, flute, oboe, clarinet, viola d'amore, and cello.[15]

Some of Vienna's principal virtuosos played concertos for the empress. Anton Weidinger, the trumpeter for whom Joseph Haydn and Johann Nepomuk Hummel wrote concertos, played a concerto on his keyed trumpet on 5 March 1802. Since Hummel had not yet written his concerto (he

---

[15] My thanks to Dexter Edge for identifying Weigl's Concertino as the work played by MT and for giving me a summary of its contents. A few dynamic indications in the cembalo part (including "cres.") suggest that Weigl intended it for piano. He probably wrote the viola d'amore part for Eybler, who on 3 October 1802 played that instrument in one of his own string quintets. MT's copy of the Concertino (*CaM*, p. 60: "Concertino per Cembalo, ed altri Stromenti") is apparently lost.

finished it in December 1803 and Weidinger first performed it before Franz and Marie Therese at a *Tafeldienst* at court on New Year's Day, 1804[16]), the concerto that Weidinger played in March 1802 was probably Joseph Haydn's. A month later Johann Stadler, brother of the clarinettist for whom Mozart wrote the Clarinet Concerto, played Eybler's Clarinet Concerto in B♭; and less than a month after that Franz Clement, who later gave the premiere of Beethoven's Violin Concerto, played a concerto whose composer Marie Therese did not name.

The empress's concerts included relatively little chamber music, probably because she did not want her orchestra and chorus to sit idly while just a few instrumentalists played. Most of the chamber music that did find its way onto her programs involved more than four players: Mozart's Quintet for piano and winds, string quintets by Eybler, and a string sextet by Albrechtsberger. The performance of string quartets she left entirely to her "beloved fiddler," Emperor Franz.

WRANITZKY'S QUODLIBET SYMPHONY

The spirit of Carnival caused Marie Therese to hold a mirror up to her private music-making by means of an instrumental depiction of a typical concert at court. In the middle of Carnival 1802 a programmatic symphony by Wranitzky portrayed a concert very much like those organized by the empress. This Quodlibet Symphony, played on 28 January 1802, consists of four movements that frame an extended medley of popular songs and excerpts from operas and ballets. In the empress's score (Mus. Hs. 11086) the movements and the quodlibet's constituent parts are labeled as follows:

I. Allegro
II. Presto
III. Ein Quodlibet.
   Erste Abtheilung:
      1. A Schüsserl und a Reindl [Austrian folksong]
      2. Mama mia non mi gridate [song of unknown origin]
      3. Nel cor più non mi sento aus der Molinara [Paisiello]
      4. Le Nozze di Figaro. Non più andrai [Mozart]
      5. Marcia Richard Löwenherz [ballet by Weigl] Ende der ersten Abtheilung
   Zweite Abtheilung:
      6. Ouverture von der Zauberflöte [Mozart]

---

[16] John A. Rice, "The Musical Bee: References to Mozart and Cherubini in Hummel's 'New Year' Concerto," *Music and Letters* 77 (1996), 401–24.

    7. Quartetto aus der Palmira. Silenzio facciasi [Salieri]
    8. L'Amor Marinaro. Pria ch'io l'impegno [Weigl]
    9. aus Lodoiska. Oh quanto l'anima [Mayr]
   10. aus Lodoiska. Contento il cor nel seno [Mayr]
   11. Menuett von der Venturini. Le Nozze Disturbate [ballet by Jacob Haibel]
IV. Finale
 V. Andante

Jan LaRue discussed the Quodlibet Symphony in the 1950s, before its connection with Marie Therese was known. He cleverly dubbed it the "Hail and Farewell Symphony" because, while in the final Andante (obviously inspired by Haydn's "Farewell" Symphony) the orchestra gradually diminishes in size, in the opening Allegro the musicians enter one after the other, sit down, tune their instruments, and begin to play.[17]

The entrances are carefully planned. The score contains indications in red ink of when each player, including a pianist (a part written for Marie Therese herself?) should enter the room. LaRue pointed out that the intervals between the time the musicians enter and the time they begin to play vary greatly: "If we study these intervals, interesting orchestral personalities emerge: a fussy viola needs twenty bars to settle down, while the prodigious first bassoon manages to enter and begin to play in six bars, and a similarly rough-and-ready timpanist tunes in only nine bars of *alla breve*." At m. 283, according to the score's instructions, ten players "run in hurriedly one after another as if they were late." As Marie Therese's concertmaster, Wranitzky was in a good position to know the idiosyncracies of her instrumentalists and who among them was habitually late for concerts; this opening movement gave him an opportunity to make fun of them.

The second and fourth movements are conventional symphonic movements that, in LaRue's words, move "through the rather routine paces of the typical opera overture of the period." The analogy with an opera overture suits the second movement especially well: it represents the overture with which Marie Therese's concerts often began.

The third movement, the quodlibet proper, likewise reflects the empress's concerts, which included operatic excerpts by most of the composers represented here. As many as four of the numbers quoted by Wranitzky had a place in Marie Therese's music-making. On 14 March 1802 Marchesi sang "Eine Polonoise mit Chöre auß Lodoiska von Mayer" that was probably "Contento il cor nel seno." The "Cavatina auß der Lodoiska" that Marchesi

---

[17] Jan LaRue, "A 'Hail and Farewell' Quodlibet Symphony," *Music and Letters* 37 (1956), 250–9.

sang on 27 December 1801 was probably "Oh quanto l'anima," borrowed from Mayr's *Lauso e Lidia* for the Viennese production of *Lodoiska*. The "Aria auß Nozze di Figaro von Mozart gesungen von Weinmüller" on 10 April 1803 could have been "Non più andrai." Even the concert in which the Quodlibet Symphony was performed included one of the quoted numbers, Salieri's "Silenzio facciasi."

Marie Therese's concerts did not include folksongs or ballet music, making "A Schüsserl und a Reindl," the march from Weigl's *Richard Löwenherz*, and the "Menuett von der Venturini" seem out of place. Yet Süssmayr had given "A Schüsserl" a certain operatic legitimacy by using it in a *Singspiel, Der Marktschreier* (Vienna, 1799).[18] And a theme from a ballet by Weigl, *Alceste* (Vienna, 1800), served the harpist Müllner as the basis for variations in a concert on 31 January 1802, three days after the performance of the Quodlibet Symphony.

Wranitzky treated the borrowed material in several different ways. He presented the march from *Richard Löwenherz* and the overture to *Die Zauberflöte* in their entirety, and largely in their original orchestration (the most important change being the omission of the trombones from the overture). Some of the arias are likewise faithful copies of the originals, with the vocal line played by a cello in "Non più andrai" and "Contento il cor nel seno," and a violin in "Oh quanto l'anima." Wranitzky's treatment of "Silenzio facciasi" falls into the same category. He altered Salieri's a cappella quartet only to the extent of scoring it for two clarinets and two bassoons. In other cases he borrowed only a melody and varied it, reminding us that variations on operatic tunes were occasionally played in Marie Therese's concerts. The piano dominates the most elaborate set of variations, on "Nel cor più non mi sento," which approach in quality those Beethoven wrote on the same theme.

When LaRue commented on "the extraordinary length of the symphony, in itself enough for a whole concert," he came close to the circumstances of the performance on 28 January. According to Marie Therese's diary, Wranitzky's symphony was performed in three parts: at the beginning, in the middle, and at the end of the concert. Movements 1 and 5 must have served to accompany the assembling of musicians and their dispersal. Played together, movements 2, 3 and 4 presented a depiction of a typical concert at court: the beginning of the first half of the concert with an operatic overture, a series of excerpts from theatrical – mostly operatic – works, divided into two parts, and an operatic finale.

---

[18] Ibid., 234.

Unlike most of Wranitzky's symphonies, the Quodlibet Symphony was not published, and it circulated very little in manuscript. (A copy in Florence was owned by Ferdinand, who witnessed its performance in Vienna.[19]) This was probably one of the works that Wranitzky "composed for the personal use and private pleasure of Empress Maria Theresia." She and her musicians alone were in a position to understand its meaning.

[19] I-Fc, F.P. S 122, listed in "Catalogo delle Opere ridotte Sinfonie &^{ra}" (Florence, Archivio di Stato, I. R. Corte 5429).

CHAPTER 5

Celebrations of Franz's birthday and nameday

Marie Therese's records of presents she gave to members of her family on their birthdays and namedays show how she enjoyed keeping track of and celebrating such occasions, very frequent in her large family. But no days mattered more to her than the birthday of her husband, 12 February, and his nameday (the feast of St. Francis of Assisi), 4 October. Having grown up at the Neapolitan court, where sovereigns' birthdays and namedays were customarily celebrated with operatic productions at the Teatro San Carlo, she naturally gravitated to the emperor's festive days as opportunities for music-making. Vienna too had witnessed many such festivities during the reign of her grandmother Maria Theresa, including musical productions in which the younger members of the imperial family took part. The widower Joseph II abandoned this tradition in the 1770s. Marie Therese reestablished it, but with an important change. While the musical celebrations of namedays and birthdays in Naples and Maria Theresa's Vienna were generally open to the public, Marie Therese tended to celebrate her husband's festive days within a relatively small circle of family members and courtiers.

The empress planned these events many months in advance, arranging a wide variety of music, which she often presented at Laxenburg, but sometimes at Schönbrunn and at least twice at Hetzendorf, another imperial residence nearby (Table 5.1). According to Seyfried, who wrote music for Franz's nameday in 1805, Marie Therese celebrated the occasion every year "with a rustic festivity" (mit einem ländlichen Feste).[1] A similar phrase appears in the subtitle of another work written for Franz's nameday. A manuscript libretto of Weigl's cantata *Der gute Wille* (dated, in Marie Therese's hand, 4 October 1803) designates it as "a rustic musical entertainment" (Eine ländliche musikalische Unterhaltung).[2] The word "ländlich" probably refers more to the place of performance than to the contents of the works, which occasionally incorporate rustic elements (such as the

---

[1] Seyfried, *Scizze meines Lebens*, 17.   [2] HHStA, Fa, Sb, Kart. 66, fol. 606–11.

Table 5.1 *Music for Emperor Franz's birthday and nameday, 1797–1807*

Year	Day/ month	Composer	Title (genre)	Place of performance	Source (see below)
1797	4/10	Wranitzky	?	?	a
1798	4/10	Wranitzky	?	?	a
1799	4/10	Wranitzky	?	?	a
1800	4/10?	Eybler	*Missa S. Wolfgangi*	?	b
1801	12/2	Wranitzky	*Die Binder* (divertissement)	?	c
	12/2	Weigl	*Il miglior dono* (cantata)	?	d
	4/10	M. Haydn	*Missa S. Theresiae*	Laxenburg	e
	4/10	Wranitzky	Ball	?	c
1802	4/10	Eybler	*Missa S. Theresiae*	Laxenburg	e
1803	13/2	Wranitzky	Divertissement, Quodlibet	?	c
	13/2?	Albrechtsberger	*Missa S. Francisci*	?	b
	2/10	Schenk	*Der Dorfbarbier* (Singspiel)	Redoutensaal	a, f
	4/10	Paer	?	?	a
	4/10	Weigl	*Der Gute Wille* (cantata)	Laxenburg	a, g
	4/10?	M. Haydn	*Missa S. Francisci*	?	e
	4/10	Wranitzky	?	Hetzendorf	a
1804	12/2	Wranitzky	*Das Picknick der Götter* (play with music)	Schönbrunn	c
1805	12/2	Paer	*Il conte Clò* (cantata)	?	a
	12/2	Eybler	ballet	?	a
	4/10	Seyfried	*Serenata con una cantatina*	Hetzendorf	c
	4/10?	Schacht	Mass in C minor	?	b
1806	12/2	Weigl	*Il sacrifizio interrotto* (cantata)	?	g
	4/10	Weigl	*Il principe invisibile* (opera)	Laxenburg	c, g
1807	12/2	Weigl	*Das Bacchantenfest* (divertissement)	?	c

Sources:

[a] Marie Therese's records of gifts, HHStA, Fa, HKF, Kart. 24

[b] Date of performance extrapolated from date of composition, as recorded in autograph score (see Table 5.2)

[c] Manuscript score or parts with date of performance

[d] Weigl, "Zwei Selbstbiographien," 52

[e] See Table 5.2

[f] Robert Haas, "Josef Leopold Edler von Eybler," *Mozart-Jahrbuch* 1952, 64

[g] Dated manuscript libretto

Berchtesgadner Instrumente in Wranitzky's *Ball zum 4ten Octob. 1801* and Paer's cantata *Il conte Clò*) but are not consistently rustic in subject matter or musical style.

To celebrate her husband's festive days Marie Therese commissioned settings of the mass, secular cantatas, operas, ballets, plays, and sets of social dances. She distributed commissions widely, ordering two masses from Michael Haydn, various *divertissements* from Wranitzky, cantatas from Paer and Weigl, a *Serenata con una cantatina* from Seyfried, and a spoken comedy with music from Franz Xaver Gewey. Another playwright who benefited from her patronage on the occasion of Franz's nameday was Joseph Richter, best known today as the author of the *Eipeldauer Briefe*, a long-running commentary, in Viennese dialect, on life in the Habsburg capital. The diary records gifts to Richter for unspecified services on 4 October 1797 and for a comedy on 4 October 1803.[3]

Given the festive nature of the birthday and nameday performances, it is not surprising that Marie Therese reinforced her regular musicians with others who rarely if ever performed privately with her. In recording her gifts to those who participated in the celebration of Franz's nameday in 1803, she mentioned, in addition to many of her regular collaborators, two musicians who never appear as performers in the records of her private concerts: the singer Gaetano Lotti and the pianist and composer Anton Eberl.[4] Franz himself may have participated in the performance of some of the birthday and nameday works. Following Marie Therese's instructions, Paer made the overture to *Il conte Clò* especially difficult for the violins so as to amuse the emperor, who, she wrote, "would also play."[5]

PLENARY MASSES

Of the two masses that Michael Haydn wrote for Marie Therese, the first, the *Missa S. Theresiae*, was performed on Franz's nameday in 1801, and the second, the *Missa S. Francisci*, was commissioned for the celebration of the same occasion two years later. This suggests the possibility that the performance of a newly composed mass was a regular part of the celebration of Franz's nameday.

In fulfilling both commissions Haydn set to music not only the Ordinary but also pieces called gradual and offertory, and the Te Deum. (I say "pieces called gradual and offertory" because their texts are not proper to

[3] HHStA, Fa, HKF, Kart. 24, diary, fol. 114r and 171v.   [4] Ibid., fol. 171r–v.
[5] See appendix 5A.

any particular feast.) In the case of the *Missa S. Theresiae*, the chronological proximity of the Ordinary, the gradual "Petite et accipietis," the offertory "Magnus Dominus," and the Te Deum in D, Sherman 800, all completed in August 1801, leaves little doubt that they were all composed for Franz's nameday. In the case of the *Missa S. Francisci*, we have Haydn's own testimony (in a letter quoted in chapter 8) that the commission included a gradual, an offertory, and a Te Deum.

Several of the works listed simply as masses in the *Kathalog der Kirchen-musickalien* (for example, the masses of Theodor Schacht and Francesco Bott di Pierot) contain not only settings of the Ordinary but pieces called offertory (between the Gloria and the Credo) and gradual (between the Credo and the Sanctus); Bott's mass contains, in addition, a Te Deum (with a separate title page). But also in cases where settings by one composer of the Ordinary and of graduals, offertories, and the Te Deum are catalogued separately, it often turns out that he wrote a mass, a gradual, an offertory, and a Te Deum around the same time. In such cases it seems likely that he wrote them to be performed together and conceived them as a single, compound work. For example, since Eybler wrote the *Missa S. Francisci*, the gradual "Exaltate Dominum Deum," and the offertory "Lux est orta," all scored for double chorus, in 1806, he almost certainly wrote them, together with the two-choir version of the Te Deum in B♭, for one occasion.

That all four of Eybler's masses from Marie Therese's library were composed as part of composite works is confirmed by the organization of his autograph scores. Each setting of the Ordinary is bound together with a gradual, an offertory, and a Te Deum (the Te Deum for the *Missa S. Francisci*, being an arrangement for double chorus of the Te Deum for the *Missa S. Theresiae*, is inserted into the score of the earlier mass). Labels written out by Eybler and glued onto the front cover of each manuscript make clear that he considered each manuscript as a musical unit, and that the date of composition applies to the manuscript as a whole, not just the Ordinary (see Table 1.7).

Michael Haydn's autographs likewise confirm that he thought of the *Missa S. Theresiae* and the *Missa S. Francisci* and their accompanying pieces as two single works. In the autographs from the collection of Grand Duke Ferdinand both settings of the Ordinary are bound together with their respective gradual, offertory, and Te Deum; a single title page (not, however, in Haydn's hand) refers to all four elements.[6] For another autograph score

---

[6] I-Fc, F.P. Ch 317 and 318.

Haydn himself supplied the title: *Missa / Sub Titulo / Sanctae Theresiae. / Graduale, / Offertorium, / et / Te Deum.*[7]

Even when individual pieces from Marie Therese's collection cannot be dated, or when autograph scores do not survive, they appear to constitute a unit when the *Kathalog der Kirchenmusickalien* lists one mass, one gradual, one offertory, and one Te Deum by the same composer. This is the case with Johann Anton Kozeluch, represented in the empress's library by a mass, the gradual "Benedictus es," the offertory "Benedictus sit," and a Te Deum. Marie Therese commissioned a grand mass from Georg Lickl in 1804;[8] she probably ordered the gradual "Specie tua," the offertory "Haec est virgo," and the Te Deum at the same time.

A few such composite works had been written before Marie Therese began commissioning them. Dittersdorf dedicated a *Missa Solemnis cum Gradual. et Offertor.* to the archbishop of Breslau in 1797; Salieri wrote a Mass in C for double chorus, with gradual, offertory, and Te Deum, in 1799.[9] But the empress took a particular interest in the plenary mass, a subgenre of the concerted mass whose existence – in a period dominated by Joseph Haydn's settings of the Ordinary alone – has hardly been noticed in the musicological literature. Reflecting this lack of interest, and helping to perpetuate it, is the tendency of library catalogues, thematic catalogues, and modern musical editions to split these works into their constituent parts.[10]

Although I refer to the genre to which these composite works belong as the plenary mass, this term is not quite accurate, since the Proper is not complete. None of these masses, for example, contains an introit. And of course the Te Deum is not part of the mass from a liturgical point of view. Yet Marie Therese and the composers associated with her had no better term. Albrechtsberger wrote on the title page of the autograph score of the *Missa Nativitatis*, commissioned by Emperor Franz, a poem in Latin hexameters:

---

[7] Sherman, 240, 247.   [8] See appendix 1.

[9] On Dittersdorf's mass see Hubert Unverricht, ed., *Carl Ditters von Dittersdorf, 1739–1799: Sein Wirken in Österreich-Schlesien und seine letzten Jahre in Böhmen*, Würzburg, 1993, 78. My thanks to Jane Schatkin Hettrick and Brigitte Lenz for telling me of Salieri's Mass in C, which Ignaz Mosel, *Ueber das Leben und die Werke des Anton Salieri*, Vienna, 1827, 157, refers to as "eine feierliche Messe mit Graduale, Offertorium und einem Te Deum."

[10] Herrmann's Eybler thematic catalogue provides a particularly egregious example of the splitting up of plenary masses by which scholars have obscured their existence. Ignoring the evidence of the autograph scores, Herrmann assigned Eybler's Ordinaries, graduals, offertories, and Te Deums to separate parts of the catalogue, and made no reference even to the idea of a composite work consisting of all four of these elements.

Me pius hanc Missam iussit componere Caesar*
In mense Aprili; scripsi bis quinque diebus,
Confecique melos Gradualis et Offertorii.
Anno 1800[11]

*Franciscus II^dus

A pious emperor ordered me to compose this mass in the month of April; I wrote for twice five days, and I made settings of the gradual and offertory.

Although the composition of the gradual and offertory was presumably part of the imperial commission, for Albrechtsberger the word "Missam" still stood for the Ordinary alone. Michael Haydn, referring to the future *Missa S. Francisci* as "eine Messe sammt *Graduale, Offertorium* und *Te Deum laudamus*,"[12] probably took his terminology from the empress herself, who used very similar words in recording in her diary her performance on 3 October 1802 of "Eine Meß von Eibler sambt Graduale und Offertorio" and, on the following line, "Te Deum d^to." Eybler was just as verbose in the titles he gave the autograph manuscripts of church music he wrote for the empress.

Table 5.2 is a list of groups of pieces owned by Marie Therese that represent, or may represent, plenary masses. I have also included groups consisting of only three pieces, since these may represent incomplete plenary masses. I have included two offertories with Eybler's *Missa S. Wolfgangi*, one of which is liturgically connected to Marie Therese's nameday. If Eybler built the plenary mass around the *Missa S. Wolfgangi* of August 1800 for Emperor Franz's forthcoming nameday, he may have replaced the offertory "Fremit mare" with "Haec est dies" for a performance on Marie Therese's nameday a week and a half later.

Before discussing the function that plenary masses may have served in Marie Therese's music-making, I should point out that the titles by which some of the masses are known do not necessarily go back to their composition or first performance. In the case of Albrechtsberger's *Missa Nativitatis*, the date of the autograph score, April 1800, makes it unlikely that it was originally intended for Christmas. (If, as is more likely, Emperor Franz commissioned it for Marie Therese's birthday on 6 June, he may have given her the idea of commissioning similar works for him.) The autograph scores of the four masses by Eybler of which Marie Therese owned sets of parts are all identified by labels that originally referred to the works simply as "Missa"; the names of the saints were added later (see Table 1.7).

---

[11] Schröder I, 37.

[12] Michael Haydn to Werigand Rettensteiner, 7 April 1803, transcribed in *Biographische Skizze von Michael Haydn*, 26–7; the letter is quoted at greater length in chapter 8.

Table 5.2 *Plenary masses in Marie Therese's library, in chronological order*

Curly brackets enclose items bound together in autograph manuscripts identified at the bottom of the table.

Composer	Liturgical unit, title	Key	Date	Remarks
Anonymous	*Missa ex Creatione mundi*	A	1798 or later	Based on
	Gradual, "O sancta spes"	C	1798 or later	Haydn's
	Offertory, "Ad sonum"	A	1798 or later	*Die Schöpfung*
J. Haydn	Te Deum (see chapter 10)	C	1799–1800	
Albrechtsberger	*Missa Nativitatis*	D	April 1800	Commissioned by
	a { Gradual, "Paratum cor meum"	D	?	Emperor Franz
	Offertory, "Te invocamus"	D	?	
	Te Deum, Schröder J.4	D	May 1800	
Eybler	b { *Missa S. Wolfgangi*	d	1800	For Franz's
	Gradual, "Nocte surgentes"	D	[1800]	nameday?
	Offertory, "Fremit mare"	d	Aug. 1800	
	Te Deum, Herrmann 118	D	July 1800	
	Offertory, "Haec est dies"	D	Oct. 1800	For Saint Theresa's Day
M. Haydn	c { *Missa S. Theresiae*	D	3 Aug. 1801	For Franz's
	Gradual, "Petite et accipietis"	Bb	8 Aug. 1801	nameday
	Offertory, "Magnus Dominus"	d	11 Aug. 1801	
	Te Deum, Sherman 800	D	3 Aug. 1801	
Teyber	*Missa S. Vincenti Ferreri*	A	Jan. 1802 or earlier	Perf. by MT, 22 Jan. 1802
	Gradual, "Gloriose Pater"	D	?	
	Offertory, "In virtute tua"	D	?	
Eybler	d { *Missa S. Theresiae*	Bb	Sept? 1802	For Franz's
	Gradual, "Magnificate"	Bb	[Sept? 1802]	nameday
	Offertory, "Levavi in montes"	g	[Sept? 1802]	
	Te Deum, Herrmann 120	Bb	[Sept? 1802]	
Albrechtsberger	e { *Missa S. Francisci*	C	Feb. 1803	For Franz's
	Gradual, "Benedictus es"	C	Jan. 1803	birthday?
	Offertory, "Gloria Patri"	G	3 Mar. 1803	
	Te Deum "für die Kaiserin"	C	March 1803	
M. Haydn	f { *Missa S. Francisci*	d–D	3 Aug. 1803	For Franz's
	Gradual, "Cantate Domino"	A	30 Aug. 1803	nameday
	Offertory, "Domine Deus"	G	23 Aug. 1803	
	Te Deum, Sherman 829	D	20 Sep. 1803	

Table 5.2 *(cont.)*

Composer	Liturgical unit, title	Key	Date	Remarks
Eybler	*Missa S. Michaelis*	C	1804	
	Gradual, "Cantate Domino"	C	[1804]	
	g Offertory, "Ad te levavi"	F	[1804]	
	Te Deum, Herrmann 117	C	[1804]	
Lickl	Mass	E♭	1804	
	Gradual, "Specie tua"	E♭	?	
	Offertory, "Haec est virgo"	E♭	?	
	Te Deum	E♭	?	
Schacht	Mass	c	Oct. 1805	For Franz's
	h Gradual, "Amavit eam"	F	[Oct. 1805]	nameday?
	Offertory, "Plaude turba angelica"	C	[Oct. 1805]	
Paer	Mass	D	1805–6	
	Gradual, "Exaltate Dominum"	C	?	
	Offertory, "Laetamini coelites"	A	?	
	Te Deum	C	?	
Bott di Pierot	Mass	B♭	6 June 1806	For MT's birthday
	Gradual, "Justus ut palma"	G	[6 June 1806]	
	i Offertory, "Laetamini in Domino"	B♭	[6 June 1806]	
	Te Deum	C	[6 June 1806]	
Eybler	*Missa S. Francisci*	B♭	1806	Double chorus
	Gradual, "Exaltate Dominum Deum"	E♭	[1806]	Double chorus
	j Offertory, "Lux est orta"	B♭	[1806]	Double chorus
	Te Deum, Herrmann 120	B♭	[1806]	Double chorus
J. A. Kozeluch	Mass	D	?	
	Gradual, "Benedictus es"	G	?	
	Offertory, "Benedictus sit"	B♭	?	
	Te Deum	D	?	
Pichl	Mass	C	?	
	Offertory, "Confitemini Domino"	C	?	
	Te Deum	C	?	

Sources:
[a] H-Bn, Ms. Mus. 2293
[b] A-Ws, 567 (436)
[c] I-Fc, F.P.Ch. 318
[d] A-Ws, 570 (417)
[e] D-Bds, Mus. ms. autogr. Albrechtsberger 3
[f] I-Fc, F.P.Ch. 317
[g] A-Ws, 566 (435)
[h] A-Wn, Mus. Hs. 16210
[i] A-Wn, Mus. Hs. 15585
[j] A-Ws, 699 (708)

The only plenary masses that we know to have been performed on Franz's nameday are Michael Haydn's *Missa S. Theresiae* and Eybler's *Missa S. Theresiae*. Marie Therese participated in performances of Haydn's mass on 4 October 1801 and of Eybler's on 4 October 1802.

A public rehearsal of Haydn's *Missa S. Theresiae* in the church of St. Peter in Salzburg on 25 August 1801 gave the composer an opportunity to correct copyists' mistakes and a distinguished audience that included the emperor's brother Archduke Johann a chance to hear Haydn's latest work.[13] Haydn came to Vienna in early September. He wrote to his wife: "On the 9th of this month I had an audience with Her Majesty the empress. Her kindness, gentleness, and affability completely enchanted me, and I had to remind myself again and again that I was speaking with an empress so that I might not fall into too familiar a tone."[14] On 23 September Haydn directed the rehearsal of which he wrote to his wife the account quoted in the introduction to this book. He conducted the performance of his plenary mass at Laxenburg on 4 October, with Marie Therese singing the solo soprano part.[15]

A similar rehearsal schedule preceded the nameday performance of Eybler's *Missa S. Theresiae* a year later. Marie Therese's execution of "a mass by Eibler" and "Te Deum by the same" on 21 September 1802 was almost certainly a rehearsal of the *Missa S. Theresiae* and its accompanying Te Deum in B♭. She rewarded Eybler for the mass on 1 October with an ebony clock decorated with bronze and alabaster and 300 Gulden in cash.[16] On 3 October she performed "A mass by Eibler together with gradual and offertory, Te Deum by the same," thus assembling, on the eve of St. Francis's Day, all the elements of the plenary mass. Finally, on 4 October, she performed a "mass by Eibler." She did not mention where the performance took place, but we know from another source that it was at Laxenburg, like that of Haydn's mass a year earlier. In November 1803 Grand Duke Ferdinand

[13] Croll and Vössing, *Johann Michael Haydn*, 142–3.

[14] Michael Haydn to his wife, Vienna, 24 September 1801, quoted in Jancik, *Michael Haydn*, 239. Translation (used here, with small changes) in the introduction to Michael Haydn, *Missa sub titulo Sanctae Theresiae*, ed. Charles H. Sherman, Stuttgart, 1995.

[15] The date of performance we know from MT's diary; on 19 November 1801 she performed "Mass, Te Deum, and Gradual by Michel Haydn made for 4 October." The *AmZ* revealed the location of the nameday service and confirmed that Haydn took part in it: "Auch von unsrer Monarchin, die vorzügliche Kennerin und Freundin der Tonkunst nicht nur genannt wird, sondern wirklich ist, ist Michael Haydn mit vieler Achtung empfangen, für einige ihm aufgetragene Kirchenkompositionen, die er in Laxenburg aufführte, kaiserlich beschenkt worden, und hat neue Aufträge von seiner hohen Gönnerin erhalten" (*AmZ* 4 [1801–2], col. 264, letter from Vienna dated 29 December 1801).

[16] "Dem 1ten [October 1802]. Dem Eibler für die Meß. Eine Uhr von schwartzen Ebenholtz mit Bronze und Alabasterne Fayence. 300 fl. in Geld" (HHStA, Fa, HKF, Kart. 24, diary, fol. 138r.).

(in a letter quoted at more length in chapter 2) asked Marie Therese to send him a copy of "the most recent mass and Te Deum written by Eybler for Laxenburg two years ago, I believe." Ferdinand miscounted by one year – Eybler's "most recent mass" was the *Missa S. Theresiae* – but there is no reason to think that he got the place of performance wrong.

Three of Marie Therese's plenary masses share a title – *Missa S. Francisci* – that hints at a connection with Franz's festive days. We know from Michael Haydn himself that he composed his *Missa S. Francisci* for Franz's name-day in 1803.[17] The empress rewarded Albrechtsberger for a mass on 29 April 1803: probably the *Missa S. Francisci*, completed in February 1803.[18] The reward, the date of composition, and the title together suggest that Albrechtsberger wrote it for Franz's birthday. If he wrote the gradual "Benedictus es" (January 1803), the offertory "Gloria Patri" (March 1803), and the Te Deum "für die Kaiserin" (March 1803) for the same occasion, he obviously did not finish the offertory and Te Deum on time. Knowing just the year of composition of Eybler's *Missa S. Francisci* for double chorus, 1806, we can only speculate that Eybler composed it – along with the gradual "Exaltate Dominum," the offertory "Lux est orta," and the double-chorus version of the Te Deum in B♭ – for Franz's birthday or nameday of that year.

Eybler's *Missa S. Francisci* probably originated in the visit to Salzburg that the emperor and empress made in June 1805. On that occasion, as we saw in chapter 2, Ferdinand introduced Marie Therese to Michael Haydn's "Missa hispanica." She may have commissioned Eybler to write the *Missa S. Francisci* in the hope of celebrating one of her husband's festive days with a plenary mass that would match the grandeur of Haydn's polychoral masterpiece.

The music of plenary masses reveals two contradictory tendencies. Some composers, perhaps afraid that adding the gradual, offertory, and Te Deum to the Ordinary would create a cycle lacking in musical coherence, wrote the added movements in the same key as the Ordinary. Others used the gradual, offertory and Te Deum as opportunities to enhance the cycle's internal variety.

Table 5.2 shows that Albrechtsberger belonged in the first category. In composing the *Missa Nativitatis* he set the gradual "Paratum cor meum,"

---

[17] Whether it was actually performed on that day is unknown. The composer wrote to Dr. Stifft on 29 October 1803 (see chapter 3) that the mass was performed under Eybler's direction, but mentioned neither the date nor the place of performance.

[18] "1803 April . . . Dem 29. Dem Albrechtsberger für eine Meß / Eine Goldene Dose 110 fl. werth / 300 fl im Geld" (HHStA, Fa, HKF, Kart. 24, diary, fol. 162r).

the offertory "Te invocamus," and the Te Deum Schröder J4 all in D major, the key of the Ordinary. Likewise Lickl's Ordinary, offertory, gradual, and Te Deum are all in E♭.

Kozeluch had more confidence in his ability to maintain coherence on the large scale. Into an Ordinary in D major he brought tonal variety by choosing G major for the gradual and B♭ for the offertory; yet he imposed a sense of unity on the whole by setting the Te Deum in D. Eybler chose a middle path between Albrechtsberger and Lickl on the one hand and Kozeluch on the other. He usually ventured away from the tonic in the offertory but never in the gradual or Te Deum.

Michael Haydn's tonal adventurousness matched Kozeluch's. In the D major *Missa S. Theresiae* he used the gradual and offertory as opportunities to explore third relations ("Petite et accipietis" in B♭) and the parallel minor ("Magnus Dominus"). These movements also contribute to the mass's variety of meter and tempo. The Gloria (in both versions) ends and the Credo begins in duple meter. In between, the gradual's 3/4 time offers a metrical respite. The slow tempo with which the offertory begins likewise comes as welcome relief after the long fast movement preceding it.

Haydn also used the gradual and offertory to enhance the stylistic variety of the mass. "Petite et accipietis" and "Magnus Dominus" introduce styles quite different from anything in the Ordinary. The offertory's text, from Christ's sermon on the mount (Matthew 8, 7–8) – "Ask, and it shall be given you; seek, and ye shall find; knock, and it shall be opened unto you" – was well suited to a nameday mass; as addressed by a wife to her husband, moreover, it could have conveyed an erotic subtext. Haydn set it to a sonata-form movement dominated by balanced, antecedent-consequent phrases, completely homophonic in texture. "Magnus Dominus," after a slow introduction in D minor, continues with a setting of the psalm-like text "Laudate populi": a kind of rondo in which a recurring cantus firmus, sung by the chorus in unison, is reharmonized on each appearance, and ensembles of soloists sing the episodes. Soprano and alto sing the first episode, tenor and bass the second, and all four soloists the third.

Although the gradual and offertory differ considerably from the movements that surround them, Haydn took care to anchor "Petite et accipietis" and "Magnus Dominus" into the cycle as a whole by creating relations between them and a crucial movement at the very center of the Credo (which is of course the center of the Ordinary). In the "Et incarnatus est" we can hear the soprano solo in B♭ and triple meter (Marie Therese's performance of which Haydn singled out for praise) as a distant echo of the gradual. The movement shifts to D minor at "Crucifixus," where not only the key but the orchestration and the tempo anticipate the slow introduction of "Magnus Dominus."

Many composers of masses chose to ignore the spirit of the last words of the Agnus Dei, "Dona nobis pacem," in order to bring their music to an exciting conclusion. Composing a plenary mass, Haydn had no need to do that, because the Te Deum furnished plenty of opportunity for closing the cycle in the most brilliant style. Haydn set the Agnus Dei of the *Missa S. Theresiae* as an Adagio non troppo of eighty-four measures. The last cadence, a diminished-seventh chord resolving to the tonic over a tonic pedal, *piano*, is a lovely expression of peace, but perhaps not the right ending for a festive nameday mass. That comes in the Te Deum, with the short but exhilarating fugue "Non confundar in aeternum."

DAS PICKNICK DER GÖTTER, A BIRTHDAY–CARNIVAL SPECTACLE

We can learn something about the organization of Franz's birthday and nameday celebrations from the diary of Joseph Carl Rosenbaum, the husband of the soprano Therese Rosenbaum, who sang in *Das Picknick der Götter*, a spoken play with music by Wranitzky, on 12 February 1804. Therese Rosenbaum was most definitely not one of the empress's "faithful believers." As mentioned in chapter 2, she is not known to have ever sung in Marie Therese's private concerts. The empress's decision to ask her to sing in *Das Picknick* can be traced back to December 1803, when she recommended her as a participant in the *Tafeldienst*, the concert traditionally given at court during a ceremonial meal on New Year's Day.[19] On 3 December Rosenbaum went to court to thank Marie Therese for her patronage. "The empress assured Th[erese] that she had already spoken to the emperor...she said: The poor dear has not sung for some time, she really should sing again."[20]

The New Year's concert – for which Rosenbaum received a gift of 135 Gulden[21] – must have been a success, because on 13 January her husband wrote of a conversation with Franz Xaver Gewey, a Viennese playwright, journalist, and government official: "Gewey confided to me that Th— will have a role in the play he has written for the empress; it is to be given at Schönbrunn on the emperor's birthday...he said...she will play Ceres;

---

[19] On the New Year's *Tafeldienst* see Rice, "The Musical Bee," 405–10.

[20] "Der arme Narr habe schon lang nicht gesungen, man muß sie wieder einmahl singen lassen" (Rosenbaum, "Tagebücher," 117; translation [used here], "Diaries," 116).

[21] Rosenbaum, "Tagebücher," 118.

Wranitzky has written an aria for her, and the first reading rehearsal is on Monday."[22] Monday was only three days away, indicative of the haste with which the celebration was being organized.

This haste probably resulted from a delay in the arrival of *Il conte Clò*, the development and postponement of which we will follow in chapter 9. Although Marie Therese intended to present Paer's cantata on Franz's birthday, the composer warned her in a letter of 5 January that all the parts had not yet been copied. It was probably in response to that letter that she decided to go ahead with a performance of *Das Picknick der Götter* and to postpone *Il conte Clò* until the following year.

The rehearsal of *Das Picknick* took place, as planned, on 16 January: "This afternoon at 3 o'clock Th— had a reading rehearsal of Gewey's play in the empress's chambers. She dressed very properly and went off… Th— returned from the rehearsal at about 6 o'clock… told me with satisfaction of the empress's kindness – she spoke twice with Th—, apologizing for the small role – and of the courtesy of all the others."[23] Another rehearsal took place ten days later: "At about 4:30 Th— went to the empress's chambers for the music rehearsal of *Götter Picknick* by Wranitzky. The empress was in the next room. Constanze Streffler asked Th— to come in after the rehearsal… and handed her a ticket to a ball. On it was printed: 'By the grace of Her Majesty the Empress, invitation to a masked ball.' She also spoke with the empress, who was most gracious to her."[24]

This invitation, presented to Rosenbaum by one of Marie Therese's chamber servants and musical collaborators, illustrates how the empress's musical activities involved social interaction as well as performance. Although many of her musicians received money and presents in exchange for their services, they also valued the prestigious access to the court that their musical activities gave them. Rosenbaum's husband was evidently not invited to the ball (which took place on 6 February): "Th— dressed for the empress's ball. She wore white satin with gold lace, a bonnet of velvet and fur with a broad gold *point Espagne*, and had some around her arms as well… Th— returned from the ball at about 2:30, laden with presents. The empress gave her little silk stockings, the emperor gave her a pocket-book with a check etc."[25]

Finally Franz's birthday arrived:

---

[22] Rosenbaum, "Tagebücher," 118; translation (used here), "Diaries," 117.
[23] Rosenbaum, "Tagebücher," 118; translation (used here), "Diaries," 117–18.
[24] Rosenbaum, "Tagebücher," 118; translation (used here), "Diaries," 118.
[25] Rosenbaum, "Tagebücher," 119; translation (used here), "Diaries," 118.

Production of *Götter Piquenique* at Schönbrunn. Farce in 2 acts by Gewey, music by Wranitzky, ballet by Frühmann, scenery by Platzer... At about 3 o'clock... we drove to Schönbrunn. It was raining heavily... Th— went immediately to the dressing room and began putting on her costume... The court arrived at a quarter to 7, and the spectacle began. I saw it from the parterre... The play has a great deal of wit. The idea of the delightful twelve signs of the zodiac, the Carnival procession, the gallopade of masked figures, and at the end the march of the gods was charming... Afterwards, there was a lavish supper... We drove back into town at about 11. The rain changed to steady snow. Th— and I chatted about the successful performance, the lovely, truly imperial theater, the extravagant costumes, and the fact that everything was badly done despite it, because Pfersmann had his hand in it, which everyone deplored.[26]

If the full staging of *Das Picknick* in the theater at Schönbrunn, with costumes and scenery, was typical of the theatrical productions organized by Marie Therese to celebrate Franz's birthday and nameday, they apparently differed in this respect from her private performances devoted to single operas, for which we have no evidence of staging. Paer's instructions for the performance of *Il conte Clò* mention the possibility of a performance halfway between a concert and a full staging. The cantata could be performed "either in a small theater or in a chamber; costumes for everyone seem to me indispensable."[27] Paer sanctioned, in other words, a concert performance using costumes.

Since Franz's birthday fell within the Carnival season, Marie Therese sometimes turned the celebration into a kind of Carnival masquerade. *Das Picknick*, as one might guess from Rosenbaum's description, was one such work: a theatrical extravaganza involving spoken comedy, music, dance, and elaborate costumes and sets, but with very little in the way of plot.

---

[26] "*Sonntag (Fasching) am 12ten Production des Götter Piqueniques in Schönbrunn*. Farce in 2. A. vom Gewey, Mus. vom Wranitsky, Ballet vom Frühmann, Decorationen vom Platzer... Um 3 Uhr... wir führen nach Schönbrunn. Es regnete sehr stark. Th. gieng gleich in die Garderobe und fieng gleich sich anzukleiden... Am 1/4 auf 7 Uhr kam der Hof an, und das Spectakel began. Ich sah es im Parterre... Das Stück hat viel Witz, der Gedanke mit den reizenden 12 Himmelszeichen, der Einzug des Fasching, der Callopad von Masken, und zum Schluß Marsch von Göttern war sehr artig... Nach dem Schauspiel war ein sehr wohl besetztes Souper... Um 11 Uhr fuhren wir in die Stadt. Der Regen verwandelte sich in einen anhaltenden Schnee. Th— und ich plauderten von der gelungenen Aufführung, den schönen wirklich kais. Theater, dem Aufwand an guarderobe, und doch alles schlecht gemacht, weil Pfersmann die Hand im Spiel hatte, auf den alles gar jämmerlich schimpfe" (Rosenbaum, "Tagebücher," 119; translation [used here], "Diaries," 119; several short passages omitted from the edition are supplied here from the manuscript in the Österreichische National-bibliothek, Handschriftsammlung. My thanks to Rita Steblin for help in deciphering Rosenbaum's handwriting). Pfersmann (according to Rosenbaum, "Tagebücher," 61) was secretary to the management of the court theaters. I do not know what role he played in the production of *Das Picknick der Götter*.

[27] See Appendix 5C.

A manuscript copy of the play preserved among the empress's theatrical papers is entitled *Das Picknick der Götter, oder Das Fastnachtsfest im Olympe, Gelegenheitsstück in zwey Aufzügen* (The Picnic of the Gods, or The Shrove-Tuesday Party on Olympus, an Occasional Play in Two Acts).[28] Marie Therese's score, inscribed "den 12ten Februar 1804 aufgeführt in Schönbrunn," and parts are now in the Österreichische Nationalbibliothek (Mus. Hs. 11005–7). The play features a huge cast. A vast panoply of Olympian gods are joined by naiads, furies, fauns, the twelve signs of the zodiac, and various personifications related to the season: Carnival, Dance, Play, *Trinklust*, and so forth. After an overture in which Wranitzky's music foreshadows the procession of the gods, the play begins with several comic conversations – between Iris and Ganymede, Jupiter and Momus, Juno and Jupiter – about a forthcoming Carnival party. It is only in scene 12 that the music returns, with what Gewey referred to in his stage directions as a march that accompanies the entrance of the gods. He carefully organized this scene, specifying the order in which the gods appear and describing their costumes and accouterments in great detail. Wranitzky used the orchestra to further differentiate each god. Diana and her nymphs enter to the sound of two horns playing hunting fanfares; Apollo and the muses are accompanied by harp (which returns frequently later in the drama); Bacchus and his bacchantes by Turkish instruments.

The chorus that the assembled deities sing, "Es lebe Vater Jupiter / Des Himmels und der Erde Herr," was undoubtedly addressed to Franz as well as the king of the gods. The chorus includes a solo for Ceres, written for and sung by Rosenbaum. Act 1 ends with another procession involving elaborate costumes. The march of the twelve signs of the zodiac, like much of the rest of this play, must have pleased Joseph Carl Rosenbaum more for the brilliance of the spectacle than for the interest of the drama.

Much of the play's comedy comes from the anachronism of the Greek gods celebrating Carnival, and doing so by indulging in delights unknown to the Greeks. Apollo (bass), instead of driving the chariot of the sun, praises a fizzy drink that sounds like champagne: "Hoch sprudelt im Becher der göttliche Saft." At the beginning of act 2 the chorus celebrates another drink – "Kaffee, du Lieblingstrank der Schönen!" – while the gods drink punch as well as coffee, and partake of yet another comically anachronistic pleasure, snuff. The masquerade ball with which the play ends is interrupted by the entrance of Momus and his entourage, welcomed by the gods with a

---

[28] HHStA, Fa, Sb, Kart. 65, fol. 262–332.

chorus (the final vocal number) that makes the work's function as Carnival entertainment explicit:

> Heil dem Abgott aller Städter,
> Heil dem großen Carneval!
> Ihm verdanken selbst die Götter
> Heute diesen Maskenball.

Hail, idol of every city, hail, great Carnival! The gods themselves thank you for this masked ball.

Although Marie Therese loved to give presents, she was not always prompt in doing so. Therese Rosenbaum had to wait until August to be rewarded for her birthday performance in *Das Picknick*. Her husband wrote in his diary on 23 August: "The empress's Paul brought Th— a present: a silver cup, coffee pot, milk jug, and sugar bowl and a lovely blue and gold porcelain dish. This lovely gift came as a most agreeable surprise to Th— and myself."[29]

SEYFRIED'S *SERENATA CON UNA CANTATINA*

Ignaz von Seyfried served from 1797 as music director in Emanuel Schikaneder's Theater auf der Wieden and its successor the Theater an der Wien, for which he wrote and arranged vast amounts of dramatic music: ballets, *Singspiele*, and adaptations of *opéras-comiques*. His memoirs contain valuable information about the celebration of Franz's nameday on 4 October 1805. The festivities, rather oddly, began with the witnessing of three weddings:

On this occasion three bridal couples were outfitted and joined in matrimony in the chapel of the imperial villa at Hetzendorf, and in the garden they enjoyed Their Majesties' splendid hospitality at a banquet. After the dessert, the subjects, charmed by the condescending grace of their affable sovereigns, were left to the expression of their joy, while the imperial family rose and proceeded to the middle of the park, where coffee was served on a grass-covered terrace, surrounded by a bed of sweet-smelling flowers.

This moment was to be enhanced with music, and the gracious empress's choice of composer fell undeservedly on me. An orchestra suited to the place of performance, consisting of only eighteen wind instruments, played, as an introduction,

---

[29] Rosenbaum, "Tagebücher," 120; translation (used here), "Diaries," 120. Paul Haas was one of MT's personal footmen (*HSS*, 1804, 431). MT registered the gift and its value in her diary: "Der Rosenbaum für die Götter Comedie am 12. Ein Kaffee Dejeuné von Silber von 150 fl" (HHStA, Fa, HKF, Kart. 24, diary, fol. 206r; see Fig. 9.3.). The diary shows that Weinmüller, Vogl, Wallaschek, and Rathmayer also sang in *Das Picknick*.

a concertante echo-serenade, which produced an authentically romantic color through the echo that sounded from a distant thicket.

This was followed by a brief vocal piece (the *cantatina* referred to in the title) in celebration of the imperial nameday for three soloists and chorus. Marie Therese sang soprano, Simoni tenor, and Vogl bass.

"The whole production went like clockwork; it won for the illustrious commissioner the heartfelt thanks of the gracious head of the family, and I received, out of imperial munificence, a valuable golden snuffbox as a keepsake."[30] That last statement is confirmed by the empress's diary. In November 1805 she wrote in her list of presents: "To the Kapellmeister Seyfried for the little composition on 4 October, a golden snuffbox worth 180 Gulden."[31] From the same document we learn that Seyfried's brother Joseph (a prolific writer for the Viennese theater during the early nineteenth century) provided the text, for which the empress rewarded him with two silver candlesticks worth eighty Gulden.[32]

The *Serenata con una cantatina* is preserved in a manuscript score and a set of parts from Marie Therese's library (Mus. Hs. 11105–6). Annotations in the score confirm that it was performed at Hetzendorf on 4 October 1805. Seyfried divided the wind band into two ensembles (called "due orchestre d'armonia" in the score) throughout the work, not just in the echo serenade. Each ensemble includes pairs of oboes, clarinets, horns, and bassoons, with the bass reinforced by a contrabassoon; band 2 also includes two basset horns and an English horn. (This was not the first occasional piece commissioned by Marie Therese whose accompaniment was largely limited to wind instruments. Paer's *Operetta cinese*, the autograph score of which

---

30 "Dießmal wurden drey Hochzeitspaare ausgestättet, in der Burgcapelle des kais: Lustschloßes Hetzendorf getrauet, u. in dem dortigen Hofgarten an einer Tafel mit beyden Majestäten fürstlich bewirthet. Nach dem *Dessert* wurden die durch die herablassende Huld ihrer humanen Beherrscher hoch entzückten Unterthanen den Gefühlen ihrer Fröhlichkeit überlassen; die kaiserlichen Familie aber erhob, und verfügte sich in den Mittelpunkt des Parkes, wo auf einer Rasen-Terrasse, umgeben von einem aromatisch duftenden Blumen-Teppich der Caffeh servirt ward; dieser Moment sollte nun durch Musik gewürzt werden, u. der gütigen Monarchinn Wahl eines Tonsetzers war unverdientermassen auf mich gefallen. Ein der Localität angemessenes, bloß auf 18 blasenden Instrumenten bestehendes Orchester spielte zur *Introduction* eine concertante Echo-Partie, welche durch den aus einem fernen Bosket herübertönenden Nachhall ein ächt romantisches Colorit gewann ... Den Beschluß machte eine *Cantate*, als Glückwunsch zu dem in allen Herzen des weiten Kaiserreiches segnend gefeyerten hohen Namensfeste. Die drey Hauptstimmen sangen: den *Sopran*, Ihro Majestät, die Kaiserinn; *Tenor*, u. *Bass*, die Hofkammer-Sänger *Simoni* und *Vogel* ... Die ganze Production gieng wie am Schnürchen zusammen, erwarb der erlauchten Anordnerinn den herzlichen Dank des humanen Familien-Oberhauptes, u. ich erhielt aus kaiserlicher Munifizenz eine köstbare goldene *Tabatiere* zum Andenken" (Seyfried, *Scizze meines Lebens*, 17–18).

31 "Dem Kapellmeister Seyfried für eine kleine Musik am 4. 8. Eine goldene Dose von 180 fl." (HHStA, Fa, HKF, Kart. 24, diary, fol. 222 r.)

32 "Dem Poet Seyfried für die Poesie dazu: 2 Silberen Leuchter von 80 fl." (ibid., fol. 222 v.)

is dated Laxenburg, 1803, requires an ensemble of oboe, clarinet, pairs of bassoons and horns, double bass, and various percussion instruments; two violins, played pizzicato, appear in one number only.)

Seyfried's work consists of five movements, each called "Serenata" in the score. An elaborate symmetrical structure serves to focus attention on the central movement, the *cantatina* (Serenata No. 3), which is itself symmetrical: two choruses frame a canonic ensemble for the soloists. The *cantatina* is flanked by big instrumental numbers. Serenata No. 2, "Divertimento per l'armonia a due orchestre a l'eco," is the echo piece whose "romantic color" Seyfried remembered fondly. Serenata No. 4 is a quodlibet, a medley of popular tunes, mostly operatic (to be discussed in chapter 6). Serenatas No. 1 and No. 5 serve as the outermost frame. They are both transcriptions of marches from *opéras-comiques* recently performed in Vienna: Grétry's *Raoul Barbe-bleue* and Cherubini's *Les Deux Journées*. Hummel quoted the march from *Les Deux Journées* earlier, in the trumpet concerto he wrote for the New Year's *Tafeldienst* at court (1 January 1804); evidently it was a favorite of the imperial family.

DANCE

Dance played an important role in Marie Therese's celebrations of Franz's birthday and nameday. This can be seen most obviously in Wranitzky's music for the festive days, almost all of which involved dance. His *Ball zum 4ten Octob. 1801*, his *divertissement, Die Binder*, his *Divertissement den 13ten Februar 1803*, and his *Quodlibet 13ten Februar 1803* are all suites of dances. The quodlibet is an international tour reminiscent of Dittersdorf's *Sinfonia nazionale nel gusto di cinque nazioni*: it consists of a Strassburger, a Cosacca, an Altvater, a Contredanse, a Fandango (from Mozart's *Figaro*), a Massur, a Russisch, and a Furlana. And the second act of *Das Picknick der Götter* is dominated by a masked ball. It is rarely clear who actually danced to this music: the boundary between performers and audience at Marie Therese's festivities was often thin and porous.

That the empress took part in the preparation not only of the music for these dances but also the choreography is suggested by several choreographic plans in her theatrical *Nachlass*. The most elaborate of these was made in preparation for the celebration of the empress's own birthday in 1800, but it gives us an idea of what some of the dancing on Franz's nameday and birthday might have looked like (Fig. 5.1).

Entitled *Ventiquatro Figure di Contradanza eseguitta il Giorno Sei di Giugno 1800*, the choreography calls for eight dancers of unspecified

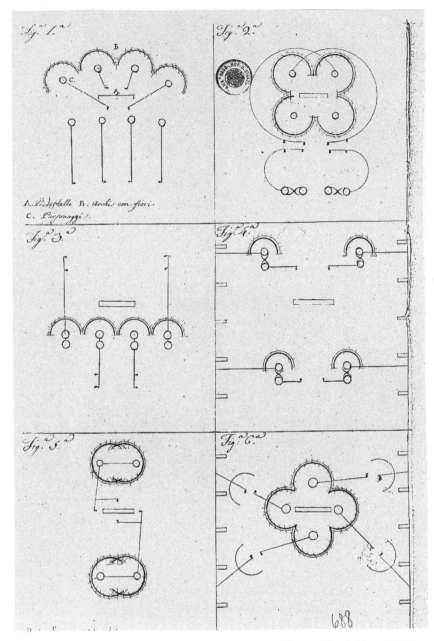

Figure 5.1 *Ventiquatro Figure di Contradanza eseguitta il Giorno Sei di Giugno 1800*, figures 1–12.

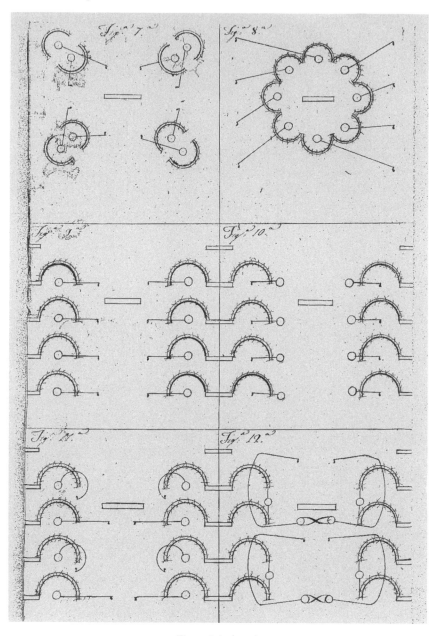

Figure 5.1 (*cont.*)

gender.[33] Around a central pedestal that serves as a point of orientation (represented in the drawings by a rectangle) the dancers create a varied series of symmetrical patterns, or figures. Small circles indicate the positions of the dancers at the beginning of each figure, lines indicate the direction of movement required for the next figure.

In many respects this notation resembles that used in France in the second half of the eighteenth century to record contredanses. French dance masters likewise composed contredanses for eight dancers (four men and four women, which they differentiated in their notation) and notated the dances as a series of symmetrical figures formed within a square space.[34]

Different from the French choreography of contredanses, however, is the incorporation into the *Ventiquatro Figure di Contradanza* of props that transform it into a garland dance, a kind of dance frequently encountered in nineteenth-century ballet.[35] The cross-hatched semicircles (at first four, later eight) represent "archi con fiori," according to the legend in figure 1. Most of the time these "arches with flowers" remain behind or above the dancers as they move from figure to figure, indicating that they are held by or somehow connected to the dancers. But figures 9–12 seem to call for the arches to be attached to unidentified objects protruding from the side of the space, allowing the dancers to move away from the arches (in figure 9), to return to them (in figure 10), and to go under pairs of them (in figure 12). With these floral arches frequently shifting position, and with the dancers wearing extravagant costumes of the kind praised by Rosenbaum in his description of *Das Picknick der Götter*, Marie Therese's birthday contredanse must have presented a delightfully kaleidoscopic sight to whoever was watching it. This contredanse, indeed, was probably closer to a ballet than a social dance: a spectacle performed for the pleasure of those assembled to celebrate the empress's birthday.

---

[33] HHStA, Fa, Kart. 66, fol. 687–90. I am grateful to Carol Marsh for several useful observations about the notation of the contredanse and for much valuable information about the history of this dance.

[34] On the contredanse in France during the second half of the eighteenth century and the revolutionary and Napoleonic periods see Jean-Michel Guilcher, *La Contredanse et les renouvellements de la danse française*, Paris, 1969, 88–167, which includes reproductions of French contredanse notation.

[35] I am grateful to my father, Eugene F. Rice Jr., for this point.

CHAPTER 6

Musical caprice

Queen Maria Carolina criticized her daughter Marie Therese for her *caprice très, mais très marqué* for (that is, her very obvious infatuation with) the male soprano Marchesi, her *impetuosité du caprice* (impetuosity of mood), and her "headstrong and intemperate disposition."[1] Baroness Du Montet called her "strange, ignorant, and ill-bred... She was *capricieuse*, her activities trivial, and her games often common."[2] They were not alone in finding in her a strong tendency toward the irrational and the playful that she probably inherited from her sometimes childish father, King Ferdinand, and which became increasingly prominent as the number of her children increased. In the amusements she organized for her family and courtiers she broke down distinctions between the activities of children and of adults, creating a pleasant and irrational world of *Laune*, or caprice. So much of the music that she collected and performed reflected this part of her personality that the compiler of *CaM* invented a category for it alone; he called it *Scherzmusick*.

Life at Laxenburg, the empress's favorite residence, was full of play. Games of blindman's bluff alternated with boat rides and fishing in the lake, among other "capricious undertakings" (*launige Unterhaltungen*).[3] Evenings were devoted to fancy-dress balls, puppet shows, and performances of plays and operas in which the empress, her family, and her household took part. The plays included comedies in the Hanswurst tradition such as Philipp Hafner's *Megära die fürchterliche Hexe*, in which Marie Therese took the leading role, according to a gossipy account of court life during the reigns of Joseph II, Leopold II, and Franz, published anonymously in 1799.[4]

---

[1] Maria Carolina to Gallo, 6 March 1802, quoted at greater length in chapter 2.
[2] Du Montet, *Souvenirs*, 6.
[3] Friedrich Anton von Schönholz, *Traditionen zur Charakteristik Österreichs*, ed. Gustav Gugitz, 2 vols., Munich, 1914, I, 66–8.
[4] *Beytrag zur Charakteristik und Regierungs-Geschichte der Kaiser Josephs II. Leopolds II. und Franz II.*, Paris, year 8 (1799), 285–6. Several studies, including Ernst Wangermann, *From Joseph II to the*

In expressing fondness for another artless comedy, the empress earned the disapproval of those who considered themselves upholders of good taste, if we are to believe hearsay from the same source:

Once, in the empress's presence, the conversation turned to the theater, and someone expressed great regret at the loss of good taste that Lessing had brought to the German stage. Maria Theresia responded: "I do not share your opinion. I heard Lessing's *Emilia Galotti* once, and that was enough, for it bored me terribly, while I could see *Der Bettelstudent* one hundred times in a row." And in fact this farce is a favorite at court, and I have been assured that if both Their Majesties wish to have a really enjoyable evening in the theater, *Der Bettelstudent* must be performed. This may serve as evidence of their taste.[5]

Der Bettelstudent, a comic play by Paul Weidmann, enjoyed enormous popularity in Vienna, and not only with Franz and Marie Therese. Between 1773 and 1810 it was performed 113 times in the court theaters.[6]

THE HAUS DER LAUNE

The empress's caprice is perhaps most concretely exemplified by the Haus der Laune that she had built in the vast English landscape park at Laxenburg: a building whose entire function, as Du Montet put it, was "to stand reason on its head."[7] Although today it lies in ruins, a large and meticulously built model that, to judge by comparison with early nineteenth-century depictions, represents it quite accurately, gives a good idea of what it was like (Fig. 6.1). It presented a bizarre mixture of architectural styles, combining the rough-hewn stones of a grotto with Egyptian and gothic motifs. A balustrade consisted of a row of cats standing on their hind legs; a tower of

---

Jacobin Trials, Oxford, 1959, 24, have attributed this book to Franz Xaver Huber. Others, including Denis Silagi, *Ungarn und der geheime Mitarbeiterkreis Kaiser Leopolds II*, Munich, 1961, 59, have not accepted the attribution as definitive. Parts of the *Beytrag* have been proven false by documentary evidence; but that does not lessen its value as a repository of rumors, mostly hostile to the court, circulating in Vienna during the 1790s.

5   "Als in Gegenwart der Kaiserinn die Rede vom Theater vorkam, und man den Verlust des guten Geschmackes, welchen Lessing auf die deutsche Schaubühne gebracht hatte, sehr beklagte, erwiederte Maria Theresia darauf: 'Da bin ich nicht ihrer Meinung. Ich habe Lessings Emilia Galotti mit einem Mahle genug, denn das Stück macht mir erschreckliche lange Weile; hingegen den Bettel-Studenten kann ich hundertmahle hinter einander sehen.' In der That ist diese Posse das Lieblings-Stück des Hofes; und man hat mich versichert, daß wenn beyde Majestäten sich einen recht vergnügten Abend im Theater machen wollen, so muß der Bettel-Student gegeben werden. Dieß mag als Beweis ihres Geschmackes dienen" (*Beytrag zur Characteristik*, 210–11).

6   Franz Hadamowsky, *Die Wiener Hoftheater (Staatstheater) 1776–1966*, 2 vols., Vienna, 1966, I, 17–18.

7   Du Montet, *Souvenirs*, 6. Brock, *Das Haus der Laune*, subjects this extraordinary folly to sustained study.

Figure 6.1 Model of the Haus der Laune at Laxenburg.

an enormous birdcage. The Haus der Laune did not ignore the dark side of caprice. The hideous, nightmarish decoration of another tower, with grotesque animal skulls and deformed human heads with tongues jutting out (Fig. 6.2), brings to mind the dictum chillingly illustrated by Goya in his *Caprichos*, "El sueño de la razon produce monstruos."

Marie Therese's passion for music intersected with her caprice in the music room of the Haus der Laune. A visitor to Laxenburg in 1800 described this "temple of music":

On the frescoed walls are real title pages and pieces of music by famous composers of both sexes and of every nation. Of some of these, entire volumes attached to the wall can be leafed through. Even the chairs and tables consist of wind instruments,

Figure 6.2 Model of the Haus der Laune. Detail.

and the chandelier is a little kettledrum, around which the hunting horns represent the arms. Tasseled hangings represent a bagpipe. Behind the door stands a double bass that can also be used as a music chest. Even on the floor lie sheets of musical manuscripts.[8]

Confirmation of parts of this description can be found not only in the model (Figs. 6.3 and 6.4) but also in watercolors representing the walls. They were covered with music, title pages as well as pages from scores; but the model and the watercolors do not agree on what music was actually used.

In the model tiny printed pages (several copies of each page) have been pasted on the walls. The music is entirely instrumental. Although the title pages refer to a keyboard sonata by Haydn, a violin duet by Fodor, and a quartet by Gramer (= Cramer?), the notation itself does not make sense and was probably the product of the model maker's imagination. The only watercolor in which one can read a considerable number of titles (Fig. 1.2) includes excerpts from operas ("Aus der Cosa rara," "Aus der Zauberflöte"), dance music ("Minueten," "Minuet," "Deutsche aus dem...", "Contra und Deutsche"), chamber music ("Quarteto"), a symphony ("Sinfonie v: H: M:" [Herrn Mozart?]), and individual orchestral parts ("Corno prim," "Corno secondo"). The multiplicity of genres is very much in keeping with Marie Therese's musical taste.

In another watercolor, the musical wallpaper, mostly illegible (though "Aus der Zauberflöte" and "La molinara" can be made out at the top left), frames the portraits of a man and a woman (Fig. 6.5). The man has been unpersuasively identified as Mozart.[9] It is much more likely that these pictures represent the emperor and empress whose lives were enriched by the music that surrounds them. While the scores seem to be hanging loosely from the wall, another watercolor depicts a wall to which sheets of music have been pasted more firmly (Fig. 6.6).

QUODLIBETS

A description of Laxenburg published in 1846 called the Haus der Laune "an architectural grotesque, or a quodlibet in the grand style."[10] The term "quodlibet" suggests an analogy between the garden folly's visual and

---

[8] Franz de Paula Anton Gaheis, *Wanderungen und Spazierfahrten in die Gegenden Wiens*, Neueste Aufl., 9 vols., Vienna, 1801–8, IV, 165–94, quoted in Géza Hajós, *Romantische Gärten der Aufklärung: Englische Landschaftkultur des 18. Jahrhunderts in und um Wien*, Vienna, 1989, 227.

[9] *Zaubertöne: Mozart in Wien, 1781–1791*, exhibition catalogue, Vienna, 1990, 515.

[10] "Jedenfalls war dieses Haus der Laune eine architektonische Groteske, oder ein Quodlibet im großen Style" (Realis [pseudonym of Duetzele Gerhard Coeckelberghe], *Das k. k. Lustschloss Laxenburg*, Vienna, 1846, 25).

Figure 6.3 Model of the Haus der Laune. Music room.

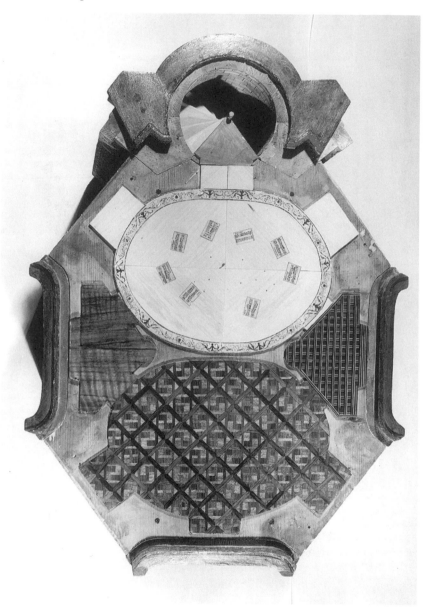

Figure 6.4 Model of the Haus der Laune, taken apart to reveal the decoration
of the floor of the music room.

Figure 6.5 Watercolor illustrating the decoration of a wall in the music room
of the Haus der Laune.

architectural caprice and the musical caprice expressed by Marie Therese in
a series of quodlibets that quickly and unexpectedly shift from one opera to
another, juxtaposing utterly different dramatic situations. In these works
she contributed to a tradition of quodlibets as musical representations of
nonsense that went back well beyond the *Galimathias musicum* ("Musical
nonsense"), a quodlibet the ten-year-old Mozart wrote in the Netherlands
in 1766.

The fourth movement of the *Serenata con una cantatina* that Seyfried
wrote to celebrate Franz's nameday in 1805 (discussed in chapter 5) is a
quodlibet of twenty-four tunes arranged for alternating ensembles of wind

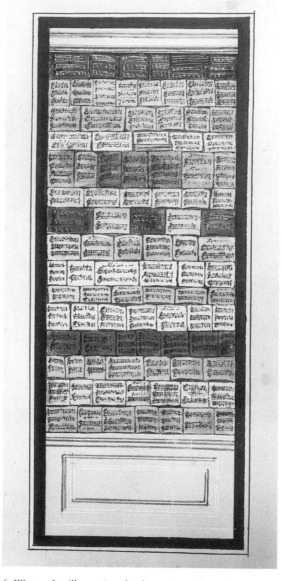

Figure 6.6 Watercolor illustrating the decoration of a wall in the music room
of the Haus der Laune.

instruments. Seyfried recalled that neither the decision to write a quodlibet nor the choice of quotations were his, implying that he composed it under Marie Therese's direction: "As second movement a potpourri was specified, whose constituent parts were assigned to me; and although the lack of words did not allow for the sequence of ideas to be easily understood, the juxtaposition of heterogeneous, mostly diametrically opposed motives was far too grotesquely comic not to draw frequently from the illustrious audience an involuntary smile."[11]

Of the twenty-four tunes that Marie Therese assigned to Seyfried, twenty have so far been identified.[12] All but three are from operas. Mozart's music predominates, at least among the excerpts most recognizable today (Table 6.1; I have included incipits of the hitherto unidentified items in the hope that readers will identify them).

Seyfried's reference to "the sequence of ideas" in his quodlibet suggests that Marie Therese, in choosing quotations (and presumably the order in which they appeared), intended not only to amuse her husband but to convey a message to him: an elaborate and entertaining nameday greeting.

The quodlibet began with music written to celebrate the coronation of Franz's father. Quoted here, the overture to Mozart's *La clemenza di Tito* identified Franz not only with Leopold II but with a Roman emperor famous for his generosity and virtue. This evocation of the noble ruler was comically undercut by two references to the abuse of power: a song from Méhul's *Une Folie* known in Vienna as "In des Tyrannen Eisenmacht" ("In the tyrant's iron grip")[13] and Gluck's famous portrait (immortalized by Mozart's variations for piano) of the mendicant dervish who lives like a king. Wenzel Müller's "Wer niemals einen Rausch hat g'habt" and Weigl's "Pria ch'io l'impegno" were both popular favorites about the satisfaction of baser appetites: the former a song in praise of drink, the latter (used by Beethoven as the theme for a set of variations in his Trio for clarinet, piano,

---

[11] "Als 2tes Stück war ein *Potpourri* bestimmt, dessen Bestandtheile mir angegeben wurden, und, wiewohl zur Verständlichkeit der Ideen-Folge die Worte ermangelten, so war die Zusammenstellung heterogener, meist contradicktorisch opponirter Motive doch gar zu barok komisch, um dem erlauchten Auditorium nicht öfters ein unwillkührliches Lächeln zu entlocken" (Seyfried, *Scizze meines Lebens*, 17).

[12] My thanks to Erich Benedikt for identifying Nos. 5 and 22; to David Buch for identifying No. 15 and for sending me his transcription of the text; and to Elizabeth Bartlet, Michel Noiray, and Patrick Taïb for sending me copies of the original French version of the text of No. 2.

[13] That Méhul's tune was known in Vienna under this title is suggested by the poster advertising a concert given by the pianist Josepha Auernhammer in the Burgtheater on 23 March 1805, just a few months before the performance of Seyfried's Serenata. It announced that she would play variations on "In des Tyrannen Eisenmacht" (Morrow, *Concert Life*, 328).

Table 6.1 *Contents of the quodlibet in Seyfried's* Serenata con una cantatina

No. 1	Mozart, *La clemenza di Tito*, beginning of overture
No. 2	Méhul, *Une Folie*, "Je suis encore dans mon printemps" ("In des Tyrannen Eisenmacht")
No. 3	Gluck, *La Rencontre imprévue*, "Les hommes pieusement" ("Unser dummer Pöbel meint")
No. 4	Müller, *Das Neusonntagskind*, "Wer niemals einen Rausch hat g'habt"
No. 5	Mozart, *Die Zauberflöte*, "Dies Bildnis ist bezaubernd schön" (embellished)
No. 6	Weigl, *L'amor marinaro*, "Pria ch'io l'impegno"
No. 7	Paisiello, *L'amor contrastato* (*La molinara*), "Nel cor più non mi sento"

Scherzando

No. 8

p

No. 9	Umlauf, *Das Irrlicht*, "Zu Steffen sprach im Traume"
No. 10	Crescentini, "Ombra adorata" (insertion aria for Zingarelli's *Giulietta e Romeo*)

Moderato

No. 11

dolce **pp**

Andante sostenuto

No. 12

Allegro

No. 13

mf

No. 14	Mozart, *Die Zauberflöte*, "In diesen heil'gen Hallen"
No. 15	Süssmayr, *Der Spiegel von Arkadien*, "Seit ich so viele Weiber sah"
No. 16	Martín y Soler, *Una cosa rara*, "Pace, caro mio sposo"
No. 17	Müller, *Das Neusonntagskind*, "Wenn d'Liserl nur wolt"
No. 18	Dittersdorf, *Der Apotheker und der Doktor*, "Wenn man will zu Mädchen gehen"
No. 19	Salieri, *Palmira regina di Persia*, "Silenzio facciasi"
No. 20	"Ach du lieber Augustin"
No. 21	Mozart, *Le nozze di Figaro*, "Non più andrai"
No. 22	Nägeli, "Freut euch des Lebens"
No. 23	Mozart, *Die Zauberflöte*, "Zum Ziele führt sich diese Bahn" (beginning of the finale of Act 1)
No. 24	Haydn, "Gott erhalte Franz den Kaiser"

and cello, Op. 11) a request for a snack. Seyfried juxtaposed these with the nobler, more passionate longing felt by Tamino on first seeing Pamina's portrait – the first of three quotations identifying Franz with the young hero of *Die Zauberflöte*.

The duet from Paisiello's *L'amor contrastato* begins "In my heart I no longer feel youth's spark"; its quotation on Franz's nameday teased the emperor for not being as young as he used to be, and perhaps reminded him of an earlier birthday piece, Paer's *Il conte Clò*, in which (as we will see in chapter 9) Marie Therese herself sang Paisiello's melody. "In diesen heil'gen Hallen" may have served as a testament to the imperial couple's conjugal devotion. But that devotion did not make Franz immune to the charms of women other than his wife. The quotation from Süssmayr's *Der Spiegel von Arkadien* (labelled "Scherzando") probably teased him for his roving eye: "Since I have seen so many women, my heart beats so warmly; it buzzes and rumbles here and there, like a swarm of bees..." If such feelings led to quarrels between him and Marie Therese, they were soon reconciled. That seems to be the message of "Pace, caro mio sposo," a duet that begins with lovers in conflict but ends with an erotically charged reconciliation. Dittersdorf's advice – "If you wish to court a girl, you must be happy and cheerful" – alluded again to the theme of relations between the sexes while encouraging Franz to be joyful on his nameday.

After Salieri's call for silence, the old Viennese folksong "Ach du lieber Augustin" made affectionate fun of the emperor, one of whose traditional appellations was Augustus. "Non più andrai" took up the entomological imagery of Süssmayr's aria but replaced bees with a butterfly. Mozart's music playfully equated Franz with Cherubino: he would no longer be free to enjoy the irresponsibilities of youth. Yet he should still rejoice in life's pleasures, Hans Georg Nägeli's song reminded him; while the excerpt from the finale of act 1 of *Die Zauberflöte* likened him once again to Tamino and urged him, on a more serious note, to be resolute, patient, and discreet. Finally, in Haydn's hymn, Marie Therese was joined by all Franz's subjects in asking God to grant him health and happiness.

One of Wranitzky's quodlibets, in the symphony that depicts and parodies a private concert organized by Marie Therese, has been discussed in chapter 4. Another, the *Quodlibet aus verschiedenen Opern* for bass and orchestra (Mus. Hs. 10233–4), illustrates some of the characteristic features of quodlibets written for the empress. The operas from which Wranitzky drew included Mayr's *Ginevra di Scozia* (1801), which means that he must have composed the quodlibet in 1801 or later. A few *Gassenlieder* (street songs) and *Volkslieder* aside, it ranges widely over some of the most popular operas performed in Vienna during the 1780s and 1790s: Martín y Soler's *Una cosa rara* and *L'arbore di Diana*, Paisiello's *L'amor contrastato*, Weigl's *L'amor marinaro* (including the ever popular "Pria ch'io l'impegno"), and several quotations from Süssmayr's *Soliman der zweite*. But again Mozart's music comes up most frequently. In quoting *Figaro*, *Don Giovanni*, and – most often – *Die Zauberflöte*, Wranitzky testified to the extent to which these operas had, by the beginning of the nineteenth century, become part of Vienna's musical culture.

Despite the use of very similar material in all three quodlibets, Wranitzky's *Quodlibet aus verschiedenen Opern* differs significantly from those in his Quodlibet Symphony and in Seyfried's *Serenata con una cantatina*. The latter are loosely linked chains of instrumental movements, some complete numbers, others substantial excerpts. The *Quodlibet aus verschiedenen Opern*, in contrast, is a tightly knit quilt of very short vocal excerpts, one of the chief pleasures of which is the ingenious way one fragment leads to another. A phrase from "Bei Männer, welche Liebe fühlen" from *Die Zauberflöte*, for example, is followed, after a fermata, by a phrase from "Nel cor più non mi sento." The G with which that excerpt ends (the third degree of Eb major) is reinterpreted as a new tonic as a modulation up a third and a change of tempo accompany a return to Mozart (*Don Giovanni*, "Giovinette che fate all'amore," in German translation; Ex. 6.1).

UNCONVENTIONAL INSTRUMENTS

Marie Therese owned several works that call for unconventional instruments. Although it is rarely possible to tell who played these pieces, her ownership of them is another indication of her musical caprice. An interest in such instruments was nothing new to a woman whose father played the *lira organizzata*, a kind of hurdy-gurdy for which he commissioned works by Joseph Haydn and others.

The little-known Viennese violinist Ignaz Schweigl composed several works for the empress that have parts for xylophone.[14] Schweigl's Concerto for *Holzspiel* and violin in C (Mus. Hs. 11096) is dedicated to Marie Therese, "first protectress of music," in celebration of her nameday,

---

[14] My thanks to Dexter Edge and Harrison Powley for calling my attention to Schweigl's works. Powley, whose study of the xylophone works from the Kaisersammlung ("Eighteenth-Century Xylophone Music: Ignaz Schweigl's Hausmusik for Kaiser Franz I," presented at the conference "Austria, 996–1996: Music in a Changing Society," Ottawa, 6 January 1996) and editions of several of them are forthcoming, kindly sent me copies of the title pages of Schweigl manuscripts containing dedications to Franz and/or Marie Therese.

Ex 6.1 Paul Wranitzky, *Quodlibet aus verschiedenen Opern*, mm. 295–307

15 October 1798 (Fig. 6.7).[15] But the parts for the two soloists have separate dedications: the violin part to Emperor Franz on *his* nameday, 4 October 1798, and the xylophone part to Marie Therese. Schweigl evidently wrote the concerto for her in the hope that it would be played by both sovereigns. On another occasion Schweigl put all his dedicatory eggs in one basket: his Xylophone Sextet (Mus. Hs. 11408) is "dedicated *in its entirety* to Her Majesty the Most Gracious Empress"[16] (italics mine). Among other works from her collection that call for xylophone are Wranitzky's Variations on "Ach du lieber Augustin" (Mus. Hs. 11375) and three pieces by Kauer: the cantata *Der Einsiedler*, the Four Variations for violino piccolo, zither, xylophone, and bassoon (Mus. Hs. 12036), and the *Sei variazioni* for orchestra.[17]

[15] "Pastorale Duetto Concerto / welches gewitmet / In aller unterthänigster und Tiefester Erfurcht den 15ten October / 1798 zu den aller Höchsten und Glorreichen Namensfest Seine / Güttigsten Majestet der Kaiserin Maria Therese der zweyten. / Und Erste Protectorin der Thon Kunst . . . von Ignaz Schweigl / Concert Maister."

[16] "Neuere Art / Sextetto / Holz-Spiel / Welches ganz gewitmet / Seine Majestet der Allergnädigster Kaiserin in Allertiefester Erfurcht / von / Ignaz Schweigl / Concert Maister / Copirt von Lorenz Schweigl."

[17] On Kauer's use of xylophone and other unconventional percussion instruments in works owned by MT see Longyear, "Ferdinand Kauer's Percussion Enterprises," 2–8.

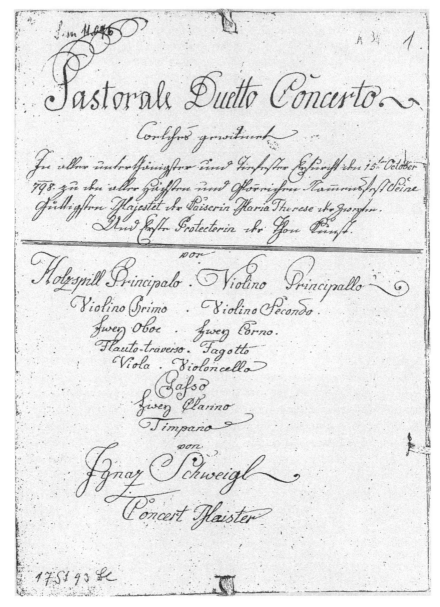

Figure 6.7 Title page of Ignaz Schweigl's Pastorale Duetto Concerto for xylophone, violin, and orchestra, dedicated to Marie Therese, "first protectress of music," on the occasion of her nameday, 15 October 1798.

Although the double dedication of Schweigl's concerto suggests that he wrote the xylophone part for Marie Therese and the violin part for Franz, the emperor too may have amused himself with the xylophone. According to an anecdote from the time of his marriage to Elisabeth of Württemberg, young Archduke Franz "passed time each evening with his wife playing chamber music; the archduchess played the double bass and the archduke the so-called 'woodfiddle,' or, as they call it in Vienna, 'das hölzerne Gelächter' (the wooden laughter)."[18]

The xylophones played at the Habsburg court may have resembled the pair of hanging xylophones that entered the collection of Grand Duke Ferdinand around 1794 (Fig. 6.8). A little more than half a meter long, they consist of sixteen rosewood bars ranging in length from twelve to twenty-six centimeters suspended vertically on two strings.[19]

Marie Therese's rapidly growing brood of archdukes and duchesses encouraged her to indulge in another kind of musical caprice: commissioning and playing music for toy instruments, frequently called Berchtesgadner Instrumente because craftsmen in and around Berchtesgaden (in the Bavarian Alps south of Munich) specialized in their manufacture.[20] These instruments are best known today from the "Toy Symphony" formerly attributed to Leopold Mozart and Joseph Haydn, but generally considered an anonymous composition of which several musicians made arrangements.[21]

For a glimpse of toy instruments in their natural habitat we can consult Joseph Richter's play *Kinder sollen Kinder seyn*, of which the empress owned a manuscript copy, making it likely that this *Kinderkomedie* was one of the plays Richter wrote for her.[22] We might reasonably guess that her offspring portrayed the children. Left alone for a few hours by their mother, Frau

---

[18] *Beytrag zur Characteristik*, 188–9, quotes a newspaper report to the effect "daß der Erzherzog sich mit seiner Gemahlinn durch eine Cammermusik täglich Abends die Zeit verkürzte, wobey die Erzherzoginn die große Baßgeige, der Erzherzog aber die sogenannte Holzfidel, oder wie man es zu Wien benennet: das hölzerne Gelächter spielte." That "das hölzerne Gelächter" was a xylophone Harrison Powley has demonstrated by showing that in several works from the Kaisersammlung parts described as being for "das hölzerne Gelächter" are in fact xylophone parts.

[19] For a more detailed description see *La musica e i suoi strumenti: La collezione granducale del Conservatorio Cherubini*, exhibition catalogue, Florence, 2001, 226–7.

[20] See the introduction to *Musik mit Kinderinstrumenten aus dem Salzburger und Berchtesgadener Land*, ed. Gerhard Croll (Denkmäler der Musik in Salzburg, vol. 2), Munich, 1981. Many of the same instruments sound in *The Nutcracker*; in the "Scène et danse Gross-Vater" in act 1 Tchaikovsky called for *Tromba infantile*, *tamburi infantili*, *raganella*, *cuculo*, *quaglia*, and *piatti infantili*. In late eighteenth-century sources "Berchtesgadner" was frequently corrupted, especially in manuscripts, to "Pertelsgadner," "Petersgarner," and other names equally distant from that of the Bavarian village.

[21] See Robert Münster, "Wer ist der Komponist der 'Kindersinfonie'?", *Acta Mozartiana* 16 (1969), 76–82, and Robert Illing, *Berchtolds Gaden Musick*, Melbourne, 1994.

[22] HHStA, Fa, Sb, K. 65, fol. 465–503.

Figure 6.8 Xylophone, one of a pair that entered the collection of Grand Duke
Ferdinand around 1794.

Figure 6.9 Marie Therese surrounded by her husband Franz and children Maria Luisa, Ferdinand, and Leopoldina, around 1798. Painting, probably by Joseph Kreutzinger, the location of which is unknown.

v. Gutmann (if, as is likely, Marie Therese took this part, Richter chose the name as a compliment to her husband, known as Franz der Gute[23]), the children decide to put on a show with dance and music, which they provide with an orchestra of "Pertelsgadner-Trommeln, Pfeifferl, Trompeten und Geigen."[24]

A painting of Marie Therese and her family that dates from around 1798 depicts her oldest daughter Maria Luisa at the keyboard of what is probably a piano, while her little brother, the future Emperor Ferdinand, plays a toy drum (Fig. 6.9).[25] It may have been from situations

[23] Langsam, *Francis the Good*, vii.
[24] [Joseph Richter], *Kinder sollen Kinder seyn*, eine Kinderkomedie in zwey Aufzügen . . . vom Verfasser der Eipeldauerbriefe, Vienna, 1809, 21.
[25] I am grateful to Wilfried Slama of the Bildarchiv of the Österreichische Nationalbibliothek (e-mail, 24 August 2001) for confirming the identity of Marie Therese and Franz; Slama attributes the painting, formerly in Schloß Schwarzenberg, Neuwaldegg, to Joseph Kreutzinger. My thanks also to Daniel Heartz for his comments on the painting.

such as this, in which an instrument was played by a child and treated as a toy, that Berchtesgadner Instrumente found their way into more general use in the empress's music-making. She owned several works with toy instruments. Paer used them, at her request, in *Il Conte Clò*; Georg Druschetzky called for them in a partita (Mus. Hs. 11377); Wranitzky wrote a mass with Berchtesgadner Instrumente (Mus. Hs. 10235) and two divertimenti for strings and toy instruments (Mus. Hs. 11107–8); Marie Therese owned a copy of the "Toy Symphony" (*CaM*, p. 99; present location unknown).

The manuscript parts that preserve this music refer to the toy instruments with words whose meaning is not always clear, or which can mean more than one thing; but almost all of them belonged to the wind or percussion families.

Most of the wind instruments fell into two categories: bird calls and imitation trumpets and horns. The bird calls included *Kuku* or *Kuckuck* (playing two notes a minor third apart[26]), *Wachtel* (quail, playing a single note), *Meisenpfeifchen* (titmouse pipe), *Trillerpfeifchen* (trill pipe, possibly the same as *Wasserpfeife* or *Nachtigall*, in which air blown through water created a warbling sound), and *Papageno-Pfeifchen* (Papageno pipe, playing the five-note scale that Papageno uses for calling birds in *Die Zauberflöte*). The trumpets and horns, made of wood or metal, were not brass instruments proper (with cup-shaped mouthpiece and without reeds) but contained internal reeds that allowed each of them to play only one pitch.

The percussion instruments included *Trommel* (drum) and *Kindertrommel*. *Glocken* were bells with definite pitch, sometimes perhaps organized as a glockenspiel. *Schellen* and *Glöckel* were little bells or chimes, without definite pitch (*Schellenkappe* means fool's cap). Two jingles ("sistri a circhio") entered Grand Duke Ferdinand's collection of instruments around 1794: networks of thick iron wires from which hang spherical bells of three different sizes (Fig. 6.10).[27] The *Glöckel* or *Schellen* of the Berchtesgadner ensemble probably resembled these instruments. *Gläser* were glasses with definite pitch, but it is not clear whether the player rubbed or struck them. The *Ratsche* was a ratchet or cog rattle.

The nature of three other toy instruments used by Wranitzky is unclear. The *Rodel* was a composite, percussion–wind instrument. In his mass with

---

[26] Although the cuckoo's call is sometimes imitated by composers as a major third (e.g. Beethoven in the "Pastoral" Symphony), all the music for Berchtesgadner Instrumente that I have seen requires an instrument that plays a minor third.

[27] For a more detailed description see *La musica e i suoi strumenti*, 229–31.

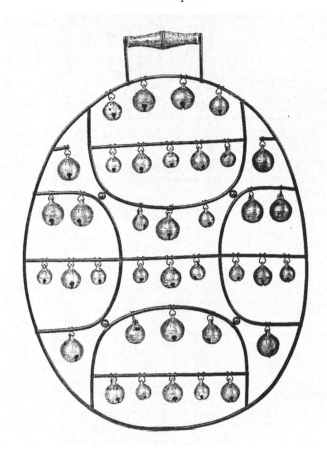

Figure 6.10 Jingle, one of a pair of *sistri a cerchio* that entered the collection of Grand Duke Ferdinand around 1794, probably similar to the Glöckel or Schellen used in Wranitzky's Mass with Berchtesgadner Instrumente.

Berchtesgadner Instrumente, Wranitzky notated the Rodel part with two notes: A above the treble staff and middle C. He explained in a note: "The As are blown, the Cs are shaken" ("die A werden geblasen; die C werden geschüttelt"). This particular Rodel could apparently play a single pitch, A, and could also serve as a rattle. A nineteenth-century dictionary of Viennese dialect defines the Rodel, not very helpfully, as "a children's toy, woven out of reeds, with a spherical knob containing a bell."[28] Like the names of many of the toy wind instruments, the *Orgelhenne* ("organ-hen") suggests a bird

[28] Franz Seraph Hügel, *Der Weiner Dialekt: Lexikon der Wiener Volksprache*, Vienna, 1873, 129.

Ex 6.2 Wranitzky, Mass with Berchtesgadner Instrumente, Kyrie, mm. 1–5

Ex 6.2 (*cont.*)

call. Yet the parts Wranitzky wrote for it (notated with C in the bass clef, which he used for most percussion instruments) indicate that it produced an indefinite pitch. So did the *Zimbelstern*, possibly similar to the device of the same name on some organs: a star from which bells hang that produces a tinkling sound as it revolves.

In the concerts documented in the empress's diary she programmed only one piece with Berchtesgadner Instrumente. The "Meß mit Berchtesgadner Instrumenten von Wranitzky" performed on 28 February 1802 must have been the Mass in C. In addition to conventional violins, trumpets, timpani, and organ (playing a figured bass line that may have been doubled by cello, double bass or bassoon), it calls for the following toys: a horn that plays only the note C, a horn that plays F, trumpets that play Gs an octave apart, glasses in C and E, bells in B, C, and D, cuckoo in G and E, quail in F, tamburino (Kindertrommel? tambourine?), Glöckel, Schellen, Ratschen, Rodel, Zimbelsterne, and Orgelhenne. With the parts Wranitzky left instructions on how his notation for the toy instruments should be realized, concluding: "The cuckoo, the glasses, and all the instruments that have one specific pitch must be well in tune with one another. The violins can take their pitch from these instruments."[29]

The Kyrie begins with a five-measure passage played by the orchestra before the chorus enters (Ex. 6.2). The violins and organ take primary responsibility for melody and harmony, while the crowd of toy instruments contributes color, loudness, and rhythmic details. They also enhance the effect of certain harmonic gestures. The cuckoo announces the completion of V–I cadences in the tonic. The quail and the horn in F are silent until m. 4, where they accentuate the movement's first taste of subdominant harmony.

The empress's interest in toy instruments was related to her fondness for Turkish instruments, amply demonstrated by Wranitzky's frequent use of them in works from her library. The Symphony in D (Mus. Hs. 11052) calls for an orchestra that includes a piccolo, four trumpets, *tamburo turchese*, cymbals, triangle, two *grosse Trommel zum Cannoniren* (two large drums to imitate the firing of a cannon), *grosse Ratschen* and tamburino.[30] The Sixteen German Dances performed, according to the title page, at Laxenburg on 30 October 1803 (Mus. Hs. 11187) are scored for an orchestra

---

[29] "Kuku, Gläßer, und alle Instrumenten, die einen bestimmten Ton haben, müssen gut zusamge-stimmt werden. Die Violinen kann man nach den Instrumenten stimmen" (Wranitzky, autograph instructions filed with parts for the Mass with toy instruments, Mus. Hs. 10235).

[30] This was either the "Synf. in D colla Mus. militare" or the Sinfonia strepitosa, both listed in *CaM*, p. 120.

that includes two piccolos, triangle, cymbals, military drum, Turkish drum, and four *Pfeifferln* (flageolets?). Wranitzky also used Turkish instruments to accompany the entrance of Bacchus and his retinue in *Das Picknick der Götter*.

It was particularly in the percussion section that Berchtesgadner Instrumente resembled the instruments of the janissary band, which had long served to represent middle-eastern and oriental subjects on the Viennese stage. In describing the premiere of Gluck's *Le cinesi* near Vienna in 1754 Dittersdorf mentioned several percussion instruments (none of which Gluck actually notated) that would have been equally at home among Berchtesgadner Instrumente: "little bells, triangles, small hand-drums, tambourines, and so forth."[31] Clearly the line between Turkish and toy instruments was fine: they both appealed to the same taste for noisy effects, and toy versions of percussion instruments were among the easiest to make and to play.

EXOTIC LANGUAGES

Another product of Marie Therese's musical caprice was the mixing of languages in several of the works she commissioned. Bits of French, German, and Turkish made occasional appearances in Italian comic opera of the eighteenth century, but Marie Therese went further, incorporating into the works whose composition she oversaw not only these languages but Czech, Hungarian, Spanish, Chinese, and Hebrew.

At least one of the empress's foreign languages may have been entirely made up, while others combined authentic words with nonsense. Paer's *Operetta cinese*, performed at Laxenburg in 1803, contains a chorus in a language that purports to be Chinese, but is unrecognizable to speakers of contemporary Mandarin[32]: "Sa alamara ciun pagoa tetri minubar foè foè fò."

The Hebrew that Paer set to music in *La lanterna magica*, in response to Marie Therese's instructions that one of the pictures to be represented in this series of *tableaux vivants* was "la sinagoga degli Ebrei," consists at least in part of real Ashkenazi Hebrew.[33] The printed libretto for *La lanterna*

---

[31] Carl Ditters von Dittersdorf, *Lebensbeschreibung*, ed. Norbert Miller, Munich, 1967, 81.

[32] My thanks to Ping Yang and Bosheng Yang for attempting to make sense of this line and another "Chinese" passage quoted below.

[33] Marie Therese's plan for *La lanterna magica* is preserved in HHStA, Fa, Sb, Kart. 65, fol. 139r–140r. I am grateful to David Buch for identifying the language as Hebrew. An article by Buch about the synagogue scene is forthcoming.

magica contains a transliterated version of the Hebrew text and an Italian translation.[34] They begin:

RABINO   Posachti schiero belschaun Tehaurò
          Ki se jaum Lessincho brurò.
          Mandrey bauh un horim Kaulenù,
          Ki se hajaum jemalle mischàlaussenù.

CORO   Mandrei bauh un horim Kaulenù,
          Ki se hajaum jemalle mischàlaussenù.

                    Versione italiana
RABINO   Con voce allegra lasciateci cantare,
          Perché questo dì è al piacere consegrato.
          Venite amici, e accordatevi insieme,
          Giacché paghe saran le nostre brame.
IL CORO   ripete li due ultimi versi.

Rabbi: With joyful voice let us sing, for this day is dedicated to pleasure. Come, friends, and join together in song, for our prayers will be answered.
    The chorus repeats the last two lines.[35]

Paer's setting of the Hebrew is strange and beautiful.[36] Was it perhaps based on music actually sung in a synagogue? In Paer's autograph of *La lanterna magica* (from Marie Therese's library, Mus. Hs. 10046), he called this scene "Gli ebrei di Praga," suggesting that it was inspired by what he had actually heard on one of his visits to Prague.

Not satisfied with one exotic language by itself, Marie Therese sometimes commissioned works that combined several languages. In Weigl's cantata *Der gute Wille* a Spaniard, a German, a Hungarian, and a Bohemian sing a quartet, each in his or her own language. In *La stravaganza musicale*, a libretto (possibly by De Gamerra) that may never have been set to music, Pancrazio, a composer, expresses Marie Therese's taste for *plurilinguismo*:

> Per il mio dramma io penso
> Far un misto di cori
> Di nazioni diverse, e sceglier voglio
> Un coro turco per il maestoso;

---

[34] *La lanterna magica*, cantata comica, musica del Sig. Mro. Pär, n.p., n.d., 21–2.

[35] The English translation is from the Italian.

[36] David Buch, who has prepared an edition of "Posachti schiero," kindly allowed me to hear his computer's rendition of the music. It was to this part of *La lanterna magica* that Carpani referred when he wrote: "Anche il *Paer* fece, non ha molto, una sinagoga per privato divertimento di una casa sovrana; ed è molto bella ancor questa" (*Le Haydine*, 115).

Voglio per il giocoso
Porre un coro chinese, e un coro ebraico,
La di cui piagnistera cantilena
È di note nasali tutta piena.

For my drama I intend to make a mixture of choruses of different nations, and I want to choose a Turkish chorus to express majesty, and for comedy I want to compose a Chinese chorus, and then a Hebrew chorus, whose plaintive melody is completely full of nasal notes.

After the following ensemble begins with soloists alone and in various groups, the chorus sings in various pseudo-languages of which at least two include a few authentic words, first Turkish:

Salamaleck [greetings] usuf,
Amucharem orinuf,
Itascm, haluck, halà.

Then Chinese:

Musabè, corabè, funebì,
Pekenà, duremì, casebì,
Jehemè, sapebè, mimimì.

Then Hebrew:

Adonai [Lord], adonai barabà
Amamon, macmacon, sabbatà [sabbath],
Jefelin Aron barucabà [welcome].

In a final climax – a moment of true linguistic caprice – all three languages are combined.[37]

PARODY

The empress loved *travestissements*, according to the Baroness Du Montet, "and she generally chose the least elegant."[38] By *travestissements* Du Montet may have meant "disguises" or "costumes," Marie Therese's fondness for which – attested to by the many costumes mentioned in her will – was related to her love of dancing, masquerade balls, and theater. But we might also translate *travestissements* as "parodies" or "burlesques." She shared with

---

[37] *La stravaganza musicale*, manuscript in HHStA, Fa, Sb, Kart. 66. On the libretto's authorship see chapter 8, note 1. My thanks to Adena Portowitz for translating the Hebrew words.
[38] Du Montet, *Souvenirs*, 6.

her Viennese subjects a passion for theatrical parodies: comedies that made fun of serious operas and plays or used Greek myths as the basis for light-hearted entertainment.

Several of Marie Therese's papers demonstrate her interest in theatrical and musical parody. A manuscript libretto for Weigl's *Die Hochzeit im Reich der Todten, eine Posse mit Gesang* includes characters from the commedia dell'arte. A letter from De Gamerra (to be discussed in chapter 8) refers to an unspecified *parodia* that she had asked him to write. A sketch in her hand begins "Il Parnaso travestito o sia in parodia sarebbe la mia idea."[39]

That idea may never have been realized. Her request to Paer to compose a work that he referred to as *Il Pimmalione in travestimento* seems to have been no more successful.[40] But several of her parodistic projects did reach fruition. She owned scores and performance material for Wranitzky's *Das Picknick der Götter*, *Macbeth travestirt* and *Medea, ein travestirtes Melodrama*, Weigl's *Die Hochzeit im Reich der Todten*, and Paer's *Il conte Clò*. Although De Gamerra initially refused to satisfy her request for a parody unless she helped him obtain a pension, he may have eventually relented. She owned a manuscript libretto, *Parodia della Ginevra di Scozia*, that De Gamerra probably wrote. It makes fun of the serious opera by Mayr from which Marie Therese sang a duet in her concerts.[41]

Some of these titles call to mind comic plays given in the Theater auf der Wieden around the turn of the century and revived later in the Theater an der Wien: Carl Ludwig Giesecke's *Der travestirte Aeneas* (with music by Seyfried, 1799) and its sequel *Aeneas in der Hölle* (1800) and Richter's *Das Urtheil des Paris travestirt* (also with music by Seyfried, 1800) and *Die travestirte Alceste* (1800). These parodies derive much of their comedy from inserting into the tales of Greco-Roman mythology unexpected aspects of contemporary culture, such as Viennese dialect, the fashionable use of French and Italian words and expressions, and references to living persons and modern institutions and customs.[42] *Macbeth travestirt* belongs to a Viennese tradition of parodies of Shakespeare's tragedies to which Giesecke (*Hamlet travestiert*, 1794), Joachim

[39] HHStA, Fa, Sb, Kart. 66, fol. 151r.   [40] Paer to MT, 21 April [1806].

[41] As discussed in chapter 8, this libretto is one of several in MT's *Nachlass* in the same hand as librettos that De Gamerra is known to have written.

[42] See Otto Rommel, *Die alt-Wiener Volkskomödie*, Vienna, 1952, 530–40 (on "die mythologischen Karikaturen"). For a discussion of a later product of the Viennese taste for mythological parody, see Laurine Quetin, "*Die Entführung der Prinzessin Europa, oder So geht es im Olymp zu!*: Un Divertissement burlesque à Vienne en 1816," *D'Europe à l'Europe II: Mythe et identité du XIX*[e] *siècle à nos jours*, ed. Rémy Poignault et al., Tours, 2000, 41–54.

Perinet (*Hamlet, eine Karikatur*), and Ignaz Castelli (*König Lear*) also contributed.[43] Although we do not know what plays by Richter the empress performed (the only one that I have identified among her papers is *Kinder sollen Kinder seyn*), she probably found his parodies particularly appealing.

Wranitzky's *Medea* (Mus. Hs. 10230–2) is a good example of theatrical parody as cultivated at the court of Marie Therese. Christoph-Hellmut Mahling has pointed out in an essay on which the following discussion is largely based that Georg Benda's melodrama *Medea* of 1775 provided Wranitzky with the raw material from which he derived his parody.[44] With *Medea* and *Ariadne auf Naxos*, which received its first performance the same year, Benda demonstrated the potential of a theatrical genre that combined spoken drama and instrumental music. Mozart, who saw two performances of *Medea* during his stay in Mannheim in 1778, wrote to his father: "Nothing has ever surprised me so much, for I had always imagined that such a piece would be quite ineffective! You know, of course, that there is no singing in it, only recitation, to which the music is like a sort of obbligato accompaniment to a recitative. Now and then words are spoken while the music goes on, and this produces the finest effect."[45] Well known in Vienna, *Medea* was given forty-two times in the court theaters between 1778 and 1809.[46]

The anonymous librettist of Wranitzky's parody took enough from Friedrich Wilhelm Gotter's original text for a Viennese audience to be able to recognize the source, but otherwise allowed himself free rein.[47] Although the title page of Wranitzky's manuscript score preserves Benda's generic term "melodrama," the work that follows is in fact an opera. It contains extensive passages of melodrama, but it also includes arias, ensembles, and choruses. The librettist shifted the setting from Jason's palace in

[43] My thanks to David Buch for telling me of these Shakespearean parodies.

[44] Christoph-Hellmut Mahling, "Original und Parodie: Zu Georg Bendas *Medea und Jason* und Paul Wranitzkys *Medea*," *Untersuchungen zu Musikbeziehungen zwischen Mannheim, Böhmen und Mähren im späten 18. und frühen 19. Jahrhundert*, ed. Christine Heyter-Rauland and Christoph-Hellmut Mahling, Mainz, 1993, 244–95.

[45] Mozart to his father, 12 November 1778, in *Mozart: Briefe und Aufzeichnungen*, ed. Wilhelm A. Bauer, Otto Erich Deutsch, and Joseph Heinz Eibl, 7 vols., Kassel, 1962–75, II, 505–6; translation (used here) in *The Letters of Mozart and His Family*, trans. Emily Anderson, 3rd ed., New York, 1985, 631.

[46] Hadmowsky, *Die Wiener Hoftheater* I, 84.

[47] Mahling attributes the libretto to Perinet, who is known to have written a parody of another melodrama by Benda, the libretto of which MT owned (*CaM*, p. 105): "Perinet. Ariadne auf Naxos. Melodram travest." However, it is also possible that Richter, whose associations with MT her diary documents, wrote the text of *Medea*.

Greece to a contemporary Viennese *Gaststätte*, added several new characters, introduced a chorus to which he gave an important role, and changed the tragic and violent end of Benda's melodrama to a happy one. In keeping with the opera's new setting, the characters speak and sing in Viennese dialect (with occasional phrases in French and Italian) and make frequent reference to the local cuisine. All this is juxtaposed, to considerable comic effect, with bits of Gotter's original text. Compare, for example, Medea's speeches at the beginning of the two works. Benda's Medea speaks consistently in a high, tragic style. In Wranitzky's opera the tragic tone is amusingly undercut first when Medea addresses the inn by its name (The Golden Ninepin), then by her use of the colloquial *fraß*, and finally by her mouthwatering reference (in local dialect) to a Viennese culinary speciality.

Benda/Gotter	Wranitzky
Vertrauter Wohnsitz! Vormals den Schutzgöttern frommer Eintracht, häuslichen Glücks, der unverbrüchlichen Treue heilig!...Haus meines Gatten, der mich von sich stößt! Meiner Kinder – ach, die nicht mehr mein sind! Unglückliche Medea!	Wohnsitz meiner vormaligen Freuden! Vormals den Schutzgöttern frommer Eintracht, und häuslichen Glückes heilig! O geliebter goldener Kegel! Wie oft fraß ich hier nicht gebackene Hähndl mit meinem Jason. O unglückliche Medea!
Trusted abode, once sacred to the tutelary gods of innocent concord, of domestic bliss, of unbreakable constancy!...House of my husband who rejects me, of my children who are no longer mine! Unfortunate Medea!	Abode of my former happiness, once sacred to the tutelary gods of innocent concord and of domestic bliss! Oh beloved Golden Ninepin! How often did I eat fried chicken here with my Jason. Oh unfortunate Medea!

Wranitzky's musical parody paralleled the librettist's literary one. He quoted and paraphrased enough of Benda's music for his audience to recognize the source; then, having established Benda's *Medea* as a point of reference, he departed from it with increasing frequency as the work progressed. Sometimes he preserved aspects of Benda's melodic style, orchestration, and accompaniment; sometimes he produced completely new music. Responding to his librettist's direct quotation of Gotter at the beginning of the opera, Wranitzky copied the slow introduction of Benda's overture almost exactly. Much of Wranitzky's new music is in his arias and choruses, for which Benda's melodrama provided no models. This music alternates with disconcerting and comic suddenness between folklike simplicity (as in the governess's aria "Mercket doch ihr jungen Herren") and the grandiloquence

Ex 6.3 Wranitzky, *Macbeth travestirt*, No. 11 1/2, mm. 9–15

of *opera seria* (as in Medea's aria "Wart nur ich krieg dich schon").[48] Another kind of musical parody involves the use of unorthodox instruments,
played by members of the chorus: not only Berchtesgadner Instrumente
but also, in keeping with the setting, a kitchen utensil – Wranitzky specified
that a spit for roasting meat be used in place of a triangle.

Another tragedy that provided Wranitzky with material for a parody for
Marie Therese was Shakespeare's *Macbeth*, known to Viennese audiences
through a production in the Theater auf der Wieden first seen in 1796.[49]
Wranitzky's *Macbeth travestirt* (Mus. Hs. 10227–9) features melodrama,
arias, ensembles, and choruses in a mixture quite similar to that of *Medea*.
The three witches (two tenors and a baritone) gave the composer much
opportunity for ensembles.[50] Exaggeration is a crucial element of parody;
he put it to good use in *Macbeth* by giving the first witch an improvisatory
embellishment of absurd elaborateness (Ex. 6.3). Exaggeration and the
anachronistic use of foreign languages reinforce one another in Rohse's aria
in act 1. It begins with an orchestral introduction that promises something
grand and heroic, but Rohse's first words, "Votre très humble serviteur,"
comically contradict the music. He later repeats these words over and over,
to ridiculous effect. Another example of the comic contradiction of words
and music is in Macbeth's aria "Du ruhst in sanften Schlummer hier," in

---

[48] For musical examples see Mahling, "Original und Parodie," 265–6.
[49] *Chronologische Verzeichniß aller Schauspiele*, Vienna, 1807, 64.
[50] Wranitzky wrote the music for the first and second witches using tenor clef, and for the third witch
     (who often carries the bass line) using alto clef. I assume he intended the third witch to sing the
     part an octave lower than written.

Ex 6.4 Wranitzky, *Macbeth travestirt*, "Du ruhst in sanften Schlummer hier," mm. 43–54

(Tempo di Polonese)

MACBETH

Mein Weib das ist be - ses - sen, der Teu - fel steckt in ihr,___ will ich mit ihr mich mes - sen so

Basso (rest of orchestra omitted)

gibt sie Faun-zen   mir,   will ich   mit ihr mich mes - sen, so gibt sie Faun-zen mir.

which he describes Lady Macbeth's madness with music in the jolly rhythm of a polonaise (Ex. 6.4).

A CAPRICIOUS CONCERT

In most of Marie Therese's private concerts we can find no trace of caprice. They were serious, well organized explorations of a wide variety of music, with relatively little exploitation of the devices that characterize her most obvious expressions of musical *Laune*. But on 24 February 1802 she gave a concert that, exceptionally, conveyed caprice of several different kinds.

The concert began with a symphony by Wranitzky. That in itself is no cause for surprise, since Marie Therese performed several of them between 1801 and 1803; but this work, which she referred to as "Eine Sinfonie die Revolutions," must have been the *Grande Sinfonie caractéristique pour la paix avec la Republique Françoise*, of which she owned a set of parts under the title *Friedens Synfonie* (*CaM*, p. 119). This symphony depicts a series of historical events leading up to the Treaty of Campo Formio, concluded by France and Austria in October 1797.

1 The Revolution. English March. March of the Austrians and Prussians.

  Andante maestoso (C minor) – Allegro molto (C minor):
  Slow introduction, fast movement in sonata form with marches interpolated

2 The Destiny and Death of Louis XVI. Funeral March.

  Adagio affettuoso (E♭ – C minor – E♭):
  Ternary form with funeral march as middle section

3 English March. March of the Allies. Confusion of a Battle.

Tempo di marcia movibile (C) – Allegro (C):
Two binary-form marches followed by a battle

4 Peace Negotiations. Cries of Joy for the Restoration of Peace.

Andante grazioso (G) – Allegro vivace (C):
Slow introduction, fast movement in sonata form[51]

Two months after Campo Formio, in December 1797, Wranitzky's new symphony was to have been performed in benefit concerts given by the Tonkünstler-Sozietät. But Emperor Franz himself forbade the performance.[52] The symphony may have attracted his hostility for a number of reasons. The treaty was in reality a capitulation by the Austrians, involving the loss of much territory. A symphony by a Viennese composer on such a theme required a certain amount of poetic licence, as Richard Will has shown:

The otherwise stormy first movement, representing the Revolution, is interrupted by Austrian and Prussian marches, a presumed reference to their 1792 invasion of France . . . that does not, however, recognize the catastrophic defeat of that campaign. Similarly in the finale, the celebration of peace, further reference to the Austrian march tends to forget that the imperial army had given little reason to rejoice. The "Tumulte d'une bataille" omits all mention of the enemy, quoting only Austrian, Prussian, and English marches before plunging into action, and the slow movement mourns Louis XVI, uncle by marriage to Emperor Franz, with a heroic funeral march embedded within an apotheosizing Adagio affettuoso. This was history as the Habsburgs might have liked to remember it, a fantasy of royal martyrdom and military redemption.[53]

Franz may have feared that listeners would hear through this fantasy. Or he may simply have resented the celebration of a peace that military defeat had forced on him. Furthermore, Marie Therese's reference to the symphony as "die Revolutions" suggests that, despite its official title, its first movement attracted more attention and interest than its last. At a time when the Austrian government was nervous about Jacobin elements within the monarchy, Franz may have considered politically dangerous a symphony that could potentially incite interest in the French Revolution. Whatever his reasons for refusing to allow it to be performed in public, we might call his wife's performance of it in private an act of caprice both political and marital.

[51] Richard Will, *The Characteristic Symphony in the Age of Haydn and Beethoven*, Cambridge, 2002, 206. I have introduced a few minor changes of wording. I am grateful to Will for allowing me to see his typescript before publication.

[52] *Joseph Haydn in seiner Zeit*, 488. My thanks to Heinz Anderle for telling me of this episode.

[53] Will, *The Characteristic Symphony*, 206.

The second piece on the program of 24 February 1802 was a mass by Hasse, presumably one of the six of which Marie Therese owned sets of parts. Nothing capricious about that; but unlike most of the concerts that included liturgical music, this one also included secular vocal music, although vocal music of a very odd kind, as we shall see. Given her normal segregation of sacred and secular, this mixture was in itself capricious.

The concert concluded with "Die Vocal Sinfonie von Bohdanowicz." Basyli Bohdanowicz, a violinist at the Theater in der Leopoldstadt, put on several public concerts in Vienna featuring his large family, a kind of musical circus whose activities failed to amuse one historian of the period:

> But for the truly bizarre, no one could top the antics of the Bohdanowicz family, whose concerts featured everything from standard pieces to outlandish program-matic works…The programs generally opened fairly normally with his daugh-ters singing several popular opera arias but then would inevitably deteriorate to selections for one violin played with four bows and sixteen fingers and similar nonsense.[54]

Bohdanowicz specialized in the composition and performance of a cap-pella vocal works without text. He presented a "symphony in 24 vocal parts, without text and instruments" in the Burgtheater on 5 March 1785 and a similar piece in the Leopoldstadt Theater ten years later. He and his family sang another "vocal symphony without text" in Ignaz Jahn's restau-rant (a popular site for concerts) on 8 April 1802, a little more than two months after Marie Therese's concert.[55] His detailed description of this work suggests that it, the vocal symphony performed by Marie Therese, and the vocal symphony of which she owned a set of parts were one and the same.[56]

The *Sinfonia vocale ed originale senza parole* (*CaM*, p. 99; Mus. Hs. 10887) consists of three movements. The first is a study in dynamic con-trast. The second, based on bird songs, must have amused an empress who delighted in the sound of cuckoo and quail calls. The finale is a hunt as vividly pictorial as the symphony by Wranitzky "mit der Jagd" that the em-press had performed on 22 January. A note in the manuscript explains some of its programmatic content and some of the more complicated aspects of its performance, and dedicates it to Emperor Franz:

---

[54] Morrow, *Concert Life*, 157. See also "Basilius Bohdanowicz und seine musikalische Familie," in Emil Karl Blümml and Gustav Gugitz, *Von Leuten und Zeiten im alten Wien*, Vienna, 1922, 238–56.

[55] Morrow, *Concert Life*, 288, 312.

[56] Translated in Morrow, *Concert Life*, 313–14.

Ex 6.5 Bohdanowicz, *Sinfonia vocale*, first movement, mm. 1–16

Vocal and original symphony without words for eight voices, namely first and second soprano, first and second alto, first and second tenor, first and second bass, with three accompanying cellos and a contrabass (these instruments are added to help the singing voices stay in tune).

This symphony consists of a first Allegro, an Andante, and a final Allegro. The first movement is sung in a lively manner, with all the gradations between forte and piano. The Andante expresses the crowing of cocks and hens and the call of the cuckoo, and imitates the woodpecker, a bird of the forest. The final Allegro, entitled "The Hunt," expresses the noise of the hunters, the excitement and the baying of the hounds, the growling of the bears, and the shooting of guns.

Annotation for the Andante. In the Andante the chorus is divided into three parts, namely the visible part and the first and second echoes. N.B.: At the beginning of the Andante and in the first tempo, the first and second echoes remain

Ex 6.6 Bohdanowicz, *Sinfonia vocale*, second movement, mm. 1–8

distant from the visible part, behind closed doors on the right and left; but at the Allegretto con moto both echoes approach the visible part behind open doors.
    Conceived and composed by Basilio Bohdanovicz. For the best Monarch.[57]

   The beginning of the first movement gives one an idea of the contrasts of dynamics explored throughout this movement (Ex. 6.5); the beginning of the Andante shows that this movement has moments of lyric beauty in addition to its echo effects and depictions of birdlife (Ex. 6.6). Both excerpts illustrate some of the nonsense syllables used by Bohdanowicz throughout the symphony. The finale, as one might guess from the description, is a fast movement full of triadic motives; although Bohdanowicz notated it in

---

[57] "Sinfonia vocale ed originale senza parole, per otto voci, cio è: Soprano primo e secondo, Alto primo e secondo, Tenore primo e secondo, Basso primo e secondo, con tre accompagnati Violoncelli, ed un contrabasso: Questi stromenti sono aggiunti per mantener le voci cantanti in ugual' intonazione.
    Questa Sinfonia consiste d'un prim' Allegro, d'un Andante, e d'un ultimo Allegro. Il primo Allegro è decantato frescamente con tutti per i gradi del forte, e del piano. L'Andante esprime il grido dei galli, e delle galline, la voce del cuculo, ed imita il picchio (o un uccello della selva). L'ultimo Allegro (intitolato: la caccia) esprime il clamore de' venatori, l'incitamento e l'abbajamento dei cani, il mormoramento degli orsi, ed i tiri degli schioppi.
    Annotazione dell'Andante. All'Andante divide s'il choro in tre spartimenti, cio è: in Parte visibile, in primo e secondo Echo. N.B. In principio dell'Andante ed al tempo primo l'uno e l'altro Echo restano lontano dalla parte visibile dentro delle porte chiuse alla destra e sinistra, ma all'Allegretto con moto approssimano si ambi Echi alla parte visibile dentro delle porte aperte.
    Dell'invenzione e composizione di Basilio Bohdanowicz. Per ottimo Monarca."

3/8 meter, it would have sounded the same if he had used the 6/8 meter more typical of hunting music.

The program of Bohdanowicz's concert of 8 April 1802 was published in the *Allgemeine musikalische Zeitung*. Following a description of the vocal symphony similar to the one quoted above, a correspondent or editor asked: "Who has ever heard such a vocal (N.B. non-instrumental) symphony, without text, of such *Laune*, such programmatic interest, and such extremely amusing, entertaining, and ingenious composition anywhere in Europe, which is capable of drawing a smile even from the most lugubrious pedant?"[58] Although the parts belonging to Marie Therese were dedicated not to her but to her husband, the fact that she performed the *Sinfonia vocale* in her concert of 24 February 1802 suggests that its very obvious caprice appealed to the playful, irrational side of her personality.

[58] *AmZ* 4 (1801–2), cols. 494–6, transcribed in Morrow, *Concert Life*, 521.

CHAPTER 7

Marie Therese's influence on music in the public sphere

Although Marie Therese's musical activities rarely had as their principal aim the shaping of public taste or the directing of musical or theatrical policy outside the court, it was impossible for an empress so intensely and constantly involved with music not to influence Vienna's musical life. Even the marriage that brought her to Vienna (part of a triple marriage that tied even closer together the already closely allied Bourbons of Naples and Habsburgs of Austria) had musical repercussions: it coincided with, and probably helped to bring about, a shift in Viennese operatic repertory in favor of Neapolitan comic opera.[1] Her influence was largely limited at first to the expression of her personal tastes through her patterns of attendance in the theaters and her informal comments to members of her family. "Yesterday I went to the Prater," she wrote to Franz in August 1791, "and from there with your father [Emperor Leopold] to the theater. The *Pastorella nobile* was performed, and Tomeoni received much applause."[2] Guglielmi's *La pastorella nobile* was one of the Neapolitan operas most frequently performed in Vienna during the year following Marie Therese's arrival; and Irene Tomeoni, who had sung almost exclusively in Naples during the late 1780s, personified the Neapolitan taste toward which the court steered Viennese opera in the early 1790s. Even without making her own opinion clear, Marie Therese's attendance and her report of the audience's approval helped to solidify the repertorial shift represented by *La pastorella nobile* and Tomeoni. So too did her report of the favorable reception of Cimarosa's *Il matrimonio segreto*, an early product of the "Neapolitanization" of Viennese opera. King Ferdinand of Naples wrote to his daughter a month after the premiere, evidently in response to a letter that has

---

[1] Rice, *Salieri*, 507–26.
[2] MT to Franz, 6 August 1791, HHStA, Fa, Sb, Kart. 30, quoted in John A. Rice, *Emperor and Impresario: Leopold II and the Transformation of Viennese Musical Theater, 1790–1792*, Ph.D. dissertation, University of California, Berkeley, 1987, 182.

not survived: "I hear with pleasure that Cimmarosa's new opera was so successful."[3]

BARON BRAUN AND OPERA

It was not until the mid-1790s that Marie Therese took a first public step into the arena of operatic policy, encouraged perhaps by her personal acquaintance with Baron Braun, who became manager of the court theaters in 1794. A rich banker and manufacturer of silk and cotton, Braun took a personal interest in entertaining the empress. No expense was too great, if we can believe the rumor that "Braun ruined himself for the sake of a lady of high rank (the second wife of Emperor Franz), for whom, whenever she and her children visited Schönau [his estate near Vienna], he always prepared expensive surprises."[4] Another way in which he may have surprised and delighted the empress was to give private concerts featuring her favorite genres, works, and composers. He had Guglielmi's *Debora e Sisara* performed on 26 March 1802, about two months after she sang a quartet from it. Two weeks later, on 10 April, he presented Cimarosa's *Gli Orazi e i Curiazi*, of which she performed several excerpts in 1801–2. He displayed Weigl's talents with the performance on 30 March 1803 of excerpts from the opera *I solitari*, which she sang a year earlier.[5] And he remained open to her suggestions about what operatic genres, composers, and particular works to present in the court theaters.

When Braun became impresario he inherited an operatic repertory consisting exclusively of works in Italian. He made one of his first major changes, bringing German-language opera back into the court theaters, at the empress's suggestion and with her full support. The German troupe made its debut on 11 May 1795 with a performance of Wranitzky's *Die gute Mutter*, the libretto of which, dedicated to the empress, contained a letter from Braun stating clearly that the reintroduction of German opera reflected her wishes:

Your Majesty most graciously demonstrates at every opportunity how much you wish for German diligence, German art, and German merit to be recognized, encouraged, and rewarded.

---

[3] Ferdinand to MT, 6 March 1792, HHStA, Fa, Sb, Kart. 53, Alt 122, fol. 14r-v, quoted in Rice, *Emperor and Impresario*, 183.

[4] *König Jérome und seine Familie in Exil: Aus dem Tagebuch der Frau von B.*, ed. Ernestine von L., Leipzig, 1870, 84.

[5] Braun's concerts are documented in Morrow, *Concert Life*, 396–400.

German opera too owes its existence to your patriotic hint: for this hint was for the management a command. And just as Your Majesty had in mind, above all, the pleasure of the public, so the management dares to hope for the public's satisfaction next to that of Your Majesty, and to lay this libretto at the feet of their monarch with full confidence in her all-highest grace.[6]

Although Marie Therese sometimes performed excerpts from *Singspiele* in private, her public support of German opera was probably more a product of political calculation than of musical and theatrical taste. Braun's reinstatement of *Singspiel* to the court theaters and his characterization of that act as a recognition of specifically German virtues acknowledged nationalistic feelings inflamed by the war with France. Such feelings might have given rise to hostility toward the Neapolitan princess who was now empress and queen, unless she could somehow turn them to her advantage. How better to demonstrate her "Germanness" than to declare publicly (or allow Braun to declare) her patriotic support of German opera?

Marie Therese's influence on operatic repertory did not end with her contribution to the return of *Singspiel* to the court theaters. Paer's *Achille*, one of the most important Viennese operas of the early nineteenth century, owed its existence to her. Its librettist De Gamerra wrote his sister on 17 December 1800: "The empress wanted from me a grand *opera seria*, and I have obeyed. It is now in the hands of the composer Weigl."[7] Despite his naming Weigl as the composer, this opera must have been *Achille*: Weigl wrote no serious operas and De Gamerra no serious librettos besides *Achille* around this time. Furthermore, in a later letter De Gamerra referred explicitly to *Achille* as "my grand *opera seria*."[8] Paer's opera reached the stage of the Kärntnertortheater on the empress's birthday, 6 June 1801.

Librettists and composers who accepted commissions from Marie Therese did so with the understanding that she was in a position (thanks largely to her contacts with Braun) to put their work before the public. Paer, writing in 1804, alluded openly to her influence and its source:

[6] "Eure Majestät geben bey allen Gelegenheiten huldreichest zu erkennen, wie sehr Allerhöchst Dieselbe Deutschen Fleiß, Deutsche Kunst, Deutsche Verdienste hervorgezogen, ermuntert, belohnt wissen wollen.

Auch das Deutsche Singspiel verdankt dem patriotischen Winke Eurer Majestät sein Daseyn: denn dieser Wink war für die Hofdirection ein Befehl; und so wie Eure Majestät hierbey vorzüglich das Vergnügen eines Publicums vor Augen hatten, das Sie anbettet; so wagt es die Hofdirection nebst der allerhöchsten auch die allgemeine Zufriedenheit zu hoffen, und dieses erste Opernbuch voll Zuversicht auf Allerhöchst Dero Gnade zu den Füßen Ihrer Monarchinn zu legen" (*Die gute Mutter*, eine comische Oper in zwey Aufzügen Ihrer Majestät der Kaiserinn zugeeignet, Vienna, 1795).

[7] De Gamerra to Maria Casimira Caterina Gamerra Berte, Vienna, 17 December 1800, in "Lettere di Giovanni De Gamerra (III)," ed. Federico Marri, *Studi musicali* 30 (2001), 117–18.

[8] De Gamerra to Berte, Vienna, 28 April 1801, in "Lettere di Giovanni De Gamerra (III)," 121–2; see especially note 1273.

A favor that I would like, after having served Your Majesty [by fulfilling a private commission], would be to be able to write an opera for Baron von Braun, that is, for the theater and the public, but I would like the invitation to come from the aforementioned in particular. The company of the theater of Vienna needs an opera right now, and I would desire, after *Achille*, to write another adapted to the company.[9]

Since Paer had written several operas for the court theaters besides *Achille*, he probably singled it out because of Marie Therese's role in its creation.

An invitation from Braun was not long in coming. In May 1805 Paer wrote from Bologna, where he had just presented a new opera, *Sofonisba*: "Baron Braun was here in passing before the opening of the theater. He talked to me about staging *Sargino* in German, which I would desire with all my heart as long as it would please Your Majesty."[10] But Paer evidently preferred to present *Sofonisba* in Vienna. In promising to adjust it for a private performance by Marie Therese, he again alluded to her influence on the repertory of the public theaters: "I am ready to make it completely new, so as to give Y. M. an opera that can be given first in Your Imperial Royal apartments and then (if Y. M. commands) in the theater in Vienna."[11]

Another theatrical artist who hoped that his association with Marie Therese, and hers with Braun, would lead to performances of his work in public was Carpani. Shortly after Braun extended his impresarial control over the Theater an der Wien in 1804, Carpani wrote to the empress of his desire to have *L'uniforme*, which he and Weigl had written for her private performance in 1800, presented in public:

Now that the Teatro della Wieden is at the disposition of Baron Braun, I am unable to hide from the most humane clemency of Y. M., at whose feet I lay everything in my soul, that I would hope to see my aforementioned *Uniforme* in that theater, in which grand spectacles are much more effectively mounted than in the two imperial theaters of the city.[12]

Carpani got part of his wish. Less than a year later, on 15 February 1805, Weigl's opera was performed in a new German translation by Georg Friedrich Treitschke ("tedescamente tradotta in tedesco da un tedesco," as Carpani put it[13]), but in the Kärntnertortheater, not the Theater an der Wien.

---

[9] Paer to MT, Eisenberg, 18 August 1804.   [10] Paer to MT, Bologna, 25 May 1805.

[11] Paer to MT, no date, but probably written between May and August 1805; appendix 3, letter No. 21.

[12] Carpani to MT, 4 April 1804, in Jacobs, *Carpani*, 238. The poet confused the name of the new Theater an der Wien with its predecessor, the Theater auf der Wieden. He preferred a production of *L'uniforme* in the larger suburban theater because of the opera's spectacular battle scenes.

[13] Carpani to Isabella Teotochi Albrizzi, Vienna, 20 February 1805, in Jacobs, *Carpani*, 245.

MAYR IN VIENNA

The closeness of Marie Therese's relations with Braun and the effect of those relations on both her private music and his management of the theaters were apparent during the visit to Vienna in 1802–3 of Johann Simon Mayr. Born in Ingolstadt, Bavaria, in 1763, Mayr moved to Italy as a youth and made it his home for the rest of his life. He studied in Venice, where he achieved his first operatic triumph in 1796 with *Lodoiska*. During the next quarter century he supplied the theaters of Italy with a succession of works, mostly *opere serie*, in which he sought to mediate between his admiration for and knowledge of Mozart's music and his understanding of Italian theatrical practice and musical taste. His operas were frequently performed in Vienna and enjoyed a prominent place in the empress's concerts and library. His visit almost certainly resulted from consultation between Braun and Marie Therese, for he came to Vienna to serve both: to compose two operas for him and one for her.

The librettos for the first of the public operas, *Ercole in Lidia*, and for the opera for Marie Therese, *Caio Coriolano*, were both by De Gamerra. The empress owned manuscript copies of both librettos.[14] Since De Gamerra left Vienna before the rehearsals of *Ercole* (a strange circumstance at a time when theatrical poets usually served as stage directors), it is possible that she supplied the libretto from her collection.[15] *Ercole* belongs to a genre, *opera seria*, that Braun used mostly as a vehicle for the male sopranos who made occasional appearances in Vienna between 1798 and 1804. But *Ercole* has no role for a *musico*, in this respect resembling *Achille*, which was written for a very similar cast: the same singers created the principal male roles in both operas.[16] The similarities of Mayr's opera to one Marie Therese is known to have helped bring into existence, her possession of a manuscript copy of the libretto, and the librettist's absence from Vienna together suggest that the empress was involved in the commission that resulted in *Ercole*.

Mayr's letters allude to the intertwining interests of the impresario and the empress. On 20 November 1802 he wrote:

My opera [*Ercole in Lidia*] has been scheduled for the first of the year. The libretto of the opera that I will set to music for the empress has likewise been selected, and

---

[14] MT's collection of manuscript librettos by De Gamerra will be discussed in chapter 8.

[15] Mayr wrote on 1 December 1802 of rehearsals for *Ercole*: "Mi sono esse un po' pesanti, perché è assente il poeta" (Girolamo Calvi, *Di Giovanni Simone Mayr*, ed. PierAngelo Pelucchi, Bergamo, 2000, 64). I am most grateful to Iris Winkler for calling this source to my attention and for sending me a photocopy of the relevant pages.

[16] The heroic tenor Antonio Brizzi sang Achille and Ercole, Vogl sang Agamennone and Euristeo, Saal sang Patroclo and Filotete, and Felice Angrisani sang Briseo and the high priest of Juno.

it is *Coriolano*. I will have to write this opera in Vienna as well, and then in Italy I will write the other opera semiseria for the theater. That is the arrangement that has been reached by the empress and signor barone di Braun; and he has offered to give me a permanent position in his theaters, since one of his composers [Paer?] is now absent.[17]

One might think that the decision about whether Mayr was to stay in Vienna to write his second opera for the theater was Braun's alone; but that decision affected Marie Therese too because on it depended the amount of time that Mayr would be able to devote to *Caio Coriolano*. By encouraging Braun to allow Mayr to write the second public opera after his return to Italy, she gave Mayr more time to compose an opera for her. So it is not surprising that the composer, on 1 December, attributed to her the decision to allow him to postpone the composition of the second opera for Braun:

The day before yesterday I went to H. M. the empress to thank her for having decided that I could write the second opera for the theater in Italy. At the same time she gave me a plan for the opera that will serve for her and that I have to write after *Ercole in Lidia*, rehearsals for which will begin on Saturday.[18]

Throughout December 1802 and January 1803 Mayr juggled rehearsals for *Ercole* with discussions with the empress about *Coriolano*, the composition of which she eventually permitted Mayr to postpone, along with the second opera for Braun. Even on the day of the premiere of *Ercole* Mayr was thinking about his opera for the empress:

Never has any production so exhausted me with unending cares and troubles as this *Hercules*, which will reach the stage this evening, after the public has awaited it so long. I thought I would be able to leave on Monday, but I will have to delay my departure for two reasons. First, I have to wait for a concert that the empress wants to give so that I may be able to adapt my composition to the voices that will perform it; and second, it is said that snow has been falling over the last fifteen days and has been continuously increasing to the point where the passes might be closed.[19]

It must have been in reference to *Coriolano* that Weigl, later in 1803, wrote to Carpani, who addressed his answer directly to the empress:

Weigl relayed to me some time ago the most honorable command of Y. M. that I find out if Majer is composing for Y. M. On that subject I am happy to be able

---

[17] Calvi, *Mayr*, 63.   [18] Calvi, *Mayr*, 63–4.

[19] Mayr to Lucrezia Venturali, Vienna, 29 January 1803, Bergamo, Fondazione Donizetti, II, 273. My thanks to Paolo Fabbri, editor of a forthcoming edition of Mayr's letters, for sending me a transcription of this letter, the original of which is in French. An excerpt in Italian translation is in Calvi, *Mayr*, 65.

to submit the news that the day before yesterday he arrived in Venice and that he immediately departed for the country with the sole intention of dedicating himself fully, without distractions, to the opera commissioned by Y. M.[20]

Despite that promising news Mayr never finished *Coriolano*. Marie Therese's desire to perform new music by him had to be satisfied with excerpts from *Ercole in Lidia*.

As for the opera that Mayr owed Braun, all we know of it for sure (from Mayr's letters) is that it was to be an *opera semiseria*. From the fact that Vienna presented no premieres of operas by Mayr after *Ercole* it is tempting to conclude that he never wrote that opera either. However, in 1805 he presented a *farsa sentimentale* in Padua, *L'amor coniugale*. Because that work combines elements of two dramas in which Marie Therese was particularly interested (as we will see in chapter 10), I believe it was the *opera semiseria* originally destined for the Viennese court theaters. Having gained the empress's permission to compose the opera in Italy, Mayr apparently took it upon himself to have it performed in Italy as well.

PUBLIC BENEFIT CONCERTS

Because the theaters Braun controlled served as important sites for concerts, he helped shape not only Viennese opera but also concert life. Through him the empress exerted influence over public concerts, as demonstrated by Georg August Griesinger in one of his reports to Breitkopf & Härtel:

It is in fact difficult to organize a financially profitable concert. The Burgtheater and Kärntnertortheater are let to a Baron Braun, who has many friends at court. He doesn't easily lend his orchestra for accompanying, or on the day when the concert is supposed to take place, he announces [for performance in the other theater] a new or very popular piece and ballet, and thereby deprives the poor musician of his numerous public. Would you believe it, but even Haydn, when he performed his *Schöpfung* for the first time [in public], had to get the empress to put in a special word for him in order to get a satisfactory day for the performance of his masterpiece.[21]

In several respects the empress's private concerts resembled public concerts given around the same time, but they also differed. The two-part structure of many of her programs was common elsewhere in Vienna, as was her practice of beginning a concert with a symphony or operatic overture. Some of the musicians who performed with her also performed in

---

[20] Carpani to MT, 19 September 1803, in Jacobs, *Carpani*, 226.

[21] Griesinger to Breitkopf & Härtel, 6 November 1799, in *Griesingers Korrespondenz*, 37; translation (somewhat altered here) from Landon, *Haydn* IV, 457.

public, sometimes the same music. Perhaps the most important difference between her concerts and public ones was that she emphasized vocal music at the expense of instrumental while public concerts generally sought a balance between vocal and instrumental music. Only occasionally did Marie Therese's concerts approach the alternation of vocal and instrumental music typical of public concerts. On 25 April 1802 she participated in a program that could have easily been presented in public. It began with a *Sinfonie* (probably an operatic overture) by Mayr, continued with a chorus from Sarti's serious opera *Alessandro e Timoteo*, an aria with chorus from Guglielmi's *dramma sacro, Gionata Maccabeo*, a violin concerto played by Clement, an operatic trio by Tarchi, a duet from Paisiello's *Elfrida*, and a fantasy played on the harp by Müllner, and concluded with the finale from the first act of Mayr's *Adelaide di Guesclino*. Not only the prominence of instrumental music reminds us of public concerts; so does the participation of Clement and Müllner, both of whom performed often in public.

If that program betrayed the influence of public concerts on Marie Therese's private music, the programs of several public concerts show that her influence on the public sphere was also strong. She enjoyed combining music and fundraising, and used benefit concerts as opportunities to bring before the public music and musicians she favored. Her influence came partly from her generosity. On the occasion of a concert in the Grosser Redoutensaal on 16 January 1801, organized for the benefit of wounded soldiers, she gave 1,000 Gulden.[22] Aware of her willingness to make such large donations, organizers of charity concerts must have been tempted to accomodate her musical tastes. On at least one occasion a program she gave in private was incorporated into a benefit concert given shortly afterward. Other musical fundraisers included or consisted entirely of music chosen by her, while still others were dominated by works in genres and by composers she particularly liked.

On 7 April 1802 the empress participated in a concert that consisted mostly of excerpts from *opera seria*. She wrote in her diary:

Academy at my place with the following pieces:
An overture by Hayden Joseph
A quartet with chorus from Ratto delle Sabine by Zingarelli, sung by Wiesenthal, Altamonte, Ratmayer, Weinmüller
An aria by Righini, sung by Weinmüller
A duet from Alessandro by Tarchi, sung by Wiesenthal and Ratmayer
An aria from Alceste by Gluck, sung by me.

---

[22] Rosenbaum, "Tagebücher," 89.

A quartet with chorus from Lodoiska by Mayer, sung by me, Marchesi, Ratmayer,
   Weinmüller
A clarinet concerto by Eibler, played by Stadler
A quartet from Ratto delle Sabine by Zingarelli, sung by Wiesenthal, Altamonte,
   Ratmayer, Weinmüller
An aria with chorus by Nasolini, sung by Altamonte
A duet from Ezio by Tarchi, sung by me and Weinmüller
An aria with chorus from Artemisia of Cimarosa, sung by Ratmayer
A trio from Ines by Bianchi, sung by me, Altamonte, and Ratmayer
A rondò from Alessandro by Tarchi, sung by Marchesi
A quartet with chorus from *I sciti* by Mayer, sung by me, Wiesenthal, Ratmayer,
   Weinmüller

Less than a week later, on 13 April, two of the same performers appeared in
a concert in the Burgtheater for the benefit of former theatrical personnel
who had been reduced to poverty:

Symphony by Haydn
Quartet by Zingarelli, sung by Rosenbaum, Therese Saal, Vogl, and Weinmüller
Aria by Righini, sung by Weinmüller
Duet by Tarchi, sung by Rosenbaum and Antonio Brizzi
Fantasy on the harp, played by Müllner
Aria by Sarti, sung by Therese Saal
Quartet by Mayr, sung by Rosenbaum, Therese Saal, Brizzi, and Weinmüller
Aria, sung by Rosenbaum
Duet by Tarchi, sung by Therese Saal and Brizzi
Clarinet Concerto by Eybler, played by Johann Stadler
Aria by Cimarosa, sung by Brizzi
Quartet by Mayr, sung by Rosenbaum, Therese Saal, Brizzi, and Vogl[23]

Although the playbill for the public concert does not mention the titles
of the operas from which excerpts were taken, this program obviously
resembled Marie Therese's very closely, the main difference being that she
and the other amateur singers Wiesenthal, Altamonte, and Rathmayer were
replaced with the professionals Rosenbaum, Saal, Vogl, and Antonio Brizzi.
Having performed with the empress on 7 April, Weinmüller and Stadler
may have sought and received her permission to bring some or all of the
performing materials to the Burgtheater, where they served as the basis for

---

[23] Morrow, *Concert Life*, 314–15. My thanks to Theodore Albrecht for checking the *Zettel* for
this concert (in A-Wth) and confirming that the clarinettist who played Eybler's concerto on
13 April (and thus presumably also on 7 April) was Johann Stadler (not Joseph, as given by
Morrow).

the public concert on 13 April. Or perhaps her concert was intended from the beginning as a rehearsal for the public concert six days later.

One of Marie Therese's earliest direct interventions in Vienna's public concerts was recorded by Rosenbaum's husband in his diary (28 November 1798) as a bit of gossip, "that the empress had given Salieri a requiem to perform at the academy of the Society, and had requested Therese [Gassmann, later Rosenbaum], Saal, and Simoni as the leading singers."[24] The "academy of the Society" was the pair of concerts that the Tonkünstler-Sozietät, of which Salieri was president, traditionally gave near the end of Advent for the benefit of musicians' widows and orphans. According to Rosenbaum, Marie Therese had discussed with Salieri not only the program but also the vocal soloists, urging him to engage one of her favorite singers and two others to whom she gave less frequent patronage.

With the possibility of a large donation from the empress in mind, Salieri and the directorate of the Tonkünstler-Sozietät probably felt obligated to perform the music she offered it, and to follow, at least in part, her recommendations about singers. The concert took place on 22 and 23 December 1798. It included symphonies by Haydn and Eybler; an aria by Haydn; a concerto by Leopold Kozeluch for the peculiar combination of piano, mandolin, keyed trumpet (*tromba organizzata*, played by Anton Weidinger), and double bass; and a sacred cantata (not a requiem) by the very obscure Italian composer Ettore Romagnoli for four soloists (including Therese Gassmann and Ignaz Saal, but not Simoni) and chorus.[25] The playbill announced that Marie Therese had provided the music not only for the cantata but the concerto: "Her Majesty the Empress, on account of her innate pity and maternal love for widows and orphans, and also of the patronage that she deigns to give to artists, has had the clemency to present to the Society all the performance materials for the above-mentioned concerto and cantata."[26] She owned Kozeluch's concerto (Mus. Hs. 11072) and Romagnoli's setting of Psalms 45 and 46 (Mus. Hs. 9934–6), presumably the cantata performed by the Tonkünstler-Sozietät.

The empress's name was not enough to guarantee the success of Romagnoli's cantata. In writing of the first concert, Joseph Carl Rosenbaum referred to the cantata in such a way as to show he was fully aware of

---

[24] Rosenbaum, "Tagebücher," 54; translation (used here), "Diaries," 54.

[25] Morrow, *Concert Life*, 299–300.

[26] "S. M. l'imperatrice per l'innata pietà, e materno amore verso le vedove e pupilli, egualmente che per la protezione che si degna accordare agli artisti, ha avuta la clemenza di regalare alla Società tutto ciò che compone il Concerto, e la sacra Cantata suddetta" (playbills in A-Wgm and A-Wth; this passage is not quoted in Morrow).

its origin: "Haydn's Military Symphony was the best, the concertino with mandolin and organized trumpet was also well received; Teyber, at the pianoforte, was extremely wretched and confused, and the empress's cantata fell straight into the pit. No one other than Therese was applauded."[27]

We do not need proof that Marie Therese provided music for a concert to recognize her influence. A concert given in the Grosser Redoutensaal on 30 January 1801 for the benefit of soldiers wounded at the Battle of Hohenlinden, ostensibly organized by Christine Frank, clearly reflected the empress's musical practices and tastes:

First part

Symphony by Haydn, conducted by the composer
Scena and aria with chorus from Nasolini's *Merope*, sung by Frank
Sonata for piano and horn by Beethoven, played by Beethoven and Giovanni
    Punto (Johann Wenzel Stich)
Scena and duet from Nasolini's *Merope*, sung by Frank and Simoni

Second part

Symphony by Haydn, conducted by the composer
Trio with chorus from Cimarosa's *Gli Orazi e i Curiazi*, sung by Johanna
    Willman Galvani, Frank, and Simoni
Aria with horn obbligato by Salvatore Rispoli, sung by Simoni and accompanied
    by Punto
Scena and finale with chorus from *Gli Orazi e i Curiazi*, sung by Willman
    Galvani, Frank, and Simoni[28]

In presenting excerpts from *Merope* and *Gli Orazi* this program gave pride of place to one of the empress's favorite genres, to one of her favorite composers, and to a work of which she frequently performed excerpts (the trio with chorus from *Gli Orazi* was "Germe d'illustri eroi"; the scena and finale the *sotterraneo* at the end of act 2). Two of the singers who took part, Frank and Simoni, regularly performed with her. The participation of a chorus in several of the operatic numbers was also characteristic of her concerts. Finally, the presence on the program of music by an obscure Italian, Rispoli, hints at a possible intervention by her similar to the one that resulted in the performance of music by Romagnoli three years earlier.

Another benefit concert that projected Marie Therese's tastes took place in the Burgtheater on 8 April 1800. It featured a performance of Guglielmi's

[27] Rosenbaum, "Tagebücher," 55; translation (used here), "Diaries," 55.
[28] Morrow, *Concert Life*, 307.

Neapolitan dramma sacro *La morte di Oloferne*, of which she owned both score and parts (Mus. Hs. 9899–900) and of which she performed excerpts in 1802.

CONCERTS FOR THE WOHLTHÄTIGKEITS-ANSTALTEN

Marie Therese played a particularly prominent role in a series of concerts given from 1804 for the benefit of a group of charities that adopted the rather colorless name "Charitable Organizations" (Wohlthätigkeits-Anstalten). The concerts took place in the Grosser Redoutensaal three times a year, on Easter Sunday, Pentecost, and St. Leopold's Day (15 November – the nameday of her husband's father). They generally consisted of performances of oratorios or operas.

The Charitable Organizations received the proceeds of these concerts; but who actually organized them? In some cases, at least, the empress herself. Among her papers is a manuscript libretto entitled *Die Früchte der Wohlthätigkeit: Eine Kantate zum Vortheile des Fonds für die neu organisirende Wohlthätigkeits-Anstalten* (The Fruits of Charity: A Cantata for the Benefit of the Fund for the Newly Forming Charitable Organizations).[29] That libretto may never have been set to music, but the empress's possession of it suggests that she was associated with the concert series from its inception. The original inventory of *CaM* (p. 101) documents Marie Therese's ownership of *raddoppiamenti* – extra sets of parts – for several works performed for the Wohlthätigkeits-Anstalten: Cherubini's opera *Anacréon*, Paer's opera *Sofonisba* and his oratorio *Il trionfo della chiesa*, Vogler's oratorio *Atalia*, and Winter's opera *Castore e Polluce*. These extra parts probably served as performance materials for the concerts.

Letters to the empress occasionally allude to her participation in concerts for the Wohlthätigkeits-Anstalten. On 6 November 1804 (see Fig. 2.1) Eybler wrote her about arrangements for a forthcoming concert involving Vogler: "I could not carry out your supreme command until yesterday because Abbé Vogler did not come back from Prague to Vienna until the evening of the day before yesterday. According to him, he chooses the two Sessi as sopranos, the younger Brizzi as tenor, and Weinmüller as bass."[30] The concert in question was the benefit for the Wohlthätigkeits-Anstalten

---

[29] HHStA, Fa, Sb, Kart. 65.

[30] "Allerhöchsten Befehl konnte ich erst gestern vollziehen, indem auch Abbè Vogler erst vorgestern abends von Prag nach Wien zurückkamm. Seiner Sage nach wählt er sich die beyden Sessi zum Sopran, den jungeren Brizzi zum Tenor, und Weinmüller zum Basso" (Eybler to MT, Vienna, 6 November 1804, HHStA, Fa, Sb, Kart. 63, fol. 154 r–v).

that took place nine days later, on St. Leopold's Day, when a cast that included Vittoria Sessi, Ludovico Brizzi, and Weinmüller performed *Atalia* under the composer's direction.[31] In May 1806 the soprano Francesca Riccardi Paer visited Vienna. Before the trip, on 21 April, her husband wrote the empress: "she will always be at Your Majesty's command in case she might be of use to you for the poor." He was referring to a forthcoming concert for the Wohlthätigkeits-Anstalten. On 25 May (Pentecost) Riccardi Paer sang the title role in a concert performance of her husband's *Sofonisba* in the Large Redoutensaal.[32] Paer had sent Marie Therese a copy of the score from which she probably produced the parts used in the concert.

The empress certainly supplied the music for two other concerts for the Charitable Organizations. On 14 April 1805 (Easter) Cherubini's *Anacréon* was given a concert performance "out of the all-highest grace of Her Majesty the Empress," in the words of the *Wiener Zeitung*.[33] From Richter's *Eipeldauer Briefe* we know what the empress's "grace" consisted of: "On Easter Sunday we had a cantata in the Redoutensaal for the benefit of the Wohlthätigkeits-Anstalten, and our gracious empress, who has previously done so much good for the poor, provided the music for it."[34] She also provided music for a performance of Paer's *Il trionfo della chiesa* in which her participation is particularly well documented in letters written to her by the composer.

At the end of 1803 Grand Duke Ferdinand, now settled in Salzburg, sent Marie Therese a copy of *Il trionfo della chiesa*, which he had commissioned, and the copying of which he mentioned in a letter quoted in chapter 2. She thought of having the Tonkünstler-Sozietät perform it during its regular fundraiser the following Lent and began consultations to this effect with Paer and Salieri. When it became apparent that the performance could not be prepared in time (*Die Schöpfung* was performed instead) she arranged

---

[31] Morrow, *Concert Life*, 326. MT owned Vogler's Italian oratorio in score and parts: Mus. Hs. 9917–18.

[32] Morrow, *Concert Life*, 339.

[33] The *Wiener Zeitung* announced on 6 April 1805: "Aus allerhöchster Gnade Ihrer Majestät der Kaiserin wird am Ostersonntage als den 14. April, Abends um halb 8 Uhr in dem k. k. großen Redoutensaale Anacreon, Musik von Cherubini zum Vortheile der Wohlthätigkeits-Anstalten aufgeführt werden." Quoted in Joseph Richter, *Die Eipeldauer Briefe*, ed. Eugen von Paunel, 2 vols., Munich, 1917–18, II, 441.

[34] Richter, *Eipeldauer Briefe* II, 206. MT had received the printed score of *Anacréon* a few weeks earlier from the Marchese di Gallo, who announced the shipment in a letter of 11 February 1805: "Ho compreso nel medesimo l'importo di un pacchetto di musica che oggi collo stesso corriere ho l'onore di spedirle, e che contiene la musica di *Anacreon*, che Cherubini ha publicato" (HHStA, Fa, Sb, Kart. 64, fol. 11). She also owned a German version of *Anacréon* in a manuscript score and set of parts (Mus. Hs. 10163–4), presumably used for the performance of 14 April 1805.

that Paer's oratorio be given for the Wohlthätigkeits-Anstalten on 20 May (Pentecost).

Paer's letters record the empress's involvement in several aspects of the concert's organization. She requested his permission to perform the oratorio in public; she invited him to direct the performance. But most of the correspondence involved casting, and in particular the problem of who was to sing La Religione (soprano). Paer urged that a woman be assigned the role; but Marie Therese preferred the *musico* Crescentini, whom Braun had engaged to sing in serious operas – Zingarelli's *Giulietta e Romeo* and Mayr's *Alonso e Cora* – during the coming months, and who at some time after April 1803 became a regular participant in her concerts. If we did not know Paer was writing to the empress, we might guess his long, rambling discussion was addressed to an impresario. Typical of her musical correspondence was the involvement of a third party, in this case Salieri, who had been in direct contact with Paer:

No one could execute the role of La Religione as perfectly as Crescentini, and it would really be a pleasure if, being in Vienna, he sang it; but if the younger Signora Sessi does not accept the part (as Signor Salieri has written me) because she has not yet made her debut in the theater, perhaps Crescentini too will consider his [operatic] debut as something entirely new, and will not want to perform elsewhere before the opera. Forgive me, Your Majesty, perhaps I am mistaken, but it is always prudent to anticipate the future. In any case, since Sig. Salieri says the part would suit Mlle. Sessi better than anyone else but because she has not made her debut she could not perform beforehand, then even this difficulty would be overcome since by 20 May *La clemenza di Tito* will already have been performed.

Here Paer referred to the first production of Mozart's *La clemenza di Tito* in the court theaters, with Marianna Sessi as Sesto and, making her Viennese debut, Vittoria Sessi as Vitellia; opening night was 12 April 1804. He continued:

Your Majesty is perfectly correct to say that maybe these women's hesitation will be easier to overcome after my arrival. I will do everything, both what Your Majesty commands and what is necessary to perform this music well and to satisfy whoever will take the trouble to perform it.

Among the amateurs who would be able to sing the role of La Religione the most suitable would be Sig. Catterina Bianchi, who has a superb middle register. But I do not know if the doctor, or the great stage fright that she suffers, would prevent her. Sig. Frank is excellent, but the notes G, A, and B in her middle register would not be heard well in a large hall. The example of the last-mentioned, who gives her services in the public performance of oratorios, could serve for many other amateurs, so I take the liberty of saying it, but only in passing, submitting myself to the authority, experience, and sensible ideas of Your Majesty, who has the wisdom to know better than anyone else.[35]

In response Marie Therese must have reiterated her preference for Crescentini. Paer's next letter made no mention of female sopranos:

I would be truly happy if Crescentini would sing in the oratorio; indeed I beg you to secure for me the favor of giving the music to him to look at and persuading him that despite the fact that the style is sacred, and that he cannot expect to be treated as he deserves, the part, as I adjusted it for Your Majesty, should suit him well. He cannot please any less than Marchesi in oratorio.[36]

The reference to Marchesi probably alludes to that soprano's participation in performances of Paer's *Per il santo sepolcro* in Tonkünstler-Sozietät concerts a year earlier, in April 1803.

Crescentini did indeed sing La Religione in the Redoutensaal, along with two of the empress's most faithful collaborators, Simoni and Weinmüller, and another soloist, Saal, who occasionally sang with her. The Hofkapelle made up the chorus, and Müllner played a harp solo.[37] This Wohlthätigkeits-Anstalten concert, then, fully embodied Marie Therese's musical tastes.

Paer's oratorio was not well received, according to a notice in the *Allgemeine musikalische Zeitung*, partly because of its operatic character, and partly because it suffered from inevitable comparisons with Haydn's late oratorios:

A new cantata of Pär, *Il trionfo della Chiesa*, given in the Grosser Redoutensaal for the benefit of the poor, was not a full success, and it must be understood that one can find very few traces in Pär's work of what one is entitled to expect in a *religious* cantata. Only the concluding chorus of the first act and the last Amen have fugues, and even those are of a kind that cannot satisfy the expectations of strict composition, which is all the more unpleasantly noticeable here since Haydn produced in *Die Schöpfung* and *Die Jahreszeiten* such brilliant examples of choruses that are fugal and at the same time full of effect. The rest of the cantata is very pleasant to hear, nicely orchestrated; but, as already said, one might bet anything that the experienced music-lover, if he did not understand the words, would think of this piece as anything but a *religious* cantata.[38]

---

[35] Paer to MT, Dresden, 2 April 1804.   [36] Paer to MT, 12 April 1804.

[37] Morrow, *Concert Life*, 324.

[38] "Eine neue Kantate Pärs: Il triomfo della chiesa, welche im grossen Redoutensaale zum Besten der Armen gegeben wurde, wollte nicht recht gefallen, und man muss gestehen, dass von dem, was man von einer *religiösen* Kantate zu erwarten berechtiget ist, sehr wenige Spuren in Pärs Werke anzutreffen sind. Nur ein Schlusschor des ersten Theiles und das lezte Amen ist fugirt, aber auch das

It is tempting to read a nationalistic agenda between the lines of this comparison of Haydn and Paer, which seems to stand for a comparison of German and Italian music. Without mentioning the empress, the critic alluded to a characteristic feature of her musical background. That she could love an Italian oratorio that sounded much like an Italian opera was undoubtedly a result of her childhood in Naples, where the generic border between opera and oratorio was thin indeed. As a princess she probably enjoyed, in the theaters of Naples, fully staged productions of *drammi sacri*: serious operas in all but biblical subject and time of performance (Lent). In Vienna she performed excerpts from several Neapolitan *drammi sacri*, including Cimarosa's *Il sacrificio d'Abramo* and Guglielmi's *Debora e Sisara*, *La morte di Oloferne*, and *Gionata Maccabeo*. *Debora e Sisara*, one of the most widely performed of such works, was first presented at the Teatro San Carlo by a cast that included Crescentini himself. By insisting on his participation in *Il trionfo della chiesa*, Marie Therese came close to restaging an event she had almost certainly witnessed sixteen years earlier in Naples.

auf eine Art, womit der strenge Satz nicht zufrieden seyn kann, und die hier um so unangenehmer auffällt, seit uns Haydn in der Schöpfung und den Jahrszeiten so glänzende Muster fugirter und doch zugleich effektvoller Chöre aufgestellt hat. Das Uebrige der Kantate ist ganz angenehm zu hören, hübsch instrumentirt, aber, wie schon gesagt, es wäre alles darauf zu wetten, dass der geübteste Kenner, wenn er die Worte nicht verstünde, hier eher auf jedes andre Musikstück, als auf eine *religiöse* Kantate, rathen würde" (*AmZ* 6 [1803–4], col. 620).

CHAPTER 8

The empress as conceiver, commissioner, and shaper of musical works

Eager to further the careers of leading composers and to associate her name with theirs, Marie Therese commissioned many works. Her role in their creation went far beyond simply paying for them. At one time or another she participated in every stage of the process except that of actually writing the text and music: she set down on paper preliminary sketches of possible works, chose librettists and composers and oversaw the interaction between them, distributed roles, took part in rehearsals and performances, rewarded librettists, composers, and performers, and finally filed scores and parts away in her music library. Her papers tell us much about how she brought new works to completion and performance; they also offer insight into relations between her and the poets and composers she patronized.

MARIE THERESE AND LIBRETTISTS: DE GAMERRA AND CARPANI

Among several theatrical poets with whom the empress had dealings, De Gamerra and Carpani maintained particularly productive relations with her; but they differed in what they did for her. De Gamerra wrote several librettos but seems to have done little to encourage composers to set them to music; most of them remained in manuscript and unset. Carpani, in contrast, developed close relations with several composers and repeatedly took the initiative in bringing his words to musical life.

As house poet to the Viennese court theaters from 1794 to 1803 De Gamerra had plenty of opportunity to ingratiate himself with the empress, and he succeeded in doing so. She commissioned from him the texts for at least two cantatas, *L'amor filiale* and *La festa di Carolina negli Elisi*, and asked him for "a grand opera seria" that resulted in Paer's *Achille*. She owned manuscripts of several librettos by De Gamerra:[1]

---

[1] HHStA, Fa, Sb, Kart. 66 and 66a. Although none of these manuscripts contains De Gamerra's name, the librettos can be attributed to him because autograph copies of all of them except *L'isola*

180

Caio Coriolano, dramma per musica, 1802
Il carbonaro, commedia per musica in due atti
La corona del merito, o sia Il Torquato Tasso, opera eroi-comica in due atti
Ercole in Lidia, dramma per musica, 1802
L'isola di Luciano, farsa in due atti con prosa e musica e piccolo ballo
   unito
Il pianeta di Giove

A letter from De Gamerra to Marie Therese gives us an idea of how she assembled this collection. Writing from Italy in July 1803, shortly after leaving his post in Vienna, he refused her request for an otherwise unknown parody unless she provided him with financial help; he evidently still hoped for the imperial pension he had sought since the late 1790s.[2]

August Protectress,
With pleasure I received the command of Y[our] C[aesarean] M[ajesty], but, finding myself ill for the last four months and sapped of my strength, it is not possible for me to carry it out for the time being, nor indeed to write anything, unless Y. C. M. grants me some aid so that I may be able to provide myself with adequate food and a decent living.

   Y. M. knows that a light does not burn without fuel, and this vital fuel I expect from the beneficent concerns of Y. S[acred] C. M., after which I will be able to put myself in a position to execute the parody commanded of me, for which are necessary a light-hearted spirit, a healthy body, and a free and lively mind.

   In the meantime I await, with my family, the desired help, in order to be able to demonstrate immediately to Y. M. with my miserable labors the great gratitude and deep submission with which I grant myself the glory of being,
Of Y. C. M., August Protectress,

> The most faithful subject
> and most humble servant

Vicenza, 26 July 1803

Even before mailing this letter De Gamerra regretted its brusque tone. He added a postscript, telling the empress that in place of the parody he was sending another libretto, *L'isola di Luciano*, and adding another plea for money:

di Luciano are preserved among his papers in the Archivio Guadagni Dufour Berte in Florence; see "Lettere di Giovanni De Gamerra (I)," ed. Federico Marri, *Studi musicali* 29 (2000), 111–14. De Gamerra's authorship of *L'isola di Luciano* is confirmed by the poet himself in the letter transcribed below. The handwriting used in all these manuscripts is similar to De Gamerra's, but according to Federico Marri (email, 8 February 2002) the scribe was not in fact De Gamerra.
   MT also owned three anonymous librettos copied out in the same hand as those known to be by De Gamerra, who was possibly the author of these as well: *Parodia della Ginevra di Scozia*, *Selimo*, opera eroi-comica in due atti, and *La stravaganza musicale*.
[2] He was pleading for the pension already in 1798; see "Lettere di Giovanni De Gamerra (I)," 114.

P.S. In order that my most respectful letter does not present itself at Your Caesarean Feet all by itself, it comes with the operetta *L'isola di Luciano*: eccentric, rich in images, and visually oriented. In any case, it will serve to amuse Y. C. M. for half an hour, and to inspire the sublime generosity of Y. M. for the needy author. Costume designs as well will be found inside. As a father, I inform Y. M. that my poor daughters have lost 25 Gulden from their pension out of 100, as Sig. Smithmayer can learn from the banker Borchetta. I hope that Y. M., our only heavenly star, will, by helping the father, repair the grave harm done to his daughters, of whom she has declared herself so many times not only Caesarean Protectress but also beneficent and tender mother.[3]

The manuscript of *L'isola di Luciano* that De Gamerra sent is apparently the only source for this libretto, its value further enhanced by the beautiful costume designs in watercolor (*figurini*) pasted into it.

De Gamerra's letter and its postscript suggest that Marie Therese obtained librettos from him in two ways. Some, like the parody he refused to write, she commissioned; others, like *L'isola di Luciano*, she accepted as unsolicited gifts (which he naturally hoped would inspire her "sublime generosity" in return).

De Gamerra made no reference in his postscript to a possible musical setting of *L'isola di Luciano*. Only one of De Gamerra's librettos in the empress's collection, as far as I know, was set to music more or less complete. Mayr, during the Viennese sojourn discussed in chapter 7, presented *Ercole in Lidia* in the Kärntnertortheater on 29 January 1803: a production in

---

[3] "Augusta Protettrice.

   Con gioja ho ricevuto il comando della C. M. V, ma trovandomi da quattro mesi ammalato, ed esausto di forze non mi è possibile per ora d'eseguirlo, nè di scrivere io stesso, se la C. M. V. non mi somministra qualche soccorso da poter provvedere ai miei bisogni con buoni cibi e un buon governo.

   Sà La M. V. che il lume non arde senza alimento, e quest' alimento vitale lo attendo dalle benefiche cure della S. C. M. V. ond'io possa pormi in stato d'eseguire la comandatami *Parodia*, per cui è necessario spirito lieto, corpo sano, e mente libera e vivace.

   Intanto colla mia Famiglia attendo il bramato soccorso, per poter subito comprovare alla M. V. colle mie misere fatiche l'alta riconoscenza, e profonda sommissione, che mi porge la gloria d'essere

Della S. C. M. augusta Protettrice
Wicenza, 26 Lulio 1803
fedelissimo Suddito, e umilissimo Servo

   P.S. Perchè l'ossequioso mio Foglio non si offra ai Cesarei piedi senza compagnia, egli si presenta coll'Operetta bizzarra, immaginosa, ed ottica dell'*Isola di Luciano*. In ogni caso, servirà a divertire una mezz'ora La C. M. V, e a più eccitare della M. V. sublime generosità per il bisognoso Autore. Vi troverà uniti anche i Figurini. Prevengo V. M, come Padre, che le povere figlie hanno perduto sulla loro pensione 25 F.[i] per ogni 100 come il Sig[r] de Smithmayer può sapere dal Banchiere Borchetta. Spero che la M. V, nostro unico Astro celeste, nel soccorrere il Padre riparerà a così grave danno delle Figlie, di cui tante volte si è dichiarata, non solo Cesarea Protettrice, ma benefica e tenera Madre" (HHStA, Fa, Sb, Kart. 62, Verschiedene an Kaiserin Marie Therese 1803, fol. 190r–191r).

which De Gamerra played no role. The other librettos by De Gamerra probably represent unfinished projects: she collected them with the intention of having them set to music.

Marie Therese had partial success with *Caio Coriolano*. After Mayr failed to keep his promise to compose it for her private use, Eybler set to music two extracts from it: a quartet and an aria, both preceded by orchestrally accompanied recitative (Mus. Hs. 10357–8, 10363–4; Herrmann 151, 152).[4] Her unsuccessful attempt to transform one of De Gamerra's other librettos into an opera is documented in an exchange of letters with Paisiello, to be discussed later in this chapter.

More fruitful was Marie Therese's collaboration with De Gamerra on the cantata *L'amor filiale*, performed with music by Weigl in honor of the visit of Queen Maria Carolina to Vienna in 1800. We can follow the development of this project in letters from De Gamerra to his sister, which show that Ferdinand (who, as grand duke of Tuscany, may have taken a special interest in this Tuscan poet) acted as both intermediary and performer. On 3 August 1800 De Gamerra wrote:

Fifteen days ago Rosellini, secretary to the grand duke, came to tell me on behalf of the grand duke that I should go immediately to Hetzendorff and announce myself in the antechamber of H. M. the empress, who wished to speak to me. You can believe that I rushed there as soon as I received the command. I was immediately admitted, and that incomparable sovereign told me in the most attractive terms that I was to compose a cantata for five voices and chorus for the arrival of her august mother, leaving to me the choice of the contents. Having seen how moved she was when she deigned to speak with me of her royal mother, I responded to her that I was thinking of choosing a theme befitting the circumstance so precious to her most sensitive heart, and the project received the sovereign's approval.

The "circumstance" to which De Gamerra alluded was presumably her love for her mother, to judge from the cantata's title:

After three days the cantata was finished, and, returning to Hetzendorff, I had the honor of laying it at the royal feet. It was received with her customary clemency and she found it perfectly suited to the occasion so ardently desired by her filial love, having as its title *L'amor filiale*. In my presence she assigned the roles. H. R. H. the grand duchess of Tuscany [Maria Luisa, Ferdinand's wife and Marie Therese's sister] will portray the mother, H. M. the empress the daughter, and H. R. H. the grand duke the daughter's husband. That leaves two minor roles,

---

[4] These excerpts date from fall 1804. On 6 November 1804 Eybler wrote to MT: "Die Kopiatur von den beyden Szenen aus dem Coriolan wird bis 13ten dieses Monaths fertig" (HHStA, Fa, Sb, Kart. 63, fol. 154r, reproduced as Fig. 3.1).

which will be sung by two members of the royal chapel. Maestro Weigl is setting it to music right now, and it will be completed by the 10th of this month.[5]

De Gamerra mentioned here one crucial aspect of the compositional process that the empress almost always reserved for herself: the distribution of roles.

Weigl must have finished the music on time, for on 18 August De Gamerra, referring to Marie Therese as *la padrona*, wrote:

A week ago Saturday the patroness wished to hear the music, and in the presence of the composer and me it was performed from three to half past four in the afternoon. I turned the pages of the music, and was able to witness the effect on her sensitive heart of the sentiments of the words, clothed in expressive and suitable music. Tears often fell from her eyes. She sang the part of the daughter, and in more than one emotional outburst she cried out, deeply moved: "How could one not be touched by such tender and attractive words?" Oh what a sublime soul our august protectress has, being at once the most affectionate daughter, tender mother, and sensitive wife![6]

Thus Marie Therese was able to participate in a performance of *L'amor filiale* less than a month after she commissioned the libretto. A year and a half later she organized a revival of the cantata in one of her private concerts (17 January 1802). The concert, which included the finale of the first act of Mozart's *La clemenza di Tito* and his Quintet for piano and winds, ended with "the cantata *L'amor filiale* by Weigl, sung by me, Marchesi, Ratmayer, Weinmüller, the grand duke, and chorus."

Carpani's letters show him to have taken a much more active role in the musical side of theatrical creation than De Gamerra. Occasionally his activities formed part of a three-way collaboration between librettist, composer, and patron. In February 1802, for example, he sent from Venice a plan for the oratorio *La passione*, for which Weigl was to supply the music. A few weeks later he expressed happiness at Weigl's news of her approval of the poetry.[7] Weigl, in Vienna, was evidently in direct communication with both the empress and Carpani. More often, however, she allowed Carpani free rein in choosing composers and stayed clear of the interaction between him and the Italian musicians with whom he worked.

Pilade e Oreste, a serious opera on which Carpani, at the behest of Marie Therese, worked with Zingarelli in 1803 and 1804, received an unusual

---

[5] De Gamerra to Maria Casimira Caterina Gamerra Berte, Vienna, 3 August 1800, in "Lettere di Giovanni De Gamerra (III)," 111–14.

[6] De Gamerra to Maria Casimira Caterina Gamerra Berte, Vienna, 18 August 1800, in "Lettere di Giovanni De Gamerra (III)," 114–15. MT said: "Come non intenerirsi da parole così tenere e interessanti!"

[7] Carpani to MT, 3, 17, 23 February 1802, in Jacobs, *Carpani*, 214–15.

amount of attention in the letters, which contain information not only about how Carpani supervised the production of this opera, but also about the potentially awkward period that followed its delivery, as the librettist and composer wondered how the empress would receive it and how – if at all – she would reward them.

Carpani kept Marie Therese informed of the slow progress on *Pilade e Oreste*, which began as a *pasticcio* but evolved, during the composition of the second act, into a mostly new work. On 4 January 1803 he wrote:

I hope to be able humbly to present to you in twenty days the first act of my *Pilade e Oreste*, to which Zingarelli has composed all the recitatives, and four new pieces, that is two concerted choruses (or, to put it better, two scenes), an aria for the prima donna, and one for the bass. If the second act is as successful as the first, I hope Y. M. will honor the work by looking on it with kind eyes. But my duties as censor do not permit me to apply myself to poetry at the moment; and the composer did not wish to remain here at his own expense and has returned to Loreto, hence he will send the pieces one by one as he finishes them. That will result in some delay, which will however find compensation in the generous clemency of Y. M., who will surely be willing to believe that this delay does not come from a lack of energetic desire on our part to match the eagerness with which we obeyed such an important commission.[8]

In the manuscript score of *Pilade e Oreste* from Marie Therese's library (Mus. Hs. 10019) the following numbers in what is apparently Zingarelli's hand correspond to the "four new pieces": "Fermati che fai" and "Scendi fausta dall' alta tua sfera" (scenes with chorus and soloists), "Senti ritorna" (aria, Ifigenia), and "Vanne, t'intesi omai" (aria, Tonante). The rest of the act, written out by various copyists, consists of excerpts from operas by Johann Gottlieb Naumann, Mayr, and Cimarosa, with their texts altered by Carpani (with red ink) so as to make sense within the story of Iphigenia at Tauris. For the finale of act 1 Carpani chose one of Marie Therese's favorite scenes, the *sotterraneo* from Mayr's *Gli sciti*.

"Twenty days" turned into two months, and in March Carpani had recourse to an excuse that must have been familiar to Marie Therese: "la lentezza di questi copisti."

Finally I have been able to get from the composer Zingarelli the new pieces for *Pilade e Oreste*, and I do not delay a moment in laying at the feet of Y. M. the first act of this opera, which is truly new of its kind. If the celebration of the birthday of H. M. the Emperor had not taken so much time I would have possibly been able

---

[8] Carpani to MT, 4 January 1803, in Jacobs, *Carpani*, 219–20.

humbly to present to you the second act as well.[9] But this duty – dear to me – has caused me to delay the other, hence there is nothing for me but to invoke the great clemency of Y. M.... The slowness of these copyists discouraged me from having the whole first act copied here, and I have written to maestro Weigl everything necessary for it to be done there [i.e. in Vienna]. I would be truly happy if the new pieces succeed in satisfying the refined and rare taste of Y. M. The aria of Ifigenia seems to me a masterpiece in the grand tragic style; but my judgment could be influenced by my desire, hence I do not dare deceive myself until Y. M. has pronounced hers. Now I look forward with the greatest enthusiasm to writing the second act, inserting the pieces that Y. M. ordered from me.[10]

Carpani left Weigl responsible not only for having the parts extracted but also for some musical adjustments. In reference to a passage in Mayr's *sotterraneo* originally sung by two characters ("Ah! non so dirti addio") but that Carpani wished to be sung by three, he wrote in the score: "N.B. In this duet it will be necessary for Maestro Weigl to add the third vocal part, which is Ifigenia, who will say 'Parti, lascialo' to Pilade and Oreste; and at the cadence she will serve as *pertichino* with these two verses: 'Mi sento il cor dividere / Chi non ne avria pietà!' "[11]

In September the second act of *Pilade* was still unfinished. This time among Carpani's explanations for the delay was a change of plans. Instead of simply replacing some of the numbers in act 2, he decided to rewrite the entire act:

Maestro Zingarelli is now there [in Milan], and is writing *Ines de Castro* for the new theater; he has therefore regretfully had to suspend work on the second act of my *Pilade ed Oreste*, to which he is fully committed and of which he has already done more than half. Inserting the pieces that remained from other authors resulted in an act that was very cold in its action and that repeated the situations of the first act; thus I believed I was responding better to the faith that Y. M. placed in my scarce talents by redoing it from the top, both the music and the poetry, and the result has been very exciting, so much so that if the music does not betray me, it will have nothing to fear in comparison with the first [act].

The composer writes me that he is so happy with the poetry that he has never written with so much enthusiasm, and especially when he thinks of the honor to which his work is destined. I have no doubt that it will be sent to Vienna before the end of next October.[12]

---

[9] For Franz's birthday Carpani had written the libretto for a cantata, *L'incontro*, set to music by Ignazio Gerace.

[10] Carpani to MT, 9 March 1803, in Jacobs, *Carpani*, 220–1.

[11] "N.B. In questo duetto si deve aggiungere dal Maestro Weigl la terza parte cantante che è Ifigenia, la quale dirà 'Parti, lascialo' a Pilade ed Oreste. Ed alla cadenza farà loro il pertichino con questi due versi 'Mi sento il cor dividere / Chi non ne avria pietà!' " (Mus. Hs. 10019, fol. 158r).

[12] Carpani to MT, 29 September 1803, in Jacobs, *Carpani*, 226.

Again Carpani missed his self-imposed deadline. It was not until April 1804 that he sent act 2:

> Finally I have fulfilled my promises. After so many difficulties, here at the feet of Y. M. is the second act of my *Pilade e Oreste*, finished and polished, as good as it can be, although not worthy of the highest honor of being humbly presented to Y. M., to whose sovereign order it owes its existence. Whoever loves music that is strong, expressive, and full of feeling will find nothing displeasing, I hope, in this work of maestro Zingarelli, who has labored on it an entire year. To such an extent was he inflamed by the desire to satisfy the genius of so great a sovereign and so demanding a connoisseur of all the fine arts! As long as there is, in addition to an excellent Oreste in Brizzi, an excellent Ifigenia in Sessi, I would dare to hope that, properly staged, this tragedy in music ought to obtain the most favorable reception. The action will bring out all the beauties of the music that, without it, cannot reveal themselves clearly. But its future that I foresee above all is that of making a good effect in the royal apartments of Y. M., to whom I send all my most humble best wishes. The composer will be perfectly happy if he learns that his tireless efforts have been honored by the sovereign satisfaction, and I will feel the same way already to have been able to fulfill the commission with which Y. M. honored me.[13]

Even after *Pilade* was complete, Carpani did not know whether Marie Therese intended to have it performed by professional singers in the Burgtheater or Kärntnertortheater or to perform it herself in private.

The score of act 2 that Carpani sent the empress was, as his letters suggested, very different from the score of act 1. What is probably Zingarelli's hand, found only intermittently in act 1, is found through most of act 2. The interventions in red ink by which Carpani turned the *pasticcio* of act 1 into a coherent drama are absent in act 2, which appears to be the new work he promised.

Now began Carpani's wait for praise and payment. A month after sending the second act of *Pilade*, he left no doubt about what he and Zingarelli wanted:

> I am most impatient – and I cannot hide this from my most merciful sovereign – to know what grace the diligently written music of *Pilade e Oreste* of Zingarelli has elicited from the refined taste with which she is endowed. He is on tenterhooks as much as I am in fear of not having met with the most honorable, hoped-for approval.[14]

Marie Therese must have ignored this plea, for Carpani repeated it a few weeks later:

---

[13] Carpani to MT, 4 April 1804, in Jacobs, *Carpani*, 235–6.
[14] Carpani to MT, 5 May 1804, in Jacobs, *Carpani*, 242.

I live continuously in the most anxious impatience to hear what grace my *Pilade e Oreste*, with Zingarelli's diligently written music, has elicited from the refined taste of Y. M. The composer torments me continuously from Loreto with this most natural desire. If Y. M. would deign to let us know something, we would bless the labors spent with such pleasure in earning for ourselves, at least in part, the sovereign's satisfaction and grace.

Why was the empress silent for so long? I believe she had no opportunity to perform or to hear *Pilade*. Carpani, having decided not to have parts copied out in Venice for act 1 with the expectation that Weigl would do so in Vienna, probably made the same decision in regard to act 2. But Weigl did not apparently fulfill Carpani's expectation. Marie Therese owned no parts for *Pilade* – only the patchwork score that Carpani sent from Venice. That score, moreover, may have been misplaced. *CaM* refers to *Pilade e Oreste*, but attributes it to Naumann, not Zingarelli. The cataloguer, confused by the fact that act 1 begins with a chorus from Naumann's opera *Protesilao* (title page: "Protesilao / Coro / Fra lutto e gemito / Del Sig. Naumann"), failed to recognize Zingarelli's much more important role in the opera's composition and attributed it to Naumann. Unperformed and miscatalogued, the work of Carpani and Zingarelli probably went unrewarded by the empress.

PAISIELLO AND *LA CORONA DEL MERITO*

Marie Therese must have been familiar with Giovanni Paisiello and his music from her youth in Naples, where he presented many of his most celebrated operas and where her father named him Compositore della Musica de' Drammi in 1783 and Maestro della Real Camera in 1787. In 1802 Napoleon summoned Paisiello to Paris, and it was there that Marie Therese initiated a correspondence with him of which four letters are transcribed in appendix 4.[15] Referring to herself as "an old acquaintance of yours," she asked him on 18 July 1802 to set to music one of the librettos written for her by De Gamerra. The letter's charm, warmth, and sincerity make it easy to see how she won the hearts of so many musicians:

Signor Paisiello,
I have too much respect for you as a person and for your unique merit not to turn to you in the hope that you might wish to set to music the opera that you will find enclosed herein, under the title *La corona del merito, o sia Il Torquato Tasso*. I know

---

[15] I am grateful to Michael F. Robinson for bringing these letters to my attention and for sending me copies of them.

well that you are besieged with many duties, and that this new labor might arrive at an inopportune time, yet I am pleased to flatter myself that you will not refuse an old acquaintance of yours the satisfaction of her desire.

In this hope, I will now communicate to you some points that you must keep in mind as you undertake this work. First of all, you must remember that this opera must be suited to the chamber, not the theater.

If you wish to introduce a concertante instrument into some arias or other pieces, keep in mind that we have an excellent cello, oboe, and clarinet. The bass who will take the part of Gherardo sings perfectly.

I would like to have this opera, if possible, for the month of January of next year; if that cannot be, I am also willing to wait as long as you want rather than hurrying the work, which would produce a result less perfect than I would desire.

Other observations that might occur to me will be communicated to you later.

The kindness with which I have no doubt you will satisfy my request will be most delightful and pleasing to me, and will give you a new claim on my admiration and benevolence, of which I am now pleased to assure you.

Your affectionate
Teresa

The bass whom Marie Therese singled out for praise was probably Weinmüller. In specifying January 1803 as the time she wished to receive the opera she may have hoped to rehearse it in time for Franz's birthday on 12 February.

She did not send the letter directly to Paisiello, but instead used Count Cobenzl, the Austrian ambassador in Paris, as a go-between. He relayed Paisiello's response: "In executing the gracious orders with which Your Majesty deigned to honor me, I delivered to Paesiello the parcel addressed to him, as Your Majesty will deign to see from his response, which is enclosed."[16]

Paisiello's answer was diplomatic:

Your Imperial and Royal Majesty,
The honor with which Your Imperial and Royal Majesty has overwhelmed me by honoring me with Your Imperial and Royal commands, with which Your Majesty has deigned to order me to set to music *La corona del merito, o sia Il Torquato Tasso*, will be a greater glory for me, which I will attempt to earn with the utmost diligence, when I am able to satisfy the wishes of Your Imperial and Royal Majesty.

My only regret is that I cannot obey you at the moment, and satisfy the desires of Your Imperial and Royal Majesty, because I am presently occupied on a French libretto given to me by the First Consul, for performance in the great theater

---

[16] "En execution des ordres gracieux dont Votre Majesté a daigné m'honorer j'ai remi a Paesiello le pacquet qui lui etoit destiné ainsi que V. M. daignera le voir de sa reponse cy jointe" (Cobenzl to MT, Paris, 2 August 1802 [*sic*, but the letter must have been written after 4 August, unless Paisiello misdated his letter], HHStA, Fa, Sb, Kart. 62, Verschiedene 1802, fol. 208r–209r).

of the Opéra, which has for its title *Il ratto di Proserpina*, on which I have been working for eight days, and which, to be brief, will keep me busy for about four months. Therefore, Your Imperial and Royal Majesty having foreseen that I could be busy for the time being, and having for that reason granted me a delay, I promise Your Imperial and Royal Majesty that as soon as I have finished my present work I will immediately go to work setting to music *Il Torquato Tasso* with as much attention, care, and zeal as my weak talent permits, in order to earn from Your Imperial and Royal Majesty a simple indulgence, not overlooking all the remarks and observations given to me relative to the subject.

I therefore humbly beseech Your Imperial and Royal Majesty to wish to deign to continue Your beneficial Imperial Protection, and I place myself at the feet of His Imperial and Royal Majesty the Emperor, and the entire imperial family, and with the most profound and respectful reverence I humbly declare myself,

> Your most humble, most obedient, most devoted,
> and most respectful servant, Giovanni Paisiello

Paris, 4 August 1802

Paisiello did not keep his promise, but the empress was too generous, and too eager for new music from him, to hold a grudge. About two and a half years later, the composer having returned to Naples, she wrote again, referring to her earlier commission in such a way as to spare the composer embarrassment over his failure to compose *La corona del merito*. She asked him to abandon that libretto and to choose a plot for a new Italian opera from one of two French dramas enclosed with her letter (although she called them *libretti*, from her next letter it emerges that they were in fact *mélodrames* – plays accompanied by instrumental music). Resorting to the arrangement she sometimes imposed when commissioning works from Paer, she asked Paisiello to engage a poet of his choice to transform one of the plays into a libretto. She adopted a warmer tone than in her first letter, addressing Paisiello as "Caro" and signing herself "affezionatissima" instead of just "affezionata":

Dear Signor Paisiello,
In the hope that you have not been able to begin composing the music that some time ago I asked you to write, or that your work on it has not progressed too far, I would like the libretto that I sent you, which, to tell you the truth, is not completely to my liking, to be replaced with a better one.

Enclosed I send you two French librettos so that you may choose the one that you prefer, asking you, after you have extracted the plot, to have an Italian libretto made from it and to set it to music yourself. Please send the other libretto back to me.

In composing this music I ask you to keep in mind that the opera must be no longer than two hours and a half, and that in the whole first part there should be only one aria, or at most two, and a cavatina, since I wish that the rest of the opera contains many choruses, ensembles, finales, and little simple recitative.

The persons for whose voices it is desired that the parts be written are to be found written in both librettos, and the compasses of the voices are written in this letter.

I do not specify the time at which your work must be finished: I leave it to you, desiring that the resulting opera be worthy of the excellent composer.

The sentiments that you have always demonstrated to me, and which I remember with satisfaction, are my assurance that you will treat my desire with good will, certain that you will thereby acquire a new claim on the gratitude and admiration of your

> Most affectionate
> Teresa

Marie Thcrese's request that the opera contain few arias and little simple recitative but many choruses and ensembles is consistent with the repertory she favored for her own private concerts. Her instructions, if Paisiello had followed them, would have resulted in an opera offering her plenty of opportunity to participate. Her indications of the vocal compass of the singers for whom Paisiello was to write have not survived.

A positive response from Paisiello (apparently lost) encouraged her to write again, on 6 July 1805:

Dear Sig. Paisiello,

I have received your letter of 11 May, in reply to which I am happy first of all to express to you my particular satisfaction for the care with which you undertake the assignment I gave you. The translation of the melodrama that you chose in preference to the other, *I mori di Spagna*, has met with my pleasure: beautiful music, such as one has the right to expect from the classic and excellent composer who writes it, cannot but enhance the book and ensure its success. Relative to the dances separate from the singing, we will need the right amount of time: for the character of the music I leave the choice to your taste, since I do not yet know the ballet master who will have to stage it. Whoever he is, he will have to adapt his ideas to your music. You will kindly let me know for which voices you will have written the parts of *Settimio* and *Pubblio*.

In the meantime, dear Sig. Paisiello, assuring you of my esteem and my particular benevolence, I am

> Your most affectionate
> Teresa

From the Italian title of the piece Paisiello rejected, *I mori di Spagna*, we know that the French drama in question was René Charles Guilbert de Pixérécourt's *Les Maures d'Espagne*, a *mélodrame* in three acts first performed in Paris in 1804. The names of two of the characters in the drama he preferred, Settimio and Pubblio, indicate that this was another *mélodrame*, Louis-Charles Caigniez's *Androcles, ou Le Lion reconnaissant* (Paris, 1804), of which Marie Therese owned an Italian translation in manuscript.[17] But she waited in vain for Paisiello's *Androcle*; he never wrote it.

PAER'S *LE MINE DE POLONIA* AND CHERUBINI'S *FANISKA*

Marie Therese's letters to Paisiello document a change in her theatrical taste that reflected and reinforced one of the most important developments in Viennese opera at the beginning of the nineteenth century: its embrace of modern French drama. The libretto by De Gamerra that she asked Paisiello to set in 1802 was, two and a half years later, "not completely to my liking," as she put it before asking him to set to music an Italian adaptation of a *mélodrame*. The *opéras-comiques* that, in German translation, dominated the repertory of the court theaters and the Theater an der Wien during the first decade of the nineteenth century found in Marie Therese an enthusiastic admirer. With the help of the Marchese di Gallo she collected *opéras-comiques* by Berton, Boieldieu, Cherubini, Dalayrac, Nicolò Isouard, Rodolphe Kreutzer, Lesueur, and Méhul.

Paisiello was not the only composer whom Marie Therese asked to write an Italian opera based on a French play. In letters of 1804 and 1805 Paer frequently referred to an opera he was writing for her, *Le mine di Polonia*, based on another *mélodrame* by Pixérécourt. *Les Mines de Pologne*, first performed at the Théâtre de l'Ambigu-Comique in Paris on 3 May 1803, is a rescue drama whose plot closely resembles that of Cherubini's *Lodoiska*. It had been brought to Marie Therese's attention by her sister Amalia, who wrote enthusiastically of a performance of Pixérécourt's play by noble amateurs in Naples on 5 February 1804:

Yesterday, in the evening, the play organized by [the Prince of] Caramanica was given in the little court theater; it was entitled *Floriska et Zamoisky, ou Les Mines de Pologne*; it was truly beautiful and interesting, the scenery superb, the costumes magnificent, and all the actors played their roles wonderfully well. Above all Brigadier Tardella portrayed the tyrant Zamoisky to perfection, and a little girl of eight, the princess's daughter, acted and danced like an angel. Between each act there were charming instrumental pieces, very well played; the orchestra consisted entirely of amateurs; the Prince of Caramanica played the double bass.[18]

---

[17] HHStA, Fa, Sb, Kart. 66, fol. 314–53.

[18] "Hier au soir on à donné la comedie de Caramanica sur le petit theatre de cour, elle est intitulée *Floriska et Zamoisky, ou les mines de Pologne*; elle est vraiment jolie et interessante les décorations

The mines that give the play its title are tunnels under the palace of the wicked Zamoski, who lusts after Floreska, wife of Edwinski. When Floreska rejects Zamoski's advances he locks her up with her daughter Angéla. Edwinski tries to rescue them by entering the castle in disguise but Zamoski recognizes him and imprisons the whole family in the mines. It is only with the help of Polina, a lively young woman (Zamoski's *femme de confiance* and the drama's main source of comic relief) that Floreska and her family escape.

Les Mines de Pologne came up in Paer's letters for the first time about two months after the performance in Naples. In response, presumably, to a request from Marie Therese that he set to music an Italian libretto based on the play, he expressed admiration for it and then touched on a decision that had to be confronted as part of the adaptation of many French dramas of the time – plays as well as *opéras-comiques* – that mixed the heroic with the comic. Rather than turning *Les Mines* into an *opera seria*, along the lines of Mayr's *Lodoiska*, as a vehicle for Crescentini (evidently the empress's first intention), Paer recommended that the mixed character of the original be preserved:

I have the honor of submitting to you that the book *Les Mines* was excellent, but not for making a pure *opera seria*; if however Your Majesty should desire it for Crescentini, then it could be translated, as was done with *Lodoiska*, in the completely serious style. But then Polina, whose vivacity comes to the rescue of that unfortunate family, could not be preserved, hence I say it should be left as it is so as not to lose the many beauties of the French original.

Paer had asked Giacomo Cinti, a singer, teacher of Italian, and poet resident in Dresden, to turn Pixérécourt's melodrama into an Italian libretto:

I have already given it to the poet of the aforementioned cantata [*Il conte Clò*, discussed in chapter 9] to be translated and arranged; but he will not accomplish it quickly, because he is a singer in the chapel, a language teacher, and has already accepted many commissions that cannot be abandoned. However, he will make every effort to make the translation as soon as possible. It will be necessary to pardon him, because he is not a great poet, but only serving temporarily to adjust librettos from Italy.[19]

superbes, les habits magnifiques, et tous les acteurs jouent leur rôle a merveille, surtout le Brigadier Tardella fait le tiran Zamoisky à perfection, et puis une petite fille de huit ans de la Princesse, joue et danse come un ange, entre chaque acte il y à eu des sinfonies charmantes et fort bien executées, l'orchestre etant tout composé de *dilettanti*, le Prince de Caramanica jouoit la basse" (Amalia to MT, 4 February 1804 [this passage with the internal date 6 February], HHStA, Fa, Sb, Kart. 63, fol. 120r–v).
[19] Paer to MT, Dresden, 2 April 1804.

Duties more pressing than the composition of an opera for the empress's private use – the composition of *Leonora* for the Dresden court theater and a commission from Rome for a Carnival opera – forced Paer to put off the composition of *Le mine di Polonia*. In promising to write the opera on his return from Rome, he showed that his interest in the work extended beyond music:

I will pass through Vienna [during Lent 1805] in order to receive from you some gracious and precious command, and if Your Majesty wishes, I will then compose *Le mine di Pollonia*, which is succeeding in the translation of our customary un-known poet. But it is absolutely necessary to obtain from Paris a simple drawing (even one done in pencil) of all three sets that were done for this play in the Teatro dell'Ambigu.[20]

Cinti finished his libretto by early 1805, as we know from a letter in which Paer reported that a copy of it had mistakenly fallen into the hands of Prince Lobkowitz.[21] But despite repeated reassurances that he was writing the music (see, for example, Fig. 8.1), Paer did not send the score of *Le mine*. When an operatic version of Pixérécourt's drama finally reached the Viennese stage, it was not with Paer's music.

On 25 February 1806 Cherubini presented his only Viennese opera, *Faniska*, in the Kärntnertortheater. The librettist was Joseph Sonnleithner, court secretary and, from 1804, secretary of the court theaters. Based on *Les Mines de Pologne*, *Faniska* gave rise to an early and important articulation of the concept of rescue opera: "This piece obviously belongs to the now dominant genre of rescue stories, without distinguishing itself from the others."[22] The plot of *Les Mines*, and even its title, made it inevitable that Cherubini's opera should contain a *sotterraneo*. Act 2 begins with an orchestral prelude in slow tempo that, as in many underground scenes of the period, depicts the darkness and mystery of a subterranean chamber. Typical of *sotterranei* is the ensuing monologue in recitative, in which Faniska, the heroine, expresses her horror: "Welche Wohnung des Schreckens!"

But Sonnleithner did not derive his German libretto directly from Pixérécourt. Hoping to disarm critics of the libretto's literary shortcomings,

---

[20] Paer to MT, Dresden, 26 July 1804. Paer's interest in stage design helps to explain a remark about him by the Dresden *directeur des plaisirs* Count Vitzthum von Eckstädt in a memorandum of 23 November 1803: "The talent and manifold ability of the still young Kapellmeister as singer as well as theater director has been recognized by everyone" (quoted in Kobuch, "Ferdinando Paer in Dresden," 36).

[21] Paer to MT, Bologna, 2 April 1805. The episode will be discussed briefly in chapter 10.

[22] "Dieses Stück gehört offenbar zu der jetzt herrschenden Gattung der Befreiungsgeschichten, ohne sich eben vor den übrigen auszuzeichen" (*Wiener Journal für Theater, Musik und Mode*, 1806, 170).

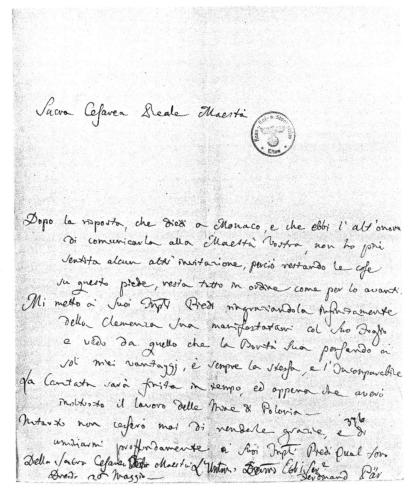

Figure 8.1 Letter from Paer to Marie Therese, dated Dresden, 26 May [1804?], promising he will complete an unidentified cantata for her after making progress on *Le mine di Polonia*. Transcribed in appendix 3.

he explained in a note that he had translated an Italian libretto that Cherubini had already set to music (in other words, he had been forced to adjust his translation to existing music).[23] That Cherubini wrote *Faniska* on an Italian libretto Bouilly confirmed in the preface to an edition of

---

[23] "Anmerkung. Herr Cherubini hat nach Italienischen Worten componirt, die übersetzt werden mußten. Hiernach sind die Deutschen Verse zu beurtheilen" (*Faniska*, Vienna, 1806).

Pixérécourt's *mélodrame*.[24] Was that libretto the one Cinti had prepared for Paer? If so, did Marie Therese, having lost patience with Paer, pass Cinti's libretto to Cherubini?

Writing to the empress less than two weeks after the premiere of *Faniska*, Paer alluded to it, to the commission for *Le mine di Polonia*, and to another commission that Marie Therese (through Simoni) was now cancelling by asking Paer to return the libretto:

> I heard that the opera of M[aestro] Cherubini was successful, as no one could have doubted. Because the occasion for doing oneself honor in our profession comes from the good fortune of finding a good libretto, I cannot deny that such good fortune, in the form of the opera *Le mine di Polonia*, of which I should have been the first composer, was taken from me by adverse destiny... Our friend Sim[oni] orders me to send to Your Majesty the superb book of *Androcle*, and this is yet another source of hope that has been taken away from me in this manner. I obey blindly, but I cannot restrain myself from begging Your Majesty to remember that I would have been happy to have been able to compose it first and to produce it, as Cherubini did *Les Mines*.[25]

The libretto the empress wanted back, *Androcle*, was yet another Italian adaptation of a French play: one that she earlier hoped Paisiello would set to music. She apparently offered it to Paer after Paisiello failed a second time to fulfill his promise to write an opera for her. Without saying it outright, Paer implied she had similarly cancelled Paer's commission for *Le mine di Polonia* and transferred the libretto to Cherubini.

Yet aside from the derivation of *Faniska* from *Les Mines de Pologne*, there is very little about Cherubini's visit to Vienna that can be connected with the empress. The *Allgemeine musikalische Zeitung* published reports from which it appeared that Braun alone was responsible for bringing Cherubini to Vienna. On 5 July 1805 a correspondent wrote from Vienna: "Baron Braun will arrive from Paris any day now. It is generally known that he will bring with him Cherubini, who has agreed to write two operas for the theater here."[26]

Given the close connections between Braun and Marie Therese, however, we have reason to suspect that the impresario's actions were motivated, at least in part, by the court. That suspicion is confirmed by Bouilly, who,

---

[24] Of *Faniska* Bouilly wrote: "à son retour à Paris, le Maestro se proposa d'arranger en français ce même opéra, écrit en italien" (Jean-Nicolas Bouilly, "Notice sur Les Mines de Pologne," in René Charles Guilbert de Pixérécourt, *Théâtre choisi*, 4 vols., Paris, 1841–3, I, 342).

[25] Paer to MT, [Dresden], 7 March 1806.

[26] "Baron Braun wird nächstens aus Paris zurückkommen. Man versichert hier allgemein, er werde Cherubini mitbringen, der sich zwey Opern für das hiesige Theater zu schreiben verpflichtet habe" *AmZ* 7 (1804–5), col. 691.

in his preface to *Les Mines de Pologne*, mentions the *mélodrame*'s favorable reception and continues: "It was after these well-deserved panegyrics that the emperor of Austria called our famous composer Cherubini to Vienna in order to set to music this drama, which was performed under the title of *Faniska*."[27] It would have been completely out of character for Franz to commission an opera. More likely he summoned Cherubini to Vienna at his wife's behest or Bouilly erred in attributing to the emperor a commission from his wife. That Marie Therese's copy of *Faniska* (Mus. Hs. 10180–81) contains the original Italian text rather than Sonnleithner's German one is a further hint of her involvement in the opera's development.

INSTRUCTIONS TO COMPOSERS: MICHAEL HAYDN'S
MISSA S. FRANCISCI

With no single composer did the empress establish warmer and more productive relations than Michael Haydn, whose two plenary masses and unfinished Requiem in B♭ are certainly, of all the works written for her, among the grandest in scale and finest in quality. We are fortunate to have, in the case of one of these works, reliable information about the instructions that came with the commission, which show how deeply she involved herself in the compositional process.

Haydn received the commission for the *Missa S. Francisci* on 5 April 1803, by way of a third party whose identity is unknown. He accepted it immediately, writing to the man who had relayed the empress's instructions:

I received your most pleasant letter today and hasten to answer it. The desire of Her Majesty the Empress is the highest command for me, and to obey the same a most exceptional delight and pleasure. I will follow most exactly everything that is requested in order (as far as my small talents are able) to deliver something respectable.[28]

---

[27] "Ce fut d'après ces éloges mérités, que l'empereur d'Autriche fit venir à Vienne notre célèbre compositeur Chérubini, pour composer la musique de cette pièce, qui fut représentée sous le titre de *Faniska*" (Bouilly, "Notice sur Les Mines de Pologne," 342).

[28] Autograph in the Pierpoint Morgan Library, New York; published for the first time, in English translation (used here), in Landon, *Haydn* V, 259. Here is the complete text:
"Salzburg den 5ten April 1803.
Wohlgebohrner Gnädiger Herr!
Dero höchst-angenehmes Schreiben habe ich unter obigem dato empfangen, und am nämlichen beantworte ich dasselbe. Das Verlangen Ihrer Majestät der Kaiserinn ist für mich der höchste Befehl, und denselben zu gehorchen eine übergrosse Gnad und Freude. Alles was vorgeschrieben ist, werde ich auf das genaueste befolgen, um nur (so viel es meine geringen Kräfte vermögen) etwas Anständiges zu liefern.

Two days later Haydn shared with his friend Werigand Rettensteiner not only his joy at the commission but also the detailed instructions that came with it:

The day before yesterday a letter from Vienna brought me the news that Her Majesty the empress wishes to receive from me, for the nameday celebration of His Majesty the emperor, another newly composed mass together with *gradual*, *offertory*, and *Te Deum laudamus*. Now the instructions: the whole thing should have the same length as two years ago. The mass should have small solos, as before; of these the *Et incarnatus est* should be in four voices, and accompanied only by cello and double bass. The *Benedictus* will be a duet for soprano and bass, with a chorus at the end. The *offertory* a four-part canon. The whole thing should have two fugues. This is all copied word for word from the letter. But there's more! The empress inquires whether I am inclined to undertake this work. Oh, what princely grace! I would like to shout with pleasure.[29]

Haydn's claim that he was repeating word for word the instructions from Vienna finds partial confirmation in a query he made to the empress's representative in his letter of 5 April:

I would only like to have clear information on one point. You write: *The Offertorium will be a 4-part Canon*. Should it then be composed like my 4-part songs? Or should it be interpreted as a most strict canon, in which one voice after the other begins, and sings in a circle that which the other has sung? – I would ask you please, when the occasion offers, to let me know.[30]

Nur über Eines möchte ich eine klärere Auskunft haben. Sie schrieben: *das Offertorium wird ein 4 stimmiger Canon*. Soll nun dieser wie meine 4 stimmigen Lieder eingerichtet seyn; oder soll er *strictissime Canon* heißen, wo eine Stimme nach der andern anfängt, und immer kreisförmig singt, was das Andere gesungen hat? – Über dieses bitte ich recht sehr, mich nach Gelegenheit zu belehren.

Es geschieht mir dadurch eine grosse Gnade; zu welcher, wie zu fernern, mich gehorsamst empfehle, und mit wahrer Hochschätzung verharre

Eurer Gnaden

unterthäniger Diener

Joh: Michael Haydn Mpia

N: S: Hier ist Alles in Spannung auf die Ankunft unsers neuen Landes–Herrn, Sr Königl: Hoheit des Erz–Herzogs Ferdinand."

[29] "Vorgestern brachte mir ein Brief aus Wien die Nachricht, daß ihre Majestät die Kaiserin von mir für das am 4 Oktober fallende Namensfest Sr. Maj. des Kaisers wieder eine Messe sammt *Graduale*, *Offertorium* und *Te Deum laudamus* neu verfertigt zu erhalten verlangen. – Nun die Vorschrift: das Ganze soll beyläufig von der nämlichen Dauer seyn, wie vor 2 Jahren. Die Messe soll, wie damals, kleine Solo's haben; davon soll das *et incarnatus est* vierstimmig seyn, und nur vom Violoncell und Violon begleitet werden. *Benedictus* wird ein Duett für Sopran und Baß; am Ende Chor. Das *Offertorium* ein vierstimmiger Canon. Das Ganze soll zwey Fugen haben. Dieses alles ist wörtlich aus dem Briefe abgeschrieben. Noch nicht genug! Höchstselbe lassen mich überdieß noch fragen: Ob ich gesonnen sey, diese Arbeit zu übernehmen? – O der fürstlichen Huld! Ich möchte jauchzen vor Lust" (*Biographische Skizze von Michael Haydn*, 27).

[30] Landon, *Haydn V*, 259.

Haydn quoted here from the instructions a sentence almost identical to one in the letter to Rettensteiner.

The empress's instructions show that she wanted Haydn's second name-day mass to differ significantly from his first, despite its being about the same length. Most important, she wanted her own musical role to be different, since the two texts that were to be composed as ensembles had both been set in the *Missa S. Theresiae* as solos for her. At the same time, by not specifying where she wished to sing by herself, she invited Haydn to surprise her. He did so, writing, in the two biggest soprano solos in the *Missa S. Francisci*, music very different from most of what she had sung in the *Missa S. Theresiae*. In place of the sweetness and lyricism of the earlier "Et incarnatus est" and Benedictus, he wrote music full of fire and excitement, sometimes violent (in the "Christe eleison" in D minor, quoted and discussed in chapter 3), and sometimes festive (at "Quoniam tu solus sanctus" in the Gloria). Both these solos are aria-like in size; both are preceded by long orchestral introductions. The soprano interacts dramatically with the chorus, which in the "Quoniam" repeatedly sings just the words "Tu solus" in unison, simultaneously underlining the meaning of the words and creating a wonderful contrast to the soloist's florid line.

The request for two fugues and for a canonic offertory insured that imitative textures played a more important role in the second mass than in the first, which contained only a single fugue (not including the one at the end of the Te Deum, Sherman 800). The two fugues in the *Missa S. Francisci*, in the Kyrie and at "Cum sancto spiritu" in the Gloria, helped call attention to the empress's new role as soloist. Both fugues followed her great solos without a break, crowning her virtuosity with polyphonic glory.

Marie Therese made only one request in regard to orchestration, specifying that the quartet of soloists in the "Et incarnatus est" be accompanied "only by cello and double bass." This stipulation Haydn realized with a tender cello solo – one of the most beautiful of many cello solos in works composed for the empress – above a figured bass (Ex. 8.1). Thus, despite her wish not to predominate vocally in the "Et incarnatus est," she nevertheless imprinted it with her musical personality. Haydn enhanced the effect of the appearance of the solo cello by setting this movement, in the middle of the D major Credo, in F major. But a more remarkable tonal effect emphasizes the text at "Passus et sepultus est": a modulation from Db major to D minor, the key in which this stunning ensemble ends. The cello, which plays mostly in its high register, descends into the depths to illustrate "sepultus est."

Ex 8.1 Michael Haydn, *Missa S. Francisci*, Credo, mm. 118–39

Ex 8.1 (*cont.*)

Ex 8.1 (*cont.*)

The empress's directions are just as interesting for what they leave out as for what they include. They do not address an issue of great importance in the composition of any plenary mass: the choice of texts for the gradual and offertory. She must have left these decisions to Haydn. A crucial musical choice that she left to him was the mass's tonal plan. It was apparently Haydn who decided to follow his brother's "Nelsonmesse" and Eybler's *Missa S. Wolfgangi* (both of which the empress owned) in setting the *Missa S. Francisci* in D minor but with several movements in D major.

ORATORIOS ON THE LAST JUDGMENT

Marie Therese had a particular interest in commissioning oratorios, probably because this genre allowed her to partake in the creation of large-scale vocal works that, like requiems and plenary masses, did not require staging. She commissioned oratorios not only from some of her favorite composers, such as Weigl and Eybler, but from musicians who wrote for her no major works in other genres, such as Salieri and Cartellieri. By energetically and repeatedly promoting the Last Judgment as a subject for oratorio, she helped to initiate the vogue for eschatological themes that characterized the genre in the nineteenth century.[31]

The empress recorded her thoughts on an oratorio about the Last Judgment in undated plans in Italian and German. In the Italian sketch, entitled *I quattro novissimi*, she envisioned "the four last things" as being depicted in an oratorio in four parts: *La morte*, *Il giudizio*, *L'inferno*, and *Il paradiso*.[32] The German sketch, untitled, contains the same four parts: *Tod*, *Gericht*, *Hölle*, and *Himmel*.[33] The plans differ only slightly in their casts of characters. Both call for a father (tenor) whose sick wife dies in part 1, their daughter (soprano), Adam (bass), various archangels and souls, both blessed and damned, and choruses of family members, angels, blessed souls, and damned souls. The Italian version has a part for Lucifer (bass) while the German version has a part for the judge (i.e. Christ, bass).

The empress demonstrated in these sketches her experience as a performing musician, her intimate knowledge of the musical forces available to her, and her awareness of the challenges facing both librettist and composer. She chose the number of soloists and their voice types; distributed solos,

[31] Howard E. Smither, *A History of the Oratorio*, 4 vols., Chapel Hill, NC, 1987–2000, IV, 97–8, points to the importance of the Last Judgment as a subject for oratorio in the nineteenth century.

[32] HHStA, Fa, Sb, Kart. 65, Schriften der Höchstsel. Kaiserin: Theatralische Gegenstände, fol. 149r–150v.

[33] Ibid., fol. 135r–136v.

ensembles, and choruses so as to produce a sense of variety; provided for dramatic interest by moving from the personal tragedy of a mother's death in part 1 to the universal theme of judgment in part 2, and finally to the spectacle of hell and heaven in parts 3 and 4. Within this variety she was able to find unity by calling for the reunion of the mother and her husband and children in heaven. In her deployment of the chorus she envisioned a daring contrast at the end of part 2, when half the chorus, having been sentenced to eternal damnation, expresses despair, while the other half, about to go to heaven, rejoices and praises God. She specified tempos in the programatic overture to the first part, not the normal slow introduction followed by a fast movement, but vice versa: "The Allegro expresses the world's pleasures. This is followed by a very dark Adagio, which shows how all these pleasures are dissolved by death; and the emptiness that death makes in human society is expressed by the end of the overture."[34] As in her instructions to Michael Haydn, here too she avoided most technical aspects of the music; she made no demands or recommendations in regard to meter, mode, key, or instrumentation.

Marie Therese's projected oratorio, like her fascination with the requiem, seems to have embodied a preoccupation with death; but it also expressed admiration for an oratorio about the beginning of life. Haydn's *Die Schöpfung* depicted the beginning of the world; her oratorio would depict the end. It would be Omega to Haydn's Alpha, or the third and final work in a great trilogy that included *Die Jahreszeiten*. Her inclusion of both Adam and archangels in *I quattro novissimi* reminds us of *Die Schöpfung*. But the most compelling reason to think that she considered her oratorio as a kind of sequel to *Die Schöpfung* and *Die Jahreszeiten* is that in 1801 and 1802 she tried to persuade Haydn himself to write an oratorio on the Last Judgment (those efforts will be discussed in chapter 10).

Old and tired, Haydn did not of course write an oratorio for Marie Therese; she, probably aware of his reluctance or inability to compose another big work, began preparations for an oratorio in Italian rather than German. An undated manuscript in her *Nachlass* contains summaries, in the elegant hand of a professional secretary, of the contents of two projected Italian oratorios, *Il giudizio finale* and *Il diluvio universale*. In reference to the former, the author, possibly the empress herself, explained in an introductory note:

---

[34] "L'Allegro esprime i piaceri del Mondo. Questo passa in un Adagio molto tetro che esprime come tutti questi piaceri sono disciolti dalla morte ed il vuoto che questa fa nella società umana esprime la fine della Sinfonia" (ibid., fol. 149r).

Some time ago I had the idea of writing a cantata, or drama, on this subject, by analogy with Haydn's *Creation*, that is, divided into three parts with angels as interlocutors ... with the addition of several characters according to verisimilitude and arias and ensembles arranged in the manner of *The Creation*."[35]

Having invoked Haydn's name, the writer mentioned the composer who seems to have succeeded Haydn in Marie Therese's plans:

Sig. Cherubini will be able to add, to omit, and to make suggestions in both plans concerning what pleases him and what appears to him to be most suitable to his great talents and musical genius, which is already known to me. And fully aware of the great energy and profundity of his art, I realize how much I need to match these in both emotional and intellectual content.[36]

The plan for *Il giudizio finale* differs from the sketch for *I quattro novissimi* in several respects. It is in three parts instead of four. Part 1 depicts not the death of a young mother and her family's grief, but the end of life in general in a series of violent events: a storm, an earthquake, a plague. With human beings largely excluded from the oratorio, most of the solo material goes to the three archangels, who describe and comment on the great spectacle of dissolution and death taking place before them. Part 2 ends with "Tenebre eterne, e Caos antico" – perhaps an invitation to Cherubini to write something like Haydn's "Vorstellung des Chaos." But since part 2 begins with a depiction of "Sterilità universale delle cose," this part of the oratorio provides little opportunity for musical contrast and development. Part 3, The Last Judgment, concludes with a depiction of Heaven and Hell and a dialogue between infernal and celestial choruses.

Cherubini's name allows us to assign an approximate date to this proposal. From a letter written from Paris by the Marchese di Gallo on 8 January 1803, we know that around this time the empress hoped to interest Cherubini in composing two works. Although Gallo did not mention their titles, they were possibly the two oratorios in question. Gallo implied that she had tried (unsuccessfully) to keep her role as commissioner secret:

---

[35] "Tempo fa mi venne in idea di comporre una Cantata, o Dramma su tal soggetto a similitudine della Creazione di Hayden, cioè diviso in tre parti con gli angeli interlocutori ... con aggiunta altresì di qualche Personaggio tratto dal verisimile, con distribuzione d'arie e pezzi concertati a somiglianza della detta Creazione" (HHStA, Fa, Sb, Kart. 66, fol. 547–54).

[36] "Il Sig. Cherubini potrà aggiungere, togliere, suggerire in ambedue gli Argomenti, quello, che gli piacerà, e parrà più gradevole a' suoi gran talenti, e genio musicale a me ancora cognito. E sapendo bene quanta è l'energia e profondità della di lui Arte, vedo, quanto mi bisogna corrisponderli col sentimento, e colla ragione" (ibid.).

Your Majesty should know that Cherubini does not want to declare his intentions concerning the desired compositions. He has learned from Vienna that the interest in him originated with Your Majesty, and he would like either to give you the compositions as a present in the hopes of furthering his own interests or to sell them at a very high price. This was the inclination that he expressed before leaving for the country, and since then I have not learned anything new, nor have I wanted to put pressure on him, because he would then make me pay twice as much, since I am not able to accept the two works as presents. I have waited for him to return from the country to have him contacted by a third, unknown party, and as soon as I have an answer that suits me, I will have the honor of informing Y. M.[37]

Cherubini wrote no oratorio for Marie Therese. But she did not give up on the Last Judgment. It was probably after having been disappointed by Haydn and Cherubini that she turned to two composers younger than the former and much closer than the latter. Salieri and Eybler accepted commissions that resulted in not one but two oratorios, one in Italian and one in German.

On 24 April 1803 (less than four months after receiving Gallo's discouraging news about Cherubini) the empress and her musicians performed Salieri's oratorio *Gesù al Limbo*, on a text by Prividali (the librettist of Paer's massive cantata *Arianna consolata*). The score and parts from her library (Mus. Hs. 9915–16) were almost certainly used for this performance. A printed libretto probably served as a gesture of gratitude to the poet and composer as much as it enhanced the enjoyment of the performers and an audience that, if it existed at all, was surely very small. Three days later she recorded in her diary a gift for Salieri for his "cantata": a blue enameled snuffbox worth 300 Gulden and 50 ducats in cash. Prividali was also generously rewarded; for the librettos of the oratorio and an unnamed opera he received a gold watch and chain worth 100 Gulden and 300 Gulden in cash.[38]

Gesù al Limbo identifies itself as a sequel to *Die Schöpfung* in several ways. While the libretto is not directly related to Marie Therese's sketches for *I quattro novissimi*, it does preserve several elements that they shared with

[37] "Sappia V. M. che Cherubini non si vuole spiegare sulle sue pretensioni per le musiche desiderate. Egli ha saputo da Vienna che le premure che riceve sono per V. M. e vorrebbe o farne un Regalo interessato, o venderle a cariss[im]o prezzo. Queste erano le sue disposizioni, andò poi in campagna e non ne ho saputo più nuove, ne allora io volli spingere perchè mi avrebbe fatto pagare il doppio, non potendo io accettare le due musiche in regalo. Ho aspettato che ritornasse dalla campagna per farli parlare da una terza persona sconosciuta, ed appena avrò una risposta che mi conviene, mi darò l'onore di informarne V. M." (Gallo to MT, Paris, 8 January 1803, HHStA, Fa, Sb, Kart. 62, Verschiedene an Kaiserin Marie Therese, 1803, fol. 147r–148v).

[38] "Dem Salieri für seine Cantate / Ein frantzblau geschmoltzene Dose 300 fl. werth / Im Geld 50 Dukaten . . . Dem Brividale für eine Oper und eine Cantate die Poesie dazu componirt / Eine goldene Uhr an d^{to} Kette 100 fl. werth / 300 fl im Geld" (HHStA, Fa, HKF, Kart. 24, diary, fol. 162r, 166r–v).

Haydn's oratorio, including the character of Adam. Prividali went further in the direction of *Die Schöpfung* by writing a role for Eve as well. Awaiting the Last Judgment, Adam and Eve recall the pleasures of Eden in a duet, "Quando i beati istanti," that in its playful listing of these delights ("l'erbe, le piante, i fior") reminds us of their duet in *Die Schöpfung*, which Marie Therese sang several times. The libretto makes frequent reference to God as creator, as in the chorus "Dio d'Abramo e di Giacobbe," which ends

> Cieli, stelle, terre, mari:
> Opre tutte del Signore,
> Benedite il Creatore
> Per il corso d'ogni età.

And the final chorus ends with a fugue on the words "Il potentissimo voler sovrano / Del Creator."

Salieri assigned to sopranos the roles of Eve and the personification of faith. He wrote three tenor roles. In making Adam a tenor he ignored both *Die Schöpfung* and the empress, whose plans referred to Adam as a bass. In regard to Christ, Salieri had no guidance from either Haydn or Marie Therese. Like Beethoven, whose *Christus am Oelberge* was first performed nineteen days earlier, he made Christ a tenor.

The empress's diary tells us that she sang one of the soprano roles in *Gesù al Limbo*. If she sang Eve, she returned to a character whose musical depiction by Haydn she had frequently realized in performance. Three of Vienna's leading tenors, Simoni, Brizzi, and Rathmayer, sang in Salieri's oratorio. From the *parti cantanti* for Christ and Adam, on which the singers' names are written, we know that Simoni portrayed Christ and Rathmayer Adam. That left the role of the Archangel Gabriel to Brizzi. Weinmüller sang the only bass part in the oratorio, that of Abraham.

Among the operatic roles for which Weinmüller was long remembered was that of the violent and wicked King Axur in a German version of Salieri's *Axur re d'Ormus*. So it is not surprising that the music Salieri wrote for him in *Gesù al Limbo* should recall one of the most brilliant arias in *Axur*. In "Dalla pietra del deserto" Abraham announces the arrival of Christ as death's conqueror with loud, martial music in D major, orchestrated with trumpets and drums, and with a tune related to Axur's "Dove andò quel maschio ardire" (act 2 in the five-act version of *Axur*, act 1 in the four-act version; Ex. 8.2). This music, in which the bass line doubles the voice most of the time, enhancing its power, made the most of what Wurzbach described as Weinmüller's "truly masculine, powerful, and brilliant bass." And just as Wurzbach also praised Weinmüller's "tender style of performance that went straight to the heart," so Salieri suddenly shifted from martial

Ex 8.2 Salieri, *Gesù al Limbo*, "Dalla pietra del deserto," mm. 8–24

Ex 8.3 Salieri, *Gesù al Limbo*, "Dalla pietra del deserto," mm. 49–58

Ex 8.4 Salieri, *Gesù al Limbo*, "Sotto il giogo del peccato," mm. 66–73

brilliance to tender lyricism for Abraham's words "Ma in grembo alla pace" (Ex. 8.3). The trumpets and drums are silent; the bass line, pizzicato, is now completely independent of the voice, while the triplet arpeggiation in the second violins anticipates the same accompanimental device, transferred to the harp, in Salieri's depiction of heaven later in the oratorio.

In writing Christ's music Salieri could look back for inspiration on roles he had composed for Simoni in his late operas; the veteran tenor had created Ford in *Falstaff* and the title role in *Cesare in Farmacusa*. But it was for Brizzi as Gabriel that Salieri wrote the oratorio's most striking scene. Woodwinds, horns, and harp playing in Eb major depict paradise. The archangel, guarding the gates, orders the wicked souls into the abyss, and sings a triumphant aria, "Sotto il giogo del peccato," whose coloratura and wide leaps convey his supernatural power. At the aria's center a beautiful contrasting section features a harp solo (probably written for Müllner) accompanied by two solo cellos and pizzicato bass (Ex. 8.4).

Among Marie Therese's theatrical papers is a detailed plan in Eybler's hand for an oratorio to be entitled *Die vier letzten Dinge* – a translation of the empress's title *I quattro novissimi* in words that pay tribute to Haydn's *Die sieben letzten Worte*.[39] The plan follows her German sketch in its overall organization, calling for a work in four parts: "Der Tod," "Das Gericht," "Die Hölle," and "Der Himmel." But in its details it has much more in common with the Italian plan destined for Cherubini. Again, individual human beings are largely absent. Archangels do most of the solo singing; Satan has a role in part 3. Adam and Eve sing a duet, as in Salieri's oratorio, but to judge from Eybler's plan it contains no nostalgic reminiscence of Eden's pleasures.

Marie Therese responded to a proposal that must have been similar to Eybler's in a memorandum that, following her regular practice, includes instructions about who is to sing each role. She assigned the roles of the three archangels to Simoni, Weinmüller, and herself; to Ignaz Saal, in tribute to his versatility, went the roles of both Adam and Satan.[40] But with the exception of this cast list, the document is less interesting for its contents than as an illustration of the give and take that characterized her relations with librettists and composers as they brought complex musical works into existence.

Eybler went on to compose *Die vier letzten Dinge*, but he did not finish it until after Marie Therese's death. The autograph score is dated 1810. The manuscript score and parts from the Kaisersammlung (Mus. Hs. 9886–9) are listed near the end of *CaM* (p. 138), in the addendum that I believe was compiled after the empress's death. Eybler later wrote that he composed the oratorio "at the express command of His Majesty the Emperor for his all-highest consort [his third wife Maria Ludovica] in 1810."[41] He probably meant that Franz asked him to finish the oratorio and paid him for it.

Some time after Eybler submitted his plan for *Die vier letzten Dinge* to Marie Therese, Sonnleithner developed the material in Eybler's sketch into a libretto. He preserved Marie Therese's title and stayed very close to Eybler's sketch in most respects. For example, the plan calls for the oratorio to begin with an overture depicting "the end of all things"; in Sonnleithner's printed libretto (Vienna, 1810), the oratorio begins with an overture depicting "the

---

[39] HHStA, Fa, Sb, Kart. 66, fol. 645–6.

[40] HHStA, Fa, Sb, Kart. 65, Schriften der Höchstsel. Kaiserin: Theatralische Gegenstände, fol. 137r–138v.

[41] In an autobiographical sketch Eybler referred to *Die vier letzten Dinge* as having been "auf ausdrücklichen Befehl Sr. Maj. des Kaisers für Allerhöchst-Sie geschrieben" (*AmZ* 28 [1826], col. 339).

anxious expectation of the general destruction of things." The plan calls for a recitative for the First Archangel at the beginning of part 2: "Recitative describes how God will now stand in judgment. The trumpet sounds..." In Sonnleithner's libretto the First Archangel's speech at the beginning of part 2 includes the words "the trumpet sounds," taken directly from Eybler's sketch.

But Sonnleithner abandoned the idea that the title should be embodied in a four-part structure. He reduced Eybler's four parts to three by the simplest means: he omitted part 3, "Hölle." Since the three remaining parts are untitled in the printed libretto, the identity of the "four last things" may have been unclear to audiences. But the advantages of omitting hell from the oratorio were two: it made the work shorter and it allowed for the omission of Satan. While his appearance might have been acceptable in a private performance of Eybler's oratorio by Marie Therese, Sonnleithner (or the censors) may have felt that a public representation of the prince of evil might cause offense.

The Tonkünstler-Sozietät presented *Die vier letzten Dinge* on 15 and 16 April 1810; it was performed again as a benefit concert in the Grosser Redoutensaal on 22 April.[42] Simoni and Weinmüller took part in all three performances, creating roles to which Marie Therese herself had assigned them. The participation of two of her favorite singers may have reminded listeners that despite its being finished and performed three years after her death, Eybler's oratorio was very much a product of Marie Therese's fascination with the idea of oratorios on the Last Judgment.

---

[42] Morrow, *Concert Life*, 360.

CHAPTER 9

Il conte Clò: *A birthday cantata from inception to performance*

Marie Therese's papers document with exceptional fullness the development of *Il conte Clò*, a big comic cantata by Paer in which she celebrated her husband's birthday by parodying her own private concerts. The documents include a preliminary sketch in her hand with comments written in the margin by Paer; a plan in his hand; several letters in which he discusses the cantata; two sets of instructions by him for its performance; records of rewards the empress gave for its composition and performance; and finally the autograph score and a set of parts (partly autograph) from her library.

PLANS AND CONSULTATIONS

Among the empress's sketches is an untitled manuscript dated "805: 12 February" (appendix 5A, Fig. 9.1). The 5 is darker and larger than the other digits; it covers a digit that appears to be a 4, recording her original intention of presenting the work described in the document a year earlier. The manuscript contains two parallel columns of text. On the left is Marie Therese's plan for a musical work to celebrate Emperor Franz's birthday. On the right is Paer's response to the plan.

The empress began with a general statement of her intentions: "The idea that I have (since this year the emperor's birthday falls in Carnival) is to make a little vocal and instrumental concert in the carnivalesque genre, that is, very comic, composed of the following pieces." She mentioned nothing here or elsewhere in the sketch about plot or characters. Indeed, in referring to the work as an *accademia*, she called for a more or less plotless succession of numbers. But her subsequent comments clearly conveyed the tone of the proposed work, summing it up in one word (used twice): *bambinata* (child's play). Parody was to be the work's principal musical and comic device, especially parody of serious opera.

Marie Therese gave specific directions about the number, distribution, and types of musical pieces. She envisioned a series of ten items:

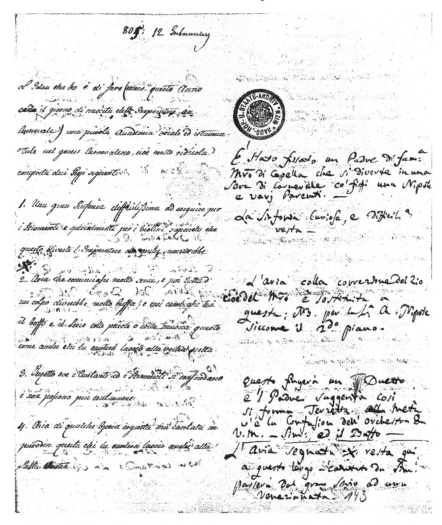

Figure 9.1 Marie Therese's sketch for the cantata *Il conte Clò* on the left, with Paer's comments on the right.

1. A grand sinfonia, very difficult for the instruments to play...
2. Aria that might begin in a very serious style, and then would suddenly become very comic...
3. Trio in which the singers and instrumentalists become confused and cannot continue.
4. Aria from some well-known opera, but sung in parody...

5. A piece of instrumental music to your taste; I would only desire that, if possible, you introduce some of those small instruments called Bertolsgadner.
6. A chorus with small solos and duets . . .
7. A quartet in which each of the singers would propose and try to imitate, but comically, some well-known singer in the serious style.
8. A serious aria with choruses that sneeze, cough, yawn, thereby making it comic.
9. Duet in which one character is completely phlegmatic and the other raving mad, with comic passages.
10. Finale mixing together singing and noisy playing . . .

Marie Therese invited Paer to change the order of these numbers or to replace any of them as he saw fit. Following her normal practice, she specified which singers were to take part, assigning the principal roles to those she called "the faithful believers": the empress herself, the amateur soprano Altamonte, the tenor Simoni, and one of three basses – Paer himself (if he were able to come to Vienna), the *basso buffo* Giambattista Brocchi, or Vogl. This was to be a domestic affair, also requiring the services of the empress's lady-in-waiting Ursula Schosulan, her chamber servants Constanze Streffler and Sebastian Schmidtmayer, and Thomas Peter Young, one of Emperor Franz's private secretaries. These courtiers "would sing in the chorus, and would also be able to play some little instruments" – presumably the Berchtesgadner Instrumente Marie Therese called for in No. 5. She told Paer that Franz himself would participate in the performance, and that the challenge posed by an unusually difficult violin part in the overture would amuse him. This was as close to musical technicality as she came in these instructions, which, like those for Paisiello and Michael Haydn, made no mention of key, mode, or meter.

In a passage that is not as clear as we might like, the empress asked Paer to prepare the text:

Because the words do not have to be in once sense [i.e. they do not have to represent a coherent drama?], each piece being by itself, I would like you to take responsibility for them as well, because I desire that the thing remain secret [from the emperor? from everyone outside the court?] and here I fear that it would not be, if the regular poet were used.

She did not say whether she expected Paer to assemble or write the words himself or to engage a poet of his choice.

Marie Therese asked Paer to supervise the copying of parts, again for the sake of secrecy. She let him decide whether or not to come to Vienna to oversee rehearsals and to take part in the performance; if he decided not to come, he was to send detailed instructions for the performance.

Without mentioning anything about paying him for his work, she ended her proposal with a characteristically charming apology and a hint of future patronage: "I am sorry about bothering you with this child's play, but I am sure that in your hands it will be a great success, and will give pleasure to him for whom it is being done, and finally the faithful [believers] must continue to receive my patronage in the new year."

In his response Paer did not mention a librettist. But the impersonal expression with which he began his remarks – "It has been decided" – suggests he was already in consultation with someone else. In other documents it emerges that he collaborated on the work that was to become known as *Il conte Clò* with Giacomo Cinti, who also prepared the libretto of *Le mine di Polonia*. Since Paer knew the empress's concerts – as a singer he took part in several of them in 1801 and 1802 – he probably helped Cinti come up with the idea of giving Marie Therese's concert a semblance of dramatic coherence and motivation by making the participants members of a family who, under the direction of a father who is also a music director, put on a private concert during a long Carnival evening. Beyond that, Paer stayed close to the empress's sketch, fleshing out her ideas with some specific names of singers and some musical titles. In response to her vague reference to "some well-known singer in the serious style" who was to be the object of imitation and parody, he mentioned Gaetano Guadagni, who had created the role of Orfeo in Gluck's *Orfeo ed Euridice* some forty years earlier; in response to her request for a serious aria rendered comic by accompanying voices that "sneeze, cough, yawn," he mentioned "Ombra adorata," the aria composed by Crescentini for Zingarelli's *Giulietta e Romeo*. He assigned arias and ensembles to the four singers who were to create the principal roles and changed the order of several numbers.

Paer informed Marie Therese in more detail about his intentions in another early plan (Appendix 5B) that gives the work a title, later abandoned: *I dilettanti di musica in famiglia*. He began with a list of roles and of the singers who were to create them. The casting of one role was still uncertain: it depended on whether Paer was able to come to Vienna himself.

A father	for me or Brocchi
A daughter	Your Majesty
A son	Sim[oni]
A niece	Alt[amonte]
The other parts are secondary	

We can see here the family taking shape. In reacting to Marie Therese's initial proposal Paer had written only of a father, "his children, a niece, and various relatives"; now the children had emerged more clearly as a son and a daughter. But he and Cinti had apparently not yet thought of names.

Paer's plan for *I dilettanti di musica in famiglia* differs only a little from his earlier remarks. He went further in specifying some of the objects of parody. Instead of mentioning one *opera seria* singer in the "Quartetto dell'imitazione" he named three (one of whom, Giacomo David, was later replaced with Matteo Babini). And taking the idea of parody even further than the empress, he referred to the finale as "L'incendio di Troia in parrodia."

Paer asked for clarification of one part of the empress's sketch. Her request for Berchtesgadner Instrumente left him mystified: "Despite extensive research I cannot identify the instrument that was described to me in the first plan, so I beg to know how one writes for it; that could be done by having sent to me a part written for such an instrument in another cantata."

COMPOSITION, COPYING, AND REHEARSALS

In Paer's letters we can follow his efforts to finish *Il conte Clò* and have it copied in time for it to be sent to Vienna (along with instructions for performance), rehearsed, and performed on 12 February 1804. He started shipments of music with some of the *parti cantanti* (announced in the undated Letter 2, probably written in late 1803), so that the soloists, including Marie Therese, could begin studying their music. The delay in the shipment of the other parts he repeatedly blamed on copyists, and he demonstrated his zeal by reporting that he himself served as copyist for some of the vocal parts.[1] On 7 February, just five days before Franz's birthday, he wrote: "I am impatient, trembling, and in the greatest state of anxiety as I wait for news of the arrival of the parts sent only on the 5th, at 8 in the morning."

With the music came letters and separate sheets of instructions that show Paer playing from afar the combined roles of conductor and stage director. Although Marie Therese had referred to the work as an *accademia* and Paer, in his letters, called it a cantata, in the score itself he called it an *opera comica*. This term helps to explain why for him the performance should constitute not a concert but the realization of a drama. Whether performed on a small stage or in a room, he wrote in his "Carta d'Istruzione per la Cantata" (appendix 5C), the work required the singers to be in costume and to act as well as sing. It was only as time grew short that he reluctantly

---

[1] Some of the vocal parts from MT's library are indeed in Paer's hand.

sanctioned a performance of the entire cantata with music in hand (rather than from memory), writing on 7 February: "Finally, it would not result in a great defect even if everything were sung from the parts." In the same letter he asked for "at least twenty-four choristers: 6 tenors, 6 altos, 6 sopranos, and 6 basses," while on a separate sheet headed "Annotazioni" (appendix 5D, Fig. 9.2) he recommended an orchestra "consisting of 8 excellent violins, as usual, and two cellos, and two double basses, etc." If we add the violas – probably two – that he inadvertently omitted, we arrive at a string ensemble of fourteen, within the range indicated by many of the empress's sets of parts.

In looking at the choral parts for *Il conte Clò* in Marie Therese's performing materials (Mus. Hs. 10043) it is difficult to tell if her choir was as large as Paer recommended, because the parts are in a state of disarray. Many of those who sang minor solo roles may have also sung in the choir, but the surviving sources do not indicate clearly who did and who did not. The string parts, however, survive in numbers exactly in keeping with the composer's recommendations: two for violin I, two for violin II, one for viola, and two for basso.

Some of Paer's comments in the "Carta d'Istruzione" give us a good idea of what he might have said at a rehearsal had he been in Vienna:

Enrichetta must be careful to observe the *forte* and the *piano* precisely... The confusion in the orchestra [an intended effect] will be clearly evident if everyone will pay attention to his part and observe the tempo exactly... I urge the rest of the choir to sing with energy and spirit, but without allowing the tempo to get too fast, which unfortunately often happens... Above all I recommend that the beginning [of the Romanza], being a pleasant, rustic melody, not be taken too slowly or too fast.

Paer, who seems to have finally understood Marie Therese's request for toy instruments, recognized the challenges presented by the *concertone*, the big instrumental piece in which they were to be played; his "Carta d'Istruzione" deals with this piece at more length than any other:

[Ubaldo's] relatives will come forward and will play the instruments described. To Sig. Brocchi will fall the playing of the horn, but only two notes ⸬ of the horn in F; and he need only count the beats, the rest will amuse. The little pipe will be tuned in high C: only that one note, of course. When the parts for this big instrumental piece arrive please bind them into the parts of each of those to whom they belong, so as to avoid confusion.

Figure 9.2 Paer's instruction for the performance of *Il conte Clò* with an illustration of "the little bells of different pitches played in Turkish bands by a single person shaking his arm." Transcribed in appendix 5.

Further instructions for playing the unconventional instruments came in the "Annotazioni":

In the instrumental piece I have marked the little bells, but these are the little bells of different pitches played in Turkish bands by a single person shaking his arm [here Paer drew a picture of the instrument he had in mind, which resembled the so-called Turkish crescent]. I have tried to see to it that the triangle goes with the little pipe, so that Sig. Ebler (or Calassanzio), in playing the triangle, will be able to conduct the little pipe, which will be played by Mad. Constanze; and they play in unison... The instruments that Ubaldo (or Brocchi) distributes should all be prepared before the concert and close at hand. The cembalino or tamburino that I desire is the one that belongs to Your Majesty, which is played with a little stick. The triangle that I prefer would be of silver, if possible, and not the bad one from the theater.

Paer suggested, in addition, a last-minute change that involved some music being shifted from one character (and one instrument) to another: "As for the harp, the adjustment can easily be achieved by changing the name – 'Tu, Luigina' (instead of Enrichetta) 'suonerai il cembalo' – and thus Your Majesty will play the cembalo, instead of asking Enrichetta to play the harp." Such improvisation must have been a frequent part of the hastily organized productions conceived and brought to fruition by Marie Therese, and it probably enhanced the excitement and pleasure that they gave her.

Again, the performance materials from Marie Therese's library document the preparations of which Paer wrote. The instrumental parts for the *concertone* include the names of the characters (and in one case the musician) who were to perform them. And Paer wrote out in his own hand the alterations that he recommended involving the transfer of Enrichetta's music to Luigina.

POSTPONEMENT

Evidently some of the parts did not get to Vienna in time for rehearsals. In her diary Marie Therese recorded gifts for Paer: "For the Kapellmeister Pär for the cantata of Clò for the 12th. A writing set of silver worth 300 fl., 500 fl. in cash."[2] But the entry is crossed out, leaving us in doubt as to whether he received the presents (Fig. 9.3). The diary mentions no other rewards or payments that can be connected to a performance of Paer's cantata in February 1804. *Das Picknick der Götter* seems to have served as the main theatrical event in celebration of Franz's birthday that year. If *Il conte Clò* was not performed until a year later that would account for the change of date on Marie Therese's sketch.

---

[2] "Dem Kapellmeister Pär für die Cantate von Clò für dem 12ten. / Ein Schreibzeug von Silber von 300 fl. / 500 fl. im Geld" (HHStA, Fa, HKF, Kart. 24, diary, fol. 206r).

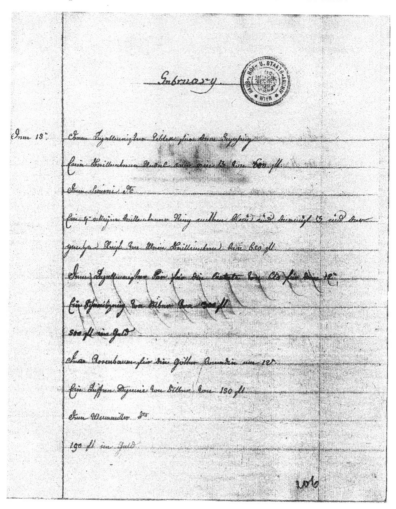

Figure 9.3 Marie Therese's diary, documenting rewards to musicians who contributed to the celebration of Emperor Franz's birthday, 12 February 1804. The record of a reward to Paer for the cantata *Il conte Clò* ("Dem Kapellmeister Pär für die Cantate von Clò für dem 12ten") has been crossed out, probably because the music arrived too late for it to be performed. At the bottom of the page are recorded gifts to Therese Rosenbaum and Carl Weinmüller for singing in Wranitzky's *Das Picknick der Götter* ("die Götter Comedie am 12ten").

On 18 August 1804 Paer promised to come to Vienna in February 1805 to take part in the postponed production of *Il conte Clò*; he confirmed his intention on 1 December, writing from Rome, where he was preparing a new opera. But just a few days before her husband's birthday Marie Therese received disappointing news, sent from Parma on 22 January 1805:

Sacred, Caesarean, Imperial, and Royal Majesty!
Following the confirmation that I submitted to Your Majesty when I was in Rome, and in accordance with the promise repeated to you that I would be in Vienna for the 12th of next February, I had cheerfully refused operatic commissions from Venice and Milan, and, because of the pleasure with which my music was heard in Rome, I was also invited to compose an opera for Naples.

All that meant more to me[3] than the high honor of placing myself at Your Majesty's Imperial and Royal Feet, and having taken the road to Lombardy with all possible speed, I intended briefly to embrace my mother in Parma and to depart again for Vienna. Before my arrival in Bologna my coach was damaged; thank God I was not hurt, but I had to travel almost a whole post on foot in the bitter cold, and on a treacherous road, which resulted in my developing a nagging constipation and a recurring fever, and although doctors have told me it will not result in serious consequences, I have however been advised to take care of myself. I am in bed, and I have been advised under no circumstances to risk the trip to Vienna, all the more so since in the last few days the weather has gotten worse. This is the only reason that I have had to break the promise I made to Your Majesty, and the only thing that consoles me is the knowledge that Your Majesty has always shown a particular goodness and mercy to me, and that even without the statement of the doctor, which I could have quoted, Your Majesty will be fully convinced of my indisposition, and that only the wish not to put my life in danger keeps me in Parma and, what is worse, without anything to do; but above all I am overflowing with sadness at not being able to be in Vienna.

Paer's sadness, I suspect, came primarily from the fear that his absence from Vienna might lead to his not receiving a reward for *Il conte Clò*. That is probably what happened. The job of conducting the cantata fell to Eybler, who further contributed to the birthday festivities by composing a ballet. For conducting the empress gave Eybler a very valuable diamond ring, for the ballet 300 Gulden in cash.[4] She also gave presents to the principal singers who joined her in the performance of *Il conte Clò*. But Paer may never have received any reward for his cantata.

---

[3] Paer wrote "Tutto era superiore," a Freudian slip. He meant to write "inferiore": "All that meant *less* to me."

[4] "February. [1805] / dem 14ten Dem Kapellmeister Eibler für die gespielte Cantate von Clò / Ein Brillantener Ring von 750 fl. / d^to für die Musik vom Ballet für dem 12. / 300 fl im Geld" (HHStA, Fa, HKA, Kart. 24, diary, fol. 216r).

PERFORMANCE

Finally performed on 12 February 1805, *Il conte Clò* lasted (if Paer's own estimate was accurate) "almost two hours."[5] It began with a trumpet fanfare "like the one in *Alceste* of Kluk," as Paer explained in his instructions.[6] In Gluck's opera (an aria from which Marie Therese sang in her concert of 7 April 1802) a fanfare precedes the herald's somber announcement that King Admetus is about to die. Paer's fanfare, in parodistic reversal, preceded the comically pompous announcement by Ubaldo, a music director (bass – the name comes from the story of Armida and Rinaldo, a favorite subject for *opera seria*), that he had organized a family concert:

> Figli, parenti, e amici filarmonici,
> Qui tutti in buona unione
> Cantar suonar si deve e star allegri.
> Siamo di carnevale
> Vicino, si può dire,
> All'ultimo momento;
> Giust'è che ci prendiamo
> Qualche divertimento:
> Del buon umor fui sempre intimo amico.

Children, relatives, and music-loving friends! Gathered here in good fellowship, we should sing, play instruments, and be jolly. We are nearly at the last moment, one might say, of Carnival; it is right that we should enjoy some entertainment, for I have always been good humor's intimate friend.

Ubaldo handed out the *parti cantanti*, referring to all the singers by name; they included his son Ambrogio (tenor), daughter Luigina (soprano), niece Enrichetta (soprano), and various friends and relatives. The concert was to be led from the keyboard by Calassanzio, to whom Ubaldo also gave his part. The other instrumental parts, he said, had already been distributed to the orchestra.

All this must have sounded amusingly familiar to the musicians assembled to perform *Il conte Clò*; they included, in addition to Marie Therese herself, in the role of Luigina, several who participated frequently in her concerts. Simoni portrayed Ambrogio, Altamonte sang Enrichetta. Eybler, as Calassanzio, took a role he often played in real life. Brocchi sang Ubaldo, the role that Paer would have sung if he had been in Vienna.

---

[5] Paer to MT, 4 January [1804].
[6] The following discussion is based on the autograph score from MT's library, Mus. Hs. 10042, and on the documents in appendix 5.

Under Ubaldo's direction his family and friends performed twelve pieces, about the same number as Marie Therese normally programmed. The concert included only two instrumental numbers, reflecting the predominance of vocal music in the empress's concerts. It began with an overture and ended with an operatic finale. The numbers in between were mostly excerpts from operas real or imagined. Just as Marie Therese's operatic concerts featured excerpts from serious or comic operas, but rarely both, this concert was dominated by a single genre, *opera seria*.

In her sketch the empress envisioned the overture as "very difficult for the instruments to play, and especially the violins, knowing that this amuses the emperor, who would also play."[7] Paer responded by giving the violins fast runs, repeated high notes, sudden changes of register, and special effects (*sul ponticello, punta d'arco*).

After the overture, as after most other numbers in the cantata, Ubaldo and his family discussed the music they had just performed or listened to. The conversation probably approximated the banter with which the empress and her musicians entertained one another during their concerts:

AMBROGIO	Signor padre mio caro,
	Mi dica, chi ha composto, in cortesia,
	Codesta stravagante sinfonia?
UBALDO	Quel che compose Achille.
AMBROGIO	Lo stile è così strano
	Ch'io ne credei l'autor un ottomano.
ENRICHETTA	Ell'è un tantin difficile,
	Ed eseguita l'hanno senza prova.
LUIGINA	L'idea è tutto nuova e sorprendente.

AMBROGIO My dear father, please tell me, who composed that peculiar symphony?
UBALDO The composer of *Achille*
AMBROGIO The style is so strange that I thought its author was a Turk.
ENRICHETTA It is a little difficult, and they played without a rehearsal.
LUIGINA The idea is completely new and surprising.

Such conversations allowed Paer to parody himself, the empress, and her private concerts with one little in-joke after another.

The reference to Paer as "the composer of *Achille*" must have been appreciated by musicians who knew Paer's serious opera and who had performed excerpts from it (including the overture) in Marie Therese's concerts. For

---

[7] The emperor's interest in musical difficulty brings to mind a comment of Grand Duke Ferdinand quoted in chapter 2. Of the musicians he had recently formed into his private orchestra he wrote: "I want to surprise them by giving them that symphony that can break one's neck, just to see what happens."

the empress herself the mention of this opera had special meaning. First performed on her birthday in 1801, *Achille* originated in a request she made to its librettist, De Gamerra. Enrichetta's reference to the lack of a rehearsal alluded amusingly to what must have been a frequent practice for Marie Therese and her musicians. And when the empress, as Luigina, commented on the *sinfonia*, she probably smiled with the knowledge that the idea of an exaggeratedly difficult overture was far from new or surprising to her, since it was her idea in the first place.

The fun continued with Enrichetta singing the aria "Qui fa le mie ritorte," while Ubaldo, *sotto voce* and *parlante*, coached her:

> Un tantinel più forte…
> Sbandite quel timore…
> Cantate un po più piano…
> Non tanto stiracchiato…
> Brava così ben va.

A little louder…Banish your fear…Sing a little more quietly…Not so strained…Brava, that's the way.

Thus Paer, Weigl, Wranitzky, Eybler, Michael Haydn, and others who wrote music for the empress probably encouraged her and her musicians during rehearsals. Likewise the compliments that Enrichetta received after her performance may have echoed the conversation during Marie Therese's concerts:

LUIGINA	Brava, cugina mia.
AMBROGIO	Brava, Enrichetta.
ENRICHETTA	Il coraggio mi manca qualche volta.
LUIGINA	Eppur cantato avete molto sciolta: Vorrei poter anch'io far lo stesso.

LUIGINA Brava, cousin.
AMBROGIO Brava, Enrichetta.
ENRICHETTA My courage fails me sometimes.
LUIGINA And yet you sang very fluently; I wish I could do the same.

Enrichetta's excuse for not doing better anticipated the empress's words to Seyfried before the rehearsal of his serenata later in 1805: "You must have patience with me; stage fright bothers me a great deal."

Ubaldo encouraged Luigina and Ambrogio to sing the next number, a duet, from memory. He offered to serve as prompter, but in doing so constantly mixed up the words. The first two lines:

> Aura amica, aura cortese,
> Zeffiretti ameni e grati

Friendly breeze, courteous breeze, zephyrs soft and gentle

became:

> Aura antica, aura cortese,
> Zuffoletti ameni e grati

Ancient breeze, courteous breeze, flageolets soft and gentle.

A sudden change in tempo led to a concluding Allegro vivace in which the two singers scolded Ubaldo for his verbal confusion.

Ambrogio's aria "Vieni al cimento" offered another kind of parody. It began as a conventional serious aria; but a switch from duple to compound meter signaled a shift to the popular style, a shift also expressed in a text in Venetian dialect. Ambrogio threw the music away in disgust:

> AMBROGIO Signor padre perdoni; io più non canto.
> UBALDO E cosa ti è saltato ora nel capo?
> AMBROGIO Di me può divertirsi quanto vuole,
> Ma non mi dee così sacrificare.
> Farmi far l'Arlecchino? E che gli pare?
> UBALDO Sei un vero lunatico!
> AMBROGIO Un cantabile in lingua veneziana?
> Si può sentir composizion più strana?

AMBROGIO Forgive me father, I will sing no more.
UBALDO What has now come into your head?
AMBROGIO You may amuse yourself at my expense as much as you like, but you must not sacrifice me thus. To make me portray Harlequin? What are you thinking?
UBALDO You are truly mad!
AMBROGIO A lyrical melody in Venetian? Is it possible to hear a stranger composition?

A wedding chorus with many short solo passages, "De' sposi novelli," gave an opportunity for the secondary characters – Ubaldo's relatives and friends Cecchina, Filippa, Menghino, Bastiano, and Carlone – to take part in the concert.

Preparations for the *concertone*, the big instrumental number that followed, involved the distribution of instruments to the singers. Fulfilling the empress's wishes, Paer included toy instruments, giving even those singers who were not able to play a conventional instrument a chance to take part:

UBALDO	Or siamo al concertone.
	Chi vuol suonar s'accosti.
	Qui vi son dei strumenti;
	Si prenda ognuno quello che gli pare.
	Tu, Luigina, che cosa vuoi suonare?
LUIGINA	Se mel permette
	Il cembalo quallor l'esecuzione
	Difficile non sia...
UBALDO	Anzi ella è molto facile.
BASTIANO	Io suonerò il flautino.
CALASSANZIO	Io prenderò la viola.
MENGHINO	Io il zuffolino.
AMBROGIO	Mi favorisca il triangolo.
CARLONE	A me il corno.
ENRICHETTA	Ed a me il tamburello.
UBALDO	Per me mi prenderò il campanello:
	Questo è quel che di meglio io posso fare.

UBALDO Now we are at the big instrumental piece. Whoever wants to play come here. Here are the instruments: everyone should take the one he or she prefers. Luigina, what do you want to play?

LUIGINA The cembalo, if you will allow me, as long as the part is not too difficult to play...

UBALDO On the contrary, it is very easy.

BASTIANO I will play the piccolo.

CALASSANZIO I will take the viola.

MENGHINO And I the flageolet.

AMBROGIO The triangle, please.

CARLONE For me the horn.

ENRICHETTA And for me the little drum.

UBALDO As for me, I will take the little bell. That is what I can play best.

Similar negotiations probably took place among Marie Therese's musicians before the performance of Wranitzky's mass with toy instruments on 28 February 1802. Luigina's line concerning the difficulty of the cembalo part recalled the empress's question to Michael Haydn about his *Missa S. Theresiae*: "You haven't made the soprano part too difficult for me? I'm singing it myself."

The young people's boasting of their ability to imitate various *opera seria* singers led to a quartet in which they did just that. Enrichetta impersonated Gasparo Pacchierotti singing "Sognai tormenti affanni" in Paisiello's *I giuochi d'Agrigento*, Luigina copied Guadagni's performance of "Che farò senza Euridice" in Gluck's *Orfeo*, and Ambrogio did Babini singing "Io t'offro in questo petto" in Paisiello's *Pirro*. (Excerpts from all these operas were performed in Marie Therese's concerts.) Ubaldo made this ensemble into a quartet by singing a comic commentary throughout. Continuing his malapropisms, he referred to the aria from *I giuochi d'Agrigento* as "l'aria dell'argento" and to Gluck's piece as "quell'aria del Morfeo"; *Pirro* he called "quel Birro di Paisiello."

The following aria with chorus, "Le dolci catene," sung by a soprano (probably Enrichetta) in the character of Circe, was evidently added to the score of *Il conte Clò* very late: no mention is made of it in documents that record the cantata's preparation. This scene made use of yet another kind of comedy by depicting the moment when Circe turns Odysseus's men into beasts. When the singers in Marie Therese's chorus portrayed the animals with nonsense syllables – "gnau" (cats), "ih ah" (donkeys), "bu bu bu" (identity unknown) – some of them probably thought of the *Sinfonia vocale* by Bohdanowicz that she had performed on 24 February 1802, with its vocal approximations of the sound of cocks, hens, cuckoos, woodpeckers, bears, and dogs.

Luigina took on the role of a shepherdess to sing a Romanza in which the carnivalesque spirit of parody was suddenly abandoned and the person for whom Marie Therese conceived the cantata openly addressed:

> Preparar pel caro sposo
> Vo di fiori una ghirlanda

I wish to prepare a garland of flowers for my dear husband.

When the empress sang these words before her husband on his birthday, one of her favorite musical devices, an accompaniment featuring a solo cello, helped to convey to Franz that the words came not from Luigina or the unnamed shepherdess she portrayed, but from Marie Therese herself. And when the chorus entered with the words

> Questo il fior ch'egli dimanda
> Nel dì sacro al suo natal

This is the flower that he demands on the day sacred to his birth.

no one participating in or listening to the performance could doubt that the birthday in question was Franz's.

Ubaldo's comic garbling of operatic titles continued in "Ombra ammalata," a parody of Crescentini's famous insertion aria for the opera that Ubaldo called *Giuletta e Borromeo*. The chorus rendered the parody even more ridiculous by frequently interrupting him with coughs, sneezes, and yawns. Marie Therese owned "Ombra adorata" in a vocal score, a full score, and a set of parts; her concert of 22 November 1801 included a performance of Crescentini's aria.

It was not until the cantata's penultimate number, a duet for Ambrogio and Luigina, that its audience discovered the meaning of its mysterious title, mentioned for the first time by Ubaldo:

> Orsù che si fa tardi, a voi miei figli,
> Al famoso duetto
> Dell'opera novella intitolata
> *Le insane gelosie del conte Clò*
> Scritta da Montezuma di Salò.

Now that it's getting late, let's move on to you, my children, and to the famous duet from the new opera entitled *Le insane gelosie del conte Clò*, written by Montezuma of Salò.

Ambrogio portrayed the insanely jealous Count Clò, Luigina his playful wife in this study of exaggeratedly contrasting personalities. Paer had recourse here to yet more operatic quotation, this time from a comic opera, Paisiello's *L'amor contrastato*. The familiar melody of "Nel cor più non mi sento," skillfully varied by Wranitzky in his Quodlibet Symphony, perfectly expressed the countess's gentle personality as she tried to calm down her raging husband. The performance won Ubaldo's applause:

> Bravi bravissimi,
> Ottimo effetto
> Fece il duetto
> Del conte Clò.

Bravi, bravissimi. The duet of conte Clò made an excellent effect.

Like most of the concerts organized by Marie Therese that consisted of excerpts from operas, Ubaldo's ended with an operatic finale. This one depicted the fall of Troy, giving Ubaldo and his family an opportunity to join together in staging an event that inspired the greatest poets and playwrights of antiquity. But Paer's reference to the finale as "L'incendio di Troia in parrodia" suggests that his intention was to make fun of a more recent treatment of the subject: Antonio Muzzarelli's heroic ballet *L'incendio e distruzione di Troia* (Vienna, 1796), whose music by Weigl Marie Therese knew; she owned an arrangement of it for piano and violin (Mus. Hs. 10993–4). Changing identity once again, Ambrogio portrayed Aeneas, Ubaldo Aeneas's father Anchises, Luigina his wife Creusa, and Enrichetta Lissandra.

Turning tragedy into comedy is often a matter of a single word here, a single unexpected sound or gesture there. Anchises made a joke of the burning of Troy by coughing in the smoke; Lissandra's stock *seria* exclamation "io gelo per l'orror" invited laughter when the orchestra's conventional depiction of shivering – repeated sixteenth notes – threatened to take over the whole finale. And any chance that someone might take this finale seriously was eliminated for good when the entire cast suddenly dropped its multiple characters, addressed Emperor Franz and his court, and, with the comic bows and curtsies prescribed by Paer in his instructions, bid them good night.

CHAPTER 10

Joseph Haydn and Beethoven between court and nobility

A certain coldness characterized relations between the Viennese nobility and the court of Franz and Marie Therese. Instead of sharing its pleasures with the aristocracy, the court tended to enjoy them in private, often in the relative isolation of Schönbrunn and Laxenburg.[1] The withdrawal of the imperial family fed resentment and rumors, as one chronicler of the time remembered:

> In the early years of the reign of Franz I, the empress's joyful caprice [*frohe Laune*] brought gaiety into Vienna's court life. In the Midsummer Night's Dream of the pleasure palace Laxenburg fantasy and humor were the favorite guests. Whoever could not offer these stayed home and subsisted on a diet of anecdotes and descriptions of the cheerful goings-on at court spread about by the usual rumor-mongers.[2]

One tale that circulated in Vienna in the late 1790s concerned Baron Gottfried van Swieten, "a patriarch of music" with "taste only for the great and the sublime."[3] As director of the court library he occupied a spacious apartment in the Hofburg. But an unpleasant incident reported in 1799 led eventually to his moving to new quarters:

> Baron van Swieten, a great friend of music, himself a good keyboard player and a skillful composer, often organized musical events at his residence, at which the music of the greatest masters was performed. One day, when great music was being given at the baron's residence before a gathering of several hundred, it happened that Their Majesties the emperor and empress were amusing themselves in the moat below, and Franz is said to have been giving the heir apparent, the little Archduke Ferdinand, a ride in a wheelbarrow. One of Van Swieten's guests saw the game and shouted out the window: "An emperor could occupy himself with more useful and respectable activities!" This voice from above struck the imperial ears like a thunderbolt.[4]

[1] Brock, *Haus der Laune*, 268–9.
[2] Schönholz, *Traditionen zur Charakteristik Oesterreichs* I, 42–3.
[3] Schönfeld, *Jahrbuch der Tonkunst von Wien und Prag*, 72.
[4] "Baron van Swieten, ein großer Freund der Musik, selbst ein guter Clavierspieler, und geschickter Tonsetzer, hat öfters Musiken bey sich, wo die Werke der größten Meisters gegeben werden. Man

Annoyed and humiliated by the aristocratic rebuke, the emperor asked Van Swieten to identify the person at the window, but he was unable or unwilling to do so. Franz later forced him to move out of his imperial apartment in punishment for his failure to identify the insulting guest.

That Van Swieten vacated his apartment is a matter of fact.[5] But even if some other parts of the story are not true, it illustrates how the aristocracy, stung by the court's self-imposed isolation, perceived its own cultural values as different from the court's, which it rejected as frivolous and childish, and saw its own musical patronage as emblematic of its superior taste.

Who were the composers whose "great music" Van Swieten presented while the emperor and empress frolicked below? He and his fellow noble connoisseurs would have agreed that Joseph Haydn and Beethoven were among "the greatest masters" living in Vienna around 1800. Van Swieten himself, a champion of Handel's oratorios, prepared the texts of *Die Schöpfung* and *Die Jahreszeiten* and encouraged Haydn to set them to music. He and Prince Joseph Johann Schwarzenberg led a society of noblemen, the Gesellschaft der Associierten Cavaliers, that presented the first performances of these oratorios in Schwarzenberg's palace and planned a performance of *Die sieben letzten Worte* that did not take place.[6] These and other members of the aristocracy also represented Beethoven's most important source of patronage. Tia DeNora has argued that the Viennese nobility's support of Beethoven constituted a self-conscious cultivation of musical greatness (at the expense of music that it viewed as merely entertaining) that bolstered its perception of itself as the vanguard of Viennese culture.[7]

As far as we know, Haydn wrote only one work for Marie Therese, the Te Deum in C. She owned relatively little music by Beethoven, and none

fügte sich, daß an einem solchen Tage, wo eben bey dem Baron große Musik und eine Gesellschaft von einegen hundert Personen war, Ihre Majestäten der Kaiser und die Kaiserin in dem Graben sich erlustigten, und Franz, seinen künftigen Thronfolger, den kleinen Erzherzog Ferdinand, in der Schieb-Truhe [footnote: Im Schiebkarren] herumgefahren haben soll. Einer der anwesenden Gäste sah dieses Spiel, und rief zum Fenster hinaus: Ein Kaiser könnte sich auch auf eine nützlichere und anständigere Art beschäftigen! Diese Stimme aus der Luft war ein Donnerschlag in den kaiserlichen Ohren" (*Beytrag zur Characteristik*, 233).

5 Walther Brauneis, "Marginalien zur Biographie von Gottfried van Swieten: Kulturminister, Bibliothekar und Musikfreund," typescript of a forthcoming article; my thanks to Brauneis for allowing me to see a copy.

6 *Griesingers Korrespondenz*, 49; Landon, *Haydn* IV, 253; Morrow, *Concert Life*, 400.

7 Tia DeNora, *Beethoven and the Construction of Genius: Musical Politics in Vienna, 1792–1803*, Berkeley, 1995.

of it found a place in the concerts documented in her diary.[8] Clearly her relations with them were not as close or as fruitful as those she maintained with Michael Haydn, Wranitzky, Weigl, Paer, and Eybler. It is tempting to view her relations with Joseph Haydn and Beethoven as symptomatic of the cultural divide that separated the court from the aristocracy and of the isolation to which the empress and her court sometimes withdrew, isolation not only physical but also psychological and aesthetic.

Yet the distance between the court and the aristocracy was not as great as it might appear, at least in musical matters. The empress and the nobility patronized many of the same musicians. Aristocratic music lovers enjoyed the works of her favorite composers. Although Joseph Haydn and Beethoven were never among her "faithful believers," they nevertheless accepted her patronage and allowed her tastes to shape some of their music.

We know the complete contents of very few of the nobility's private concerts during the period covered by the empress's diary, but what we do know suggests some of those concerts resembled hers quite closely. Prince Schwarzenberg, Count Moritz Fries, and Baron Braun presented concerts that to a large extent shared their repertory with Marie Therese's.[9] Van Swieten bestowed patronage more widely than his reputation as "patriarch of music" might suggest. He distributed tickets for a concert in 1786 in which Dittersdorf presented the first six of his characteristic symphonies on Ovid's *Metamorphoses*, which Marie Therese probably owned.[10] He attended a rehearsal of church music by Gyrowetz, some of whose sacred works the empress owned, and praised the composer personally.[11] The second Prince Nicolaus Esterházy, Joseph Haydn's employer since 1794, shared Marie Therese's interest in the music of Michael Haydn (whom he tried to engage) and Albrechtsberger. After their deaths, he bought from their widows vast quantities of their autograph manuscripts, including most of the music they had written for Marie Therese.[12]

---

[8] In addition to the Septet, Op. 20 (to be discussed below), MT owned the Piano Trios, Op. 1 (*CaM*, p. 71), three sets of variations for piano (*CaM*, p. 80), and keyboard transcriptions of the Twelve Minuets (WoO 7, *CaM*, p. 90) and the Twelve German Dances (WoO 8, *CaM*, p. 92).

[9] Morrow, *Concert Life*, 395–400.

[10] Dittersdorf, *Lebensbeschreibung*, 230. MT owned a set of "6 characterische Synfonien" by Dittersdorf (*CaM*, p. 57), almost certainly the first six Ovid symphonies.

[11] Adalbert Gyrowetz, *Biographie*, ed. Alfred Einstein, Leipzig, 1915, 108–9. For MT's holdings of church music by Gyrowetz see appendix 1.

[12] On Prince Esterházy's acquisition of these autographs, now in H-Bn, see Carl Ferdinand Pohl, *Joseph Haydn*, 3 vols. (3rd. vol. completed by Hugo Botstiber), Berlin and Leipzig, 1875–1927, III, 252, and László Somfai, "Albrechtsberger-Eigenschriften in der Nationalbibliothek Széchényi, Budapest," Part 1, *Studia Musicologica Academiae Scientiarum Hungaricae* 1 (1961), 176–7.

The empress respected the aristocracy's musical taste and learned from it. Her private performances of oratorio and church music, for example, probably owed something to the example of Van Swieten's private concerts in the 1780s. Weigl, who witnessed some of those concerts and could have told her about them, remembered: "Every Sunday at twelve noon there was music at his residence. Only compositions by Bach, Handel, Graun, and others among the oldest and most famous masters were performed. Mozart accompanied at the fortepiano. Salieri, Starzer, Teiber and the baron sang. The pleasure that we experienced cannot be imagined."[13] The empress's concerts included Graun's Te Deum and *Der Tod Jesu* and choruses from Handel's *Judas Maccabaeus*; she owned the arrangement of *Messiah* that Mozart made for Van Swieten (Mus. Hs. 9879–80) and works by Michael Haydn that Van Swieten may have performed.[14] (But Weigl's account suggests two ways in which her private performances of church music and oratorio differed from Van Swieten's. He was satisfied with a piano accompaniment and one singer on a part; she performed with orchestra and chorus. He preferred Protestant composers, she Catholic.)

Marie Therese also differed from Van Swieten and some members of his circle in her cultivation of contemporary liturgical music. Less of an antiquarian than the baron, she commissioned many masses, as we have seen, some of them to celebrate her husband's birthday and nameday. In this respect she closely resembled Prince Esterházy, who between 1794 and 1810 commissioned over fifteen masses – from Albrechtsberger, Beethoven, Gyrowetz, Joseph Haydn, Hummel, and others – several of them performed in celebration of his wife's nameday.[15]

Although Esterházy's cultivation of the mass paralleled Marie Therese's very closely in both function and chronology, in one respect they differed. He did not share her interest in the plenary mass. Most of the Esterházy masses consisted of settings of the Ordinary alone (an apparent exception: Albrechtsberger's *Missa Assumptionis*, for which he probably wrote the gradual "Propter veritatem" and the offertory "Assumpta es Maria"[16]).

---

[13] Weigl, "Zwei Selbstbiographien," 53.

[14] Writing to his father on 12 March 1783, Mozart asked him to send scores of some of his (Wolfgang's) masses and vespers, and a score of Michael Haydn's "Tres sunt"; he expressed a wish that Van Swieten's musical collaborators might hear Haydn's "Lauda Sion" (*Mozart: Briefe und Aufzeichnungen* III, 259). MT owned copies of both "Tres sunt" and "Lauda Sion."

[15] Jeremiah W. McGrann, "Of Saints, Name Days, and Turks: Some Background on Haydn's Masses Written for Prince Nikolaus II Esterházy," *Journal of Musicological Research* 17 (1998), 195–210.

[16] Schröder A.I.18, B.II.8, and C.I.13. The prince's payment to Albrechtsberger in 1809 for a "Coral Messe samt graduale und Offertorium" was probably for the *Missa Assumptionis*; see Somfai, "Albrechtsberger-Eigenschriften," Part 1, 176.

But in her advocacy of the plenary mass Marie Therese did have at least one follower in the aristocracy, as we will see below.

PRINCE LOBKOWITZ AND THE EMPRESS

Prince Joseph Franz Maximilian Lobkowitz, remembered mostly for his patronage of Beethoven, was no more exclusive than other noble music lovers; indeed his tastes seem to have been particularly close to Marie Therese's. Exactly the same age as she, he shared with her a passion for contemporary Italian opera, collecting as many operas by Mayr and Paer as she did.[17] Among several musicians who benefitted about equally from Marie Therese and Lobkowitz was Anton Reicha, who arrived in Vienna in 1802 and spent about six years there. The empress commissioned from him an Italian opera, *Argene regina di Granata*, and performed excerpts from it; Lobkowitz gave a concert performance of the opera *L'Ouragan*.[18]

Marie Therese's commissioning of two oratorios from Cartellieri paid tribute to Lobkowitz, whom he served from 1798 to 1807 as violinist, composer, and singing teacher. The prince, in turn, bought copies of several cantatas Weigl had written for the empress's private use.[19] Since he obtained these cantatas between January 1806 and July 1807, and since Weigl is unlikely to have sold him copies while the empress was alive, I suspect Weigl took advantage of her death in April 1807 to make music written for her available to Lobkowitz. In 1811 the prince paid Weigl 1,000 Gulden for the dedication of another score written for the empress (and for which she had already generously rewarded him), *La passione di Gesù Cristo*.[20]

Marie Therese's interest in the plenary mass probably inspired Lobkowitz to acquire at least two such pieces. In 1803 or 1804 he bought a manuscript

[17] Milada Jonásová, "Le rappresentazioni delle opere di Giovanni Simone Mayr a Praga. Le fonti a Praga, a Dresda e in Italia," paper read at the conference "Simon Mayr und Wien," Ingolstadt, 4–7 Oktober 2001. My thanks to Jonásová for sending me a copy of part of the inventory of the Lobkowitz-Sammlung recording its extensive holdings of operas by Paer.

[18] *Notes sur Antoine Reicha*, 24. About *Argene* Reicha states: "Cette musique était destinée à être exécutée dans les appartemens de l'Impératrice, ce qui eut lieu en effet et Marie-Thérèse elle-même y chanta." That MT performed the whole opera is doubtful, because although she owned a score (Mus. Hs. 9993), she owned parts for only a finale (Mus. Hs. 10687) and for a cavatina, recitative, and duet (Mus. Hs. 10688).

[19] On 13 January 1808, Lobkowitz signed a bill from the copyist Sukowaty that refers to music acquired by the prince between January 1806 and July 1807, including Weigl's *Le pazzie musicali*, *La festa di Carolina negli Elisi*, *Il miglior dono*, and *L'amor filiale* ("Conto Für gelieferte Musikalien und Copiaturen S.ʳ Durchlaucht Fürst v: Lobkowitz von ersten Jänner 1806. bis letzten July 1807," reproduced in facsimile in Jaroslav Macek, "Die Musik bei den Lobkowicz," *Ludwig van Beethoven im Herzen Europas*, ed. Oldřich Pulkert and Hans-Werner Küthen, Prague, 2000, 194 and 199).

[20] Jaroslav Macek, "Franz Joseph Maximilian Lobkowitz: Musikfreund und Kunstmäzen," *Beethoven und Böhmen*, ed. Sieghard Brandenburg and Martella Gutiérrez-Denhoff, Bonn, 1988, 170.

described in the copyist's bill as "Missa. Graduale. Offertorium. Introitus d'abb: Vogler," a plenary mass that differed from Marie Therese's in having an introit instead of a Te Deum.[21] In 1811 he celebrated the marriage of his eldest daughter with a mass with gradual and offertory composed by his Kapellmeister Anton Wranitzky.[22]

Paer's letters give the impression that during his occasional visits to Vienna (after establishing himself in Dresden in 1802) he divided his time fairly evenly between Lobkowitz and Marie Therese. Their competition for his services led to an embarrassing incident that resulted from his using the Lobkowitz palace as his postal address in Vienna. The empress having commissioned Paer to compose *Le mine di Polonia*, he arranged with Cinti to write the libretto. But before Paer had a chance to set it to music the libretto went astray:

> My friend Cinti, who had the honor of writing for Your Majesty the cantata *Conte Clò*, applied himself with equally tireless labor to the opera *Le mine di Polonia*, which Your Majesty had the goodness of sending to Dresden last year. Thinking that I was in Vienna (when unfortunately I was unable to make the trip) he sent the libretto to me there, arranged and translated into Italian for use as a drama. The libretto – or rather the letter with a package – went to the residence of Prince Lobkowitz, and just today I received news from the prompter of the Italian opera in Vienna that the above-mentioned gentleman opened the package and kept the libretto. That does not seem possible to me. But if it happened, it is an obvious sign that the prince (whom I greatly venerate and admire) did not know that the drama was destined for Your Majesty's service.
>
> Therefore I beg my sole and adored patroness to deign to inquire after the libretto through some third party, without Your Majesty's making an appearance, but making it understood that the libretto belongs to Your Majesty.
>
> Poor Cinti, who translated it, is desolate, fearing that some conspiracy has prevented him from receiving credit for it.[23]

Lobkowitz's apparently innocent mistake masked a rivalry that had surfaced two years earlier. When Van Swieten died in 1803, the empress and the prince vied with one another to buy his music library.[24] A contest over the

---

21 "Conto Gelieferte Musikalien S.ʳ Durchlaucht Fürst di Lobkowitz von ersten April 1803 bis 18ᵗᵉⁿ Juny 1804," illustrated in Jana Fojtíková and Tomislav Volek, "Die Beethoveniana der Lobkowitz-Musiksammlung und ihre Kopisten," *Beethoven und Böhmen*, 234–5.

22 Macek, "Die Musik bei den Lobkowicz," 200.

23 Paer to MT, Bologna, 2 April 1805.

24 Griesinger to Breitkopf & Härtel, 7 May 1803, *Griesingers Korrespondenz*, 193. In this competition MT may have been partly successful. Several items in her library may have come from Van Swieten's *Nachlass*. Her score of Mozart's concert aria "Non temer amato bene," K. 505 (Mus. Hs. 10567) is inscribed with Van Swieten's name (the title page is illustrated in Edge, *Mozart's Viennese Copyists*, 721). Her copies of Mozart's arrangement of Handel's *Messiah* and of choral music of the Bach

baron's library was perhaps, in part, a contest over who was to inherit the mantle of "patriarch of music."

HAYDN

The empress frequently demonstrated her interest in Joseph Haydn and his music. She owned copies of fifteen of his symphonies and eight of his masses; helped him obtain the use of the Burgtheater for the first public performance of *Die Schöpfung*; allowed her name to appear at the top of the list of subscribers included in the first edition of the full score of that oratorio; participated in performances of *Die Schöpfung*, *Die Jahreszeiten*, and *Die sieben letzten Worte*, some led by the composer himself; commissioned an Italian translation of the text of *Die Schöpfung*; and owned a plenary *Missa ex Creatione mundi*, arranged from the oratorio by an unknown composer.

Marie Therese's dealings with Haydn's late oratorios exemplify the close connections between her patronage and that of the aristocracy and the mutual influence that characterized those connections. *Die Schöpfung* and *Die Jahreszeiten* were very much products of Van Swieten's circle, as institutionalized in the Gesellschaft der Associierten Cavaliers. The society's patronage influenced the empress's choice of musicians as well as her repertory. The three soloists in the premiere of *Die Schöpfung* in 1798 – Frank, Rathmayer, and Saal – all later sang with her. She in turn influenced the nobility's perception of *Die Schöpfung* by having Carpani make an Italian translation of the text, which the aristocracy welcomed. On 4 April 1801 Lobkowitz presented the first performance of *La creazione del mondo* in his palace in Vienna.[25]

Given Marie Therese's obvious admiration for Haydn's music, her frequent performances of it, and her personal acquaintance with him, the fact that he wrote only a single work for her calls for some explanation. Several obstacles seem to have blocked the way of commissions that might otherwise have come from her or kept him from accepting such commissions. One was his advanced age. In 1800, just as she was becoming most active as a commissioner of major musical works, his compositional energy was

---

family possibly came from the same source. On Van Swieten's library see Andreas Holschneider, "Die musikalische Bibliothek Gottfried van Swietens," *Bericht über den Internationalen Musikwissenschaftlichen Kongress, Kassel, 1962*, ed. Georg Reichert and Martin Just, Kassel, 1963, 174–8.

[25] Georg Feder, *Joseph Haydn: Die Schöpfung*, Kassel, 1999, 169. The performance might give the erroneous impression that Lobkowitz commissioned the translation; so too Carpani's account of the occasion: "Venne poi eseguita per la prima volta in casa del mecenate della musica, il generoso signor principe *Lobkowitz*, che tutto se stesso sembra aver consacrato all'aumento delle Bell'Arti ed al piacere de' suoi simili" (Carpani, *Le Haydine*, 190–1).

beginning to flag; after the completion of *Die Jahreszeiten* in 1801 and the "Harmoniemesse" in 1802 he wrote very little. Other obstacles had to do with Haydn's aristocratic patrons, at least one of whom urged him not to accept a major commission from the empress.

THE LAST JUDGMENT

Shortly after the first performance of *Die Jahreszeiten* rumors began to circulate of Haydn's interest in writing an oratorio on the Last Judgment. The subject came up perhaps for the first time in a somewhat negative report of the premiere of *Die Jahreszeiten* itself, dated 25 April 1801: "Even during the composition [of that oratorio], Herr Haydn stated he would rather have composed another subject than the four seasons, for example the Last Judgment or something similar."[26] With *Die Jahreszeiten* behind him, Haydn began work on the Last Judgment in earnest, if we can believe a report published in the *Pressburger Zeitung* on 29 September:

enjoined by his closest friends and by Europe's finest musicians, rather than acting on his own volition, he has decided, however, to muster all his powers once more before his life's end, and to set the Last Judgment. He has already made noticeable progress. Experts who have seen the beginning of the work maintain that in every chord the composer has immortalized himself anew and has placed himself quite beyond reach.[27]

Griesinger denied the report in a letter of 21 October, but in doing so revealed that not only Haydn's friends and musical colleagues were pressing him to write another oratorio:

The rumor that Haydn is composing The Last Judgment is completely without foundation, but it is true that the empress wanted to urge him to do it; and a composer with whom Haydn talked about it assured me that Haydn would have treated the subject in a very original and in no way objectionable style.[28]

The talk refused to subside, and when Griesinger addressed it again on 4 November, he referred to Marie Therese's wishes in the present tense:

The empress still wants the composition of the Last Judgment; but Swieten is very much against it. In the meantime a young poet from here is undertaking an arrangement of the text in four parts: Death, Resurrection, Hell, Heaven. Haydn

---

[26] *Zeitung für die elegante Welt*, quoted in translation (used here) in H. C. Robbins Landon and David Wyn Jones, *Haydn: His Life and Music*, Bloomington, Ind., 1988, 309.

[27] "Musik zur Zeit Haydns und Beethovens in der Pressburger Zeitung," ed. Marianne Pandi and Fritz Schmidt, *Haydn Jahrbuch* 8 (1971), 207; translation (used here), 281.

[28] Griesinger to Breitkopf & Härtel, 21 October 1801, *Griesingers Korrespondenz*, 99.

could still give in; he says the idea seems crude, but is perfect for the use of musical representation on a grand scale.[29]

In her efforts to persuade Haydn to write yet another oratorio the empress was usurping Van Swieten's place as his oratorical muse. No wonder the aged baron argued against his undertaking the project!

By the time Griesinger, on 21 April 1802, wrote of the projected oratorio as "ein grosses Werk," it had drifted nearer to reality, despite Van Swieten's objections:

The empress and many other persons, too, are urging him to *undertake one more great work*, and he would be very much inclined to do so if he only knew of a useful text... He thinks that the Last Judgment would offer rich material, namely in the first part death, in the second the resurrection, in the third hell and heaven... Haydn would work at it *con amore*, the more so since it would be fulfilling a favorite idea of the empress. Haydn also wishes that Wieland [to whom he hoped to entrust the libretto] would send the text directly to the empress with a request to Haydn to compose it. It would certainly be well received, and the empress would feel herself flattered to participate in such a work.[30]

Seven months later Haydn was "still longing for a libretto on the Last Judgment," as Griesinger put it, while Marie Therese had emerged as an arbiter of competing texts. The author of such a libretto should not expect to be paid by Haydn: "Rather he should send it, with a reference to Haydn's proposal, directly to the empress, and should take a chance on his work winning the prize among the competing entries. Haydn wants to set the text the empress sends him."[31]

Was the Last Judgment as a subject for oratorio Haydn's idea or Marie Therese's? Griesinger's letters are ambiguous, but in calling it "a favorite idea of the empress" he suggests that Haydn got the idea from her. The structure of the proposed work, especially as described by Griesinger in his letter of 4 November 1801, was very close to that of her sketches (discussed in chapter 8) that bore fruit, eventually, in Salieri's *Gesù al Limbo* and Eybler's *Die vier letzten Dinge*.

THE "SCHÖPFUNGSMESSE"

The interest in modern church music that Marie Therese shared with Prince Esterházy led them to covet each other's music. Shortly after

[29] Griesinger to Breitkopf & Härtel, 4 November 1801, *Griesingers Korrespondenz*, 104.
[30] Griesinger to Breitkopf & Härtel, 21 April 1802, *Griesingers Korrespondenz*, 161–2. Translation (used here) in Landon, *Haydn* V, 225.
[31] Griesinger to Breitkopf & Härtel, 10 November 1802, *Griesingers Korrespondenz*, 171–2.

the first performances of Joseph Haydn's "Schöpfungsmesse" at Eisenstadt (13 September 1801) and of Michael Haydn's *Missa S. Theresiae* at Laxenburg (4 October 1801), the empress asked the prince for a copy of the "Schöpfungsmesse." He responded that he would have a copy made, but only in exchange for a copy of the *Missa S. Theresiae*.[32] She must have agreed, for she eventually obtained a copy of the "Schöpfungsmesse." But she was not satisfied with merely owning it; she asked Haydn to alter it. Griesinger wrote:

In the mass that Haydn wrote in 1801 it occurred to him in the *Agnus Dei qui tollis peccata mundi* that frail mortals sinned mostly against moderation and purity. So he set the words *qui tollis peccata, peccata mundi* to the trifling melody of the words in *The Creation, Der thauende Morgen, o wie ermuntert er!* [The dew-dropping morn, oh, how she quickens all!] But in order that this profane thought should not be too conspicuous, he let the *Miserere* sound in full chorus immediately thereafter. In the copy of this mass that he made for the Empress, he had to alter the place at her request.[33]

This account, while mistakenly referring to the Agnus Dei rather than the Gloria as the site of Haydn's quotation from the amorous duet "Holde Gattin," is partly confirmed by a manuscript copy of the "Schöpfungsmesse" formerly in the archive of the Hofkapelle, which probably came there from Marie Therese's library. In it Haydn replaced the brief quotation from *Die Schöpfung* with a newly composed passage.[34]

But that leaves unanswered the question of why she asked Haydn to make this change. Did she object to Haydn's quoting from another work? To the "trifling," *Singspiel*-like (hence "profane") melody? To the words associated with the tune, especially "ermuntert," which might (in the context of a duet sung by a husband and wife) have conveyed connotations of sexual arousal?

Griesinger's implication that Marie Therese objected to the quotation from "Holde Gattin" as unsuitably "profane" does not correspond well with what we know of her. From her possession of the *Missa ex Creatione mundi* it is obvious she did not object to the quotation of music from *Die Schöpfung* in a mass. Far from avoiding the mixture of sacred and secular, she delighted in it. She performed Wranitzky's mass with toy instruments. She owned

---

[32] Griesinger to Breitkopf & Härtel, 11 November 1801, *Griesingers Korrespondenz*, 105.

[33] Georg August Griesinger, *Biographische Notizen über Joseph Haydn*, Leipzig, 1810, translation (used here) in Vernon Gotwals, *Haydn: Two Contemporary Portraits*, Madison, Wis., 1968, 62–3.

[34] Landon, *Haydn* V, 200–1; *Joseph Haydn in seiner Zeit*, 495; Karl Pfannhauser, "Glossarien zu Haydns Kirchenmusik," *Joseph Haydn: Bericht über den Internationalen Joseph Haydn Kongress*, ed. Eva Badura-Skoda, Munich, 1986, 596–601.

the comic "Schulmeister-Messe," evidently not sharing Michael Haydn's unwillingness (stated when he denied authorship of it) "to make serious or devout texts laughable."[35] When she organized a public performance of Paer's *Il trionfo della chiesa* in 1804 she expressed no qualms about what one critic perceived as the music's lack of sacred tone.[36] Her musical celebrations of Franz's nameday and birthday, bringing together plenary masses, balls, plays, and secular cantatas, rejoiced in the musical juxtaposition of sacred and profane. Nor did she object to Michael Haydn's introduction of sexual innuendo into the *Missa S. Theresiae* by setting to music, in a gradual commissioned by her to celebrate her husband's nameday, the words "knock, and it shall be opened unto you."

I suggest that the empress, frustrated by her inability to persuade Joseph Haydn to write anything other than the Te Deum, and at the difficulty in obtaining even a mass that he had written for a competing collector of church music, used his quotation from "Holde Gattin" as an excuse to ask him to do something, even something small, for her alone: as a way to impose her individuality on a work written for someone else.

THE "THERESIENMESSE"

Another way in which Marie Therese could approximate the effect of having a piece written for her by Haydn was by accepting from him a copy made under his supervision, and perhaps even an autograph score. Although Haydn almost certainly wrote his mass in Bb of 1799, like his other late masses, for Prince Esterházy, by 1815 it was known as the "Theresienmesse."[37] H. C. Robbins Landon has suggested that the nickname arose from Haydn's having "rededicated the work, as it were, to his Empress" by giving her a set of manuscript parts and possibly the autograph score as well. Landon discovered in the archive of the Hofkapelle a manuscript of the mass copied partly by Johann Elssler, one of the copyists closest to Haydn. He concluded that it "is now certain" that Haydn gave Marie Therese a copy of the "Theresienmesse."[38] The presence of parts copied by Elssler in the Hofkapelle does not prove that she owned those parts, but it certainly

---

[35] See chapter 1, n. 59.   [36] *AmZ* 6 (1803–4), col. 620, quoted in chapter 7.

[37] According to Landon, *Haydn* IV, 475, "authentic performance material of the Mass in the Eisenstadt Archives, where it is entitled 'Anno 1799', and contains many corrections and additions in Haydn's hand," indicates "that the first performance *probably* took place at Eisenstadt" (italics mine); see also McGrann, "Of Saints, Namedays, and Turks." Günter Thomas, in the foreword to his edition of the mass in the Joseph Haydn Werke, Messen Nr. 9–10, Munich, 1965, traced the title "Theresienmesse" back to 1815.

[38] Landon, *Haydn* IV, 475.

increases the probability that she did, given that her collection of church music went to the Hofkapelle after her death.

As for the autograph score, Landon wrote: "It seems likely that the Empress had the autograph manuscript for a time (it is now owned by the Austrian National Library)."[39] Consistent with her ownership is the fact that, of eight masses by Haydn in her collection, only one, in Bb, was in score as well as parts (see appendix 1). Could that score have been the autograph of the "Theresienmesse," transferred to the Hofkapelle in 1807 and later to the Hofbibliothek or its successor the Nationalbibliothek?

An inventory preserved in the Nationalbibliothek suggests the answer is no. It indicates that the autograph of the "Theresienmesse" came not from the Hofkapelle but from a private collection, as part of a donation made on 3 February 1826 by one Michael Bartenschlag.[40] A financial official at court (*Hofzahlamtskontrolleur*), Bartenschlag was an amateur composer and timpanist, and evidently a collector of some importance.[41] When and how he obtained Haydn's autograph is unknown. But it is unlikely that he got it from the empress or, after her death, from the Hofkapelle.

THE TE DEUM FOR THE EMPRESS

We do not know the occasion for which Haydn wrote the Te Deum in C major for Marie Therese. She may have owned the autograph score (the inventory of her church music lists a "Te Deum in C maggiore. Partitura e parti cavate"); but the autograph, which was probably dated, is lost. An approximate date can be deduced from two of Griesinger's letters to Breitkopf & Härtel and from a receipt for copying expenses signed by Haydn. On 25 May 1799 Griesinger reported that Haydn had "to take care of old orders for the empress, Prince Esterhazy, and many other wealthy Viennese."[42] The Te Deum must have been finished by October 1800, when Haydn signed a receipt "for the copying of my Te Deum."[43] A little more than a year later, on 11 November 1801, Griesinger included in a list of Haydn's recent works "a Te Deum that he wrote for the empress two or

---

[39] Ibid.

[40] *Erwerbungs-Nachweis*, A-Wn, Suppl. Mus. 2485, INV III Tabulae 2), fol. 10r. My thanks to Sven Hansell for consulting this inventory and examining the autograph score of the Theresienmesse. I am also grateful to Robert von Zahn (Haydn-Institut, Cologne) for valuable help in tracing the provenance of the autograph. For further discussion of the autograph's history see Thomas's foreword to the edition of the mass in the Joseph Haydn Werke.

[41] Holschneider, "Die musikalische Bibliothek Gottfried van Swietens," 176. My thanks to Dexter Edge for sharing with me his notes on Bartenschlag.

[42] *Griesingers Korrespondenz*, 27.   [43] Landon, *Haydn* IV, 562.

three years ago."[44] Haydn probably wrote the Te Deum in 1799 or 1800; but for what reason?

The empress owned several settings of the Te Deum that were apparently independent works, by Ferdinando Bertoni, Graun, Gyrowetz, Hasse, Justin Heinrich Knecht, Paisiello, and Sterkel. She might have commissioned Haydn to add to this group. However, her practice of commissioning and performing plenary masses that include the Te Deum suggests the possibility that she ordered Haydn's Te Deum to complete a plenary mass consisting mostly of Haydn's music. Earlier I called the *Missa ex Creatione mundi* a plenary mass; but it is incomplete, containing only the Ordinary, a gradual, and an offertory. Was it perhaps to complete this plenary mass that she commissioned the Te Deum? In the introduction to a recent edition of the Te Deum, the editor points to musical parallels between it and *Die Schöpfung*.[45] Those parallels would obviously enhance the effect of the Te Deum's serving as the final part of the *Missa ex Creatione mundi*.

Several of what we might think of as the most characteristic features of Haydn's Te Deum can be explained with reference to other settings of the same text made for Marie Therese as part of plenary masses. 193 measures long, Haydn's Te Deum is matched in brevity by Albrechtsberger's Te Deum "für die Kaiserin" of 1803, which is just three measures longer. The four-part structure – a fast movement, a short slow movement beginning "Te ergo quaesimus," a fast movement beginning "Aeterna fac," and a concluding fugue beginning "In te Domine speravi" – is found in settings by Albrechtsberger, Eybler, and Michael Haydn that the empress owned. Joseph Haydn's Te Deum has no parts for vocal soloists, and in this too it resembles several of the other settings made for Marie Therese. Some early manuscript sources for Haydn's work, including sources in the Hofkapelle that may have been copied from the autograph, lack the eight-measure orchestral introduction, which led Landon to suppose that Haydn originally intended for the Te Deum to begin with chorus and orchestra together.[46] That supposition is corroborated by the many other settings of the Te Deum owned by Marie Therese that lack an orchestral introduction or have one of less than one measure. Nor was Haydn alone in his use of the Eighth Psalm-Tone as an opening theme. In three of Eybler's settings

[44] Griesinger, *Korrespondenz*, 105. See Irmgard Becker-Glauch, "Joseph Haydns Te Deum für die Kaiserin: Eine Quellenstudie," *Colloquium amicorum: Joseph Schmidt-Görg zum 70. Geburtstag*, ed. Siegfried Kross and Hans Schmidt, Bonn, 1967, 1–10.

[45] *Te Deum for the Empress Marie Therese*, ed. Denis McCaldin, Oxford, 1992.

[46] Landon, *Haydn* IV, 606.

(the Te Deum in C, Herrmann 117, and both versions of the Te Deum in B♭, Herrmann 120) the chorus enters with a quotation of the same chant.

HAYDN'S CAPRICE: MARIE THERESE AND
THE SYMPHONY "IL DISTRATTO"

One aspect of Haydn's artistic personality that Marie Therese must have found particularly attractive was his caprice, or what his German admirers often called *Laune*: his capacity for the musical expression of the bizarre, the unexpected, and the comic. A critic writing in 1803 compared the symphonies of Mozart and Haydn in terms that help to explain why the empress preferred the latter: "Mozart's symphonies are colossal, rocky peaks, wild and luxuriant, surrounding a gently smiling valley; Haydn's are Chinese gardens, composed with cheerful humor and mischievous caprice." Beethoven, wrote the same critic (who could have known only the first two symphonies), "combines Mozart's universality and wild, luxuriant daring with Haydn's humorous caprice."[47]

Within a few months of the publication of those words Marie Therese asked Haydn for performance materials for one of the most explicitly capricious of his symphonies, No. 60: "Il distratto." On 5 June 1803 Haydn wrote to Prince Esterházy's oboist Joseph Elssler, asking him to pass on a request to the prince's archivist to lend him the parts for Symphony No. 60 for a few days, because "Her Majesty the empress longs to hear the old pancake" ("den alten Schmarn").[48] Her longing for this thirty-year old symphony must have been strong indeed for it to overcome her predilection for contemporary music.

Symphony No. 60 consists of six movements that Haydn probably wrote as an overture and incidental music for a production of Jean-François

---

[47] "Die Mozartschen Symphonieen sind kolossale Felsenmassen, wild und üppig, die ein sanftes lachendes Thal umschließen; die Haydnschen chinesische Gärten, von heiterm Humor und muth-williger Laune geschaffen . . . Beethoven . . . vereinigt mit Mozart's Universalität und wilder üppiger Kühnheit Haydn's humoristische Laune" (*Musikalisches Taschenbuch auf das Jahr 1803*, ed. Julius Werden and Adolph Werden, Penig, [1803], 79. For several other instances of the word *Laune* in early Haydn criticism see Mark Evan Bonds, "Haydn, Laurence Sterne, and the Origins of Musical Irony," *Journal of the American Musicological Society* 44 (1991), 57–91, and Gretchen Wheelock, *Haydn's Ingenious Jesting with Art: Contexts of Musical Wit and Humor*, New York, 1992.

[48] Haydn, *Gesammelte Briefe und Aufzeichnungen*, ed. Dénes Bartha, Kassel, 1965, 426; translation (used here, with some changes) in Landon, *Haydn*, V, 262. On the meaning of *Schmarn* and its relevance to the symphony, see Daniel Heartz, *Haydn, Mozart, and the Viennese School, 1740–1780*, New York, 1995, 366. My thanks to Heartz for telling me of Haydn's letter.

Regnard's comedy *Le distrait* at Eszterháza in 1774.[49] Shortly after the first performance the *Pressburger Zeitung* praised it:

> One notices the same spirit that animates all of Haydn's works, this time in a caprice involving music and comedy [derselben in einer musikalisch-komischen Laune]. It alternates in a masterly way between astonishing connoisseurs and delighting ordinary listeners; it descends from the most emotional bombast into vulgarity, so that Haydn and Regnard compete with one another in capricious absentmindedness [wer am launischsten zerstreut].[50]

"Capricious absentmindedness" is the dominant quality of this symphony, as Daniel Heartz has written in reference to the comments of the *Pressburger Zeitung*:

> Musical non sequiturs such as occur in the first movement and the exotic scale in the trio of the Menuetto do indeed convey a sense of caprice and of having lost the thread of the argument. The way the *Allegro di molto* first movement gets sidetracked onto a long held subdominant chord offers another case in point. And Haydn makes use of several popular tunes, or what sound like popular tunes (one has been identified as the "Night-Watchman's Song"), which would account for the reviewer's mention of "vulgarity."[51]

Haydn's quotation of at least one popular song and an allusion in the first movement to his "Farewell" Symphony appealed to the same taste for new combinations of familiar music as the quodlibets by Wranitzky, Seyfried, and others that Marie Therese owned.[52] She must have also enjoyed Haydn's interruption of the finale by the violinists tuning up – and finding that their G-string was a whole step too low. The joke probably reminded her of the tuning of instruments in the first movement of Wranitzky's Quodlibet Symphony, played in one of her private concerts a little more than a year before she asked Haydn for a copy of "Il distratto."

BEETHOVEN'S SEPTET

On 2 April 1800 the twenty-nine-year-old Beethoven gave a grand concert in the Burgtheater. A poster announced that after a symphony by Mozart,

49   Robert A. Green, "Haydn's and Regnard's 'Il Distratto': A Re-examination," *Haydn Yearbook* 11 (1980), 183–95; Elaine R. Sisman, "Haydn's Theater Symphonies," *Journal of the American Musicological Society* 43 (1990), 311–20.
50   "Musik zur Zeit Haydns und Beethovens in der Pressburger Zeitung," 170.
51   Heartz, *Haydn, Mozart, and the Viennese School*, 366.
52   On Haydn's quotation of a popular tune see Geoffrey Chew, "The Night-Watchman's Song Quoted by Haydn and its Implications," *Haydn-Studien* 3 (1974), 106–24; on the allusion to the "Farewell" Symphony, Sisman, "Haydn's Theater Symphonies," 312.

an aria from *Die Schöpfung*, and a piano concerto composed and played by Beethoven, the concert would continue with "A septet, most humbly dedicated to Her Majesty the empress, and composed by Herr Ludwig van Beethoven."[53]

This dedication of an unpublished work might seem strange were it not for the fact that Marie Therese accepted many such dedications, though rarely so publicly announced as this one. She owned many manuscripts dedicated to her. Beethoven, who arrived in Vienna the year she became empress, was as aware as any professional musician in Vienna of her musical interests, her generosity to musicians, and her willingness to accept dedications of musical manuscripts.

In a letter of 5 December 1802 Carl van Beethoven explained to Breitkopf & Härtel the process by which his brother's instrumental works were commissioned, made available in manuscript, and finally published:

These pieces were mostly commissioned by music lovers, and with the following agreement: he who wants a piece pays a specified sum for its exclusive possession for a half or a whole year, or even longer, and binds himself not to give the manuscript to anybody; after this period the author is free to do as he wishes with the piece.[54]

Carl van Beethoven did not mention one important part of these transactions: the patrons who commissioned works and paid for temporarily exclusive ownership expected that on their publication Beethoven would dedicate the works to them. Thus in 1799 and 1800 he received 400 Gulden from Prince Lobkowitz for the Op. 18 String Quartets, of which the prince probably enjoyed ownership until they were published in 1801 in an edition inscribed to him.[55] And in 1802 Count Fries paid Beethoven for the privilege of exclusive ownership of a manuscript copy of the String Quintet, Op. 29, for six months, after which the parts, published by Breitkopf & Härtel, were dedicated to Fries.

Did Beethoven have a similar understanding with Marie Therese? Certainly he gave her a copy of the Septet before its publication. On 8 April 1802 he wrote to Hoffmeister & Kühnel, the Leipzig firm to whom he had sold publishing rights, that she had a copy, implying that someone with access to it might use it as the basis for a pirated edition: "Do send my

[53] The poster is reproduced in *Beethoven: A Documentary Study*, ed. H. C. Robbins Landon, New York, 1970, 107, and in Ludwig van Beethoven, *Briefwechsel: Gesamtausgabe*, ed. Sieghard Brandenburg, 7 vols., Bonn, 1996–8, I, 51.
[54] Beethoven, *Briefwechsel* I, 139; translation (used here) in *Letters to Beethoven and Other Correspondence*, ed. Theodore Albrecht, 3 vols., Lincoln, Neb., 1996, I, 86–7.
[55] Sieghard Brandenburg, "Beethovens Streichquartette op. 18," *Beethoven und Böhmen*, 259–309.

septet into the world a little more quickly – because the rabble is waiting for it – and you know that the Empress has it – and there are rascals in the Imperial City as there are at the Imperial Court."[56] The original inventory in *CaM* (see Fig. 1.3) confirms that she owned a copy of the Septet.[57] I have not been able to identify this copy among sources for the Septet in the Nationalbibliothek or the Gesellschaft der Musikfreunde. The fact that Pohl, who focused his attention on Haydn, Mozart, and Beethoven in choosing works to transfer from the Kaisersammlung to the Gesellschaft in 1879, did not take the Septet (it is not in Pohl's list) suggests that it had earlier been removed from the Kaisersammlung, perhaps because of an inscription in Beethoven's hand.

The empress owned several septets other than Beethoven's, including at least four involving seven different instruments: a Sonata a 7 for cembalo, viola d'amore, flauto d'amore, cello, trumpet, English horn, and glockenspiel by Weigl, and three septets for violin, xylophone, harp, piccolo, *schalmay*, *tamburino*, and cello, by Schweigl.[58] In a period when chamber works for seven different instruments were not common, the number of them owned by Marie Therese suggests she made a special effort to accumulate them. Weigl wrote his Sonata a 7 in 1799, precisely when Beethoven was writing his Septet.[59] Perhaps she commissioned Weigl and Beethoven to add to her collection around the same time.

Marie Therese's possession of Beethoven's Septet did not keep him from having it performed, even before his concert on 2 April 1800. It had been played at one of Prince Schwarzenberg's private concerts and, on 20 December 1799, at a concert in Jahn's restaurant.[60] Yet Beethoven waited until December 1800 to offer it to Franz Anton Hoffmeister,[61] and it was not published until 1802, with its dedication to Marie Therese intact

---

[56] Beethoven, *Briefwechsel* I, 105; translation (used here) in *The Letters of Beethoven*, ed. Emily Anderson, 3 vols., New York, 1961, I, 73.

[57] That this copy was a manuscript, not a print, is suggested by the absence of an opus number from the entry in *CaM*.

[58] In Weigl's Sonata a 7 (Mus. Hs. 11393) the seven instruments play together only in the fourth and final movement. The glockenspiel does not sound in the first or second movements. In the second movement the viola d'amore is replaced with an *Euphon* (an otherwise unidentified instrument whose music is notated on two staves with treble and bass clefs). My thanks to Harrison Powley for sending me copies of the title pages of the Schweigl septets (Mus. Hs. 11395–7).

[59] The autograph score of Weigl's Sonata a 7 (Mus. Hs. 19398) is dated 1799.

[60] Josephine Brunsvik reported in a letter of 21 December 1799 that the septet had been performed the previous day "dans la petite salle de Jan" (Armand de Hévésy, *Petites amies de Beethoven*, Paris, 1910, 19, cited in Brandenburg, "Beethovens Streichquartette op. 18," 274). My thanks to Rita Steblin for calling my attention to this performance. Thayer, *Beethoven*, 265, mentions the performance at Prince Schwarzenberg's without citing a source.

[61] Beethoven to Hoffmeister, 15 December 1800, in Beethoven, *Briefwechsel* I, 54.

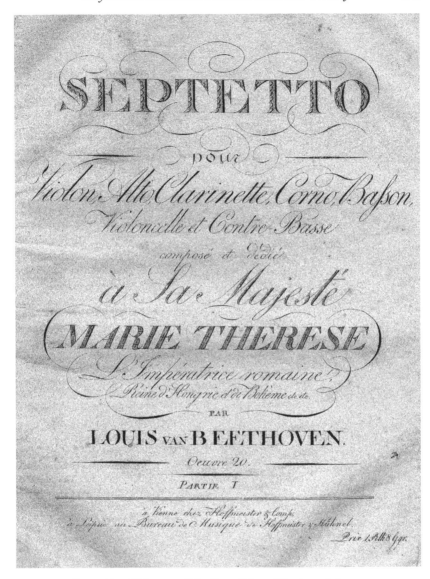

Figure 10.1 Title page of the first edition of Beethoven's Septet.

(Fig. 10.1). Beethoven's letter urging quick publication was written more than two years after the first known public performance in Jahn's restaurant. During that period he managed so effectively to keep the Septet from circulating in manuscript that even Prince Lobkowitz was unable to obtain a copy until August 1802.[62] This leads me to suspect that, having completed it in late 1799, Beethoven gave the empress a manuscript with the promise that it would not be published for two years.

Beethoven's dedication of the published Septet to the empress was almost as unusual as his reference to her as dedicatee in the poster announcing its performance in the Burgtheater. Although Marie Therese owned many manuscripts inscribed to her, she accepted the dedication of very little published music. The Septet, announcing itself as "dedié à Sa Majesté Marie Therese L'Impératrice romaine, Reine d'Hongrie et de Bohème etc. etc.," joined a handful of printed works that included the piano reduction of Leopold Kozeluch's ballet *La ritrovata figlia di Ottone II* of 1794, "dedicata a S. M. L'Imperatrice Maria Teresa de Bourbon."[63]

Marie Therese did not have the Septet, or any other music by Beethoven, performed in the concerts recorded in her diary between 1801 and 1803. But to judge by the music presented in private concerts of the nobility, her lack of performances of his music was in no way out of the ordinary. During this period Beethoven was mostly absent, as a performer and a composer, from music in aristocratic salons, possibly the result of his avoidance of these salons on account of encroaching deafness and depression. In June 1801 he wrote to his friend Franz Wegeler: "For two years I have avoided almost all social gatherings because it is impossible for me to say to people 'I am deaf.' "[64] Although the dedications of the music he published during this period – in 1801 alone he dedicated works to Schwarzenberg, Lobkowitz, Fries, and Braun's wife Josephine – show that he continued to value the patronage of that part of the aristocracy active in the organization of private concerts, none of these patrons is known to have performed in private concerts in Vienna the works that Beethoven later dedicated to them.[65]

A BALLET FOR THE EMPRESS

The great dancer and choreographer Salvatore Viganò appeared in the court theaters of Vienna from 1793 to 1795 and returned in 1799. Two years

---

[62] Lobkowitz bought a copy of the Septet on 26 August 1802 from the Prague music seller Joseph Kaspar and had it performed soon thereafter at his summer house at Jezeři; see Macek, "Franz Joseph Maximilian Lobkowitz: Musikfreund und Kunstmäzen," 157.

[63] The title page is reproduced in Rice, *Emperor and Impresario*, opposite p. 221.

[64] Beethoven, *Briefwechsel* I, 80; translation (used here) in Thayer, *Beethoven*, 284.

[65] Morrow, *Concert Life*, 394–400. How Fries used Beethoven's Quintet in C during the period in which he had paid for its exclusive ownership is unknown. Count Carl Zinzendorf attended two of Fries's concerts during 1802 and recorded their contents in his diary; they included music by Paer, Mayr, and Salieri, but not Beethoven.

later, on 28 March 1801, he presented in the Burgtheater *Die Geschöpfe des Prometheus*, "ein heroisch-allegorisches Ballett in zwey Aufzügen." A handbill advertising a performance that did not take place (on 21 March) refers to the ballet by a different title: *Die Menschen des Prometheus*.[66] The title was apparently changed just before the postponed premiere.

The poster announcing the performance on 28 March contains a synopsis of the ballet that alludes to its allegorical content: "The philosophers of Greece, to whom he [Prometheus] was known, explained the meaning of the myth as follows. It depicts him as a sublime spirit who found the men of his time in a state of ignorance, improved them by means of the sciences and arts, and taught them morals."[67] But the poster is silent on another aspect of the ballet's allegory: the "sublime spirit" of Prometheus represented none other than Marie Therese as patron of music.

It was only in 1838 that Carlo Ritorni, in his biography of Vigano, revealed the empress's place in the allegorical subtext of *Prometheus*. He referred to the ballet with an Italian version of the original title, *Gli uomini di Prometeo*. His awareness of that title and his familiarity with the action of this and other Viennese ballets he had never seen on stage suggest he had access to Vigano's papers. We thus have reason to trust his claim that *Prometheus* was "composed in honor of Empress Maria Teresa's great love of music."[68] He supplied the ballet with a subtitle, *La forza della musica e della danza*, which helps to explain why Vigano chose it as a tribute to Marie Therese's musical taste and patronage. Taking into account both the original poster and Ritorni's testimony, we can conclude that the allegory of *Prometheus* was both personal and philosophical. It honored the empress for her love of music by demonstrating the importance to human life of music, drama, and dance.

We might expect Vigano to have collaborated on *Prometheus* with a composer who enjoyed the empress's favor. Indeed the request for Beethoven's participation in the ballet came from Marie Therese herself, as was recently revealed in a document published for the first time in Sieghard Brandenburg's edition of Beethoven's correspondence. Caspar Joseph Eberl,

[66] The handbill is illustrated in *Beethoven: A Documentary Study*, 166.

[67] "Die Philosophen Griechenlands, denen er bekannt war, erklären die Anspielung der Fabel dahin, daß sie denselben als einen erhabenen Geist schildern, der die Menschen zu seiner Zeit in einem Zustande von Unwissenheit antraf, sie durch Wissenschaften und Künste verfeinerte, und ihnen Sitten beybrachte" (Theaterzettel, 28 March 1801, A-Wt).

[68] Carlo Ritorni, *Commentarii della vita e delle opere coredrammatiche di Salvatore Vigano e della coreografia e de' corepei*, Milan, 1838, 49, describes the ballet as "inventato in onore dell'amor che per la musica aveva grandissimo l'imperatrice Maria Teresa seconda moglie dell'imperatore Francesco Secondo."

manager of the publishing firm Hoffmeister & Comp. in Vienna, wrote to his associates at Hoffmeister & Kühnel on 7 March 1801 that Beethoven had received an urgent commission from the empress that would keep him from all other work for the next two weeks. Since *Prometheus* was originally planned for performance on 21 March, it must have been the "*presante arbeit*" that Beethoven received from Marie Therese.[69]

Prometheus (as far as can be judged from the explanation printed on the poster and from Ritorni's brief synopsis) contained little in the way of plot. Act 1, which served as a prelude to the much longer second act, began with a violent thunderstorm. Prometheus created the first man and woman (the *Menschen* of the original title: mythical counterparts to the biblical pair depicted in *Die Schöpfung*) and took them to Parnassus to be educated. In act 2, under the supervision of Apollo, the assembled muses, graces, and musicians mortal and immortal – Pan, Amphion, Orpheus, and Arion – shared their knowledge and skills with Prometheus's creations. Act 2 must have been a kind of pageant involving large numbers of dancers, probably decked out in splendid costumes.

Viganò may have tried to reinforce the ballet's allegory by alluding to Marie Therese's theatrical and musical tastes. The tempest at the beginning of act 1 appealed to the fondness for musical depictions of storms that led her to include in her concerts storm choruses by Dittersdorf and Mozart and the Symphony in G minor by Wranitzky that begins with a movement entitled "Donnerwetter." The synopsis on the poster for *Prometheus* mentions that the man and woman brought to life by the hero "are made susceptible by the power of harmony to all the passions of human life" ("zu allen Leidenschaften des menschlichen Lebens"). In 1801, the year of *Prometheus*, Weigl composed for the empress the Concertino in D, a series of depictions of human emotions that she referred to as *Die Leidenschaften*. The second act of Viganò's ballet had just as much mythological pageantry as Paer's cantata *Arianna consolata* and the play *Das Picknick der Götter* for which Wranitzky supplied music. In *Arianna* Bacchus (playing the same kind of supervisory role as Apollo in *Prometheus*) presents a series of short mythical scenes to entertain his bride; the first depicts "Prometheus at the Caucasus."

Das Picknick der Götter takes place on Mount Olympus, not Mount Parnassus; but in one of the empress's theatrical sketches she envisioned the home of the muses as the setting for a parody, "Il Parnaso travestito."[70]

---

[69] Beethoven, *Briefwechsel* I, 68. I am most grateful to Michael Tusa for telling me of this important document.

[70] Undated manuscript in MT's hand, HHStA, Fa, Sb, Kart. 65, fol. 151.

Her long and detailed scenario for the ballet *Alceste* culminates in a scene that, had it been realized on stage, might have strikingly resembled Viganò's Parnassus.[71] In the palace of Apollo, the god of music and poetry is surrounded by *piaceri* and *geni* and by an orchestra seated in the clouds. As in *Prometheus*, here too the focus of attention is a pair of mortals: Apollo reunites Alcestis and Admetus. He commands the performance of a contredanse, a dance for which Marie Therese demonstrated her fondness not only by specifying it here but also by preserving the choreography for the *Ventiquatro Figure di Contradanza* performed on her birthday in 1800 (see Fig. 5.1).

Beethoven too appealed to the tastes of his imperial patron. The music he wrote to accompany the depiction of Parnassus includes an Adagio followed by an Andante quasi Allegretto (No. 5 in the score) with solos for flute, clarinet, and bassoon, and even more prominent solos for cello and harp – the only harp solo he is known to have ever written.[72] The harp of course suits Apollo (in *Das Picknick der Götter* the entrance of Apollo and the muses is accompanied by harp) and Orpheus. The combination of harp and winds closely resembles the instrumentation of a work owned by Marie Therese, Weigl's Concertino for harp, flute, oboe, clarinet, and bassoon (*CaM*, p. 60). In combining harp and solo cello, Beethoven, like Weigl in *La festa di Carolina negli Elisi* (more mythological allegory!) and Salieri in *Gesù al Limbo*, brought together two of Marie Therese's favorite sonorities. If any music by Beethoven deserves to be called "Theresian" it is this. He probably wrote the harp solo for Müllner.[73] As one of the empress's most important instrumental collaborators, her participation in *Prometheus* would have served as yet another means of honoring "Empress Maria Teresa's great love of music."

Just as the empress specified a contredanse in celebration of the reunion of Alcestis and Admetus, so Viganò and Beethoven made the finale of *Prometheus* a contredanse. This finale, in the form of a rondo, takes as its principal theme the familiar tune that also appears as the seventh of the Twelve Contredanses, WoO 14, in the Piano Variations, Op. 35, and in the fourth movement of the *Sinfonia eroica*; the second episode in the finale uses dance No. 11 from the Twelve Contredanses.

---

[71] *Alceste, ballo in cinque atti*, undated manuscript in MT's hand, ibid., fol. 190–99.
[72] Barry Cooper, *Beethoven*, Oxford, 2000, 100.
[73] Haas, "'Wunschtraum und Wirklichkeit,'" 298. Evidence discovered by Theodore Albrecht for Müllner's participation in the orchestras of the court theaters during the theatrical year 1801–2, when *Die Geschöpfe des Prometheus* was still in the repertory, was cited in chapter 2, n. 59.

As if to acknowledge the tribute represented by *Prometheus*, Marie Therese suggested to Viganò the subject of his next ballet. He accepted her suggestion, and *I giuochi istmici* reached the stage in 1803.[74] But she may have agreed with the critic who wrote in the *Zeitung für die elegante Welt* that Beethoven composed *Prometheus* "too learnedly for a ballet and with too little regard for the dance."[75] *I giuochi istmici* was danced to music by Weigl, not Beethoven. And although Marie Therese had shown herself willing to accept the dedication of ballet music when Kozeluch published *La ritrovata figlia di Ottone II* in 1794, Beethoven dedicated the piano score of *Prometheus*, published by Artaria in June 1801, to Princess Christiane Lichnowsky, not the empress.

PAER'S *LEONORA*, MAYR'S *L'AMOR CONIUGALE*, AND BEETHOVEN'S *FIDELIO*

That Beethoven, despite the Septet and *Prometheus*, remained outside Marie Therese's inner circle of musical associates was demonstrated during the period from November 1805 to January 1806 when the French army under Napoleon occupied Vienna. The court fled; the empress herself left on 9 November, four days before the French entered the capital. Writing to her on 8 January 1806, Eybler responded to her request for information about musical events in Vienna during her absence:

Since I have gone out very little during this entire time, I can only pass on what I have heard from my chorus, namely, that a couple of times there were concerts in the evening, but only small ones, at Schönbrunn, where Cherubini conducted and Cambi [i.e. Antonia Campi] and Crescentini sang; the latter must have pleased very much, because he has been engaged for Paris on terms very favorable to him, and will depart within the next few days. *Buon viaggio*! Whether Weigl also conducted I do not know. There were two celebrations of the mass in Schönbrunn, at which Salieri fortunately conducted; I however had to conduct the other half of the Hofkapelle in the Burgkapelle, where only Le Clarc was present a single time. Both masses at Schönbrunn were strange: a silent mass was read, and during it only graduals and offertories were done pianissimo with sordini all the way through, without responses; the French emperor cannot stand strong, loud music.[76]

---

[74] MT's role in the creation of *I giuochi istmici* is mentioned in Ritorni, *Viganò*, 50.
[75] *Ludwig van Beethoven: Die Werke im Spiegel seiner Zeit*, ed. Stefan Kunze, Laaber, 1987, 39.
[76] "Euer Majestaet verlangen auch zu wissen, wie die von der Musick sich aufgeführt haben. Da ich diese ganze Zeit her sehr wenig ausgegangen, so kann ich auch nur das, was ich auf meinem Chor gehört, überschreiben, nämlich: ein Paarmahl war abends Concert, aber nur im kleinen, in Schönbrunn, wobey Cherubini dirigirte, Cambi, und Crescentini sangen, letzterer muß sehr gefallen haben, weil er mit sehr guten Bedingnüssen in Paris engagirt worden, und dieser Tagen

Eybler made no mention of Beethoven or of the first performance of *Fidelio* on 20 November, before an audience in the Theater an der Wien consisting largely of French officers. That omission reflects not only Eybler's limited sources of information but also the distance between Beethoven and the empress's musical circle. She owned no copy of *Fidelio*, and one might easily assume that she had nothing to do with its inception or creation.

Yet it was precisely during the preparation of *Fidelio* that Beethoven benefited from Marie Therese's musical interests and activities. During the fall of 1805, when she was still in Vienna, the censors of the Imperial-Royal police forbade the opera's performance because of its political content. The librettist Sonnleithner wrote to the police commissioner on 2 October, protesting the decision and revealing the empress's role in the opera's inception: "I have thoroughly adapted this opera from the French original of Bouilly (entitled *Léonore ou L'Amour conjugal*), primarily because Her Majesty the Empress and Queen finds the original very beautiful and assured me that no opera text had ever given her so much pleasure." Sonnleithner further tied the fate of the opera to Marie Therese by stating that *Fidelio* was "supposed to be given on the name day of Her Majesty the Empress," 15 October.[77] A day later he enlisted the help of State Councillor Philipp von Stahl, telling him that by helping to change the censor's mind, "you will eternally oblige Her Majesty the Empress (who particularly loves this piece [as] composed in Italian by Kapellmeister Paer and performed in Prague and Dresden)." He added the interesting detail that Marie Therese had "repeatedly" told him of her interest in Bouilly's libretto.[78]

Paer's opera was *Leonora, ossia L'amor conjugale*, on a libretto derived by Giacomo Cinti from Bouilly's *Léonore*, first performed in Dresden on

---

schon abreisen wird. *Buon Viaggio!* Ob auch Weigl dirigirte ist mir nicht bewußt. Ferners waren 2 Aemter in Schönbrunn, wo zum Glück Salieri dirigirte, doch mußte ich mit der anderen Hälfte der Hofmusick in der Burgkapelle dirigiren, wo ein einziges mahl blos Le Clarc gegenwärtig war. Sonderbahr waren die beyden Aemter in Schönbrunn: Es wurde eine stille Meeße gelesen, während dieser wurden blos Gradualen und Offertorien in einem fort *pianissimo* mit Sordinen gemacht, ohne zu respondiren; der franz. Kaiser verträgt keine starke und laute Musick" (Eybler to MT, 8 January 1806, HHStA, Fa, Sb, Kart. 65, Private an Kaiserin Marie Therese 1806, fol. 292r–v). For a more detailed description of one of Napoleon's concerts at Schönbrunn see Rosenbaum, "Tagebücher," 132–3.

77 Beethoven, *Briefwechsel* I, 266; translation (used here) in *Letters to Beethoven and Other Correspondence* I, 169.

78 Sonnleithner wrote the libretto because "Ihre Majestät die Kaiserin mir wiederholt sagte, daß sie kein Opernsujet jemals so sehr interessiert habe... Sie werden Ihre Majestät die Kaiserin, die dieses vom Kapellmeister Paer italienisch komponierte, zu Prag und Dresden aufgeführte Stück vorzüglich lieben... unendlich verbinden." The letter is transcribed in Karl Glossy, "Ein Gedenkblatt (Zur Erinnerung an die erste Aufführung von Beethovens 'Fidelio')," *Österreichische Rundschau* 5 (1905–6), 132–3; translation (used here) in *Letters to Beethoven and Other Correspondence* I, 171.

3 October 1804.[79] Marie Therese's love for Bouilly's libretto and Paer's opera was in keeping with her fascination with rescue operas and with stories of conjugal devotion and wifely heroism. Moreover, the presence in both dramas of a magnificent *sotterraneo* must have enhanced their attractiveness for her.

Sonnleithner's statements raise some intriguing questions about the origins of *Fidelio* and its relation to other operatic treatments of the same story by two of Marie Therese's favorite composers, Paer and Mayr. His comments also suggest parallels between *Fidelio* and another Viennese opera based on a French drama that also enjoyed Marie Therese's approval (and yet another contribution to the "now dominant genre of rescue stories"): Cherubini's *Faniska*, first performed on 25 February 1806, three months after *Fidelio*. As we saw in chapter 8, *Faniska* was the third in a series of theatrical treatments: the first French (Pixérécourt's *Les Mines de Pologne*), the second an Italian opera by Paer on a libretto by Cinti (the aborted *Le mine di Polonia*, on which Paer worked during 1804 and 1805), and the third a German opera for Vienna on a libretto by Sonnleithner. Just as Marie Therese contributed to the process that led to *Faniska* by commissioning Paer to compose an Italian version of *Les Mines* and then probably playing some role in shifting the commission to Cherubini, so she contributed to the process that led to *Fidelio* by repeatedly declaring to Sonnleithner her fondness for Bouilly's libretto.

The questions of when Beethoven got to know Paer's *Leonora* (a copy of which eventually became part of his library) and how well he knew it have frequently been discussed.[80] The evidence is contradictory. On the one hand, similarities between Paer's opera and the first version of *Fidelio* suggest strongly that Beethoven knew *Leonora* already in 1805.[81] On the other hand, the absence of any known performances of *Leonora* in Vienna before a private one given by Prince Lobkowitz sometime between 1 January

---

[79] On Paer's *Leonora* and Cinti's authorship of the libretto (previously attributed by some scholars to Giovanni Schmidt) see Enßlin, *Die Opern Ferdinando Paërs*, 532–52.

[80] Although Paer sometimes referred to his opera as *L'amor conjugale* (as for example in his letters to MT), I have adopted here the title used on the libretto for the first production (with thanks to Wolfram Enßlin for providing me with a transcription of the libretto's title page).

[81] Among the scholars who have pointed to musical parallels between *Leonora* and *Fidelio* as evidence that Beethoven knew Paer's opera are Richard Engländer, "Paërs 'Leonora' und Beethovens 'Fidelio'," *Neues Beethoven-Jahrbuch* 4, 118, Mosco Carner, *Major and Minor*, New York, 1980, 186–252, Lühning, "Florestans Kerker in Rampenlicht," Jürgen Maehder, " 'Der Kerker eine Gruft': Zum Orchesterklang in den Kerkerszenen der *Leonore*-Opern," program book of the Salzburg Festival, 1996, 92–115, and Enßlin, *Die Opern Ferdinando Paërs*, 537.

and 29 March 1806 leaves one wondering how Beethoven could have gotten to know it so soon after the Dresden premiere in October 1804.[82]

Documents related to Marie Therese's musical activities suggest new ways of thinking about the origins of Beethoven's opera. They show that she knew of Paer's *Leonora* by February 1804 and that she had a copy of it well before the premiere in Dresden.

On 27 February 1804 Paer wrote to the empress of "my new opera that I am presently composing." Since he completed no operas, as far as we know, between *Sargino* (26 June 1803) and *Leonora*, this new opera must have been *Leonora*. On 23 March he wrote: "My new opera is being copied, and a complete score is being copied for you . . . I hope Y. M. will be happy with it, and I hope to bring it to you myself on the occasion of the concert for the poor." (The benefit concert in question was the performance, discussed in chapter 7, of Paer's *Il trionfo della chiesa* on 20 May 1804.) A few days later, on 2 April, he wrote with more certainty: "When I come [to Vienna in May] I will bring the score of the new opera, which is being copied, and will humbly present it to Your Majesty." He referred to it again on 26 July, telling the empress that he intended to leave Dresden for Italy on 5 October: "for on the 3rd *L'amor conjugale* will be given here in the theater of Dresden for the first time, and I am obliged to conduct at least this single performance." Five days later he wrote: "I will send Your Majesty the second act of *L'amor conjugale* around the middle of August, for the copyist promised me it will definitely be ready by then." Marie Therese must already have owned act 1, which Paer presumably gave her in May.[83]

In his letter of 31 July 1804 Paer expressed hope that Marie Therese might arrange for a production of *Leonora* in Vienna, even naming a singer who could take the title role: "I would be delighted if Your Majesty had it performed in Vienna, but in my presence, on my return from Italy; I

---

[82] Lobkowitz's production of *Leonora* (cited in Winton Dean, "Beethoven and Opera," *Essays on Opera*, Oxford, 1990, 128) is recorded in *Journal des Luxus und der Moden* 21 (1806), 287, after a report of the revival of *Fidelio* on 29 March 1806: "Kurz zuvor wurde dieselbe Oper, von Pär componirt, unter dem Titel: L'amor conjugale bei dem Fürsten Lobkowitz vor einem auserlesenen Auditorium aufgeführt" (quoted in *Ludwig van Beethoven: Die Werke im Spiegel seiner Zeit*, 151). Lobkowitz's purchase of performance materials for *Leonora* is recorded in Sukowaty's bill covering the period 1 January 1806 to 31 July 1807 (reproduced in facsimile in Macek, "Die Musik bei den Lobkowicz," 194 and 199).

[83] The score of *Leonora* from MT's library (under the title *L'amor conjugale*, Mus. Hs. 9976) is probably the one Paer gave her, in two installments, between May and August 1804. Enßlin, *Die Opern Ferdinando Paërs*, 537, suggests that Paer's visit to Vienna in May 1804 offered opportunities for Beethoven and him to discuss their Léonore operas, and for Beethoven to see at least part of Paer's score.

have no doubt that Signora Marianna Sessi would sing it perfectly." In naming an important professional soprano as a possible Viennese Leonora, Paer made sure the empress knew he had in mind a production in Vienna's public theaters, not a private performance in which she might have been tempted to sing Leonora herself (as she had sung Giannina in an earlier rescue opera, *L'uniforme*).

Marie Therese owned another operatic version of the Leonora story. Mayr's *L'amor coniugale*, a *farsa sentimentale* in one act, was first performed in Padua in July 1805, about two and a half years after he left Vienna promising to compose an *opera semiseria* for the court theaters.[84] We saw in chapter 7 how closely Braun and Marie Therese consulted with one another during Mayr's visit to Vienna in 1802–3: Mayr thanked her, not him, for being allowed to delay the composition of the *opera semiseria* until his return to Italy. It would stand to reason that she helped to choose the libretto for that opera. That Mayr's *L'amor coniugale* had its origins at the Viennese court is suggested by the fact – hitherto apparently unnoticed – that its libretto combines Bouilly's *Léonore* with another, newer drama of which the empress was also fond: *Les Mines de Pologne*. Mayr's librettist Gaetano Rossi transferred the action to Poland. He borrowed from Pixérécourt's *mélodrame* the names of two characters: Bouilly's Marcelline became Floreska (the name of the heroine of *Les Mines*), Roc the jailor became Peters (the name of a mountain guide in *Les Mines*). Also from *Les Mines* Rossi took an important detail of the plot: the villain imprisons the hero not for political reasons but because he loves the hero's wife.

The pleasure that Marie Therese derived from Bouilly's *Léonore*, the casual manner with which Paer alluded to *Leonora* several months before it was first performed (as if she knew about the opera already) and his willingness to give her a score well before the premiere, and the incorporation of elements of *Les Mines de Pologne* into Mayr's *L'amor coniugale*: all this suggests that she played some role in the inception of both *Leonora* and *L'amor coniugale*. Moreover, Sonnleithner's claim that he derived his libretto from *Léonore* "primarily because Her Majesty the Empress and Queen finds the original very beautiful" can most reasonably be interpreted to mean that she persuaded him to use Bouilly's libretto as the basis for a German opera for Vienna. His intention of presenting the premiere of *Fidelio* on her nameday reminds us that Paer's *Achille*, which originated in her asking its librettist for "a grand serious opera," was first performed on her birthday in

---

[84] On *L'amor coniugale* see Schiedermaier, *Beiträge zur Geschichte der Oper* II, 39–50, and Carner, *Major and Minor*, 148–71.

1801. In short, the empress's personal connections with Paer, Mayr, Braun, Sonnleithner, and Beethoven placed her at the nexus of a web connecting the three Léonore operas of 1804–5.

Could Marie Therese have arranged for, or at least condoned, the more or less simultaneous production of Italian and German operas on the same subject? Paer, about four months after the first performance of *Fidelio*, thought along these lines in connection with another libretto, Carpani's *L'allievo dell'orsa* (also known as *L'orsino*), of which the empress owned a manuscript copy.[85] He proposed settings in German (by Weigl, presumably for Vienna) and Italian (for Domenico Guardasoni's Italian troupe in Prague):

> In reference to *L'orsino*, if Vaigel is writing it in German, and he does not object to my setting it to music as well, could Your Majesty grant permission to poor old Guardasoni for me to compose an opera on this book? He is without a libretto, and I promised to give him a new opera for the month of September. If Your Majesty grants him this book, he will present to you the music composed by me, and the whole thing would be done among ourselves, in absolute secrecy except while the opera is being performed in Prague.[86]

Of Marie Therese's response we know nothing; in any case, neither Weigl nor Paer apparently set Carpani's libretto to music. But the proposal is of interest nevertheless; it suggests that Paer and the empress could have been involved in a similar (and equally secretive) arrangement involving *Léonore*.

Although we do not know exactly when Sonnleithner and Beethoven began working on *Fidelio* (they preferred the title *Leonore* but were prevented from using it by Baron Braun, who probably knew from Marie Therese of Paer's eagerness to have his opera performed in Vienna[87]), it was certainly well before the first performances of Paer's *Leonora* or Mayr's *L'amor coniugale*.[88] But by the time *Fidelio* reached the stage Marie Therese had had a copy of Paer's opera for more than a year. She may have already performed it in private (she owned parts as well as a score); such a performance would have enhanced the validity of her judgment, reported by Sonnleithner, of Paer's music. Beethoven was probably as aware as Sonnleithner of the empress's fondness for Paer's *Leonora*. If the musical similarities

---

[85] *L'allievo dell'orsa*, dramma per musica in tre atti di Giuseppe Carpani in Vienna 1805, HHStA, Fa, Sb, Kart. 65, fol. 229–35.

[86] Paer to MT, Dresden, 24 March 1806.   [87] Dean, "Beethoven and Opera," 128.

[88] For an insightful and persuasive discussion of the chronology of the composition of the first version of *Fidelio* see Theodore Albrecht, "Beethoven's *Leonore*: A New Compositional Chronology Based on May–August, 1804 Entries in Sketchbook Mendelssohn 15," *Journal of Musicology* 7 (1989), 165–90.

between *Leonora* and the first version of *Fidelio* resulted from Beethoven's intentional appropriation of Paer's ideas, he probably intended those similarities as allusions to be heard and appreciated only by those few in Vienna, and especially the empress, who in 1805 already knew Paer's opera.

Sonnleithner's invocation of the empress's role in the inception of *Fidelio* succeeded in getting the censors to reverse their decision and to allow the opera's production to go forward. But due to circumstances having only partly to do with censorship the premiere was postponed until five weeks after Marie Therese's nameday. During these hectic weeks of revision, rehearsal, and staging, the French army, having defeated the Austrians at Ulm, advanced triumphantly across southern Germany and toward Vienna. When Beethoven presented *Fidelio* for the first time, the woman whose name had helped to bring it to the stage was far away.

Epilogue

Napoleon's occupation of Vienna in 1805 and the flight of the imperial family, during which Marie Therese was separated from her children, deeply upset the young empress. On 21 November (the day after the first performance of *Fidelio* in Vienna) she wrote to her mother from Olmütz, where she had taken refuge with Emperor Alexander of Russia:

> Our misfortune is very great, and it will cost me at least ten years of my life. I see myself a fugitive, driven from my house, the capital in the hands of the enemy, who advances almost at will. He is only two posts from us. Our army and the Russians are hardly an hour from here ... There, beloved mother, you have our wretched situation: and we make such a sad figure before the emperor of Russia and his entire retinue, who have been here since the 18th. You cannot imagine how infinitely unpleasant the whole company is to me ... The Czar is handsome and, I believe, a good man, but that is all: the rest is nothing. His troops are good looking, indeed splendid, but in their character they are worse than the French.[1]

It is hard to believe that only a few weeks earlier, on 4 October, in the midst of family and friends, Marie Therese had celebrated her husband's nameday with Seyfried's *Serenata con una cantatina* in the park at Hetzendorf, "where coffee was served on a grass-covered terrace, surrounded by a bed of sweet-smelling flowers."

With supplies short, Russian troops under General Mikhail Kutuzov began to suffer from hunger and cold, and they pillaged the Moravian countryside. The empress, full of foreboding, wrote to Maria Carolina of conditions and emotions that Tolstoy was later to describe in *War and Peace*:

> One must see this to believe it. Our poor peasants groan for the French to advance, so as to be freed from the Russians ... I have had no news of my poor children, and

---

[1] MT to Maria Carolina, Olmütz, 21 November 1805, quoted in German translation in Egon Caesar Conte Corti, *Ich, eine Tochter Maria Theresias: Ein Lebensbild der Königin Marie Karoline von Neapel*, Munich, 1950, 501. I have not been able to locate the originals of this and the following letters.

259

that upsets me constantly. Imagine, my dear, good mother, how, with my heart breaking every time I think about my past, my present, and my future, I have to go through with a grand dinner every day, listening to witticisms and anecdotes and seeing the jolly laughter of those who entangled us in this misfortune. I must often pray to God to grant me support, but it is impossible for me to laugh. I would prefer to hide in a corner than to play this dismal role...All this would be nothing if only we had hope that things will improve, but I confess I fear for the worst.[2]

The disastrous defeat about two weeks later of the Austro-Russian army at Austerlitz led to a humiliating peace. Marie Therese returned to Vienna and to a reunion with her children, hoping for a respite from war. "I know of – I can imagine no greater fortune," she wrote to her mother, "than to enjoy peace and quiet, as long as this is possible without losing our lands; and my husband thinks the same. It is better to have less, but to enjoy it in peace."[3] And a few months later she told Maria Carolina that she prayed "to hear nothing more of war for the rest of my life."[4]

The empress's thoughts had returned to music even before she reached Vienna. Eybler wrote to her of the music with which the city intended to celebrate the court's arrival. "The Te Deum will be performed by the orchestra of St. Stephan's, and is supposed to be newly composed by Albrechtsberger, the Kapellmeister there."[5] But in music too the French triumph frustrated her aspirations and stifled her enthusiasm. The Marchese di Gallo, who had supplied her with music from Paris, had served as one of Queen Maria Carolina's closest and most trusted advisers and confidants. With Austria and its allies near military collapse at the end of 1805, Gallo had betrayed the queen and had begun passing her letters to Napoleon.[6] No further communication between Marie Therese and the traitor was possible.

Napoleon's military success gave him an edge in his musical rivalry with Marie Therese. He found one of her favorite singers, Crescentini, in Vienna, and engaged him for Paris. He coveted one of her favorite composers, Paer, who at least had the courtesy to keep his Viennese patron informed of the courtship.[7] After Napoleon's victory at the Battle of Jena (14 October 1806), Friedrich August, elector of Saxony, made a separate peace with

[2] MT to Maria Carolina, Olmütz, 24 November 1805, quoted in German translation in Corti, 502.
[3] MT to Maria Carolina, Vienna, 26 August 1806, quoted in German translation in Corti, 541.
[4] MT to Maria Carolina, 10 January 1807, quoted in German translation in Corti, 550.
[5] "Das Te Deum wird von dem Orchester von St: Stephan gehalten, und soll von dem dasigen Kapellmeister Albrechtsberger neu komponiert seyn" (Eybler to MT, dated "Freitag abends 10 Uhr," HHStA, Fa, Sb, Kart. 65, Private an Kaiserin Marie Therese 1806, fol. 294).
[6] Corti, 503.
[7] See Paer's letters of 24 November 1806 and 14 January 1807 and the undated letter no. 32.

France and, as a symbol of his submission, freed Paer from his contractual obligations in Dresden. When Napoleon's offer of employment in Paris arrived, Paer portrayed himself to Marie Therese as reluctant to accept it. But he did so, becoming, by the terms of a contract dated 1 January 1807, "Compositeur de la Chambre de Sa Majesté."[8] He promised to make himself available to the empress during the long summer leaves granted in his new contract, but she must have suspected that her association with him had come to an end. Indeed the letter in which he belatedly announced his intention of entering Napoleon's service, dated Warsaw, 14 January 1807, was his last to her.

Marie Therese's suffering during the war of 1805 contributed to making her twelfth pregnancy her most difficult and dangerous. On 6 April 1807 she gave birth prematurely to a girl, who died after three days. Overwhelmed with fever, the empress died on 13 April, at the age of thirty-four.

Weigl remembered the event in his second autobiography:

Now I was struck by the greatest, the most painful blow possible. Maria Theresia, my benefactor, my mother, died. With me sighed many thousands of others for whom she cared. Those who knew her personally were bound to her by her kindness, charm, and virtue. With her death I lost everything, and since then I have never been what I had been earlier. The enthusiastic and energetic joy that she derived from her art, the great animation with which she was able to enliven her surroundings, the condescending sympathy with which she treated even the smallest domestic distress: all of that has disappeared since then. I am unfit for everything that the world offers and live only in my domestic circle with few possessions, happily separate from the whole world: for she was also the author of this domestic happiness that remains for me. May God reward her for all the good she did for us; her memory is permanently buried in my heart.[9]

---

[8] On Paer's engagement by Napoleon see Engländer, "Ferdinando Paer als sächsischer Hofkapellmeister," 215–16, and Kobuch, "Ferdinando Paer in Dresden," 37–8. The contract is transcribed in Fleischman, *Napoléon et la musique*, 229–30.

[9] Weigl, "Zwei Selbstbiographien," 58.

Marie Therese's collection of church music

In the annotations to this transcription of the *Kathalog der Kirchenmusickalien*, the manuscript inventory of church music bequeathed by Marie Therese to the Hofkapelle (HHStA, Fa, HKF, Kart. 10, fol. 127–33), I have tried to match items in the inventory with items in the Nationalbibliothek that were formerly in the Hofkapelle and that may have belonged to Marie Therese (see chapter 1), but this is not always possible. In some cases a work listed in the inventory (for example, the Mass in C major by Reutter) could have been any of several works from the Hofkapelle. In other cases a score or set of parts left by Marie Therese to the Hofkapelle may have been subsequently worn out by frequent use, discarded, and replaced. Generally speaking, the items of church music in Marie Therese's library that fell outside the repertory of the Hofkapelle can most easily be identified with surviving sources in the Nationalbibliothek. For example, there can be no doubt that the "Missa in B maggiore. Partitura sola" by the exceedingly obscure Francesco Bott di Pierot is the *Messa per la festa di S. Norberto* in Bb (autograph score: Mus. Hs. 15585), written by Bott in 1806.

Unless otherwise indicated, all musical sources cited here are in the Nationalbibliothek, with provenance in the Hofkapelle.

Kathalog der Kirchenmusickalien

Verzeichniß

Derjenigen Kirchenmusickalien, welche auf Allerhöchste Anordnung Seiner Majestaet des Kaisers aus dem Musickalien Archiv weiland Ihrer Majestaet der Kaiserinn in das der Hofkapelle übertragen worden.

Im Dezember 1807

A.
Albrechtsberger

I   Missa in C maggiore. Partitura, e parti cavate, in dupplo.[1]
II Missa in C maggiore. Partitura, e parti cavate, in dupplo.

---

[1] One of these two C major masses by Albrechtsberger was the *Missa S. Francisci Seraphici*, Schröder A.I.7, February 1803 (score and parts: HK 4), commissioned by MT and paid for by her on 29 April

III Missa in D maggiore. Partitura, e parti cavate.[2]

I Graduale in C maggiore (In Deo speravit). Partitura, e parti cavate, in dupplo.[3]

II Graduale in D maggiore (Paratum cor). Partitura e parti cavate in dupplo.[4]

III Graduale in C maggiore (Benedictus es). Parti cavate in dupplo.[5]

I Offertorium in C maggiore (Exaltabo te). Partitura, e parti cavate in dupplo.[6]

II Offertorium in D maggiore (Te invocamus). Partitura, e parti cavate, in dupplo.[7]

III Offertorium in G maggiore (Gloria Filio). Parti cavate in dupplo.[8]

IV Offertorium in C minore (Dextera Domini). Parti cavate in dupplo.[9]

I Te Deum in D maggiore. Partitura, e parti cavate.[10]

II Te Deum in C maggiore. Partitura, e parti cavate.[11]

Allegri

Miserere in G minore a 2 cori. Partitura sola.[12]

B.
Bertoni

Miserere in C minore. Partitura sola.[13]

Te Deum in C maggiore. Partitura sola.[14]

1803 (HHStA, Fa, HKF, Kart. 24, diary, fol. 161r). The other mass in C was the *Missa Resurrectionis*, Schröder A.I.5, 1798 (autograph score and parts: HK 3).

[2] *Missa Nativitatis D. N. J. Chr.* in D, Schröder A.I.13 (April 1800). Autograph score and parts: HK 5. Commissioned by Emperor Franz.

[3] "In Deo speravit" in C, Schröder B.I.7. Score and parts: HK 2019, HK 2377.

[4] "Paratum cor meum" in D, Schröder B.II.6. Parts: HK 2380.

[5] "Benedictus es Domine" in C, Schröder B.I.9, January 1803. Parts: HK 2373. Probably composed for performance with the *Missa S. Francisci*.

[6] "Exaltabo Te" in C, Schröder C.I.8, 1798. Parts dated 1799: HK 2388.

[7] "Te invocamus" in D, Schröder C.II.6. Parts: HK 2390. Probably composed for performance with the *Missa Nativitatis*.

[8] Probably "Gloria Patri" in G, Schröder C.I.26, 3 March 1803. Parts: HK 2387. Probably composed for performance with the *Missa S. Francisci*.

[9] "Dextera Domini" in C minor, Schröder C.I.9, 26 August 1784. Parts: HK 2391.

[10] Te Deum in D, Schröder J.4, May 1800. Score: HK 2090; parts: HK 2397. Probably composed for performance with the *Missa Nativitatis*.

[11] Te Deum in C, Schröder J.3, March 1803. Parts: HK 2396. The autograph (H-Bn, Ms. Mus. 2491) is entitled "Te Deum: in C *Novum* für die Kaiserin." Probably composed for performance with the *Missa S. Francisci*.

[12] Gregorio Allegri, Miserere. Several scores in A-Wn.

[13] Ferdinando Bertoni, Miserere in C minor. Printed score: SA.82.F.16 (provenance unknown). Carpani sent a copy of this score to MT with his letter of 4 June 1803 (Jacobs, *Carpani*, 219).

[14] Bertoni, Te Deum in C. Score: Mus. Hs. 15856.

Bott di Pierot

Missa in B maggiore.[15] Partitura sola.[16]

C.
Caffaro

Kyrie, e Gloria in B maggiore. Partitura sola.[17]

Campion

Requiem in Es maggiore. Partitura, e parti cavate.[18]
Responsoria in Hebdomata sancta.[19]

Cimarosa

Missa in Es maggiore. Partitura sola.[20]

D.
Ditters

Missa in C maggiore. Parti cavate.

Durante

I   Requiem in D minore. Partitura sola.[21]
II   Requiem in C minore. Partitura sola.[22]
III Requiem in C minore. Partitura sola.

[15] Although writing in Italian, the compiler of this inventory referred to B♭ by its German name, B.

[16] Francesco Bott di Pierot, *Messa per la festa di S. Norberto* (6 June, MT's birthday) in B♭, 1806, dedicated to MT (includes gradual "Justus ut palma" in G, offertory "Laetamini in Domino" in B♭, and Te Deum in C). Score: Mus. Hs. 15585.

[17] Pasquale Caffaro, Kyrie and Gloria in B♭. Score: Mus. Hs. 15924.

[18] Carl'Antonio Campion, Requiem in E♭. Score: Mus. Hs. 16449. This was probably the requiem by Campion that MT performed on 4 March 1802.

[19] Responsories for Holy Week. Score: Mus. Hs. 15927; parts: HK 505–7.

[20] Domenico Cimarosa, Mass in C minor (not E♭). Score: Mus. Hs. 15916.

[21] Since Francesco Durante is not known to have written a requiem in D minor, this work may be his Mass in D minor ("Missa alla Palestrina"), preserved in A-Wn in several manuscripts. For this and the following annotations I am grateful to Hanns-Bertold Dietz, who shared with me information from his typescript thematic catalogue of Durante's works.

[22] Durante is known to have written only one requiem in C minor, the *Messa di Morte*, Dietz 35. Score: Mus. Hs. 15603. One of the works listed here as "Requiem in C minore" may be the *Missa Defunctorum* in G minor, Dietz 38. Score: Mus. Hs. 15831.

I   Lytaniae in G minore. Partitura sola.[23]
II Lytaniae in F minore. Partitura sola.[24]

E.
Eybler

I   Missa in D minore. Parti cavate, in dupplo.[25]
II   Missa in B maggiore. Parti cavate.[26]
III Missa in C maggiore. Parti cavate.[27]
IV   Missa in B maggiore a 2 cori. Parti cavate.[28]
     Benedictus in G maggiore. Parti cavate.[29]
I   Te Deum in D maggiore. Parti cavate, in dupplo.[30]
II   Te Deum in C maggiore. Parti cavate.[31]
III Te Deum in B maggiore. Parti cavate.[32]
IV   L'istesso a 2 cori. Parti cavate.
     Requiem in C minore a 8 voci. Parti cavate.[33]
     Libera in G minore a 8 voci. Parti cavate.[34]
I   Salmo (De profundis) in B minore. Parti cavate.[35]

---

[23] Litaniae laurentanae in G minor, Dietz 132. Score: Mus. Hs. 15835.

[24] Litaniae laurentanae in F minor, Dietz 131. Score: Mus. Hs. 15838.

[25] Joseph Eybler, *Missa S. Wolfgangi* in D minor, Herrmann 11, August 1800. Parts: HK 2008. Jane Hettrick generously gave me much information about sources of Eybler's church music from the archive of the Hofkapelle, which I have incorporated into this and the following annotations.

[26] *Missa S. Theresiae* in Bb, Herrmann 29, commissioned by MT and first performed (or rehearsed) by her on 21 September 1802. Parts: HK 2009.

[27] *Missa S. Michaelis* in C, Herrmann 2, 1804. Parts: HK 2036. According to the title page of a set of parts for this mass (A-Ws, F 25/1), this mass was "dedicated to Her Majesty Theresia, Empress of Austria."

[28] *Missa S. Francisci* in Bb, Herrmann 30, 1806. Parts: HK 2012.

[29] *Benedictus ed Osanna* in C (not G), Herrmann 36, written in 1805 for a mass by Winter. Score and parts: HK 320.

[30] Te Deum in D, Herrmann 118, 1800. Parts: HK 2548. Composed for performance with the *Missa S. Wolfgangi*.

[31] Te Deum in C, Herrmann 117, 1804. Parts: HK 2551. Composed for performance with the *Missa S. Michaelis*.

[32] Eybler wrote two versions of the Te Deum in Bb, Herrmann 120: for one chorus and for two choruses. Eybler composed the version for one chorus in 1802 for performance with the *Missa S. Theresiae*; MT performed it on 21 September, 3 October and 4 October 1802. He probably wrote the version for two choruses in 1806 for performance with the *Missa S. Francisci*. Parts for both versions: HK 2549.

[33] Requiem in C minor, Herrmann 37, commissioned by MT and performed by her on 2 April 1803. Parts: HK 1809 and HK 2038.

[34] Composed for performance with the Requiem. Parts: HK 2545.

[35] "De profundis," Herrmann 132, 1803. MT performed it on 2 April 1803, during the same concert in which she performed Eybler's Requiem. Parts: HK 267.

II   Salmo (Laudate pueri) in B maggiore. Partitura, e parti cavate.[36]
I   Graduale in C minore (Terra tremuit). Parti cavate, in dupplo.[37]
II   Graduale in C minore (Os justi). Parti cavate in dupplo.[38]
III Graduale in B maggiore (Magnificate). Parti cavate.[39]
IV   Graduale in D maggiore (Nocte surgentes). Parti cavate, in dupplo.[40]
V   Graduale in C maggiore (Cantate Domino). Parti cavate.[41]
VI   Graduale in B maggiore a 2 cori (Exaltate). Parti cavate.[42]
I   Offertorium in Es maggiore a 2 cori (Lux est orta). Parti cavate.[43]
II   Offertorium in D minore (Fremit mare). Parti cavate.[44]
III Offertorium in G minore (Levavi in montes). Parti cavate.[45]
IV   Offertorium in C maggiore (Ad te levavi). Parti cavate.[46]
V   Offertorium in D maggiore (Haec est dies). Parti cavate.[47]
VI   Offertorium in C minore (Si consistant). Parti cavate.[48]

F.
Farinelli

Tantum ergo. Partitura sola.[49]

[36] "Laudate pueri" in B♭, Herrmann 106, 1802, performed by MT on 1 April 1802. Parts: HK 266 and HK 1752.
[37] "Terra tremuit" in C minor, Herrmann 85, 1797. Parts: HK 2521.
[38] "Os justi" in C minor, Herrmann 46, 1805. Parts: HK 2496.
[39] "Magnificate Dominum mecum" in B♭, Herrmann 67, 1802. Composed for performance with the *Missa S. Theresiae*, it was performed by MT and her musicians on 3 October 1802 ("Eine Meß von Eibler sambt Graduale und Offertorio"). Parts: HK 2493.
[40] "Nocte surgentes" in D, Herrmann 47, 1800. Parts: HK 2492. Composed for performance with the *Missa S. Wolfgangi*.
[41] "Cantate Domino" in C, Herrmann 39, 1804. Parts: HK 1804. Composed for performance with the *Missa S. Michaelis*.
[42] "Exaltate Dominum Deum" in B♭, Herrmann 68, 1806. Parts: HK 2486. Composed for performance with the *Missa S. Francisci*.
[43] "Lux est orta" in E♭, Herrmann 95 (1806). Parts: HK 2519. Composed for performance with the *Missa S. Francisci*.
[44] "Fremit mare cum furore" in D minor, Herrmann 93, 1800. Parts: HK 1807. Composed for performance with the *Missa S. Wolfgangi*.
[45] "Levavi in montes" in G minor, Herrmann 104, 1802. Composed for performance with the *Missa S. Theresiae*, it was sung by MT on 3 October 1802 ("Eine Meß von Eibler sambt Graduale und Offertorio"). Parts: HK 1747, HK 2526.
[46] "Ad te levavi" in C (not F), Herrmann 98, 1804. Parts: HK 1744, HK 2527. Composed for performance with the *Missa S. Michaelis*.
[47] "Haec est dies" in D, offertory for St. Theresa's Day, Herrmann 89, October 1800. Probably composed for performance with *Missa S. Wolfgangi*, as an alternative to "Fremit mare."
[48] "Si consistant" in C minor, Herrmann 86, 1805. Parts: HK 2526.
[49] Giuseppe Farinelli, "Tantum ergo." Score: Mus. Hs. 19334.

Fenarolli

Salmo Dixit in D maggiore. Partitura, e parti cavate.[50]

Freundthaler

I   Missa in C maggiore. Parti cavate.[51]
II Missa in C maggiore. Parti cavate.

Fux

I   Missa in C maggiore. Parti cavate.[52]
II Missa in C maggiore. Parti cavate.

G.
Gassmann

Requiem in C minore. Parti cavate, in dupplo.[53]

Gatti

Missa in C maggiore. Parti cavate.[54]
Offertorium in Es maggiore (Quando Jesus). Parti cavate.[55]

Gherardeschi

Kyrie et Gloria in D maggiore. Partitura sola.[56]
Requiem et Libera in C minore. Partitura sola.[57]

---

[50] Fedele Fenarolli, "Dixit Dominus" in D. Autograph score: Mus. Hs. 16433; parts: HK 269.
[51] A-Wn contains no masses by Cajetan Freundthaler with provenance in the Hofkapelle.
[52] This Fux is probably Johann Nepomuk Fuchs, a violinist and composer in the service of the Esterházy family from 1788; one of his masses was performed at Eisenstadt on 10 September 1797 (Rosenbaum, "Tagebücher," 25). Parts for two masses in C by Fuchs: HK 263 and HK 264.
[53] Florian Gassmann, Requiem in C minor. Parts: HK 31 and HK 245.
[54] Luigi Gatti, Mass in C minor (not major). Parts: HK 510.
[55] "Quando Jesus" in E♭. Parts: HK 536.
[56] Filippo Maria Gherardeschi, Kyrie and Gloria in D. Score in A-Wn: Mus. Hs. 15850.
[57] Requiem in C minor. Score in A-Wn: Mus. Hs. 15851.

Graun

Te Deum in D maggiore. Partitura, e parti cavate.[58]

Gyrowetz

Missa in F maggiore. Partitura e parti cavate.[59]
Te Deum in D maggiore. Parti cavate.[60]
Vespera de Beata in D maggiore. Parti cavate.[61]

H.
Hasse

I   Missa in G et D. Parti cavate.[62]
II   Missa in D minore. Parti cavate.[63]
III   Missa in Es maggiore. Parti cavate.[64]
IV   Missa in D maggiore. Parti cavate.[65]
V   Missa in F maggiore. Parti cavate.[66]
VI   Missa in F maggiore. Parti cavate.
       Requiem in C. Parti cavate.[67]
       Miserere in D minore. Parti cavate.[68]
       Te Deum in D maggiore. Parti cavate.[69]
       Regina coeli in D maggiore. Parti cavate, in dupplo.[70]

Haydn Joseph

I   Missa in B maggiore. Partitura, e parti cavate, in dupplo.[71]

---

[58] Carl Heinrich Graun, Te Deum (Leipzig, 1757), performed by MT on 24 December 1801. Printed score: SA.82.B.7 (provenance unknown); parts: HK 1836.
[59] Adalbert Gyrowetz, Mass in F, probably the "Meß von Gyrowetz" performed by MT on 10 March 1802. Score: Mus. Hs. 15852; parts: HK 502 ("composta e dedicata a sua Majestà l'Imperatrice Maria Teresa").
[60] Te Deum in D. Parts: HK 504.   [61] Vespers in D. Parts: HK 503.
[62] Johann Adolf Hasse, Mass in G and D. Parts: Mus. Hs. 17320. MT performed a mass by Hasse on 25 February 1802, but left no clue in her diary about which of these six masses it was.
[63] Mass in D minor. Parts: Mus. Hs. 17321.   [64] Mass in Eb. Parts: Mus. Hs. 17324.
[65] Mass in D. Parts: Mus. Hs. 17319.   [66] Two masses in F. Parts: Mus. Hs. 17318, 17323.
[67] Requiem in C. Although MT performed this requiem by Hasse on 1 March 1802, I found no parts in A-Wn with provenance in the Hofkapelle.
[68] Miserere in D minor. Parts: Mus. Hs. 17317.
[69] Te Deum in D. Parts (dated 18 June 1802): HK 1196.
[70] "Regina coeli" in D. Parts: Mus. Hs. 17316.
[71] The four masses in Bb in Marie Therese's collection were probably *Missa S. Bernardi de Offida* ("Heiligmesse," Hob. XXII: 10, 1796), the "Theresienmesse" (Hob. XXII:12, 1799), the

II   Missa in B maggiore. Parti cavate, in dupplo.

III Missa in B maggiore. Parti cavate.

IV   Missa in B maggiore. Parti cavate.

V   Missa in C maggiore. Parti cavate, in dupplo[72]

VI   Missa in C maggiore. Parti cavate.

VII Missa in C maggiore. Parti cavate, in dupplo.

VIII Missa in D minore. Parti cavate.[73]

I   Offertorium in C maggiore (O Jesu). Parti cavate.[74]

II   Offertorium in D minor (Insanae et vanae). Parti cavate.[75]

Stabat mater in G minore. Partitura e parti cavate.[76]

Te Deum in C maggiore. Partitura e parti cavate.[77]

Haydn Michael

I   Missa in C maggiore a 2 cori. Parti cavate.[78]

II   Missa in C maggiore. Parti cavate.[79]

III Missa in D maggiore. Parti cavate.[80]

IV   Missa in D minore. Parti cavate.[81]

"Schöpfungsmesse" (Hob. XXII:13, 1801), and the "Harmoniemesse" (Hob. XXII:14, 1802). Parts for all these masses with provenance in the Hofkapelle are preserved in A-Wn: "Heiligmesse," HK 2861; "Theresienmesse," HK 2869; "Schöpfungsmesse," HK 2868; "Harmoniemesse," HK 2860.

[72] The three masses in C major in MT's collection were probably the first *Missa Cellensis* ("Missa S. Caeciliae," Hob. XXII:5, 1766), the second *Missa Cellensis* ("Mariazellermesse," Hob. XXII:8, 1782), and the *Missa in tempore belli* ("Paukenmesse," Hob. XXII:9, 1796). Parts for all these masses with provenance in the Hofkapelle are preserved in A-Wn: the "Missa S. Caeciliae," HK 2859; the "Mariazellermesse," HK 2862; the "Paukenmesse," HK 2867. On 1 March 1802 MT performed "Die Cecilia Meß von Hayden Joseph."

[73] *Missa in angustiis* ("Nelsonmesse," Hob. XXII:11, 1798). Parts: HK 3029.

[74] "O Jesu, te invocamus" in C, adapted from the Applausus Cantata, Hob. XXIVa:6, No. 8a. Parts: HK 2593.

[75] "Insanae et vanae curae" in D minor, adapted from *Il ritorno di Tobia*, Hob. XXI:1, No. 13c). Parts: HK 2594.

[76] Stabat mater, Hob. XXbis, 1767. Parts: HK 2599.

[77] This score (probably the autograph) and this set of parts for the Te Deum in C, Hob. XXIIIc:2, written for MT in 1799 or 1800, have apparently been lost. See Irmgard Becker-Glauch, "Joseph Haydns Te Deum für die Kaiserin: Eine Quellenstudie," *Colloquium Amicorum: Joseph Schmidt Görg zum 70. Geburtstag*, Bonn, 1967, 1.

[78] *Missa a due cori* ("Missa hispanica") in C, Sherman 422. Parts: HK 2047. For this identification I am grateful to Charles H. Sherman, who kindly read a preliminary draft of my annotations to the M. Haydn entries and responded with much new information in a long and learned letter of 25 November 2000, to which I refer in the annotations as "Sherman, Letter."

[79] *Missa S. Ursulae* in C, Sherman 546 (3 August 1793), "a work whose elaborate solos for soprano the empress probably found endearing" (Sherman, Letter). Parts: HK 2046 (in Eybler's hand).

[80] *Missa S. Theresiae* in D, Sherman 796–7, autograph dated 3 August 1801, commissioned by MT and performed by her on 4 October 1801. Parts: HK 2052.

[81] *Missa S. Francisci* in D minor, Sherman 826. Commissioned by MT, completed on 16 August 1803 and probably first performed 4 October 1803. Parts: HK 2048 (copied by Eybler).

I   Te Deum in D maggiore. Parti cavate.[82]
II   Te Deum in D maggiore. Parti cavate.
III   Te Deum in C maggiore. Parti cavate.[83]
      Requiem in C minore. Parti cavate in dupplo.[84]
      Introitus da uno Requiem in B maggiore. Partitura sola.[85]
I   Graduale in B maggiore (Petite et accipietis). Parti cavate in dupplo.[86]
II   Graduale in A minore (Beatus vir). Parti cavate in dupplo.[87]
III   Graduale in A maggiore (Cantate Domino). Parti cavate in dupplo.[88]
I   Offertorium in C maggiore (Exaltabo te). Parti cavate in dupplo.[89]
II   Offertorium in D maggiore (Magnus Dominus). Parti cavate in dupplo.[90]
III   Offertorium in C maggiore (Tres sunt). Parti cavate in dupplo.[91]
IV   Offertorium in Es maggiore (Alma Dei). Parti cavate in dupplo.[92]
V   Offertorium in B maggiore (Debitam morti). Parti cavate.[93]
VI   Offertorium in G minore (Quicunque). Parti cavate.[94]

---

[82] This Te Deum and the following one, both in D, were written for performance with the two masses commissioned by MT for Emperor Franz's nameday on 4 October 1801 and 4 October 1803. The first (Sherman 800), completed on 3 August 1801, was performed by MT on 4 October and again on 19 November 1801. Parts: HK 2680. The second (Sherman 829) was completed on 20 September 1803, shortly after the *Missa S. Francisci*. Parts: HK 2678.

[83] Probably Sherman 415, a Te Deum in C composed in 1786, which "circulated widely in copies made under Haydn's supervision" (Sherman, Letter). Parts: HK 2679.

[84] Requiem in C minor (1771), Sherman 155, praised by MT when Haydn visited Vienna in 1801 and performed by her on 10 March 1802. Parts: HK 2054.

[85] "Haydn's final work, Sherman 838, left incomplete at his death. According to Pater Werigand Rettensteiner, the composer's closest friend and biographer, the autograph torso of the Requiem was sent to its commissioner, the empress in Vienna" (Sherman, Letter). Autograph score: Mus. Hs. 34232. MT commissioned the Requiem during her visit to Salzburg in 1805, according to *AmZ* 7 (1804–5), cols. 625–8: "Our revered Haydn . . . enjoyed some well-deserved distinctions in connection with the presence [in Salzburg] of the Holy Roman Emperor and Her Majesty the Empress. He had written two Latin Masses already for the empress, who holds him very dear to her; and, after an extended audience, she commissioned Haydn to write a Requiem and a Libera me, Domine in the highest church style, as this true friend of music put it . . . Haydn is now working on the Requiem" (translation in Sherman, Letter).

[86] "Petite et accipietis," Sherman 798, 8 August 1801, composed for performance with the *Missa S. Theresiae*. Parts: HK 2613.

[87] "Beatus vir, qui suffert" in A minor, Sherman 410, 1785. Parts: HK 2662.

[88] "Cantate Domino" in A, Sherman 828, 30 August 1803. Composed for performance with the *Missa S. Francisci*. Parts: HK 2621.

[89] "Exaltabo Te" in C, Sherman 547. Parts: HK 2668.

[90] "Magnus Dominus" in D, Sherman 799, 11 August 1801. Composed for performance with the *Missa S. Theresiae*. Parts: HK 2663.

[91] "Tres sunt" in C, Sherman 183, 1772. Parts: HK 2660.

[92] "Alma Dei Creatoris" in E♭, Sherman 221, composed in 1776. Parts: HK 2665.

[93] "Debitam morti" in B♭, Sherman 793, completed on 29 January 1801. Parts: HK 2666.

[94] "Quicunque manducaverit" in G minor, Sherman 259, written between 1775 and 1778. Parts: HK 2676.

VII   Offertorium in G maggiore (Lauda Sion). Parti cavate.[95]
VIII   Offertorium in G maggiore in canone (Domine Deus). Parti cavate.[96]
IX   Offertorium in F maggiore (Sicut cervus). Parti cavate.[97]
       Salmo Dixit Dominus in D maggiore. Parti cavate.[98]

Heidenreich

Missa in B maggiore. Parti cavate.[99]

J.
Jomelli

Missa in D maggiore. Parti cavate.[100]
Miserere in G minore. Partitura e parti cavate.[101]
Offertorium in F maggiore (Confirma me). Parti cavate in dupplo.[102]

K.
Kauer

Missa in C maggiore. Parti cavate.[103]

Knecht

Te Deum in D maggiore a due cori. Partitura e parti cavate.[104]

---

[95] "Lauda Sion" in G, Sherman 215, 1775. Parts (incomplete): HK 1806.
[96] "Domine Deus" in G, Sherman 827, completed 23 August 1803 for performance with the *Missa S. Francisci*. Autograph score: Mus. Hs. 19083.
[97] "Sicut cervus" in F, Sherman 143, 1770. Parts: HK 2667.
[98] "Dixit Dominus" in D, Sherman 809, Salzburg, 27 January 1802; MT performed it on 1 April 1802. Parts: HK 753.
[99] I found no mass by Joseph Heidenreich in A-Wn.
[100] Niccolo Jommelli, probably the Mass in D, Hochstein A.1.1. Parts: HK 3052.
[101] Miserere in G minor, probably "Pietà, Signore" Hochstein Anh. 42 (in Italian, 2 sopranos and orchestra, Naples, 1774), performed by MT on 24 December 1801. Parts: Mus. Hs. 19086.
[102] "Confirma hoc Deus" (not "Confirma me"), in F, Hochstein B.I.3.1, 1752. Several sources in A-Wn. MT performed "Ein Graduale Confirma von Jomelli" on 5 March 1802. The vast number of surviving sources, all over Europe, attest to this work's widespread popularity.
[103] Ferdinand Kauer, Mass in D (not C). Parts: HK 508.
[104] Justin Heinrich Knecht, Te Deum in D. Score (autograph dated 1801 and dedicated to Emperor Franz and Napoleon, probably in celebration of the Treaty of Lunéville): Mus. Hs. 15512.

Koczeluch Giovanni Antonio

Missa in D maggiore. Partitura sola.[105]
Te Deum in D maggiore. Partitura sola.[106]
Graduale in G maggiore (Benedictus es). Partitura sola.[107]
Offertorium in B maggiore (Benedictus sit). Partitura sola.[108]

L.
Leo

Kyrie e Gloria in D maggiore. Partitura sola.[109]
Miserere a 8 voci in C minore. Partitura sola.[110]
Salmo Dixit Dominus in A maggiore. Partitura sola.[111]

Lickel

Missa in Es maggiore. Parti cavate.[112]
Te Deum in Es maggiore. Parti cavate.[113]
Graduale in Es maggiore. Parti cavate (Specie tua).[114]
Offertorium in Es maggiore. Parti cavate (Haec est virgo).[115]

M.
Maschek

Missa in D maggiore colla Harmonica. Parti cavate.[116]

---

[105] Johann Anton Kozeluch, Mass in D. Autograph score: HK 313.
[106] Te Deum in D. Scores: HK 299, 300, 302.
[107] "Benedictus es" in G. Scores: Mus. Hs. 15847, 16821.
[108] "Benedictus sit" in B♭. Score: Mus. Hs. 15846.
[109] Leonardo Leo, Kyrie and Gloria in D. Score: Mus. Hs. 17021.
[110] Miserere in C minor. Score: Mus. Hs. 15519.
[111] "Dixit Dominus" in A. Score: Mus. Hs. 15527.
[112] Johann Georg Lickl, Mass in E♭, commissioned by MT in 1804 (Michael Haas, *Rede, gehalten am 12. Mai 1852, bei Gelegenheit der Enthüllung und Einweihung des dem verstorbenen Dom-Kapellmeister zu Fünfkirchen, Georg Lickl (gest. am 12. Mai 1843) von seinen Freunden und Verehrern errichteten Monumentes*, Vienna, 1852, 8). Score: Mus. Hs. 16434; parts: HK 540.
[113] Te Deum in E♭, probably composed for performance with the Mass in E♭. Parts: HK 543.
[114] "Specie tua" in E♭, probably composed for performance with the Mass in E♭. Parts: HK 541.
[115] "Haec est virgo" in E♭, probably composed for performance with the Mass in E♭. Parts: HK 542.
[116] Vincenz Maschek, Mass in D, with glass harmonica solo in the Benedictus. Parts: HK 511.

Monn

I   Missa in C maggiore. Parti cavate.[117]
II Missa in B maggiore. Parti cavate.

Monetta

Miserere in B maggiore. Partitura sola.[118]
Requiem in G maggiore. Partitura sola.[119]

Mozart

Missa in C maggiore. Parti cavate.[120]
Requiem in D minore. Parti cavate e la partitura.[121]

N.
Nopitsch

Stabat mater in E maggiore, a 8 voci. Parti cavate, e la partitura.[122]

O.
Orgitano

Requiem in G minore. Partitura, e parti cavate.[123]

P.
Paer

Missa in D maggiore. Partitura, e parti cavate.[124]
Te Deum in C maggiore. Partitura, e parti cavate.[125]
Graduale in C maggiore (Exaltate Dominum). Partitura, e parti cavate.[126]

---

[117] Matthias Georg Monn, Mass in C. The "Meß von Monn" that MT performed on 28 November 1802 was presumably this or the following mass.
[118] Giuseppe Moneta, Miserere in B♭. Score: Mus. Hs. 16648.
[119] Requiem in G. Score: Mus. Hs. 16647.
[120] This mass in C major could have been K. 257, K. 258, K. 317, or K. 337, all of which are preserved in parts from the Hofkapelle in A-Wn.
[121] Parts: HK 2879. MT performed Mozart's Requiem on 17 March 1802.
[122] Christoph Friedrich Wilhelm Nopitsch, Stabat Mater in E. Score and parts: HK 512.
[123] Vincenzo Orgitano, Requiem in G minor. Score: Mus. Hs. 16658; parts: HK 746.
[124] Ferdinando Paer, Mass in D, 1805–6. Score (with autograph corrections and alterations): HK 305.
[125] Te Deum in C. Score: HK 1876.   [126] "Exaltate Dominum" in C. Parts: HK 1383.

Offertorium in A maggiore (Laetamini coelites). Partitura, e parti cavate.
Salve Regina in F maggiore. Tenore concer[ta]to. Partitura sola.[127]

Paisiello

I   Missa in D maggiore. Kyrie, e Gloria, a 2 cori. Partitura, e parti cavate.[128]
II   Missa in G maggiore. Kyrie, e Gloria, a 2 cori. Partitura, e parti cavate.[129]
III   Missa in F maggiore. Kyrie, e Gloria, a 2 cori. Partitura, e parti cavate.[130]
IV   Missa in B maggiore. Partitura sola.[131]
       Te Deum in B maggiore a 2 cori. Parti cavate, e la partitura.[132]
I   Motetto in G maggiore (Splendete o coeli). Parti cavate, e la partitura.[133]
II   Motetto in D maggiore (Absit sonitus). Parti cavate, e la partitura.[134]
III   Motetto in C maggiore (Non est in vita). Parti cavate, e la partitura.[135]
IV   Motetto in Es maggiore (Alma fax). Parti cavate, e la partitura.[136]
V   Motetto in Es maggiore (Coeli stella amica). Parti cavate, e la
       partitura.[137]
VI   Motetto in G minore (Veni ferox). Parti cavate, e la partitura.[138]
       Salmo: Dixit Dominus in A maggiore. Partitura sola.[139]
       Miserere in A minore. Partitura sola.[140]

Pazzaglia

I   Missa in C maggiore. Partitura sola.[141]
II   Missa in D minore. Partitura sola.
       Requiem in C minore. Partitura, e parti cavate.[142]

---

[127] "Salve Regina" in F. Score: HK 1876.
[128] Giovanni Paisiello, Mass in D, Robinson 5.03. Score: Mus. Hs. 19188; parts: HK 582. This and the following masses, following Neapolitan tradition, consist of Kyrie and Gloria alone.
[129] Mass in G, Robinson 5.02. Score: Mus. Hs. 19208; parts: HK 583.
[130] Mass in F, Robinson 5.04. Score: Mus. Hs. 19209; parts: HK 584.
[131] Mass in Bb, Robinson 5.06. Score: Mus. Hs. 16618.
[132] Te Deum in Bb for double chorus, Robinson 6.01, Naples, 1791. MT performed it on 28 February 1802. Score: Mus. Hs. 19213–14; parts: HK 585.
[133] "Splendete o coeli" in G, Robinson 4.07, written for Napoleon's chapel between 1802 and 1804. Score: Mus. Hs. 16624; parts: HK 587.
[134] "Absit sonitus" in D, Robinson 4.03, written for Napoleon's chapel between 1802 and 1804. Score: Mus. Hs. 16620; parts: HK 589.
[135] "Non est in vita" in C, Robinson 4.11, written for Napoleon's chapel between 1802 and 1804. Score: Mus. Hs. 16619; parts: HK 591.
[136] "Alma fax" in Eb, Robinson 7.12. Score: Mus. Hs. 16622; parts: HK 590.
[137] "Coeli stella amica" in Eb, Robinson 4.09. Parts: HK 586.
[138] "Veni ferox" in G minor, Robinson 7.11. Score: Mus. Hs. 16621; parts: HK 588.
[139] "Dixit Dominus" in A, Robinson 6.04. No sources in A-Wn.
[140] Miserere, Robinson 6.30. Score: Mus. Hs. 18725.
[141] I found no sources for masses by Salvador Pazzaglia in A-Wn.
[142] Requiem in C minor. Score: Mus. Hs. 16666; parts: HK 513.

Pergolese

Stabat mater in F minore. Parti cavate.[143]
Miserere in F minore. Partitura sola.
I   Salmo: Laudate pueri, in D maggiore. Parti cavate.[144]
II Salmo: Laudate pueri, in D maggiore. Parti cavate, e la partitura.

Pichel

I   Missa in C maggiore. Parti cavate.[145]
II Missa in B maggiore. Parti cavate.[146]
    Te Deum in C maggiore. Parti cavate.[147]
    Offertorium in C maggiore (Confitemini Domino). Parti cavate.[148]

Platone

Missa in Es maggiore. Kyrie, e Gloria. Parti cavate, e la partitura.[149]

Pleyel

Missa in C minore. Parti cavate.[150]

Pohl

Missa in C minore. Parti cavate.[151]

Preindl

I   Missa in C maggiore. Parti cavate, in dupplo, stampate.[152]
II Missa in C maggiore. Parti cavate in dupplo stampate.[153]
III Missa in B maggiore. Parti cavate in dupplo stampate.[154]

---

[143] Giovanni Battista Pergolesi, Stabat Mater, Naples, 1736, performed by MT and Marchesi on 17 and 28 April 1802. Several sources in A-Wn.
[144] Laudate pueri in D. Parts: HK 2720.   [145] Wenzel Pichl, Mass in C. Parts: HK 328.
[146] Mass in Bb. Parts: HK 329.   [147] Te Deum in C. Parts: HK 331.
[148] "Confitemini Domino" in C. Parts: HK 330.
[149] Giuseppe Platone, Kyrie and Gloria in Eb. Score: Mus. Hs. 16659; parts: HK 535.
[150] Since no mass in C minor by Ignaz Pleyel is known, the work in question is probably Pleyel's Mass in D (Benton 756). Parts: HK 538.
[151] Pohl (first name unknown), Mass in C minor. Parts: HK 537.
[152] Joseph Preindl, Mass No. 1 in C, Op. 7. Printed parts (Vienna, n.d.): HK 1168.
[153] Mass No. 2 in C, Op. 10. Printed parts (Vienna, n.d.): HK 1263.
[154] Mass No. 3 in Bb. Printed parts (Vienna, n.d.): HK 1215.

IV Missa in C minore. Parti cavate in dupplo stampate.[155]
V   Missa in D maggiore. Parti cavate in dupplo stampate.[156]
VI Missa in Es maggiore. Parti cavate in tripplo, stampate, e scritte.[157] Da 12 Gradualia. Parti cavate in dupplo stampate.[158]
Da 12 Offertoria. Parti cavate in dupplo stampate.
Graduale scritto in As maggiore (Domine Dominus). Parti cavate, e la partitura.[159]

R.
Reutter

Missa in C maggiore. Parti cavate.[160]
Requiem in G minore. Parti cavate in dupplo.
Graduale in C maggiore (Tu de vita). Parti cavate.[161]

Righini

Missa in D minore. Partitura, e parti cavate.[162]

S.
Schacht

Missa in C maggiore. Partitura sola.[163]

Starke

Missa in C maggiore. Parti cavate.[164]

Sterkel

Missa in D maggiore. Parti cavate, e la partitura.[165]
Te Deum in D maggiore. Parti cavate, e la partitura.[166]

---

[155] Mass No. 4 in C minor. Printed parts (Vienna, n.d.): HK 1241.
[156] Mass No. 6 in D, Op. 11. Printed parts (Vienna, n.d.): HK 1221.
[157] Mass No. 5 in E♭, Op. 8, Vienna, n.d.
[158] Various graduals and offertories in printed parts (Vienna, n.d.): HK 1283–6.
[159] "Domine Dominus" in A♭. Score: HK 1886.
[160] Several masses in C major by Georg Reutter the younger are preserved in A-Wn in sources from the Hofkapelle.
[161] I found no source for this gradual in A-Wn.
[162] Vincenzo Righini, Mass in D minor. Score: HK 2281; parts: HK 2335.
[163] Theodor Schacht, Mass in C minor (later major), with gradual "Amavit eam" and offertory "Plaude turba angelica," October 1805, dedicated to MT. Autograph score: Mus Hs. 16210.
[164] I found no mass by Friedrich Starke in A-Wn.
[165] Johann Franz Xaver Sterkel, Mass in D. Score: Mus. Hs. 16208; parts: HK 496.
[166] Te Deum in D. Score: Mus. Hs. 16209; parts: HK 497.

Summer

Graduale in A maggiore (Laetamini). Parti cavate.[167]
Offertorium in C maggiore (Deum Deum). Parti cavate.[168]

Teyber Antonio

I   Missa in A maggiore. Partitura, e parti cavate.[169]
II   Missa in A maggiore. Partitura sola.[170]
III   Missa in D maggiore. Partitura sola.[171]
IV   Missa in C maggiore. Partitura sola.[172]
      Graduale in D maggiore (Gloriose Pater). Parti cavate.[173]
      Offertorium in D maggiore (In virtute). Parti cavate.[174]

Tritto

Missa in G maggiore. Kyrie, e Gloria. Partitura sola.[175]

V.
Valotti

Salve Regina a 2 cori senz' istrumenti. Partitura sola.[176]

W.
Weigl

Offertorium in G maggiore (En ipse Jesus). Parti cavate.[177]

---

[167] Georg Summer, "Laetamini in Domino" in A. Parts: HK 516.
[168] "Deum athletae" in C. Parts: HK 517.
[169] Anton Teyber, *Missa S. Vincenti Ferreri* in A. Score and parts: HK 573. This mass, the only one by Teyber for which MT owned a set of parts, was probably the "Tutti Meß von Teyber" she performed on 22 January 1802.
[170] I have been unable to find a second mass in A in A-Wn with provenance in the Hofkapelle.
[171] Mass in D. Score: HK 1107.
[172] I have been unable to find a mass in C in A-Wn with provenance in the Hofkapelle.
[173] "Gloriose Pater" in D. Parts: HK 575. Probably intended for performance with the *Missa S. Vincenti*.
[174] "In virtute tua" in D. Parts: HK 576. Probably intended for performance with the *Missa S. Vincenti*.
[175] Giacomo Tritto, Kyrie and Gloria in G. Score: Mus. Hs. 16663.
[176] Francesco Antonio Valotti, "Salve Regina." I found no score in A-Wn with provenance in the Hofkapelle.
[177] I have been unable to find in A-Wn sources for this offertory.

Winter

I   Missa in D minore a 2 cori. Parti cavate.[178]
II   Missa in F maggiore. Parti cavate.[179]
III   Missa pastorale in F maggiore. Partitura sola.[180]
      Requiem in C minore. Partitura, e parti cavate.[181]
      Miserere in Es maggiore. Partitura, e parti cavate.[182]

Ex Creatione mundi[183]

Missa in C maggiore. Parti cavate.
Graduale in C maggiore (O sancta spes). Parti cavate.
Offertorium in A maggiore (Ad sonum). Parti cavate.

Da diversi autori, cioè:
Gallus, Albrechtsberger, Haydn Giuseppe, Kauer

Missa in C maggiore. Parti cavate, e la partitura.[184]

Senza Nome[185]

I   Missa in C maggiore. Parti cavate.
II   Missa pastorale in D maggiore. Kyrie e Gloria. Partitura sola.
I   Graduale in A maggiore (Fons amoris). Parti cavate.
II   Graduale in C maggiore (In te speravimus). Parti cavate.

Fine

---

[178] Peter Winter, Mass with double chorus, performed by MT on 25 October 1802. Parts: HK 324.
[179] Mass in F. Parts: HK 323.
[180] *Missa pastoralis* in F. Score: HK 1964.
[181] Requiem in C minor. Score: HK 1965; parts: HK 326. MT performed Winter's requiem on 25 October and 15 November 1802.
[182] Miserere in E♭. Score and parts: HK 327.
[183] Anonymous arrangement of excerpts from Haydn's *Die Schöpfung* into a plenary mass in A, not C (both the Kyrie and the Agnus Dei are in A). Parts: HK 1093.
[184] I have been unable to identify a source in A-Wn for this "pasticcio" mass.
[185] I have been unable to identify sources in A-Wn for these anonymous works.

Marie Therese's musical diary, 1801–3

Source: HHStA, Fa, HKF, Kart. 24. Except where otherwise specified, all musical sources cited in the notes are preserved in A-Wn, with provenance (based on evidence presented in chapter 1) in Marie Therese's library.

Nowember [1801]

Dem 11ten   Das Fest von Carolinen im Elysium von Weigl[1]

Dem 15ten   Ackademie im Redouten Saal mit folgenden Stücken

        Ein Terzett aus Armida von Sarti[2] gesungen von der
            Wiesenthal[3] Ratmayer[4] und Weinmüller[5]

        Eine Aria von Cimarosa gesungen von der Wiesenthal

        Ein Duett aus Adelaide du Guesclin von Mayer[6] gesungen
            von mir und Marchesi[7]

        Eine Arie aus der Lodoiska mit Chöre von Weigl[8] von
            Ratmayer

        Das Finale vom ersten Act aus Adelaide du Guesclin[9] von
            mir Marchesi Ratmayer Weinmüller und Chöre

---

[1] Weigl, *La festa di Carolina negli Elisi*, cantata, text by De Gamerra. Score and parts, dated 29 October 1801: Mus. Hs. 10152–3. The title alludes to MT's mother, Queen Maria Carolina of Naples, for whose nameday on 4 November this piece was written (see chapter 3).

[2] Sarti, *Armida e Rinaldo, dramma per musica* (St. Petersburg, 1786). Score: Mus. Hs. 10002.

[3] Antonia Schleichert von Wiesenthal, chamber servant to Archduchess Maria Luisa from about 1801 (*HSS* 1802, 420).

[4] Mathias Rathmayer, amateur tenor; see chapter 2.   [5] Carl Weinmüller, bass; see chapter 2.

[6] Mayr, *Adelaide di Guesclino, dramma di sentimento* (Venice, 1799; first performed in Vienna on 24 March 1802). Score: Mus. Hs. 9954. This duet was "Ti lascio, mia vita" (score and parts: Mus. Hs. 10485–6).

[7] The *musico* Luigi Marchesi; see chapter 2.

[8] "Coraggio, Boleslao" (score and parts: Mus. Hs. 10807–8), written by Weigl for the Viennese production of Mayr's *Lodoiska* (*dramma per musica*, Venice, 1796), first performed in Vienna in 1798. The tenor Giuseppe Simoni sang an aria by Weigl in act 2 of *Lodoiska* (A-Wth, Theaterzettel; Rosenbaum, 46). Mayr later rewrote most of the opera for a production in Milan, Carnival 1800.

[9] Score and parts for the first-act finale of Mayr's *Adelaide*: Mus. Hs. 10470–1.

Der Bacchanten Chor aus der Cantata il Miglior Dono von Weigl[10]

Das Terzett d[to] gesungen von mir Wiesenthal und Ratmayer

Eine Arie d[to] mit Chöre gesungen von mir

Das Quintett d[to] gesungen von mir Wiesenthal Ratmayer Weinmüller und Wallaschek[11]

Eine Arie mit Chor d[to] gesungen von Weinmüller

Das Duett aus der Schöpfung gesungen von mir und d[to].[12]

Eine Polonoise aus der Lodoiska von Mayer gesungen von Marchesi[13]

Das Finale aus der Cantate il Miglior Dono von Weigl gesungen von mir Wiesenthal Ratmayer Weinmüller und Chöre

Dem 17ten   Das Fest von Caroline im Elysium von Weigl

Dem 19ten   Kleine Musick bey mir mit folgenden 2 Stücken
Miserere von Sarti[14] gesungen von mir Großherzog[15] Ratmayer und Weinmüller mit Chöre
Meß, Tedeum und Graduale von Michel Hayden gemacht für dem 4ten 8[ber16] gesungen von die nemlichen

Dem 22.   Ackademie bey dem Großherzog, die erste Abtheilung von ihm mit folgenden Stücken
Die Ouverture auß dem Numa Pompilio von Pär[17]
Eine Arie d[to] gesungen von Großherzog

---

[10] Weigl, *Il miglior dono*, cantata for Franz's birthday, 12 February 1801 (Weigl, "Zwei Selbstbiographien," 52); also performed under the title *Das beste Geschenk* in the Grosser Redoutensaal, 5 April 1801 (Morrow). Score and parts: Mus. Hs. 10150–1.

[11] The bass Jakob Wallaschek made his debut in the court theaters on 16 October 1795 as the druggist in Dittersdorf's *Der Apotheker und der Doktor* (A-Wth, Theaterzettel).

[12] J. Haydn, *Die Schöpfung* (Vienna, 1798), of which MT owned a score and a set of parts (*CaM*, p. 19). She and Weinmüller sang the duet "Holde Gattin" several times between 1801 and 1803.

[13] Marchesi created the role of Lowinski in both the Venetian and Milanese versions of Mayr's *Lodoiska*. This polonaise was either "Pietoso a' miei lamenti" (score and parts: Mus. Hs. 10530–1) or "Contento il cor nel seno" (Mus. Hs. 10532–3).

[14] *KK* mentions no settings of the Miserere by Sarti. A Miserere a 4 voci is among several sacred works by Sarti in score and parts in I-Fc: F.P. Ch 813–18.

[15] Grand Duke Ferdinand III of Tuscany; see chapter 2.

[16] M. Haydn, *Missa S. Theresiae*, Sherman 796–7 (3 August 1801) a copy of which MT owned (*KK*, Mass III). The Te Deum in D, Sherman 800 (21 August 1801) was one of two D major Te Deums listed in *KK*; the gradual was "Petite et accipietis," Sherman 798 (8 August 1801; copy listed in *KK*: Gradual I). These works, written for MT, were performed at Laxenburg on 4 October 1801 (St. Francis's Day) under the composer's direction, with MT singing the solo soprano part (see chapter 5).

[17] Paer, *Numa Pompilio, dramma per musica*. No public performance in Vienna is known, but a libretto was printed in Vienna in 1800 (copy in A-Wn) and MT owned score and parts (Mus. Hs. 9979–80).

Ein Terzett auß dem Opferfest von Winter[18] gesungen von
Großherzog Weinmüller und Pär[19]
Das Finale vom ersten Act des Numa von Pär gesungen
von Großherzog Bustelli[20] Vegni[21] Pär und Chöre
Eine Arie aus Debora und Sisara von Guiglielmi[22]
gesungen von Vegni
Ein Duett aus der Vendetta di Nino von Prati[23] gesungen
von Bustelli und Vegni
Das Finale vom ersten Act aus dem Opferfest von Winter
gesungen von Großherzog Bustelli Pär Weinmüller
Ratmayer und Chöre
Die zweite Abtheilung von mir mit folgenden Stücken
Ein Terzett aus Alessandro nell'Indie von Tarchi[24]
gesungen von Bok[25] Marchesi und Weinmüller
Ein Rondò aus Giulietta und Romeo von Zingarelli[26]
gesungen von der Bock
Ein Duett aus der Ginevra di Scozia von Mayer[27] gesungen
von mir und Marchesi

The first performance recorded in the *New Grove Dictionary of Opera* (4 vols., London, 1992) was in Paris in 1808; Paer probably composed the opera for the private use of MT and Grand Duke Ferdinand and later (after MT's death) revised it for Paris. The autograph score, a copy of the score, and a set of parts in I-Fc (F.P. T 339 and 597) probably belonged to Ferdinand.

[18] Peter Winter, *Das unterbrochene Opferfest* (Vienna, 1796). This trio for three male voices was "Mein Leben hab' ich ihm zu danken."

[19] Since MT normally listed female singers before male (the main exception being her tendency to place Grand Duke Ferdinand at the beginning of a list of singers), this Paer was probably the composer rather than his wife, the opera singer Francesca Riccardi Paer. Ferdinand Paer also sang in several private concerts of the Viennese nobility between 1799 and 1802 (Morrow, 392–7).

[20] I have been unable to identify the female singer Bustelli.

[21] I have been unable to identify the female singer Vegni.

[22] Guglielmi, *Debora e Sisara, azione sacra per musica* (Naples, 1789; performed in the court theaters of Vienna in 1792). Score: Mus. Hs. 9898; score and parts in I-Fc: F.P. T 146.

[23] Alessio Prati, *La vendetta di Nino, melodramma tragico per musica* (Florence, Carnival 1786; performed in Vienna in 1792). Score in I-Fc: F.P. T 398). This duet was probably "Qual gel di morte io sento," sung by Semiramide and Arsace.

[24] Angelo Tarchi presented different settings of Metastasio's *Alessandro nell'Indie* in Milan (1788), Livorno (1791), and Turin (1798). Marchesi sang the title role in Livorno. This trio was probably "Son prigioniero lo vedo" (score and parts: Mus. Hs. 10757–8).

[25] This singer, referred to as "Fräulein v. Bock" on the first page of the *parte cantante* for Artemisia in Weigl's *La festa di Carolina negli Elisi*, was probably Theresia Bockh von Pollach, chamber servant to Archduchess Maria Luisa from about 1795 (*HSS* 1796, 387).

[26] Zingarelli, *Giulietta e Romeo, tragedia per musica* (Milan, 1796). This rondò was probably Crescentini's insertion aria, "Ombra adorata" (score and parts: Mus. Hs. 10844–5).

[27] Mayr, *Ginevra di Scozia* (Trieste, 21 April 1801; first performed in Vienna on 27 October 1801). This duet was "Per pietà, deh! non lasciarmi," sung near the end of the opera by Ginevra and Ariodante (score and parts: Mus. Hs. 10494–5; see chapter 3). Marchesi created the role of Ariodante in Trieste.

> Eine Arie auß der Zauberflöte von Mozart[28] gesungen von
> Weinmüller
> Ein Rondò auß der Clemenza di Tito[29] d[to] gesungen von
> mir
> Ein Rondò auß Allesandro nell'Indie von Tarchi[30]
> gesungen von Marchesi
> Das Finale von zweiten Act auß Orazi von Cimarosa[31]
> gesungen von mir, Bok Marchesi Weinmüller Ratmayer
> und Chöre

December [1801]

Dem 20.	Der Uniform von Weigl[32]
Dem 24.	Miserere von Jomelli[33] gesungen von mir und Marchesi
	Tedeum von Graun[34]
Dem 25.	Bey dem Großherzog
	Die Hirten an der Krippe von Pär[35]
Dem 27.	Ackademie bey dem Großherzog die erste Abtheilung von
	ihm mit folgenden Stücken
	Die Ouverture aus denen Orazi und Curiazi von Cimarosa
	Ein Duett aus der Penelope von Cimarosa[36] gesungen von
	Weinmüller und Ratmayer

---

[28] Weinmüller sang the role of Sarastro in the court theaters from 1801. MT owned *Die Zauberflöte* in score and parts (*CaM, p. 19*), transferred by Pohl to A-Wgm, and a separate set of parts for "In diesen heil'gen Hallen" (Mus. Hs. 10897), probably the aria sung by Weinmüller.

[29] Mozart, *La clemenza di Tito* (Prague, 1791). Score and parts: Mus. Hs. 9969–70. This *rondò* was probably Vitellia's "Non più di fiori," of which MT owned a separate score and set of parts: Mus. Hs. 10558–9.

[30] This rondò was probably "Nel lasciarti o bene amato" (score and parts: Mus. Hs. 10755–6).

[31] Cimarosa, *Gli Orazi e i Curiazi, tragedia per musica* (Venice, Carnival 1797; first performed in Vienna on 30 June 1797). Score and parts for the second-act finale: Mus. Hs. 10285–6. For discussion of this *sotterraneo* see chapter 4.

[32] Weigl, *L'uniforme*, written for MT and first performed at Schönbrunn in 1800, with MT as Giannina (see chapter 3). Later very frequently performed in German translation in the court theaters. Score and parts: Mus. Hs. 10088–9.

[33] Of several settings by Niccolò Jommelli of the Miserere, this one was probably his setting of an Italian translation of the psalm, "Pietà, pietà Signore" for two sopranos and strings (1774). MT owned a setting in G minor (*KK*).

[34] Carl Heinrich Graun, Te Deum (Leipzig, 1757); copy listed in *KK*.

[35] The only work of this title that I have been able to identify, a Christmas cantata, is attributed to Joseph Eybler in all musical sources (Herrmann 38). However, MT did not apparently own this work, nor does I-Fc contain full score or parts.

[36] Cimarosa, *Penelope, dramma per musica* (Naples, 1795). This duet was probably "Da questo lido," sung by Ulisse and Evanore (score and parts: Mus. Hs. 10313–14).

Ein Duett aus Alonzo und Cora von Tritto[37] gesungen von
    der Bustelli und Vegni
Eine Arie mit Chöre auß die Orazi und Curiazi von
    Cimarosa[38] gesungen von Pär
Eine Scene mit Chöre auß dem Orfeo von Gluck[39]
    gesungen von Marchese
Ein Terzett auß der Penelope von Cimarosa[40] gesungen
    von der Bustelli Ratmayer und Weinmüller
Eine Arie mit Chöre auß Esther von Nasolini[41] gesungen
    von der Busletti [*sic*]
Ein Quintett auß Axur von Salieri[42] gesungen von
    Weinmüller Wallaschek, Ratmayer und Pär
Das Finale von zweiten Act von Pirro von Paisiello[43]
    gesungen von der Bustelli Ratmayer Vegni Korner[44] Pär
    Weinmüller
Die zweyte Abtheilung von mir mit folgenden Stücken
Ein Terzett aus die Sciti von Mayer[45] gesungen von der
    Wiesenthal Ratmayer und Korner
Eine Scene mit Chor aus d^{to}[46] gesungen von mir
Eine Cavatina auß der Lodoiska d^{to}[47] gesungen von
    Marchese
Ein Quartett aus die Sciti[48] gesungen von mir Wiesenthal
    Ratmayer und Weinmüller, und Chöre

---

[37] Giacomo Tritto, *La vergine del sole* (Naples, 1786), whose principal characters are Alonso and Cora.

[38] Probably "Se alla patria" (score and parts: Mus. Hs. 10336 7).

[39] Gluck, *Orfeo ed Euridice, azione teatrale per musica* (Vienna, 1762). Score: Mus. Hs. 9949. This choral scena was "Ah se intorno" (act 1), "Chi mai dell'Erebo" (act 2), or "Che puro ciel" (act 2).

[40] Probably "Perché eguale all'amor mio" (score and parts: Mus. Hs. 10296–7).

[41] I have not been able to identify an opera or oratorio entitled *Esther* by Sebastiano Nasolini.

[42] Salieri, *Axur re d'Ormus, dramma tragicomico* (Vienna, 1788). Since MT named only four singers, she probably meant quartet rather than quintet. The finale of Act 3, "Non partir, la scelta è ingiusta" (score and parts: Mus. Hs. 10703–4), consists mostly of an ensemble for four male voices and was probably the music sung here.

[43] Paisiello, *Pirro, dramma per musica* (Naples, 1787). Score and parts: Mus. Hs. 9987–8.

[44] Philipp Korner, tenor in the court theaters from 1796, probably made his debut on 4 September 1796 in Dittersdorf's *Betrug durch Aberglauben* (A-Wth, Theaterzettel); he sang in both German and Italian. From 1797 he served in the Hofkapelle.

[45] Mayr, *Gli sciti, dramma per musica* (Venice, Carnival 1800). Score and parts: Mus. Hs. 9963–4. This trio was probably "Mia destra adorata" (score: Mus. Hs. 10482).

[46] Probably "Se m'avete destinata."

[47] Probably "Ah quanto l'anima," a cavatina from Mayr's *Lauso e Lidia* that Marchesi sang in the 1798 Viennese production of *Lodoiska* (score and parts: Mus. Hs. 10526–7).

[48] Probably the *sotterraneo* in act 2.

> Eine Arie mit Chöre auß dem Pimmalione von Federici[49]
> gesungen von Weinmüller
> Ein Duett auß dem Giulio Sabino von Sarti[50] gesungen
> von mir und Marchesi
> Drey Chöre auß dem Judas Maccabäus von Händl[51]

1802

Januar

Dem 3ten   Ackademie bey dem Großherzog die erste Abtheilung von
ihm mit folgenden Stücken[52]
Ein Terzett von Tritto gesungen von der Bustelli, Vegni
und Großherzog
Eine Arie auß der Camilla von Pär[53] gesungen von Pär
Das Finale von 2tem Act von Impressario in Angustie von
Cimarosa[54] gesungen von Bustelli Vegni Pär Ratmayer
und Großherzog
Eine Arie aus der Scuffiara von Paisiello[55] gesungen von
Großherzog
Ein Quintett von Fioravanti gesungen von Bustelli Vegni
Pär Ratmayer und Großherzog
Ein Duett von Matrimonio Segreto von Cimarosa[56]
gesungen von Pär und Großherzog
Das Finale von ersten Act von Camilla von Pär gesungen
von Bustelli Vegni Pär Weinmüller Großherzog und
Chöre
Die zweyte Abtheilung von mir mit folgenden Stücken

[49] Vincenzo or Francesco Federici, *Pimmalione, azione lirica.* Score and parts: Mus. Hs. 10116–17. This aria for bass and chorus was probably "Queste lagrime ch'io verso" (score and parts: Mus. Hs. 10369–70).

[50] Sarti, *Giulio Sabino, dramma per musica* (Venice, 1781; performed in Vienna in 1785). This duet was probably "Come partir poss'io" (score and parts: Mus. Hs. 10733–4).

[51] Handel, *Judas Maccabaeus* (London, 1747). Score and parts: Mus. Hs. 9877–8.

[52] Since performance materials for several works on this program were not in MT's library but do belong to I-Fc, they were probably part of Ferdinand's library.

[53] Paer, *Camilla, ossia Il sotterraneo, dramma serio-giocoso per musica* (Vienna, 1799). Score and parts in I-Fc: F.P. T 350.

[54] Cimarosa, *L'impresario in angustie, farsa* (Naples, 1786; first performed in Vienna in 1793). Score and parts in I-Fc: F.P. T 80.

[55] Paisiello, *La modista raggiratrice*, also known as *La scuffiara, dramma giocoso per musica* (Naples, 1787). Score and parts in I-Fc: F.P. T. 311.

[56] Cimarosa, *Il matrimonio segreto* (Vienna, 1792). Score and parts in I-Fc: F.P. T 77. This duet was probably "Se fiato in corpo avete."

Ein Terzett auß der Principessa d'Amalfi von Weigl[57]
   gesungen von mir Marchesi und Ratmayer
Eine Arie auß dem Impressario in Angustie von
   Cimarosa[58] gesungen von Weinmüller
Ein Terzett von Mozart[59] gesungen von mir Ratmayer und
   Weinmüller
Eine Arie auß Prima la Musica poi le Parole[60] gesungen
   von mir
Ein Terzett auß dem Matrimonio Segreto von Cimarosa[61]
   gesungen von Ratmayer Korner und Weinmüller
Ein Quartett von Mozart[62] gesungen von mir Ratmayer
   Weinmüller und Wallaschek.
Ein Arie auß die Nozze di Figaro von Mozart[63] gesungen
   von Marchesi
Das Finale vom ersten Act d.to[64] gesungen von mir Marchesi
   Ratmayer Weinmüller Wallaschek Korner und Heller[65]

Dem 10.ten   Akademie bey dem Großherzog die erste Abtheilung von
   ihm folgenden Stücken
Die ouverture auß dem Achille von Pär[66]
Ein Duett auß der Clemenza di Tito von Mozart[67]
   gesungen von Korner und Ratmayer
Ein Terzett auß der Vendetta di Nino von Prati gesungen
   von der Bustelli Vegni und Großherzog
Ein Duett auß dem Achille von Pär[68] gesungen von der
   Bustelli und Großherzog

---

[57] Weigl, *La principessa di Amalfi*, dramma giocoso (Vienna, 1794). Score and parts in I-Fc: A. 519. This trio was either "Ah, che mai dissi" or "Alfin respiro" (separate scores and sets of parts: Mus. Hs. 10792–3, 10/94–5).

[58] This aria for bass was probably "Vado in giro" (score: Mus. Hs. 10327).

[59] Probably the trio "Mandina amabile," K. 480 (score and parts: Mus. Hs. 10553–4), written by Mozart for performance in Francesco Bianchi's *La villanella rapita*.

[60] Salieri, *Prima la musica e poi le parole*, divertimento teatrale (Vienna, 1786).

[61] *Il matrimonio segreto* contains no trios for male singers.

[62] Probably the quartet "Dite almeno," K. 479 (score and parts: Mus. Hs. 10551–2), written by Mozart for performance in *La villanella rapita*.

[63] Mozart, *Le nozze di Figaro* (Vienna, 1786). Score and parts in I-Fc: F.P. T 262.

[64] Presumably MT meant the finale to act 2.

[65] This Heller may have been Sigismund Hüller, who appeared in several Tonkünstler-Sozietät concerts between 1798 and 1801, or Johann Höller, who sang in the Hofkapelle from 1801.

[66] Paer, *Achille*, melodramma eroico (Vienna, 1801). Score: Mus. Hs. 9974.

[67] Probably "Deh prendi un dolce amplesso," with the parts (orginally for two sopranos) taken down an octave.

[68] Probably "Se il fato scrisse" (score and parts: Mus. Hs. 10587–8).

Das Finale von 1tem Act auß der Clemenza di Tito von
    Mozart gesungen von Pär Ratmayer Vegni Korner
    Großherzog und Chor
Eine Arie und Terzett auß dem Numa von Pär[69] gesungen
    von Vegni Bustelli und Korner
Ein Terzett auß der Clemenza di Tito von Mozart
    gesungen von Ratmayer Vegni und Großherzog
Ein Terzett auß dem Achille von Pär gesungen von Bustelli
    Pär und Großherzog
Das Finale von 1tem Act d^{to} gesungen von Bustelli Korner
    Pär Großherzog Weinmüller und Chöre
Die zweyte Abtheilung von mir mit folgenden Stückten
Ein Terzett auß Cesare von Salieri[70] gesungen von
    Weinmüller Wallaschek und Ratmayer
Ein Duett auß der Elfrida von Paisiello[71] gesungen von mir
    und Wiesenthal
Eine Arie mit Chöre auß Adelaide di Guesclino von Mayer
    gesungen von Ratmayer
Ein Terzett auß der Ginevra von Weigl[72] gesungen von mir
    Ratmayer und Weinmüller
Ein Duett auß der Camilla von Pär[73] gesungen von mir
    und Weinmüller
Das Finale vom 1ten Act auß Cesare von Salieri[74] gesungen
    von mir Wiesenthal Korner Ratmayer Weinmüller
    Wallaschek und Chöre
Dem 17ten Ackademie bey mir mit folgenden Stücken
Eine Cavatina auß Pigmalione von Federici gesungen von
    Marchesi
Eine Arie von Paisiello gesungen von der Schmeier[75]

---

[69] Probably the *rondò* with recitative and trio, "Son queste le catene" (score: Mus. Hs. 10585).
[70] Salieri, *Cesare in Farmacusa, dramma eroicomico* (Vienna, 1800). Score and parts: Mus. Hs. 9997–8. This trio was probably "Disciolto qual pria" (parts: Mus. Hs. 10708).
[71] Paisiello, *Elfrida, tragedia per musica* (Naples, 1792). This duet was "Un marmo istesso," for Elfrida and Adelvolto (score and parts: Mus. Hs. 10614–15).
[72] This trio, added to Mayr's *Ginevra di Scozia* by Weigl for its Viennese production (1801), was probably the partially canonic trio in the finale of Act 2, "Dopo il fremente nembo." Weigl's finale to Act 2 is included in the score entitled "Cinque pezzi di musica espressamente composti per l'opera Ginevra di Scozia dal Sig. Maestro Giuseppe Weigl" (Mus. Hs. 10799).
[73] Probably "No, crudel, tu non m'amasti" (score and parts: Mus. Hs. 10589–90).
[74] Parts: Mus. Hs. 10705.
[75] Possibly Johanna Schmierer, a soprano who made her debut at the Leopoldstädter Theater in 1801 (Rosenbaum, "Tagebücher," 99); she participated in a concert in Vienna in 1805 (Morrow, *Concert Life*, 326).

Ein Duett auß Ginevra von Mayer gesungen von d[to] und
    mir

Das Finale von 1tem Act auß der Clemenza di Tito von
    Mozart gesungen von mir Wiesenthal Marchesi
    Ratmayer Weinmüller und Chor[76]

Ein Quintett von Mozart für Fortepiano Oboe Clarinetto
    Corno und Fagotto[77] gespielt von Mesmer[78]

Die Cantata L'Amor Filiale von Weigl[79] gesungen von mir
    Marchesi Ratmayer Weinmüller Großherzog und Chöre

Dem 19ten   Bey dem Großherzog
    Die Hirten an der Krippe von Pär

Dem 20ten   Bey dem Großherzog
    Die Schöpfung von Hayden[80] gesungen von Bustelli Vegni
    und Großherzog

Dem 22ten   Bey dem Großherzog
    Die sieben lezte Worte des Heilands von Hayden[81]
    gesungen d[to]

    Ein Tutti Meß von Teyber[82]

    Eine Sinfonie mit der Jagd von Wranitzky[83]

Dem 24ten   Ackademie bey dem Großherzog die erste Abtheilung von
    ihm mit folgenden Stücken

    Die Ouverture auß dem Manasse von Zingarelli[84]

    Die Introduction auß Oloferne von Guiglielmi[85] gesungen
    von Bustelli Vegni Ratmayer Korner und Chöre

---

[76] MT had heard a performance of Mozart's finale only a week earlier.

[77] K. 452, first published (by Gombart in Augsburg) in 1799. A set of parts owned by MT was transferred to A-Wgm by Pohl.

[78] Perhaps the Herr Messner whom Schönfeld (*Jahrbuch der Tonkunst von Wien und Prag*, 43) called "one of our strongest pianists. He mostly plays compositions of Mozart and Brendt."

[79] *L'amor filiale*, cantata for the arrival of Queen Maria Carolina of Naples, 1800. Score and parts: Mus. Hs. 10146–7. On its origins see chapter 8.

[80] This and subsequent performances of *Die Schöpfung* recorded in MT's diary are not included in Brown, *Performing Haydn's Creation* (Table 1: Viennese Performances of *The Creation* to Early 1810).

[81] *Die sieben letzten Worte*, performed by the Tonkünstler-Sozietät in 1798, 1799, and 1801. Score and parts from MT's library (*CaM*, p. 19) were transferred to A-Wgm by Pohl.

[82] Anton Teyber served as *Kompositor* in the K. K. Hofmusik. Of four masses by him listed in *KK*, MT owned parts for only one, in A major, which was probably the mass that MT sang.

[83] Symphony in G minor (score and parts: Mus. Hs. 11088), the second movement of which represents "eine Jagd." This symphony includes a very elaborate solo piano part probably written for MT or Ferdinand (see chapter 4).

[84] *Manasse* is probably an alternative title of Zingarelli's *Gerusalemme distrutta, dramma sacro per musica* (Florence, Lent 1794), one of the characters in which is named Manasse. Score and parts in I-Fc: F.P. T 591.

[85] Guglielmi, *La morte di Oloferne, tragedia sacra per musica* (Naples, 1791; performed in Vienna in 1800). Score and parts: Mus. Hs. 9899–900.

> Das Gebeth auß Manasse von Zingarelli gesungen von
>   Vegni und Chöre
> Ein Terzett auß Oloferne von Guiglielmi[86] gesungen von
>   Vegni Großherzog und Ratmayer
> Ein Quartett auß Debora von Guiglielmi[87] gesungen von
>   Bustelli Ratmayer Vegni und Großherzog
> Eine Arie auß der Schöpfung von Hayden gesungen von
>   Großherzog
> Das Finale von 1tem Act von Oloferne von Guiglielmi
>   gesungen von Bustelli Vegni Ratmayer Korner
>   Großherzog
> Der Schlußchor von 2tem Act auß der Schöpfung von
>   Hayden[88]
> Die zweyte Abtheilung von mir mit folgenden Stücken
> Ein Sestett auß Gionata Maccabeo von Guiglielmi[89]
>   gesungen von mir Marchesi Korner Ratmayer und
>   Weinmüller
> Ein Duett auß der Schöpfung gesungen von mir und
>   Weinmüller
> Ein Chor auß Hiob von Dittersdorf[90]
> Ein Terzett auß Gionata Maccabeo von Guglielmi[91]
>   gesungen von mir Marchesi und Ratmayer
> Ein Duett auß Abramo von Cimarosa[92] gesungen von mir
>   und Marchesi
> Der Schlußchor vom 1ten Act auß der Schöpfung von
>   Hayden[93]

Dem 25.   Ackademie bey der Schosulan[94] mit folgenden Stücken
>   Eine Sinfonie von Hayden

---

[86] Probably "Da quel labbro."

[87] "Perfido a questo eccesso" (score and parts: Mus. Hs. 10397–8).

[88] "Vollendet ist das große Werk"

[89] Guglielmi, *Gionata Maccabeo, tragedia tratta dalle Scritture* (Naples, 1798). Score and parts: Mus. Hs. 9901–2. MT also owned a separate set of parts for the sextet "Che mora": Mus. Hs. 10425.

[90] Carl Ditters von Dittersdorf, *Giobbe*, oratorio (Vienna, 1786). This was the storm chorus "Onnipotente Dio" (score and parts: Mus. Hs. 10353–4).

[91] The trio "Se pietade un fiero affanno" for two sopranos and tenor (parts: Mus. Hs. 10426) serves as the finale to act 1 of *Gionata Maccabeo*.

[92] Cimarosa, *Il sacrificio d'Abramo, dramma sagro per musica* (Naples, 1786). This duet was probably "Consola il tuo dolore" (score and parts: Mus. Hs. 10309–10).

[93] "Die Himmel erzählen die Ehre Gottes."

[94] Ursula Schosulan (also spelled Schosselein, Schoselan, and Schosullan) served as lady-in-waiting to MT's child Maria Clementina from about 1798 (*HSS* 1799, 384) and to MT herself from about 1800 (*HSS* 1801, 399).

Ein Duett auß der Lodoiska von Mayer[95] gesungen von
    Marchesi und Bridi[96]

Variationen auß dem Don Giovanni von Mozart gespielt
    von der Zach[97]

Eine Arie auß Ines de Castro von Bianchi[98] gesungen von
    der Franck[99]

Ein Quintett von Eibler[100] gespielt von ihm den zwey
    Resik und noch zwey andern

Ein Duett auß Saldagna von Zingarelli[101] gesungen von
    der Franck und Marchesi

Variationen auß dem Trofonio von Salieri[102] gegeigt von
    der Brunner[103]

Eine Arie auß der Elfrida von Paisiello gesungen von Bridi

Variationen gegeigt von Clement[104]

Ein Terzett auß Alessandro von Tarchi gesungen von der
    Franck Marchesi und Bridi

Ein Quintett von Eibler gespielt von den nemlichen

Dem 28. Ackademie bey mir mit folgenden Stücken

Die Quodlibet Sinfonie von Wranitzky in 3 Theilen
    Anfang in der Mitte und End[105]

Ein Duett auß Telemaco von Mayer[106] gesungen von mir
    und Ratmayer

Ein Terzett auß der Zauberflöte von Mozart[107] gesungen
    von mir Ratmayer und Weinmüller

[95] Probably the duet "Dunque dirai" from the Milanese version of *Lodoiska* (score, dated Milan, Carnival 1800, and parts: Mus. Hs. 10496–7).

[96] Giuseppe Antonio Bridi, Viennese merchant and amateur singer, praised by Schönfeld (*Jahrbuch der Tonkunst in Wien und Prag*, 10) as one of Vienna's finest tenors.

[97] I have not been able to identify the female musician Zach.

[98] Bianchi, *Ines de Castro, dramma per musica* (Naples, 1794).

[99] Christine Frank (née Gerhardi), amateur soprano; see chapter 2.

[100] Several string quintets by Eybler are extant: one with two violas (Herrmann 183), two with viola d'amore and double bass (Herrmann 184–5, and three with double bass (Herrmann 186–8).

[101] Zingarelli, *Il conte di Saldagna, tragedia per musica* (Venice, Carnival 1795). Marchesi created the role of Ramiro.

[102] Salieri, *La grotta di Trofonio, opera comica* (Vienna, 1785).

[103] Probably the "Demoiselle Brunner," daughter of a dentist, whom Schönfeld called "a skillful violinist, both in quartets and concertos."

[104] Franz Clement, Viennese violin virtuoso.

[105] Wranitzky, Symphony in D major, Poštolka 27 ("Sinfonia Quodlibet"). Score and parts: Mus. Hs. 11086–7. See chapter 4.

[106] Mayr, *Telemaco nell'Isola di Calipso, dramma per musica* (Venice, Carnival 1797). Score ("Nel Nob. Teatro La Fenice il Carnevale 1797"): Mus. Hs. 9965. This *duetto* may have been "Giura che i passi miei" (score and parts: Mus. Hs. 10503–4).

[107] "Soll ich dich, Theurer, nicht mehr sehen?" (score and parts, with the Italian text "Dunque il mio bene non vedrò?": Mus. Hs. 10555–6).

Eine Arie au Pimmalione von Federici gesungen von
    Marchesi
Ein Duett von Zingarelli[108] gesungen von Marchesi und
    Ratmayer
Ein Quartett auß Palmira von Salieri[109] gesungen von
    Ratmayer Weinmüller Wallascheck, und Großherzog
Das Finale vom 1ten Act d[to] [gesungen von] d[to]

Dem 29.   Numa Pompilius von Pär bey dem Großherzog
Dem 31.   Ackademie bey mir mit folgenden Stücken
Die Introduction von der Ginevra geblasen durch die
    Harmonie[110]
Ein Terzett auß Ines de Castro von Bianchi gesungen von
    mir Altamonte[111] und Ratmayer
Variationen auß Alceste[112] gespielt auf der Harpfe von der
    Müller[113]
Ein Duett auß Saldagna von Zingarelli gesungen von
    Weinmüller und Rathmayer
Eine Arie auß Ginevra geblasen von der Harmonie
Ein Quartett auß Sciti von Mayer gesungen von mir
    Schmier Ratmayer und Weinmüller
Das Fest von Carolinen im Elysium von Weigl gesungen
    von mir Schmier Altamonte Ratmayer und Weinmüller

February [1802]

Dem 2.   Bey dem Großherzog die Hirten an der Krippe von Pär
Dem 7.   Ackademie bey mir mit folgenden Stücken
Eine Ouverture von Mayer
Eine Arie mit Chöre auß Artemisia von Cimarosa[114]
    gesungen von der Wiesenthal

---

[108] Possibly "Giura se tutto sai" (score and parts: Mus. Hs. 10849–50).
[109] Salieri, *Palmira regina di Persia, dramma eroicomico* (Vienna, 1795). "Silenzio facciasi" is a short a cappella quartet for male voices (parts: Mus. Hs. 10706).
[110] Probably an arrangement for winds of the *introduzione* of Mayr's *Ginevra di Scozia*.
[111] Probably Katherina Altamonte, lady-in-waiting to Archduchess Maria Clementina; see chapter 2.
[112] This *Alceste* was probably Gaetano Gioia's ballet (Vienna, 1800, with music by Weigl) rather than Gluck's opera.
[113] Josepha Müllner, harpist and composer active in Viennese concert life (see chapter 2).
[114] Cimarosa, *Artemisia* (Venice, 1801); the composer's last work, left unfinished at his death. Score ("Opera postuma rappresentata nel Carnovale 1801, nel Nob.[mo] Teatro La Fenice dopo la morte dell'autore"): Mus. Hs. 9945. This aria with chorus was either "Sol dal primo amato oggetto" or "Ah che la morte io veggo" (parts: Mus. Hs. 10321, 10322).

Ein Duett auß Ezio von Tarchi[115] gesungen von mir und
    Marchesi

Eine Arie mit Chöre auß Timoteo von Winter[116] gesungen
    von Weinmüller

Eine Arie auß Lodoiska von Mayer gesungen von Marchesi

Ein Terzett auß Ezio von Tarchi[117] gesungen von mir,
    Marchesi und Ratmayer

Eine Sinfonie strepitosa von Wranitzky[118]

Dem 14.   Bey mir Dom Juan von Mozart

Dem 21.   Ackademie bey dem Großherzog die erste Abtheilung von
    ihm mit folgenden Stücken

Eine Ouverture von Pär

Ein Terzett auß den Solitari von Weigl[119] gesungen von der
    Bustelli Vegni und Großherzog

Eine Arie mit Chöre auß Achille von Pär gesungen von
    Großherzog

Ein Duett auß d.to gesungen von der Bustelli und
    Großherzog

Ein Quartett auß der Principessa d'Amalfi von Weigl
    gesungen von Bustelli Großherzog Weinmüller und
    Wallaschek

Eine Arie auß dem Ezio von Tarchi gesungen von Marchesi

Ein Duett auß Orazi und Curiazi von Cimarosa[120]
    gesungen von Bustelli und Vegni

Das Finale von 2.tem Act von Ginevra von Pär[121] gesungen
    von Bustelli Rathmayer Vegni Weinmüller und
    Großherzog

Die zweyte Abtheilung von mir mit folgenden Stücken

Ein Quartett auß Demofonte von Tarchi[122] gesungen von
    mir Marchesi Ratmayer und Weinmüller

---

[115] Tarchi made at least two settings of Metastasio's *Ezio*: Vicenza, 1789 and Vicenza, 1792. This duet was "Vado a sfogar l'affanno" or "No, che pietà non voglio" (scores and parts: 10761–2, 10763–4).

[116] Winter, *Timotheus, oder Die Gewalt der Musik*, cantata (Vienna, Tonkünstler-Sozietät, 9–10 April 1797). Score and parts: Mus. Hs. 10158–9.

[117] Probably "Ecco alle mie catene" (score and parts: Mus. Hs. 10759–60).

[118] *CaM*, p. 120, lists a *Sinfonia strepitosa* by Wranitzky.

[119] Weigl, *I solitari* (Vienna, 1797). This trio was probably "Se il ciel così" (score and parts: Mus. Hs. 10796–7).

[120] Probably "Se torni vincitor" (score and parts: IIs. 10306–7).

[121] Paer, *Ginevra degli Amieri*, *tragicommedia per musica* (Vienna, 1800). Score: Mus. Hs. 9978.

[122] Tarchi, *Demofoonte*, *dramma per musica* (Milan, 1786). This quartet was probably "Padre, perdono," for two sopranos, tenor, and bass (score and parts: Mus. Hs. 10753–4).

> Ein Duett aus Alessandro d^{to} gesungen von mir und
> Ratmayer
> Eine Arie mit Chor auß Ginevra von Pär gesungen von
> Weinmüller
> Ein Quartett auß Lodoiska von Mayer[123] gesungen von
> mir Marchesi Ratmayer und Weinmüller
> Ein Duett auß Antigono von Paisiello[124] gesungen von mir
> und Marchesi
> Das Finale von 1ten Act von Achille von Pär gesungen von
> mir Marchesi Weinmüller und Großherzog

Dem 25.   Akademie bey mir mit folgenden Stücken[125]
> Eine Sinfonie die Revolutions von Wranitzky[126]
> Eine Meß von Hasse[127]
> Die Vocal Sinfonie von Bohdanowicz[128]

Dem 28.   Ackademie bey mir mit folgenden Stücken
> Ein Tedeum mit 2 Chöre von Paisiello[129]
> Eine Meß von Hayden Joseph
> Eine Meß mit Berchtesgadner Instrumenten von
> Wranitzky[130]

März [1802]

Dem 1.   Ackademie bey dem Großherzog mit folgenden Stücken
> Ein Requiem von Hasse[131]
> Ein Tedeum von Zingarelli[132]
> Die Cecilia Meß von Hayden Joseph[133]

---

[123] Probably "Dammi la destra" (score and parts: Mus. Hs. 10476–7).

[124] Paisiello, *Antigono, dramma per musica* (Naples, 1785). This duet was probably "Non temer, non sono amante" (score and parts: Mus. Hs. 10610–11).

[125] On this concert see chapter 6.

[126] Wranitzky, *Grande Sinfonie caractéristique pour la paix avec la Republique Françoise* (Poštolka 12), published in 1797. MT owned parts: *CaM*, p. 119.

[127] Hasse made at least fifteen settings of the mass, of which MT owned parts for six (*KK*).

[128] Bazyli Bohdanowicz, *Sinfonia vocale ed originale senza parole* (parts: Mus. Hs. 10887).

[129] Paisiello's Te Deum in B♭ for double chorus and soloists, Robinson 6.01 (Naples, 1791), composed to celebrate the return of King Ferdinand and Queen Maria Carolina after a long visit to Vienna. Score and parts: HK 585.

[130] Wranitzky's Mass with children's instruments. Parts: Mus. Hs. 10235. See chapter 6.

[131] Probably the Requiem in C major by Hasse of which MT owned a set of parts (*KK*).

[132] Zingarelli composed no fewer than twenty-three settings of the Te Deum, none of which is listed in *KK*.

[133] The *Missa cellensis in honorem BVM* in C major ("Cäcilienmesse," 1766), a copy of which was probably among the three masses in C by J. Haydn that MT owned (*KK*).

Dem 3.[134]	Bey dem Großherzog
	Das unterbrochene Opferfest von Winter
Dem 4.	Ackademie bey dem Großherzog mit folgenden Stücken
	Die Responsen von Todtenoffitz von Perez[135]
	Ein Requiem von Campion[136]
Dem 5.	Ackademie bey mir mit folgenden Stücken
	Eine Meß von Hayden Michael[137]
	Ein Graduale Confirma von Jomelli[138]
	Ein Offertorium von Eibler[139]
	Eine Meß von Reiter[140]
	Ein Concert auf der organisirten Trompetten von Weidinger geblasen[141]
Dem 7.	Ackademie bey dem Großherzog die erste Abtheilung von ihm mit folgenden Stücken[142]
	Die Ouverture auß dem Corsaro von Weigl[143]
	Ein Quartett auß der Pastorella nobile von Guiglielmi[144] gesungen von Bustelli Vegni Großherzog und Weinmüller
	Ein Duett von Pär gesungen von Bustelli und Großherzog
	Ein Arie auß Trofonio von Salieri gesungen von Großherzog

---

[134] Ash Wednesday.

[135] No music by David Perez is listed in *KK*. Score and parts for Responsori a 5 are among several sacred works by Perez in I-Fc (F.P. Ch 689).

[136] Carl'Antonio Campion, grand ducal maestro di cappella in Florence from 1763 to 1788. This Requiem was probably the one in Eb of which MT owned a score and a set of parts (*KK*; only the score seems to have survived: A-Wn, Mus. Hs. 16449).

[137] Of the four masses by M. Haydn that MT eventually owned, she probably had only two at this time: the *Missa S. Theresiae* and the *Missa S. Ursulae*. She had not commissioned the *Missa S. Francisci* and did not know the "Missa hispanica."

[138] Probably the offertory "Confirma hoc, Deus" for five voices and basso continuo, written in Rome in 1752; the large number of sources in which it is preserved testifies to its popularity. The offertory by Jommelli listed in *KK* as "Confirma me" was probably this work.

[139] Possibly "Laudate pueri," composed in 1802 and performed by MT on 1 April.

[140] Georg Reutter the younger made eighty-one settings of the mass, of which MT owned one, in C, probably the work performed on this occasion.

[141] Possibly Joseph Haydn's Trumpet Concerto in Eb, composed in 1796 for Anton Weidinger to play on his new keyed trumpet (*organisierte Trompete*). Hummel's Concerto in E (written for the same performer) was not completed until December 1803.

[142] Another concert at Ferdinand's residence for which he probably provided performing materials.

[143] Weigl, *L'amor marinaro, ossia Il corsaro, commedia per musica* (Vienna, 1797). Score and parts in I-Fc: F.P. T 522.

[144] Guglielmi, *La pastorella nobile, commedia per musica* (Naples, 1788; performed very frequently in Vienna from 1790 on). Score and parts in I-Fc: F.P. T 143

Ein Terzett d^{to} gesungen von Bustelli, Ratmayer und
   Großherzog

Eine Polonese auß Capricciosa Coretta von Martini[145]
   gesungen von Bustelli

Ein Quintett auß Corsaro gesungen von Bustelli Vegni
   Großherzog Ratmayer Weinmüller

Ein Duett auß Re Teodoro von Paisiello[146] gesungen von
   Bustelli und Großherzog

Das Finale von 2tem Act d^{to} gesungen von Bustelli Ratmayer
   Vegni Korner Großherzog Weinmüller Wallascheck

Die zweyte Abtheilung von mir mit folgenden Stücken

Ein Quintett auß Testa riscaldata von Pär[147] gesungen von
   mir Marchesi Ratmayer Weinmüller und Wallascheck

Ein Duett auß Cosi fan tutti von Mozart[148] gesungen von
   mir und Marchesi

Ein Terzett auß Testa riscaldata von Pär gesungen von
   Ratmayer Weinmüller Wallaschek

Eine Arie auß Amanti comici von Fioravanti[149] gesungen
   von Wallaschek

Ein Quintett auß Trame Deluse von Cimarosa[150] gesungen
   von mir Marchesi Ratmayer Weinmüller und
   Großherzog

Ein Duett auß Cosi fan tutti gesungen von Marchesi und
   Weinmüller

Das Finale vom 1ten Act d^{to} gesungen von mir Marchesi
   Weinmüller Wallaschek Ratmayer und Korner

Dem 10.   Ackademie bey mir mit folgenden Stücken

---

[145] Vicente Martín y Soler, *La scuola dei maritati* (also known as *La capricciosa corretta* and *Gli sposi in contrasto*), comic opera (London, 1795; performed in Vienna in 1796). Score and parts in I-Fc: F.P. T 198. This "polonese" was the aria "La donna ha bello il core."

[146] Paisiello, *Il re Teodoro in Venezia*, *dramma eroicomico* (Vienna, 1784). Score and parts in I-Fc: F.P. T 313. This duet was probably "Cosa far pensi" (score and parts: Mus. Hs. 10620–1).

[147] Paer, *La testa riscaldata*, *farsa* (Venice, 1800; first performed in Vienna on 23 April 1801). Score and parts: Mus. Hs. 10052–3.

[148] Mozart, *Così fan tutte* (Vienna, 1790). Score and parts in I-Fc: F.P. T 260. Since there is of course no role for male soprano in this opera, we do not know in which duets Marchesi sang here and later on this program.

[149] Fioravanti, *Gli amanti comici*, alternative title of *La famiglia stravagante* (Rome, 1792).

[150] Cimarosa, *Le trame deluse*, *commedia per musica* (Naples, 1786). This quintet was "Che tremore nelle vene" (score and parts: Mus. Hs. 10288–9).

Ein Requiem von Hayden Michael[151]
Ein Concert auf 2 Geigen von Tarchi[152]
Eine Meß von Gyrowetz[153]
Ein Tedeum von Reiter[154]

Dem 14.   Ackademie bey dem Großherzog die erste Abtheilung von
ihm mit folgenden Stücken
Eine Ouverture von Pär
Eine Arie mit Chöre auß Giuochi d'Agrigento von
Paisiello[155] gesungen von Marchesi
Eine Arie d^to gesungen von Bustelli
Ein Duett von Pär gesungen von Bustelli und Marchesi
Ein Quartett auß Cinna von Pär[156] gesungen von Bustelli
Vegni Großherzog und Marchesi
Eine Scene auß Pirro von Paisiello gesungen von Vegni
Ein Terzett auß Zulema von Portogallo[157] gesungen von
Bustelli Vegni und Großherzog
Das Finale von 3. Act von Ginevra von Pär gesungen von
Bustelli Vegni Ratmayer Weinmüller Großherzog und
Wallaschek
Die zweyte Abtheilung von mir mit folgenden Stücken
Ein Terzett mit Chöre auß Lodoiska von Mayer[158]
gesungen von mir Marchesi und Ratmayer
Eine Arie von Mozart gesungen von Weinmüller
Ein Duet auß Pirro von Zingarelli[159] gesungen von mir
und Marchesi

---

[151] Michael Haydn, Requiem in C minor, Sherman 155 (Salzburg, 1771). MT praised this work, of which she owned a set of parts (*KK*), when she met Haydn in 1801.

[152] MT owned three concertos by Tarchi in parts: two for two violins and orchestra (in C and B♭, Mus. Hs. 11097 and 11098) and one for one violin and orchestra (in A, Mus. Hs. 11099).

[153] Probably the Mass in F that Adalbert Gyrowetz dedicated to MT (*KK*).

[154] Since MT owned no Te Deum by Reutter (*KK*), Ferdinand provided the performance materials; three Te Deums are preserved among the large collection of Reutter's sacred music owned by the grand duke (I-Fc, F.P. Ch 780–2).

[155] Paisiello, *I giuochi d'Agrigento*, *dramma per musica* (Venice, 1792). This aria with chorus was probably "Nuove ognor funeste pene," a rondò for Clearco (soprano) in which five other soloists enter as *pertichini* (score and parts: Mus. Hs. 10602–3).

[156] Paer, *Il Cinna*, *dramma per musica* (Padua, 1795; score and parts in I-Fc: F.P. T 336).

[157] Marcos Antonio Portugal, *Zulima*, *dramma per musica* (Florence, 1796). Score and parts in I-Fc: F.P. T 389.

[158] "Spirto gentil, t'arresta," from the Milanese version of *Lodoiska* (score and parts: Mus. Hs. 10478–9).

[159] Zingarelli, *Pirro re d'Epiro*, *dramma per musica* (Milan, Carnival 1792). Marchesi created the title role. This duet was probably "Che l'ira mia" (score and parts: Mus. Hs. 10835–6).

Ein Terzett auß Achille von Pär gesungen von Ratmayer
Weinmüller und Wallaschek

Eine Polonoise mit Chöre auß Lodoiska von Mayer[160]
gesungen von Marchesi

Das Finale von 1. Act von Adelaide di Guesclino von
Mayer gesungen von mir Marchesi Ratmayer Wallaschek
und Chöre

Dem 17. Ackademie bey mir mit folgenden Stücken

Ein Requiem von Mozart[161]

Ein Sextett auf 2 Geigen 2 Bratschen Bassetl und Baßgeige
von Albrechtsberger[162]

Eine Meß von Eibler[163]

Dem 21. Ackademie bey mir mit folgenden Stücken[164]

Die Ouverture auß dem Uniforme von Weigl

Ein Terzett auß der Principessa d'Amalfi d[to] gesungen von
Wiesenthal Ratmayer Weinmüller

Eine Arie mit Chöre auß Miglior Dono von Weigl
gesungen von Ratmayer

Ein Duett auß Corsaro d[to][165] gesungen von Wiesenthal
und Ratmayer

Eine Arie mit Chöre auß Ginevra d[to] gesungen von mir

Das Finale vom 1ten Act von Pirro d[to][166] gesungen von mir
Wiesenthal Marchesi Ratmayer Weinmüller und
Großherzog

Ein Concert auf das Clawier die Leidenschaften vorstellend
gespielt von mir[167]

Eine Arie auß Uniforme von Weigl gesungen von der
Wiesenthal

---

[160] "Contento il cor nel seno," from the Milanese version of *Lodoiska* (score and parts: Mus. Hs. 10532–3).

[161] MT owned Mozart's Requiem in score and parts (*KK*).

[162] MT owned Albrechtsberger's *6 Sonate con le Fughe a 6*, Op. 13 (sextets for two violins, two violas, cello and double bass; Vienna, [ca. 1802]; *CaM*, p. 62).

[163] MT owned copies of four masses by Eybler (*KK*), of which only one, *Missa S. Wolfgangi* (1800), was composed before March 1802.

[164] This concert represents an unusual case in MT's composite concerts in which all the music was by a single composer, Weigl.

[165] Probably "Ah spiegarti oh Dio vorrei," sung by Lucilla and Dorimante.

[166] When Zingarelli's *Pirro* was performed in Vienna in 1798 Weigl revised the score, adding this finale (score and parts: Mus. Hs. 10788–9).

[167] Concertino in D, the autograph of which (Mus. Hs. 19398) is dated 1801; see chapter 4.

Ein Terzett auß Ginevra d^{to} gesungen von mir Marchesi
  und Weinmüller
Eine Arie auß Principessa d'Amalfi gesungen von
  Weinmüller
Ein Quintett auß Uniforme[168] gesungen von mir
  Wiesenthal Ratmayer Weinmüller und Wallaschek
Eine Arie auß Ginevra gesungen von Marchesi
Das Finale von 1tem Akt von Uniforme von Weigl gesungen
  von mir Weinmüller Wallaschek Großherzog und Chöre

Dem 25.   Die Schöpfung von Hayden gesungen von mir Simoni[169]
  und Weinmüller

Dem 28.   Ackademie bey dem Großherzog die erste Abtheilung von
  ihm mit folgenden Stücken[170]
Die Ouverture auß dem L'oro fa tutto von Pär[171]
Ein Quartett auß la Donna di testa debole von
  Portogallo[172] gesungen von Bustelli Vegni Großherzog
  und Pär
Ein Duett auß L'oro fa tutto von Pär gesungen von
  Ratmayer und Weinmüller
Eine Arie auß Griselda d^{to}[173] gesungen von Großherzog
Das Finale von 2tem Ackt von Barbiere di Seviglia[174]
  gesungen von Bustelli Vegni Ratmayer Weinmüller
  Saal[175] Großherzog
Ein Terzett auß d^{to}[176] gesungen von Großherzog
  Weinmüller und Pär

---

[168] "Dove vado? A chi mi volgo?" (act 2), in which Giannina (soprano, a role written for MT) is the center of attention.

[169] Giuseppe Simoni, tenor; see chapter 2.

[170] Another concert in which Ferdinand seems to have provided the performing materials. Most of the music was not owned by MT but does survive in I-Fc.

[171] Paer, *L'oro fa tutto*, *dramma giocoso per musica* (Milan, 1793). Score and parts in I-Fc: F.P. T 348.

[172] *La donna di testa debole* is probably an alternate title of Portugal's *La donna di genio volubile* (Venice, 1796). Score and parts in I-Fc: F.P. T 391.

[173] Paer, *La virtù in cimento, ossia Griselda*, *melodramma* (Parma, 1798). Score and parts in I-Fc: F.P. T 346.

[174] Paisiello, *Il barbiere di Siviglia*, *dramma giocoso per musica* (St. Petersburg, 1782; Vienna, 1783). Score and parts in I-Fc: F.P. T 312. In the original four-act version, act 2 ends with an aria, not a finale. Probably MT is referring to a two-act version and to the finale at the end of the opera.

[175] Ignaz Saal, a veteran bass, sang both German and Italian opera in the court theaters from 1782 to 1821, and served in the Hofkapelle from 1795. From 1787 he was also active in Viennese concerts, public and private. A regular participant in Tonkünstler-Sozietät concerts, he sang the bass solo in the premieres of both *Die Schöpfung* and *Die Jahreszeiten*.

[176] "Ma dov'eri tu, stordito" (parts: Mus. Hs. 10609).

Ein Terzett auß L'Isola Piacevole von Martin[177] gesungen
von Großherzog Korner und Pär
Ein Terzett auß la Pazza Giornata von Portogallo[178]
gesungen von Bustelli Ratmayer und Pär
Das Finale vom 2ten Act vom Corsaro con Weigl gesungen
von Bustelli Ratmayer Vegni Weinmüller Saal
Großherzog und Pär
Die zweyte Abtheilung von mir mit folgenden Stücken
Ein Terzett auß l'Accademia di Cisolfautte von Weigl[179]
gesungen von mir Ratmayer und Weinmüller
Eine Arie auß Trame Deluse von Cimarosa gesungen vom
Weinmüller
Ein Duett d^{to}[180] gesungen von mir und Marchesi
Eine Arie auß Re Teodoro von Paisiello gesungen von
Marchesi
Ein Quartett auß Re Theodoro von Paisiello[181] gesungen
von mir Ratmayer Saal Weinmüller
Das Finale vom 1ten Act von Trame Deluse von Cimarosa
gesungen von mir Marchesi Ratmayer Korner
Weinmüller und Großherzog

April [1802]

Dem 1.   Ackademie bey mir mit folgenden Stücken
Dixit von Michael Hayden[182]
Ein Concert auf dem Clarinett von Eibler[183] geblasen von
Stadler[184]
Laudate Pueri d^{to}[185]

---

[177] Martin y Soler, *L'isola piacevole*, also known as *L'isola del piacere* (London, 1795). Score and parts
in I-Fc: F.P. T 197.

[178] Portugal, *La pazza giornata, ovvero Il matrimonio di Figaro, dramma comico per musica* (Venice,
Carnival 1800). Score and parts in I-Fc: F.P. T 392. This trio was either "Amore è un traditore" or
"Presto oh là impertinente" (scores and parts: Mus. Hs 10673–4, 10675–6).

[179] Weigl, *L'accademia del Maestro Cisolfaut, commedia per musica* (Vienna, 1798). This trio was
probably "Avete ragione" (score and parts: Mus. Hs. 10790–1).

[180] "Vanne, o cara" (scores: Mus. Hs. 10317, 10318).

[181] "Permetti a mia Lisetta" (score and parts: 10606–7).

[182] M. Haydn, "Dixit Dominus," Sherman 809 (Salzburg, 27 January 1802); MT owned a set of parts
(*KK*).

[183] Eybler, Clarinet Concerto in B♭, Herrmann 160, composed in February 1798.

[184] The clarinettist was probably Johann Stadler; see note pertaining to the performance of Eybler's
concerto on 7 April.

[185] Eybler, "Laudate pueri Dominum" in B♭, Herrmann 106, composed in 1802; listed in *KK* as
"Salmo II."

Eine Sonate mit allen Instrumenten von Albrechtsberger[186]
Annibale in Capua von Salieri[187] gesungen von mir
    Altamonte Ratmayer Korner Weinmüller und Chöre

Dem 4. Ackademie bey dem Großherzog die erste Abtheilung von
    ihm mit folgenden Stücken[188]
Eine Ouverture von Pär
Die Introduction auß Orazi von Cimarosa mit Chöre
    gesungen von Großherzog
Eine Arie auß Theodoro von Paisiello gesungen von
    Großherzog
Ein Duett auß Cinna von Pär gesungen von Bustelli und
    Ratmayer
Ein Terzett auß Orazi von Cimarosa[189] gesungen von
    Bustelli Vegni und Großherzog
Ein Terzett auß Pirro von Paisiello gesungen d^to
Ein Quintett auß Hero von Pär[190] gesungen d^to Ratmayer
    und Korner
Das Finale auß Nina von Paisiello[191] gesungen d^to und
    Weinmüller
Die zweyte Abtheilung von mir mit folgenden Stücken
Ein Chor auß Idomeneo von Mozart[192]
Ein Terzett mit Chöre auß Orazi von Cimarosa[193]
    gesungen von mir Marchesi und Ratmayer
Ein Duett mit Chöre auß Numa von Pär[194] gesungen von
    Marchesi und Weinmüller
Der Chor mit dem Sturm auß Idomeneo von Mozart[195]

---

[186] Albrechtsberger, *Sonata in pieno coro* in C for orchestra, written for MT in November 1801. The dated autograph score (H-Bn) is inscribed "NB für die Kayserinn." See Somfai, "Albrechtsberger-Eigenschriften," Part 3, *Studia musicologica Academiae Scientiarum Hungaricae* 9 (1967), 219–20. MT owned a copy entitled *Sonata con più strumenti, e colla fuga* (*CaM*, p. 62).

[187] Salieri, *Annibale in Capua, dramma per musica* (Trieste, May 1801). Score and parts: Mus. Hs. 9994–5. Did MT mistakenly omit the date of this performance, which surely represented an entire concert?

[188] Ferdinand probably provided the performing materials for the first half of this concert, MT for the second half.

[189] Probably "Quando nel campo."

[190] *Ero e Leandro, dramma per musica* (Naples, 1794). Score and parts in I-Fc: F.P. T 338.

[191] Paisiello, *Nina o sia La pazza per amore, commedia in prosa ed in verso per musica* (S. Leucio [near Caserta], 1789). Score: Mus. Hs. 10059; score and parts in I-Fc: F.P. T 323.

[192] Mozart, *Idomeneo* (Munich, 1781). Score and parts: Mus. Hs. 9971–2. This chorus was probably "Nettuno s'onori" (score and parts: Mus. Hs. 10547–8).

[193] "Germe d'illustri eroi" (score and parts: 10294–5).

[194] Probably "In placida calma" (score: Mus. Hs. 10591).

[195] "Qual nuovo terrore" (score and parts: Mus. Hs. 10545–6).

            Ein Quartett mit Chöre auß Numa von Pär[196] gesungen
                von mir Ratmayer Korner und Weinmüller
            Eine Scene und Duett auß Conte di Saldagna von
                Zingarelli gesungen von mir und Marchesi
            Das Finale von 1. Act von Pirro von Weigl gesungen von
                mir Marchesi Ratmayer Korner Weinmüller Wallaschek

Dem 7.   Ackademie bey mir mit folgenden Stücken[197]
            Eine Ouverture von Hayden Joseph
            Ein Quartett mit Chöre auß Ratto delle Sabine von
                Zingarelli[198] gesungen von Wiesenthal Altamonte
                Ratmayer Weinmüller
            Eine Arie von Righini[199] gesungen von Weinmüller
            Ein Duett auß Alessandro von Tarchi gesungen von
                Wiesenthal und Ratmayer
            Eine Arie auß Alceste von Gluck[200] gesungen von mir
            Ein Quartett mit Chöre auß Lodoiska von Mayer gesungen
                von mir Marchesi Ratmayer Weinmüller
            Ein Concert von Clarinett von Eibler geblasen von
                Stadler[201]
            Ein Quartett aus Ratto delle Sabine von Zingarelli
                gesungen von Wiesenthal Altamonte Ratmayer
                Weinmüller
            Eine Arie mit Chöre von Nasolini gesungen von Altamonte
            Ein Duett auß Ezio von Tarchi[202] gesungen von mir und
                Weinmüller
            Eine Arie mit Chöre auß Artemisia von Cimarosa gesungen
                von Ratmayer
            Ein Terzett auß Ines von Bianchi gesungen von mir
                Altamonte und Ratmayer
            Ein Rondò auß Alessandro von Tarchi gesungen von
                Marchesi

---

[196] Probably "Dunque m'insulti, ingrato?"

[197] This concert served as a preview or rehearsal of one given in the Burgtheater six days later, on 13 April, which included much the same music (see chapter 7).

[198] Zingarelli, *Il ratto delle Sabine, dramma per musica* (Venice, 1800). This quartet and the other one later in the program were "In si fatale istante" and "Ah che fate, che tentate" (scores and sets of parts: Mus. Hs. 10830–1, 10832–3).

[199] Probably Vincenzo Righini's bass aria "Pensa" (score and parts: Mus. Hs. 10694–5).

[200] Gluck, *Alceste* (score: Mus. Hs. 9948).

[201] Johann Stadler performed Eybler's concerto in the Burgtheater on 13 April. Thus it was probably he (rather than his brother Anton) who played the concerto in MT's concerts on 1 and 7 April.

[202] "Vado a sfogar l'affanno" or "No, che pietà non voglio."

Ein Quartett mit Chöre auß Sciti von Mayer von mir
    Wiesenthal Ratmayer Weinmüller

Dem 10.	Die Solitari von Weigl
Dem 15.[203]	Bey dem Großherzog La Passione von Paisiello[204]
Dem 16.[205]	[Bey dem Großherzog La Passione] von Pär[206]
Dem 17.[207]	Ackademie bey mir mit folgenden Stücken

Die 7 Worte des Heilandes am Kreutze von Hayden Joseph
    gesungen von der Altamonte Ratmayer Saal
Das Stabat Mater von Pergolesi[208] gesungen von mir und
    Marchesi
Das Alleluja von Albrechtsberger[209]

Dem 18.[210]	Die Schöpfung von Hayden Joseph gesungen von mir
	Ratmayer und Saal
Dem 19.	Bey dem Großherzog die Passione von Pär
Dem 22.	Ackademie bey mir mit folgenden Stücken

Die Cantata von Böhmen von Maschek[211]
Die Battaille Sinfonie von Kotzeluch[212]

Dem 25.	Ackademie bey mir mit folgenden Stücken

Ein Sinfonie von Mayer
Ein Chor auß Timoteo von Sarti[213]
Eine Arie auß Gionata von Guiglielmi gesungen von mir
    mit Chöre
Ein Violin Concert gegeigt von Clement
Ein Terzett auß Admeto von Tarchi[214] gesungen von mir
    Marchesi und Ratmayer

---

[203] Holy Thursday.

[204] Paisiello, *La passione di Gesù Cristo*, oratorio (St. Petersburg, 1783). Score and parts: Mus. Hs. 9910–11.

[205] Good Friday.

[206] Paer, *La passione* (score and parts: Mus. Hs. 9908–9). [207] Holy Saturday.

[208] Pergolesi, *Stabat mater* (Naples, 1736); MT owned a set of parts (*KK*).

[209] A choral Alleluia by Albrechtsberger was performed at Tonkünstler-Sozietät concerts on 4 April 1789, 16 April 1791, and 22–3 December 1797 (Morrow, *Concert Life*). No copy of this work is listed in *KK*.

[210] Easter Sunday.

[211] Václav Vincenc Mašek, *Böhmens Dankgefühl* (Prague, 1796). Score: Mus. Hs. 10191.

[212] I know of no battle symphony attributed to either Leopold or Johann Anton Kozeluch. This was possibly "Maneuvre," a military piece by Leopold Kozeluch listed in *CaM*, p. 61.

[213] Sarti, *Alessandro e Timoteo*, *dramma per musica* (Parma, Spring 1782). Score: Mus. Hs. 9999.

[214] Tarchi is not known to have written an opera called *Admeto*. Either MT attributed Guglielmi's *Admeto* (Naples, 1794) to Tarchi by mistake, or she used the wrong title in referring to Tarchi's *Ademira*, of which there were at least three versions: Milan, 1784; Venice, 1787; and Pavia, 1792.

Ein Duett auß Elfrida von Paisiello gesungen von mir und
   Marchesi
Eine Fantaisie auf den Harpfe gespielt von der Müller[215]
Eine Scene auß dem Disertore von Tarchi[216] gesungen von
   Marchese
Fantasie auf der Geige gespielt von Clement
Das Finale vom 1. Act vom Adelaide von Mayer gesungen
   von mir Marchesi Ratmayer und Chöre

Dem 28.   Ackademie bey mir mit folgenden Stücken
Die sieben Worte von Hayden Joseph gesungen von
   Altamonte Ratmayer Saal
Das Stabat Mater von Pergolesi von mir und Marchese
Das Alleluja von Albrechtsberger

* * *

July [1802]

Dem 18.   Ackademie bey mir mit folgenden Stücken
Ein Terzett auß Alessandro von Tarchi gesungen von mir
   Marchesi und Weinmüller
Ein Quartett auß Sciti von Mayer gesungen d^{to} und
   Ratmayer
Dixit Deus von Michael Hayden[217]
Eine Sonate mit allen Instrumenten von Albrechtsberger
Laudate Pueri von Eybler
Ein grosser Chor d^{to}.[218]
Die Follia di Spagna mit allen Instrumenten von
   Eybler[219]

Dem 22.   Bey mir

---

[215] Müllner played fantasies on the harp in public concerts on 25 March and 13 April 1802 (Morrow, *Concert Life*, 311, 315).

[216] Tarchi, *Il disertore, dramma serio per musica* (Genoa, Carnival 1799). Score: Mus. Hs. 10006. Marchesi created the role of Gualtieri. This scene was probably the recitative and *rondò* "Nel lasciarti in questo istante" (parts: Mus. Hs. 10768).

[217] *Recte*: "Dixit Dominus," performed earlier on 1 April 1802.

[218] The only independent chorus by Eybler that MT owned was "Es töne dann in rascher Saiten Sturme" (parts: Mus. Hs. 10893).

[219] Herrmann contains no work of this title. "Follia con Variazioni," listed in *CaM*, p. 62 (see Fig. 1.3), was transferred to A-Wgm by Pohl. This anonymous orchestral version of Corelli's variations on La Follia from the violin sonatas, Op. 5 (A-Wgm XIII 29392) was probably the work performed by MT, whose diary allows us to attribute the orchestration to Eybler.

Teresa e Wilk von Pucitta[220] gesungen von mir Wiesenthal
Ratmayer Korner Weinmüller und Wallaschek

Dem 25.   Bey mir

Carlotta e Lubino von Mayer[221] gesungen von mir
Wiesenthal Simoni Korner, Weinmüller Wallaschek und
Heller.

Dem 26.   Ackademie bey mir mit folgenden Stücken

Ein Quartett auß Debora von Guiglielmi gesungen von
mir Altamonte Simoni und Weinmüller

Ein Duett auß Pirro von Zingarelli gesungen von
Altamonte und Simoni

Fantaisie auf der Harpfe gespielt von Müller

Ein Duett mit Chöre auß Achille von Pär gesungen von
mir und Weinmüller

Einige Stüke d[to] geblasen von der Harmonie

Das Finale von zweyten Akt auß Orazi von Cimarosa
gesungen von mir Altamonte Wiesenthal Simoni
Ratmayer Weinmüller und Chor

* * *

September [1802]

Dem 21.   Eine Meß von Eibler[222]
Tedeum d[to][223]

October [1802]

Dem 3.   Eine Meß von Reuter mit Clarino solo sambt
Graduale[224]

---

[220] Vincenzo Pucitta, *Teresa e Wilk, farsa* (Venice, Carnival 1802). Score and parts: Mus. Hs. 9989–91.

[221] Mayr, *Lubino e Carlotta, farsa* (Venice, 1799). Score and parts: Mus. Hs. 10035–6.

[222] Eybler, *Missa S. Theresiae* in B♭, Herrmann 29, composed in 1802. This performance and that on 3 October probably served as rehearsals for the performance on Franz's nameday, 4 October.

[223] Eybler, Te Deum in B♭ (Herrmann 120, version for single chorus), composed in 1802, listed in *KK* as Te Deum IV.

[224] Probably Reutter's Mass in C and gradual in C, "Tu de vita," listed together in *KK*. The mass with clarino solo was possibly *Missa S. Ignatii*, of which a set of parts from the Hofkapelle (HK 782) carries the note "NB Clarino sempre conc[to]."

Eine Meß von Eibler sambt Graduale und Offertorio
Tedeum d^{to}[225]
Ein Quintett von Eibler[226] gespielt auf der Geige von
Kaplan [?], Bratsche Rutsdizka, [227] Viole d'amour
Eibler, violoncello Gottlieb, [228] Violone Sedler[229]

Dem 4.   Meß von Eibler[230]
Dem 10.   Cantate von Weigl Le Pazzie Musicali[231] gesungen von mir
Altamonte Ratmayer Korner Weinmüller Wallaschek
und Chöre
Dem 17.   Ackademie bey mir mit folgenden Stücken[232]
Dem 23.   Eine Opera von Mayer Misteri Eleusini[233] gesungen von
mir Ratmayer Korner Weinmüller und Chöre
Dem 25.   Ein Requiem von Winter[234]
Eine Meß von Winter mit doppelten Chöre[235]

November [1802]

Dem 3.   Eine Cantate von Winter auf dem Frieden[236] gesungen von
mir Wiesenthal Ratmayer Weinmüller und Chöre

[225] The mass and Te Deum by Eybler were probably those performed on 21 September; the gradual was almost certainly "Magnificate Dominum mecum" (Herrmann 69), composed in 1802. With the addition of the offertory "Levavi in montes" (Herrmann 104) Eybler's plenary mass was complete.
[226] One of Eybler's two quintets for viola d'amore, violin, viola, cello and double bass, both in D major (Herrmann 184 and 185), of which MT owned copies (*CaM*, p. 62; see Fig. 1.3).
[227] Joseph Rusiczka (also spelled Ruschitzka), second organist in the Hofkapelle (HSS 1800, 344), violist in the Burgtheater orchestra (HHStA, Hoftheater SR 33 [1799–1800]), freelance violinist (VA 1800, 142) and violist (*Die sämmtlichen wienerischen Künstler*, unpaginated appendix to *HSS* 1796).
[228] Kajetan Gottlieb, freelance cellist (*Die sämmtlichen wienerischen Künstler*, VA 1800, 142).
[229] Either Georg Settler, freelance double-bass player (*Die sämmtlichen wienerischen Künstler*, VA 1800, 143) or Joseph Settler (also spelled Sedler), double-bass player in the Hofkapelle (HSS 1800, 344) and in the Burgtheater (HHStA, Hoftheater SR 33 [1799–1800]).
[230] Nameday of Emperor Franz. The mass was presumably the *Missa S. Theresiae*, rehearsed on 21 September and 3 October.
[231] Weigl, *Le pazzie musicali*, 1802; this was probably the premiere (score and parts: Mus. Hs. 10082–3).
[232] MT left this entry incomplete.
[233] Mayr, *I misteri eleusini* (Milan, 1802). Score and parts: Mus. Hs. 9961–2.
[234] Two settings of the Requiem by Winter are known: one for Joseph II (1790, in C minor) and a *Missa di Requiem* of unknown date. *KK* lists a Requiem by Winter in C minor.
[235] Winter, Mass in D minor for double chorus, of which MT owned a set of parts (*KK*).
[236] Winter, *Das Friedensfest* (score and parts: Mus. Hs. 10217–18).

Dem 7.	Eine Oper von Eibler Das Zauberschwert[237] gesungen von mir Wiesenthal Ratmayer Korner Weinmüller Vogel[238] und Chöre
Dem 15.	Requiem von Winter Meß von Hayden Joseph
Dem 28.	Eine Meß von Monn[239] Eine Meß von Fuchs[240]

December [1802]

Dem 5.	Eine Meß von Joseph Hayden Eine Meß von Michael Hayden

1803
January

Dem 5ten	Ackademie bey mir mit folgenden Stücken Ein Duett auß Ginevra von Mayer[241] gesungen von Altamonte und Simone Eine Arie auß Artemisia von Cimarosa gesungen von Ratmayer mit Chöre Ein Rondo von Capuzi[242] gesungen von Altamonte Ein Quartett auß Lodoiska von Mayer gesungen von mir Altamonte Simone Weinmüller und Chöre Eine Cantata von Weigl mit Chöre gesungen von Weinmüller Ein Duett auß der Schöpfung von Hayden gesungen von mir und Weinmüller Eine Aria von Weigl mit Chöre gesungen von mir Eine Aria mit Chöre auß der Lodoiska von Weigl gesungen von Simone

---

[237] Eybler, *Das Zauberschwert*, Herrmann 142 (Vienna, Theater in der Leopoldstadt, 1802). Score and parts: Mus. Hs. 10182–3.

[238] Johann Michael Vogl, baritone in the court theaters from 1795, singing in both German and Italian.

[239] Mathias Georg Monn (1717–50), two of whose masses, in C and B♭, MT owned (*KK*).

[240] *KK* lists two masses by "Fux," both in C. The composer may have been Johann Nepomuk Fuchs.

[241] "Vieni, colà t'attendo" (score and parts: Mus. Hs. 10492–3).

[242] Perhaps the "scena ed aria" by Antonio Capuzzi of which MT owned a score dated 1800: Mus. Hs. 10279.

Ein Quartett auß Sciti von Mayer gesungen von mir
Altamonte Simone Ratmayer und Chöre

* * *

Mertz [1803]

Dem 4.   Ein Requiem von Paisiello mit 2 Chöre[243]
            Eine Sinfonie von Wranitzky
Dem 16.   Eine Opera von Cherubini Elisa[244] gesungen von mir
            Wiesenthal Ratmayer Korner Weinmüller Vogel
            Wallaschek und Chöre
Dem 27.   Eine Sinfonie von Hayden Joseph
            Eine Sinfonie von Wranitzky
            Cantate von Weigl le Pazzie musicali gesungen von mir
            Marchesi Ratmayer Korner Weinmüller Wallaschek und
            Chöre

April [1803]

Dem 2.   Requiem von Eibler[245]
            Libera d^{to}
            De Profundis d^{to}[246]
Dem 7.[247] Stabat Mater von Pergolese gerichtet von Eibler gesungen
            von mir Altamonte Simone Weinmüller und Chöre[248]
            Der Tod Jesu von Graun d^{to}[249]
Dem 10.[250] Ackademie mit folgenden Stücken

---

[243] Paisiello, Requiem for double chorus, Robinson 5.01 (Naples, 1789; revised 1799). This work
is not listed in *KK*; the performing parts probably belonged to Ferdinand or to his wife (MT's
sister) Maria Luisa, who on 5 July 1802 wrote to MT from Schönbrunn: "j'ai reçus divers spar-
titi, dont un est Acis, et Galaté de Nauman, così così; et un nouvelle Lodoiska de Cherubini, en
Italien; et la Grande Messe de Requiem de Paesiello, que dans le moment que je vous ecris Ferdinand se met à la prouver" (HHStA, Fa, Sb, Kart. 62, Briefe der Geschwister der Kaiserin 1802,
fol. 62v).

[244] Cherubini, *Eliza, ou Le Voyage aux glaciers du Mont St-Bernard* (Paris, 1794). Score and parts: Mus.
Hs. 10165–6.

[245] Eybler, Requiem with Libera, Herrmann 37 (1803). MT owned parts (*KK*) and probably also the
autograph score.

[246] Eybler, De profundis, Herrmann 132 (1803); MT owned a copy (*KK*).

[247] Holy Thursday.

[248] Eybler's arrangement of Pergolesi's Stabat mater for four soloists (SATB) and chorus, Herrmann
244.

[249] Graun, *Der Tod Jesu*, passion cantata (Berlin, 1755). Score: Mus. Hs. 9872.

[250] Easter Sunday.

Sinfonie auß Lodoiska von Cherubini[251]
Ein Quintett auß Trame Deluse von Cimarosa gesungen
　　von mir Altamonte Ratmayer Weinmüller Wallaschek
Eine Aria auß Nozze di Figaro von Mozart[252] gesungen von
　　Weinmüller
Ein Duett auß Pirro von Zingarelli gesungen von mir und
　　Simone
Eine Arie auß Elfrida von Paisiello gesungen von
　　Bevilacqua[253]
Eine Finale auß Pirro von Weigl gesungen von Altamonte
　　mir Simone Ratmayer Korner Weinmüller
Ein Terzett auß Lodoiska von Mayer gesungen von mir
　　Altamonte und Simone mit Chöre
Eine Aria mit Chöre auß Misteri Eleusini gesungen von
　　Simone
Ein Duett auß Lodoiska von Mayer[254] gesungen von mir
　　und Altamonte
Eine Aria auß Orazi von Cimarosa[255] gesungen von
　　Bevilacqua
Ein Finale auß Misteri Eleusini von Mayer gesungen von
　　mir Simone Ratmayer Weinmüller und Chöre

Dem 17.　Eine Opera von Winter Marie von Montalban[256] gesungen
　　von mir Altamonte Weinmüller Saal Vogel Ratmayer
　　und Chöre

Dem 19.　Ackademie mit folgenden Stücken
　　Eine Sinfonie von Cherubini
　　Ein Terzett auß Artemisia von Cimarosa[257] gesungen von
　　　mir Simone und Ratmayer
　　Ein Rondò auß Conte di Saldagna von Zingarelli gesungen
　　　von Marchesi

---

[251] Cherubini, *Lodoiska* (Paris, 1791). Score and parts: Mus. Hs. 10171–2.
[252] Probably "Non più andrai" (score and parts: Mus. Hs. 10560–1).
[253] Abbé Bevilacqua, tenor in the service of Prince Esterházy; sang in concerts in Vienna in 1803 and 1805 (Morrow, *Concert Life*; Rosenbaum, "Tagebücher," 107).
[254] "Parto, ti lascio, o dio" (score and parts: Mus. Hs.: 10500–1).
[255] Probably "Se alla patria."
[256] Winter, *Marie von Montalban, ernsthaftes Singspiel* (Munich, 1800; first public performance in Vienna on 18 July 1803). Score and parts: Mus. Hs. 10219–20. The cast in the Kärntnertortheater included Saal, Vogl, and Weinmüller.
[257] "Tremante, confusa" (parts: Mus. Hs. 10302).

Ein Duett auß Hercules von Mayer[258] gesungen von
Simone Weinmüller
Eine Arie von Portogallo gesungen von Bevilacqua
Ein Quartett auß Sciti von Mayer gesungen von mir
Marchesi Simone Ratmayer Weinmüller und
Chöre
Eine Cantate auf dem Frieden von Winter gesungen von
mir Simone Weinmüller und Chöre

Dem 24.   Ackademie mit folgenden Stücken
Eine Sinfonie auß die Fuorusciti von Pär[259]
Ein Terzett auß Annibale von Salieri gesungen von mir
Simoni und Weinmüller
Eine Arie mit Chöre d[to] gesungen von der Altamonte
Ein Chor d[to]
Ein Duett d[to] gesungen von mir und Simoni
Eine Arie mit Chöre gesungen von Brizi[260]
Ein Quintett auß die Fuorusciti von Pär gesungen von mir
Brizi Simoni Weinmüller Vogel und Chöre
Eine Cantata von Salieri Gesù al Limbo[261] gesungen von
mir Altamonte Brizi Simone Ratmayer Weinmüller und
Chöre

Dem 26.   Ackademie bey mir mit folgenden Stücken
Die Ouverture auß Hercules von Mayer
Ein Duett auß Numa von Pär gesungen von mir und
Großherzog und Chöre
Eine Aria auß Ifigenia von Zingarelli[262] gesungen von
Simoni
Ein Quartett auß Numa von Pär gesungen von mir
Großherzog Simoni Ratmayer und Chöre
Ein Rondo auß Alessandro von Tarchi gesungen von
Marchese

[258] Mayr, *Ercole in Lidia*, dramma per musica (Vienna, 29 January 1803). Score: Mus. Hs. 9958. This duet was probably "Ecco il toro investo" (score and parts: Mus. Hs. 10490–1).

[259] Paer, *I fuorusciti di Firenze* (Dresden, 1802). Score and parts: Mus. Hs. 10044–5.

[260] The tenor Antonio Brizzi made his professional debut in 1787; he sang in the court theaters from June 1801 and appeared frequently in public and private concerts from 1802 to 1809 (A-Wth, *Theaterzettel*, Morrow, *Concert Life*).

[261] Salieri, *Gesù al Limbo*, oratorio (score and parts: Mus. Hs. 9915–16). This was evidently the premiere.

[262] Zingarelli, *Ifigenia in Aulide*, dramma per musica, of which at least two versions were performed: Milan, 1787 and Venice, 1795. Simoni sang Agamennone in Milan.

Das Finale von 1. Act auß Hercules von Mayer gesungen
    von mir Brizzi Großherzog Weinmüller Vogel und Chöre
Ein Terzett d$^{to\,263}$ gesungen von Brizzi, Großherzog, Vogel
Ein Rondò mit Chöre auß Sciti von Mayer[264] gesungen
    von mir
Ein Duett von Zingarelli gesungen von Marchesi und
    Simoni
Eine Aria mit Chöre auß Hercules von Mayer gesungen
    von Brizzi
Ein Duett auß Elfrida von Paisiello gesungen von mir und
    Brizzi
Ein Finale auß Sciti von Mayer gesungen von Altamonte
    Simone Ratmayer Großherzog und Chöre

---

[263] Probably the trio "L'alma anelante e cupida."
[264] Probably the *rondò* "Non t'affanni la mia sorte."

APPENDIX 3

Paer's letters to the empress

All musical sources cited in the notes, unless otherwise indicated, are preserved in A-Wn, with provenance (based on evidence presented in chapter 1) in Marie Therese's library.

1. Dresden, 1 June 1803. Source: HHStA, Fa, Sb, Kart. 62, Verschiedene an Kaiserin Marie Therese 1803, fol. 142r–143v

Sacra Real Cesarea App[ostoli]ca Maestà
Rammaricato al sommo son io nel dover rappresentare ossequiosissima-
mente alla Maestà Vostra, che mi è stato impossibile sino ad ora, malgrado ogni mio buon volere, a poter eseguire i Cenni Suoi veneratissimi col
travagliare alla Composizione della Consaputa Cant[at]a a me trasmessa
pezzo, a pezzo in varie volte.[1] Poco dopo il mio ritorno in Dresda è giunto
qui, come a V. M[aest]à è noto, S. A. R. il Gran Duca,[2] ed in tale circostanza
volendo questa Elettoral Corte procurare al medesimo qualche teatral divertimento sono stato obbligato, per debito di contratto, d'ammanare due
delle mie Opere, una delle quali *Sargino* essendo tutta affatto nuova per
codesta Compagnia, ed Orchesta[3] mi ha neccessitato ad un gran numero di
prove prima che sulla scene venisse esposta.[4] Ho dovuto eziandio preparar
l'Oratorio composto per la prefata S. A. R.,[5] cosichè a respirare mi sono

---

[1] This cantata, described later in the letter as extremely long, was probably *Arianna consolata*, an enormous "accademia per musica" in two parts on a libretto by Luigi Prividali (score and parts: Mus. Hs. 10134–5). The libretto's date of publication, 1803, suggests that empress performed it in private some time that year. *Arianna* was complete by 7 November 1803, when Grand Duke Ferdinand referred to a copy of it that MT had sent to him. It was probably for *Arianna* that MT rewarded Paer on 23 July 1803, "für seine Cantate," with presents whose lavishness matched the size of *Arianna*: a writing case of ebony worth 85 Gulden, a diamond ring worth 700 Gulden, 1,000 Gulden in cash, and a purse with 300 Gulden for travel expenses. On the same occasion Prividali received a snuffbox worth 120 Gulden and 200 Gulden in cash (HHStA, Fa, HKF, Kart. 24, diary, fol. 169r).
[2] Ferdinand, grand duke of Tuscany; S. A. R. stands for Sua Altezza Reale.
[3] This is Paer's normal spelling.
[4] *Sargino*, first performance in Dresden, 26 May 1803.   [5] *Il trionfo della chiesa*.

restate appena le poche ore del riposo. Ho insegnata a memoria la parte alla mia Moglie; [6] ho dovuto essere col G. D. spesse volte al cembalo perchè il tempo è stato quasi sempre piovoso, e vi si è anche aggiunto la malattia de' miei due figliuolini, che mi ha non poco costernato, onde e per mancanza di tempo, e per vessazion d'animo non ho assolutamente potuto accingermi ad un travaglio, che merita la più grande attenzione.

Quallora la M[aest]à V[ostr]a degni d'umanissima riflessione gli esposti veri motivi, che impedito mi hanno l'applicazione, io non dispero certamente d'ottenerne benigno perdon. Or che cessate sono le pressanti, ed indispensabili mie incombenze, or che l'animo mio più tranquillo trovasi, ad onta di sovrastarmi qualch'altro dovere con questo Elett[ora]l Teatro, tutto dedito a servir V. M. per meglio farlo mi preffiggo di partir dimani Giorno di Giovedì per Vienna; Colà arrivato, ogni momento consacrato sarà al travaglio accelerandolo più che possibil fia.

Ho esaminata la Poesia della prima Parte essendomi pervenuto collo scorso ordinario anche il Finale; confesso che v'è da farsi onore, ma è difficile assai da mettersi in musica, ed è estremamente lunga. Sono tutti gran Pezzi, e se in essa ve ne sono più di venti (senza contarne i Recit[ati]vi strumentati) per quanto breve io possa tenermi, senza mancare però all'effetto, ed alla parola, la sola prima parte ne durerà la musica tre ore almeno; onde direi d'omettere qualche cosa previo l'assenso di Vostra Maestà, e renderla con tal mezzo a regolar lunghezza, indi soggiungere al Vate Autore a tenersi breve nella Seconda Parte. Tutto ciò potremo combinare quando avrò l'onore di mettermi a Suoi Piedi appena giunto.

Supplicando intanto la Clemenza di Vostra Maestà di continuarmi l'onore dell'alto suo Patrocinio, e di accettare la mia illimitata rassegnazione a qualunque Suo Ordine ulteriore, mi protesto con profondissimo inchino: Di Vostra R[eal] Cesarea App[ostolica] Maestà

Umilissimo, Devotissimo, ed Obbligatissimo

Servitore Ferdinand Pär

Dresda primo Giugno 1803

2. No place, no date, but probably Dresden, 1803. Source: HHStA, Fa, Sb, Kart. 65, Private an Kaiserin Marie Therese, fol. 367r–v

Sacra Real Maestà Apostolica

Quanto consolante sia stato per me l'ordine Suo riguardo alla nota Cantata[7] non posso esprimerglielo. Tardi ho ricevuto la lettera che accompagna

---

[6] The soprano Francesca Riccardi Paer.

[7] Probably *Il conte Clò*, originally intended for performance on Emperor Franz's birthday, 12 February 1804, but postponed until the following year (see chapter 9).

l'Ordine suo pre[zioso?][8] perciò essendo imminente la partenza della posta d'oggi mi restringo, e mi metto soltanto a Suoi Sacri Imp[eriali] Piedi col dirle, che dimani mi abbocherò col Poeta presente di codesto nostro Teatro,[9] che in tutta segrettezza comunicherò al sud[dett]o La Sua Intenzione la quale trovo a proposito benissimo per divertir la Nota Persona,[10] e se mi permette aggiungerò tutto quello che sarà per il meglio – Eseguirò a puntino quanto V. M. mi ordina per le copie.

Mi prendo la libertà di farLe sapere, che da pochi giorni in qua la mia moglie si è sottoposta a delle convulsioni che se avessero conseguenze per l'avvenir forse mi toglierebbero l'onore di venire io stesso a mettermi a Suoi Piedi, per non abbandonarla in quest' incomodi; ma spero, che mediante la continua assistenza di Mr. Riffel medico del Principe Xaverio a cui ora è affidata non averà a ricadere in simili malattie, e così sarò felice se potrò umigliar a Vostra Maestà la nota Cantata in persona, e dirmi eternemente quale ho l'alto onore di pormi a' Suoi Reali Piedi:
Di Vostra Sacra Cesarea Maestà

Umili[ssi]mo, Dev[otissi]mo Ossequiosissimo
Servitore Ferdinand Pär

3. No place, no date, but probably Dresden, late 1803. Source: HHStA,
Fa, Sb. Kart. 65, Private an Kaiserin Marie Therese,
fol. 369r–372v

Vostra Imperial Cesarea Augusta Maestà
Ho l'onore di poter spedire la nota Cantata,[11] ma una sol porzione di Parti Cantanti – Quella di Luigina è per V. M. e non vi manca, che un solo Duetto fra Luigina, ed Ambrogio, ed il Finale. Tutto sarà terminato per Venerdì prossimo. I Copisti quanto bravi, sono altrettanto lunghi – Un lavoro di questa sorte merita almeno per la ristrettezza del tempo un benigno compatimento. Intanto Vostra Maestà potrà divertirsi, e studiare – Due prove d'Orchesta parmi, che basteranno, adunque abbia la degnazione di tener impegnati al di Lei ordine il 10, e 'l 11 dell'entrante prossimo Febb[rai]o.

---

[8] This "ordine" was probably MT's sketch, transcribed in Appendix 5A.
[9] Giacomo Cinti.
[10] Emperor Franz. Paer's assurance of secrecy was probably in response to a remark in MT's sketch that she wished to keep the project secret.
[11] *Il conte Clò.*

Quanto per me sia dispiacevole, ed amaro il non poter trovarmi presente, ne l'eseguirla Iddio lo sa, ma prostrato a' Suoi Clementissimi Piedi devo dirle che pur troppo non potrò movermi da Dresda se non dopo Quaresima in cui avrò adempiti a' miei doveri assunti, ai quali non ho potuto dar termine per la ritardata guariggione della mia moglie – Non voglio annojarla, ma più dettagliatamente ho significate le mie giustificazioni all'amico mio Sig. Simoni[12] acciò Egli gliele umilii in mio nome, e si degni onorarmi graziarmi di un benigno Perdono.

Non creda Vostra Maestà, che sebbene io non abbia l'onore di portarmi a Vienna per ora io abbia trascurata l'onorevol Comissione; nò, Vostra Maestà anzi mi sono data tutta la premura possibile, e vedrà (almeno me ne lusingo) ch'io mi son dato tutto l'impegno, acciò dopo la Cantata dell'Estate passata[13] su tal genere la presente abbi il suo luogo, e si scosti totalmente da quella come scritta da altra penna, ed a norma delle Rispettab.[i] di Lei intenzioni.

Unisco un foglio d'Istruzione sempre sotto gl'ordini e correzioni di V. Maestà.[14] Ho parimenti fatta copiare di nuovo la parte di Gioanni nell Orat[ori]o che ho l'onore d'addrizzargliela[15] – e mentre giorni sono attendeva la poesia della nuova cantata per non perder tempo ho puntata la parte suddetta, e spero che anderà meglio per la voce di V. Maestà, devo però umilmente rappresentarle, che nel duetto in E, ed in altri pezzi a più voce è assolut[ament]e impossibile puntarla senza scombussolare l'ordine dell'armonia.

La pregevolissima di Lei Carta risguardante l'ordine de' piccioli strumenti, m'è arrivata troppo tardi perciò ho sostituiti gl'istrumenti rimarcati a tenore della poesia.

Termino col prostrarmi a' Suoi Piedi implorando di nuovo la Valevolissima Sua Prottezione: l'alt'onore de' Suoi Ordini, ed umilissimamente ripetermi nel numero de' suoi *Fedelissimi*:
Dell'Imperial Cesarea Vostra Maestà
Dev[otissi]mo Umili[ssi]mo Obbl[igatissim]o Servitore
Ferdinand Pär

---

12 The tenor Giuseppe Simoni served frequently as a go-between in MT's dealings with Paer, who sometimes referred to him discreetly as "l'amico."
13 Probably *Arianna consolata*.   14 Transcribed in Appendix 5C.
15 *Per il Santo Sepolcro*, oratorio on a text by Pietro Bagnoli, performed at the Tonkünstler-Sozietät on 3 and 4 April 1803, has a character named Giovanni.

4. Dresden, 5 January [1804]. Source: HHStA, Fa, Sb. Kart. 63,
fol. 359r–360r

Sacra Cesarea Real Maestà

Sono stato questi due giorni in una mortale angoscia non essendo ancora
state in pronto tutte le parti della Cantata,[16] ed avendomi impedita la
lentezza del copista la data mia parola alla Sacra Real Vostra Maestà com'ebbi
l'Alt'Onore di dirLe coll'ultima mia. Gli ultimi del Carnevale; gl'impegni
della Capella, le Copie pel Teatro sono le ragioni addotte da quell'uomo –
Ho fin'ora bilanciato se doveva spedirle com'erano o se dovevo aspettarne il
fine – A quest'ultimo partito mi appigliai, considerando per primo punto la
segrettezza, e per secondo, che essendo terminata affatto Vostra Maestà
all'arrivo della sudd[et]ta non avea che a provarla, e cantarla – Oggi adunque
ricevo queste benedette Copie, e sia ringraziato il Cielo – Io stesso ho fatto
il Copista in diversi luoghi di queste fra cui il duetto le parti cantanti come
vedrà.

Non manca, che raddoppiare i Violini del Duetto N° 9 – e ciò deve
ordinarlo Vostra Maestà. Credo che la Cantata durerà quasi due ore – Mi
prendo la libertà di quì accludere un'altra Carta d'Istruzione pel rimanente.
Mi metto a' Suoi Piedi Vostra Maestà e le chieggo perdono se oso scriverLe
tutto ciò – Ma il desiderio che V. M.ª sii di me contenta mi farebbe intraprendere qualunque tentativo. – Dico ciò perchè ho fatto la prova colla
mia debole capacità scrivendo in sì breve tempo la presente Composizione;
Il solo Finale mi costa quattro giorni di continuo lavoro. Iddio voglia che
accompagnata dai miei voti, e dalla Esperimentata Clemenza della Maestà
vostra codesta musica possa divertire, ed aggradire alla Persona che a sì
giusto Titolo preme tanto alla Vostra Maestà, e per cui è composta. Il mio
dispiacere sarà il non esservi, e 'l giorno 12 sarò certamente in un continuo palpito. Per accellerare, ed assicurar l'arrivo della Sud[dett]a musica
mi sono servito di codesto Sig. Baron Bull[17] segrett[ari]o del Ministro di
Vostra Maestà presso Codesta Elettoral Corte; Non credo d'aver fatto male,
ma se ciò fosse le dimando umilissimamente perdono, non essendo a mia
cognizione l'ordine, o la ettiketa di tali cose.

Spero, che Vostra Maestà ora goderà una perfetta salute, e sarà ristabilita
del passato suo raffreddore – Anelo di sentire l'esito delle mie povere fattiche
che raccomando di nuovo alla di Lei Bontà, e Prottezione sotto la di Cui
Ombra m'inchino, mi prottesto ossequiosamente:

---

[16] *Il conte Clò.*
[17] Joseph von Buol-Mühlingen, secretary to the Austrian ambassador at Dresden (*HSS* 1804, p. 11).
I am grateful to Michael Lorenz for this identification.

Della Sacra Real Maestà Vostra
                    Umilissimo Dev[otissi]mo Osseq[uiosissimo] Ser[vitor]e
                                                            Ferd°. Pär
Dresda a dì 5 Genn[ai]o

5. Dresden, 7 February 1804. Source: HHStA, Fa, Sb, Kart. 63, fol. 363r–366r

Sacra Imperial Reale Cesarea Maestà
Quanto m'è di consolazione il sentire Vostra Maestà contenta di quello che ho fatto per la Nota Cantata, altrettanto si raddoppia in me il dispiacere di non esservi presente – Ma Vostra Maestà vedrà a chiara prova, che tutto anderà bene. Ora mi vedo onorato dallo desiderato scritto al quale tosto rispondo, e piacesse a Dio, che lo potessi fare in persona ma pur troppo devo scacciar la tentazione perchè troppo tardi. Pochi gesti servono a Recit[ativ]i essendo la cosa famigliare ma se si canta a memoria convien gestire, quello che averebbe il più sarebbe Brocchi.

L'orchesta parmi come quella dell'estate passata per la cantata di Vaigel[18] – Almeno ventiquattro coristi 6 tenori, 6 alti, 6 sopr. e 6 bassi per il coro nuziale e sopratutto il Finale, che tanto mi preme. È si facile quello fatto per i Dilettanti che s'impara in un momento ma se non si può allora si può servire Vostra Maestà di questa camerista di Junk e degli altri, o di Correr o di Ractmayer.[19] Per l'arpa è facile l'accomodamento col cambio del Nome – *Tu Luigina* B. E. (*in vece* d'Enrichetta) *suonerai il cembalo*, e così Vostra Maesta suonerà il Cembalo, in vece di parlare al'Enrichetta per l'Arpa, vi sii la *Müler*[20] sotto il nome di Margherita altra parente &c – Le altre annotazioni ultime saranno arrivate in tempo ed a proposito. – Se v'è il tempo di fare le tre prove accennatemi dalla Maestà Vostra io non dubito, che la cosa anderà bene: e non farebbe poi gran diffetto se anche si cantasse tutto colla parte in mano.

Sono anzioso, palpitante, e nella massim' agitazione finchè non averò riscontro quando saranno arrivate le parti spedite soltanto il giorno 5 alle 8 di mattina.

Supplico la Maestà Vostra a perdonare di nuovo le mie debolezze dopo le Feste di Pasqua conto d'esser libero affatto de' miei affari e posso essere al Suo Ordine, così anche la mia Moglie è più di contenta, e mi prega di

---

[18] Joseph Weigl.
[19] "Junk" is Thomas Peter Young; "Correr" is probably the tenor Phillip Korner; "Ractmayer" is Mathias Rathmayer, amateur tenor; see chapter 2.
[20] Probably the harpist Josepha Müllner.

metterla a Vener[atissi]mi Piedi di Vostra Maestà – La supplico onorarmi
della Valentissima ed Altissima sua Prottezione frattanto non cesserò fin
che averò vita d'essere quale ho l'Alt'onore di prottestarmi alle Sue Piante:
Della Cesarea Imperial e Real Maestà Vostra

L'Umil[issi]mo e Dev[otissim]o Ser[vitor]e

Ferdinand Pär

Dresda 7 Febb[rai]o 1804

6. Dresden, 27 February [1804]. Source: HHStA, Fa, Kart. 63, fol. 367r–369v

Sacra Cesarea Reale Imperial Maestà!
Alle due ore pomeridiane ho ricevuta la Musica speditami dalla Imperiale
Reale Vostra Maestà quest'oggi, e non manco di prontamente pormi di
nuovo a Sacri I[mperiali] Suoi Piedi ringraziandola delle comissioni con cui
Vostra Maestà si degna tutt'ora onorarmi. Per risponderLe adeguatamente,
e col più proffondo rispetto esporle quanto sinceramente io penso, le dirò
adunque, che non dubito, che il G. D. avendo fatto un presente a Vostra
Maestà dell'Oratorio il *Trionfo della chiesa* le soggiungerà di servirsene ove,
e quando piacerà a Vostra Maestà, molto più se si tratta di un Opera sì Pia,
come il benefizio delle povere Vedove.[21] Allora anch'io sarei felice se potesse
eseguirsi da quella superba Orchesta, e sotto la Direzione del M[aest]ro
Salieri giacchè non sapendo ancora quando la presente mia Opera nuova,
che attualmente compongo, andrà in scena non posso fidarmi di essere per
la Domenica delle Palme in Vienna.[22]

  In quel Caso tutto anderebbe a dovere sotto gli Auspici e Prottezione
di Vostra Maestà, e direzione di un sì celebre, ed esperto Compositore.
Ma l'applicazione delle parti è un po difficile: io però non mancherò dimani subito di applicarmici e farò di tutto per servire a' Suoi Supremi,
e Veneratissim' Ordini. Soltanto lascio nel qui accluso Suo foglietto in
bianco chi potria meglio eseguire la parte della Religione dandosi in Teatrale
Accademia, mentre non conosco pienamente ancora l'estensione delle due
Sorelle Sig.ᵉ Sessi,[23] ma direi d'affidarla ad una di esse perchè: primo, la Religione in pubblico sta meglio per una voce di donna; secondo per quanto

---

[21] Paer refers here to the possibility of presenting *Il trionfo della chiesa* during the Lenten concerts of
  the Tonkünstler-Sozietät.

[22] Paer's "opera nuova" was probably *Leonora, ossia L'amore coniugale*, first performed in Dresden,
  3 October 1804. He is not known to have written any operas between *Sargino* and *Leonora*.

[23] Marianna Sessi and Vittoria Sessi. Marianna was the older; Paer later refers to her as "Mad.ª Sessi
  mag.ʳᵉ" and to Vittoria as "Sig.ª Sessi Minore" and as "Madamoiselle Sessi."

io sia capace di puntarla più alta e trasportarla in qualche luogo sempre
rimarrà un poco bassa come l'era quando la feci per Vostra Maestà, ed
allora conviene affidarla ad una, che abbia le corde di mezzo sonore, e non
deboli come sono le altre attuali cantanti del Teatro. Mi rincresce, che non
entri il Brizzi,[24] ma nella parte dell'Angelo non è possibile l'addattargliela,
poichè essa è per un Basso effettivo, perciò ha segnato Fogel.[25] Sopratutto
Vostra Maestà rimarchi la prim'Aria, ed il coro dell'Aqua Benedetta &c. che
sono estremamente bassi. Bensi può il Brizzi Cantare il *Numa* suscettibile
d'essere puntato più alto, e d'aggiungere abbellimenti trilli e volate in gran
numero. Ma chi farà la parte dell'Egeria bassissima? E poi mi faccio un dovere di rappresentare a Vostra Maestà, che il *Numa* farebbe un grand'effetto
sul Teatro, ma accorcciato, ed *arrangé* per l'attuale compagnia; rappresen-
tato così ad uso di accademia, non rispondo dell'esito.[26] – Perciò io direi
sempre sul venerato consenso del G. D. e di Vostra Maestà di attenersi
all'*Oratorio il Trionfo della Chiesa* – Se si effettua questo io sono veramente
felice, e soltanto supplico Vostra Maestà ad ordinare, che sii stampato colla
traduzione ben fatta in lingua tedesca, se dee l'Uditore interessarsene come
uno de' principali punti di religione, e così gustare l'espressione musicale.
Supplico umilmente se però non le dispiace di tollerare fin che la mia
Opera sia costì rappresentata, e poi sono al Suo Rispett[os]o ordine verrò
più presto a Vienna, se me lo Comenderà, accomoderò il Numa pel Teatro,
e mi darò l'onore d'essere in tutto, e per tutto qual sono umilmente, ed
ossequiosamente:
Della Imperial Reale Sacra Maestà Vostra
Umil[issi]mo Dev[otissi]mo Oss[equiosissimo]
Servitore Ferdinand Pär
Dresda 27 Febb[rai]o

Enclosure (fol. 368r; Marie Therese's handwriting in boldface type)

Oratorio.
La Religione come era accomodata per me   N. N.
Davidde   Simoni   *perchè par fatto per la Sua Voce*

---

[24] The tenor Antonio Brizzi sang in the court theaters from 1801.

[25] The baritone Johann Michael Vogl.

[26] Paer wrote *Numa Pompilio* for private performances at court (probably in 1800 and 1802, the years
in which librettos were published in Vienna). The location of the autograph score in I-Fc strongly
suggests that Grand Duke Ferdinand commissioned the opera shortly after his arrival in Vienna in
1799. Here Paer refers to a projected revision of the opera for performance in the court theaters that
never took place. Paer revised *Numa* in Paris in 1808 for a performance before Napoleon.

Abramo   Vaymyler[27]
S. Angelo   Fogel

N. B. I cori dell'Eco da mettersi sopra il Cielo del palco scenico, oppure per maggior commodo da un lato della scena invisibili come pure l'arpa &c.

Numa.

Camilla   Mad.ª Sessi mag[gio]re con qualche miglioramento, essendo stata originalmente composta per una discreta dilettante

Ninfa Egeria un Contr'alto; oppure comporre un altra nuova musica non essendo affidata, che a tre, o quattro toni –

Numa   Brizzi. cogli abbellimenti ed aggiunzioni –

Lavinio   Simoni –

Mezio   Ratmayer –

7. Dresden, 23 March 1804. Source: HHStA, Fa, Sb Kart. 63, fol. 370r–v

Sacra Cesarea Real Maestà

Il contento per essere tanto felice di godere la Grazia, la Prottezione altissima della Maestà Vostra, e l'onore segnalato de' preziosi Suoi Comandi mi fa scordare il dispiacere che non s'eseguisca la nota Cantata del *Trionfo della Chiesa*. Il Sig. Maestro Salieri mi ha scritto, mi da le ragioni note alla Maestà Vostra, e credo ch'egli abbia ragione di darle, e che siano anche giustissime. Se Sua Maestà L'Imperatore vorrà la Sud[dett]a musica pel *benefizio de' Poveri*[28] (come m'accenna la Maestà Vostra) io ubbidirò venendo, e cercherò di superare tutte le attuali opposizioni sempre sotto le *Ali preziose* e *potenti* della Grazia di Vostra Maestà – Soltanto la supplico divotamente farmi accennare quando all'incirca sarebbe l'occasione di darlo, e quando mi ci dovrei trovare.

La mia nuov' Opera[29] si copia, e si copia un intera partitura per Vostra Maestà, ma l'esecuzione della sudd[ett]a non si darà che a Pelnitz – non essendovi spettacolo, ma bensì sentimento, ed interesse. Spero, che V. M.ª ne sarà contenta, e spero di portargliela io stesso all'occasione del Concerto per i Poveri. – Non ho ricevuto lettera ne libro dal Simoni; spero, che lo

---

[27] The bass Carl Weinmüller.   [28] Wohlthätigkeits-Anstalten concert on 20 May 1804.

[29] Again, this is presumably *Leonora*, although no performance at Pillnitz in advance of the Dresden premiere is known to have taken place.

riceverò colla Diligenza vent[ur]a – Non dubito che 'l libro francese sarà fondato sopra un buon soggetto, se scelto è dall'ottimo gusto Suo, e dal sensibile Suo sentimento; io non mancherò di leggerlo, ed umilmente gliene avvanzerò il mio debole avviso.[30]

Mi metto a' suoi R[eal]i ed Imp[eria]li Piedi prottestandole eternamente la più fedele servitù, e la più affettuosa, rispettosa e sommessa ubbidienza, colla quale ho l'Alt'onore di replicarmi sempre sempre:
Della Sacra Cesarea Vostra Maestà

Umil[issi]mo Dev[otissi]mo Obb[ligatissimo] Servitore
Ferdinand Pär

Dresda 23 Marzo 1804

8. Dresden, 2 April 1804. Source: HHStA, Fa, Sb, Kart. 63,
fol. 372r–373v

Sacra Cesarea Imperiale Reale Maestà
Mi prostro a' Piedi di Vostra Maestà ed accuso il grato, e prezioso suo comando, per l'esecuzione del quale non mancherò di pormi in Viaggio per Vienna ne' primi del vent[ur]o Maggio, e così avrò l'onore altissimo di bacciarle divot[issimament]e la mano, poscia dirigere il Concerto, ossia 'l mio Oratorio il *Trionfo della Chiesa*, che ai 20 del sudd[ett]o si darà nella Sala del Ridotto a prò de' poveri.

Se mi permette intanto mi prendo la libertà di umiliare a Vostra Maestà il mio debole parere. Niuno al pari di Crescentini[31] potrebbe eseguire perfettamente la parte della Religione, e ciò sarebbe un vero piacere s'ei vi cantasse trovandosi in Vienna, ma se la Sig.ª Sessi minore non accettò la parte (come mi ha scritto il Degno Sig.ᵉ Salieri) per non aver ancora debuttato sul Teatro, fors'anche Crescentini considererà il proprio suo debutto come cosa affatto nuova, ne vorrà farsi sentire in altro luogo avanti l'Opera. Perdoni Vostra Maestà forse m'ingannerò ma il prevenire è sempre cosa prudente. In tutt'i Casi giacchè il Sig. Salieri dice, che la parte sarebbe più che ad ogn'altra convenuta alla Madamoiselle Sessi ma, che per ragione del non eseguito ancora suo debutto non poteva avanti farsi sentire, in allora anche questa difficoltà sarebbe superata poichè a 20 di Maggio *La clemenza di Tito* sarà già stata rappresentata.[32]

---

[30] *Les Mines de Pologne*, a *mélodrame* by R. C. G. de Pixérécourt, which MT hoped would serve as the basis for an Italian opera by Paer (see chapter 8).

[31] Girolamo Crescentini, male soprano.

[32] Mozart's *La clemenza di Tito* received its first Kärntnertortheater performance on 12 April 1804. Vittoria Sessi made her Viennese debut as Vitellia; Marianna Sessi sang Sesto.

Dice perfett[ament]e Vostra Maestà, che al mio arrivo saranno forse più superabili le smorfie di quelle Signore. Io farò tutto, e per tutto quanto mi comanderà la Maestà Vostra, e quanto sarà neccessario per dar bene quella musica, e contentar chi si darà la pena d'eseguirla – Fra le dilettanti, che averebber potuto cantar la parte della Religione, la più adattata era la *Sig. Catt[erin]a Bianchi*, avendo delle superbe corda di mezzo, ma non so se il medico, o la gran soggezione, che soffre forse gliel avrebber impedito – La Sig. Frank è bravissima, ma le corde del G. A. B. di mezzo non si sentirebber molto in una gran sala.[33] L'Esempio della sud[dett]a che si prestò in pubblico per Opere pie, potrebbe servire per tant'altre Dilettanti e perciò mi prendo la libertà di dirlo, ma soltanto di passaggio. Sottomettendomi all'Autorità, Esperienza, e giuste disposizioni di Vostra Maestà, che per Savia esperienza le conosce meglio d'ogn'altro.

Porterò alla mia venuta lo Spartito dell'Opera nuova che si sta copiando, e lo presenterò umilmente alla Maestà Vostra; anche il libretto della cantata carnevalesca sarà accomodato per darsi in altra occasione fuori di carnevale, così non avranno da cangiar, che pochi versi, lo che eseguirò subito al mio arrivo.

Ebbi l'onore di rappresentarle che il libro le *Mines*&c[34] era eccellente ma non per far un'Opera Seria affatto, se però Vostra Maestà la desiderasse per Crescentini allora si potrebbe traddurla come han fatto della Lodoiska[35] in serio affatto, ma quella *Polina*[36] la di cui vivacità mette al salvamento quella sventurata famiglia non si potrebbe conservarla, onde io dico di lasciarla come sta per non perdere le tante bellezze dell'Original francese. L'ho diggià data a traddurre, e ridurre al Poeta della Cantata succennata; ciò non sarà eseguita però sì presto perchè costui è Cantante della Cappella, maestro di lingue ed assume tante cose che non può abbandonare, ma però Egli si darà tutta la premura possibile per traddurlo presto, e bisogna perdonargli non essendo egli gran Poeta, ma soltanto interinale per accomodar i libretti d'Opere, che vengon dall'Italia. –

Ma io incomodo Vostra Maestà col farla legger troppo; Spero che il Clemente Suo Cuore me compatirà l'ardire: Amo meglio di spiegare i miei deboli sentimenti alla Maestà Vostra, che di farli passare per altre mani, meno atte a compatire, o a soffrire le altrui debolezze.

---

[33] Christine Frank, née Gerhardi.

[34] *Les Mines de Pologne*, first alluded to by Paer in his previous letter.

[35] Mayr, *Lodoiska* (Venice, 1795; heavily revised version performed in Milan in 1800); opera based on a story (quite similar to that of *Les mines de Pologne*) that Cherubini had used as the basis for an *opéra-comique* (Paris, 1791).

[36] Polina is a character in Pixérécourt's *mélodrame*.

Col più vivo del cuore la scongiuro a compartirmi un raggio solo dell'Altissima Prottezione di Vostra Maestà, ed ansioso d'inginnochiarmi al più presto a' Suoi Piedi, con il più proffondo Ossequio, ed umilissimo Rispetto mi offro, e sono eternamente:

P. S. La mia moglie m'incombe di umilmente metterla a Suoi R[eali] Piedi. Della Maestà Vostra

Dev[otissi]mo Obbl[igatissimo] Affezio[natissim]o
Umil[issi]mo Ser[vitor]e Ferdinand Pär

Dresda 2 Ap[ri]le 1804

9. [Dresden?], 12 April 1804. Source: HHStA, Fa, Sb, Kart. 63,
fol. 374r–375v

Sacra Real Cesarea Maestà

Non manco di subitamente prostrarmi a Clementissimi Suoi R[eali] Imp[eria]li Piedi, e meco mia Moglie, che umilissimamente le porge i suoi ringraziamenti giacchè la Maestà Vostra si degna ricordarsene. Le includo come me lo ordina il piano della nuova Cantata pel Nattale venturo: Ella è di moltissimo effetto – Niuno potrà meglio trattare favorevolmente, e dignitos[ament]e un tal Sacro Soggetto, che l'Abbate Pietro Bagnoli[37] – Se Vostra Maestà m'ordina di scrivergli, io la ubbidirò subitamente in tal Caso conviene che la Maestà Vostra mi rispedisca il piano giacchè essendomi pervenute tutte le lettere di quest'ordinario assai tardi, appena ho il tempo di rispondere a Vostra Maestà e non mi resta tanto, che basta per copiarla – Colla raccomandazione accennata da Vostra Maestà l'Abbate suddetto cercherà d'essere segreto, e per certo S. A. R. il Gran Duca ambirà ch'egli abbia con quest'occasione l'alt'onore di servirla.

Ciò, che umilmente le raccomando, è di raccomandar la sollecitudine poichè questo lavoro omettendo per ora l'Opera *le Mines* &c conto di farlo subitamente appena sarò ritornato dopo il Concerto[38] a cui ho promesso alla Maestà Vostra d'assistere. Conviene, ch'io dica tutto alla Maestra Vostra conto primieramente di venire a Vienna come ebbi l'onore di dirle, poi applicarmi al lavoro della Cant[at]a qui acclusa; poi spedirla; indi passare un mese, e mezzo circa dal buon Principe di Lobkovitz (che sempre me lo raccomanda anche colla sua lettera d'oggi) in compagnia di mia Moglie

[37] MT had apparently sent Paer a sketch for a Christmas cantata in the hope that it would serve Pietro Bagnoli (librettist of *Il trionfo della chiesa*) as the basis for a libretto that Paer would set to music. (Paer and Bagnoli had collaborated on an earlier Christmas cantata, *Per la festività del S. Natale*, of which the printed libretto is dated 1801.) Although Bagnoli may have written a libretto in response to MT's plan (see Paer's Letter 12), Paer does not seem to have composed the cantata. MT owned no Christmas cantata by Paer.

[38] The performance of *Il trionfo della chiesa* for the Wohlthätigkeits-Anstalten.

a cui l'aria della campagna farà del bene non essendosi tutt'affatto ancora rimessa dalle fiere, e spesse sue convulsioni – Si degni notare Vostra Maestà ch'io sarò quindi a Vienna ossia a Laxemburgo per la metà del mese di Settembre, e se me l'ordinerà vi resterò fino alla metà di Ottobre; poscia partirò per Roma, e colà scriverò l'Opera prima di S. Steffano pel Teatro Valle, essendo l'oggetto del mio viaggio il desiderio di meco condurre la vecchia mia Madre unica cosa preziosa, che mi resta in Italia, e che non isdegnerà di voler morire presso di me; Anche il vantaggioso, ed inusitato compenso alle deboli fattiche mie, che m'offrì quel Teatro è stata la più forte tentazione potendo combinare così la Gloria, il piacere d'abbracciare mia Madre, e qualche amico ma ben raro che mi è restato avanti la mia partenza dall'Italia – Sebbene io non sarò per dirigere la Cantata che desidera Vostra Maestà, il proggetto, che mi propongo d'eseguire è di comporla fra Giugno e Luglio, cosichè Vostra Maestà potrà ordinare in Agosto e Settembre le copie, e farne qualche prova me presente in segreto fra pochi, e passarla al cembalo di Vostra Maestà fra noi.

Ho veramente rossore d'essere tanto esteso colle mie lettere, ma Vostra Maestà mi perdoni io non posso far di meno. Sarei ben felice se Crescentini cantasse nell'Oratorio; anzi la supplico di procurarmi questa *Grazia* dando a vedere la musica al sudd[et]to subito, e persuadendolo, che lo stile è sacro, perciò non può esser servito come merita, ma come l'ho ridotto per Vostra Maestà deve starle bene. Ei non può esser meno compiacente di Marchesi quando si tratta di *Opera pia.*[39] – Io non posso essere più impaziente di mettermi a Suoi Piedi, e dirmi con proffondissimo ossequio: Della Cesarea R. Maestà Vostra

Umili[ssi]mo Dev[otissi]mo Ferd: Pär

12 Ap[ri]le 1804

10. Dresden, 26 May [1804?]. Source: HHStA, Fa, Sb, Kart. 63, fol. 376r

Sacra Cesarea Reale Maestà
Dopo la risposta, che diedi a Monaco, e che ebbi l'alt'onore di comunicarLa alla Maestà Vostra, non ho poi sentita alcun altr'invitazione, perciò restando le cose su questo piede, resta tutto in ordine come per lo avanti.

Mi metto a' Suoi Imp[eria]li Piedi ringraziandola infinitamente della Clemenza Sua manifestatami col Suo Foglio e vedo da quello che la Bontà Sua pensando ai soli miei vantaggi, è sempre la stessa, e l'Incomparabile.

---

[39] The *musico* Luigi Marchesi sang in Paer's *Per il santo sepolcro* in Tonkünstler-Sozietät concerts in April 1803.

La Cantata sarà finita in tempo, ed appena che averò inoltrato il lavoro delle Mine di Polonia –

Intanto non cesserò mai di renderLe grazie, e di umiliarmi proffonda-mente a' Suoi Imp[eria]li Piedi qual sono

Della Sacra Cesarea Maestà

L'Umil[issi]mo Dev[otissi]mo Obb[ligatissimo] Ser[vitor]e

Ferdinand Pär

Dresda 26 Maggio

11. Dresden, 22 June 1804. Source: HHStA, Fa, Sb, Kart. 63, fol. 378r–v

Sacra Cesarea Real Imperiale Maestà!

Col più proffondo ossequio e venerazione mi prendo l'ardire di umi-liare la presente alla Vostra Cesarea R[eal] Imp[eriale] Maestà al solo oggetto di ringraziarla degl' onori compartitimi in Vienna, e prottestandole la più viva, ed eterna obbligazione, e la mia (sebben debole) indefessa servitù.

Mi lusingo e spero, che esaudendo il Cielo i miei sinceri voti; Vostra Maestà sarà del tutto ristabilita. Subito che andata sia l'Opera mia in scena m'applicherò al componimento della Messa, che devo a V. M.[40] e che con tanta soddisfazione, e piacere ho scommessa e perduta, quanto è stato il gaudio mio pel felice e breve successo nello sgravamento dell'Augusta ArciDuchessa[41] – Ricolmi il Cielo di benedizioni tutta l'Imp[erial]e Augusta, ed adorabile Loro Famiglia, e secondi gl'immutabili, e felici auguri del mio cuore.

Si degni la Maestà Vostra di conservarmi sotto l'ali dell'Altissima Sua Prottezione unitamente la mia famiglia, che mettendosi tutta a Suoi I[mperiali] R[eali] Piedi meco si umilia divotamente le augura ogni bene ed io umilissimamente, ossequios[issimamen]te mi offro colla più proffonda venerazione a' Suoi Piedi:

Della Cesarea Imperiale Reale Vostra Maestà

L'Umili[ssi]mo Devo[tissi]mo Obblig[atissimo] Osseq[uiosissimo]

Ser[vitor]e Ferdinando Pär

Dresda 22 Giugno 1804

---

[40] Presumably the Mass in D major owned by MT (*KK*), the bulk of which Paer does not seem to have composed until fall 1805 (letter of 28 October 1805), and which he sent to the empress in February 1806 (letter of 3 February 1806).

[41] Archduchess Maria Anna, MT's tenth child, born 8 June 1804.

12. Dresden, 26 July 1804. Source: HHStA, Fa, Sb, Kart. 63,
fol. 380r–381v

Sacra Cesarea Reale Imperial Maestà
Mi prendo la libertà di mettermi di nuovo agl'Imperiali Piedi di Sua Maestà
prima per consolarmi della ristabilita sua preziosa Salute poscia per umiliarle
la terza ed ultima parte, che mi ha inviato il Sig^r Abbate Bagnoli della quale
sono contento in quanto all'arridità del soggetto, toccato però colla maggior
delicatezza e nobiltà – Quei piccioli Duettini riesciranno lo spero di gusto
di Sua Maestà – Nel fine della prima, e della 3^{za} parte vi comporrò le fughe
descritte da Sua Maestà.[42]

Ad onta di tutt' i miei sforzi non ho potuto sciogliermi dall' *engagement*
di Roma, e per delicatezza d'onore, e per non essere forsi la disgrazia di
quell' Impresario devo far codesto per me penosissimo innavveduto sagri-
fizio stantecchè il Sud[dett]o può anche legalmente obbligarmi se vuole.[43]
In adempimento di codesto mio dovere partirò adunque per colà il dì cinque
di Ottobre giacchè il tre si darà in questo Teatro di Dresda per la prima
volta *L'Amor conjugale*, ed almeno per quella sola recita sono obbligato
a diriggerlo.[44] Io ho diggià stabilito di passare per Salzburg solamente per
mettermi a' Piedi di S. A. R. – Ma quale più segnalato onore se avessi potuto
accettare l'onore di andarvi allora quando Le Loro Maestà vi vanno? Io non
ho lingua bastante per ringraziare La Maestà Sua che almeno si degna pensare alla povera mia persona col proggetto di procurarmi col seguito della
Loro Imperial Corte una piazza per quella gita – Almeno potessi ritrovarLi
ancora colà al mio passaggio? – Diggià mi lusingo di mettermi a Suoi Piedi al
Castellaccio di cui Sua Maestà mi fa menzione nel suo venerabile scritto –
quel mede[si]mo Castellaccio, che diverrà un Eliso allorchè sarà abitato
dalle Adorabili Loro Maestà – Io non mancherò chiudermi in camera in
Eisenberg[45] sovvente e colà incominciare la Cantata di Natale, poichè am-
bisco di dargliela avanti la mia stabilita partenza terminata affatto, anzi co-
mincio a quest'ora a distribuirne, e fissarne le idee, ed i mottivi – Nel ritorno
dall'Italia ossia da Venezia ch'io ho prefferita a Milano com'ebbi l'alt'onore
di comunicare a Sua Maestà ciò sarà in Quaresima, onde passerò di Vienna
onde ricevere qualche grato e prezioso suo comando, e se vorrà La Maestà
Sua, comporrò allora le *Mine di Pollonia* le quali riescono molto bene colla

---

[42] Paer refers here probably to the Christmas cantata with a libretto by Bagnoli mentioned by Paer on
12 April 1804; he refers to it more explicitly later in the present letter.

[43] Paer had accepted a commission from Rome for an opera for Carnival 1805, *Una in bene e una in
male*.

[44] *Leonora.*

[45] Eisenberg (Jezeří), the Bohemian summer residence of Prince Franz Joseph Maximilian Lobkowitz.

traduzione del nostro solito Poeta incognito – Soltanto è assolutt[ament]e neccessario l'ottenere da Parigi un semplice dissegno (anche fatto col tocca lapis) di tutte, e tre le decorazioni che si fecero in detta Commedia al Teatro dell'Ambigu.[46]

Chieggo prostratto a terra mille perdoni a Sua Maestà. Il mio zelo, e l'onore di essere sempre ascritto nel numero de' suoi *Fedeli Servi* mi fa essere troppo prolisso, ed esteso colle mie lettere; La sperimentata Clemenza Sua supplisca a' miei trascorsi intanto, che terminando d'annojarLa ho l'altissim'Onore di umilissimamente prottestarmi:
Di Sua Cesarea Imperial Maestà
L'Umili[ssi]mo Dev[otissi]mo Osseq[uiosissimo]
Servo Ferdinand Pär
Dresda 26 Luglio 1804

13. Dresden, 31 July 1804. Source: HHStA, Fa, Sb, Kart. 63, fol. 382r–383v

Sacra Imperiale Reale Maestà!
Non poteva credere che una leggera e picciolissima Cantatina composta in poch'ore ed umiliata ai Piedi della Maestà Sua sin l'anno scorso in Laxemburg[47] avesse prodotta una sì graziosa, ed ellegante invenzione nel Degiunè, che con indicibile sorpresa, ed inesplicabil piacere ho ricevuto ieri l'altro.[48] Si vede che le persone di vero spirito, e d'ingegnosa perspicace generosità, sanno cavar partito dalle cose più insulse, e leggere. Le moltiplici teste m'hanno al solito spaventato, ed abbattuto; ma un *Altra sola* tanto Rispettabile, ed Adorata da tutti quei che hanno l'Alt'onore di conoscerla perfettamente, ha sbandito l'orror passaggero, che l'altre m'avevan ispirato.

Questo nuovo tratto della Clemenza di Sua Maestà mi ha talmente comosso, ed onorato ch'io nel pormi qui adesso alle Reali, ed Imperiali sue Piante non trovo espression bastante onde ringraziarla. Questo è per me il più onorevole il più rispettabile souvenir, che desiderar potevo, nè posso saziarmi d'ammirarlo, e contemplarlo.

Mi sono preso l'ardire di scrivere a Sua Maestà riguardo al mio viaggio importuno di Roma. Ora dimando la grazia di ritardare il soddisfamento

---

46 Théâtre de l'Ambigu-Comique, where *Les Mines* had its premiere (my thanks to Elizabeth Bartlet for this identification).
47 Probably *Operetta cinese* (autograph score [dated Laxenburg, 1803] and parts: Mus. Hs. 10048–9).
48 MT recorded the gift in her diary on 20 June 1804 as including "eine Caffée Dejeunè von Porcelaine" and "Eine Brilliantene Nadel wie eine Leyer von 150 fl" (HHStA, Fa, HKF, Kart. 24, diary, fol. 208r).

di mia scommessa per applicarmi subito alla Cantata, che spero riescirà di genio di chi me l'ha comandata. Se potrò, farò l'uno e l'altro ma non mi resta che un solo mese e mezzo ond'applicarmi al compimento de' miei doveri, e devo travagliar la Cantata con ogn'impegno.

Spedirò a Sua Maestà il 2.^{d} atto dell'Amor conjugale verso la metà del mese imminente agosto giacchè il Copista me lo promette per quel tempo indubitamente. Desidererei che Sua Maestà lo facesse eseguire in Vienna, ma me presente al mio ritorno d'Italia, non dubito che la Sig.^{a} Marianna Sessi lo eseguirebbe perfett[amen]te – Qui si parla di nuovo del 2.do Mattrimonio di S. A. R. il G. Duca con codesta Principessa e credo, che S. A. R. la principessa Teresa sia l'avvocato primario; supplico umilmente Sua Maestà a non farmi l'autore, ma già soppongo che lo saprà a quest'ora. Intanto mi prostro di nuovo a Suoi Clementissimi Piedi, e col più umile ossequio, e riverenza le auguro ogni bene, e mi prottesto:
Della Sacra Imperiale, e Reale Sua Maestà

L'umil[issi]mo, ossequios[issim]o e Dev[otissi]mo Servo

Ferdinand Pär

Dresda 31 Luglio 1804

14. Eisenberg, 18 August 1804. Source: HHStA, Fa, Sb. Kart. 63, fol. 386r–387v

Sacra Imperiale Reale Maestà!
Appena ebbi il contento avant'jeri d'esser onorato dal suo prezioso scritto, che poco dopo ricevei di nuovo per Venezia un invito per la 2.^{d} Opera del vent[ur]o Carnevale dopo quella di Roma. La fortunata combinazione d'esser ancora in tempo di ubbidire a suoi vener[atissi]mi desiderj i quali per me son gli ordini più venerabili, mi obbliga adunque di umilmente esporLe, che essendo ancora in tempo di accettare, o no, un contratto di una 2.^{d} Opera, non mi obbligherò in nessun conto affine di poter essere nei primi di Febbrajo 1805 a' comandi di V. Maestà, e così celebrare quel giorno felice che l'anno scorso attese le mie circostanze non potei colla mia debol persona celebrare, ne festeggiare.[49] Vostra Maestà allora potrà dare la Cantata del Conte Clò, e tutto ciò che Vostra Maestà mi ordinerà farò con quel core, e quella premura, che non si potrà giammai da me obbliare, come da me non si obbliano le grazie che da Vostra Maestà ho ricevute. Dopo l'Opera di Roma volerò a Vienna.

---

[49] Franz's birthday, 12 February.

Una Grazia che desiderarei, sarebbe dopo d'aver allora servita Sua Maestà, di poter scrivere un Opera pel Barone di Braun[50] cioè per il Teatro e pel pubblico, ma desiderarei che l'invito sortisse dalla parte del Sudd[ett]o particolarmente; La Compagnia del Teatro di Vienna abbisogna in ora d'Opere, ed io desiderarei dopo l'Achille scriverne un'altra addattata alla Compagnia.[51]

Sua Altezza Seren[issim]a L'Ellettore di Sassonia[52] mi ha graziato d'una pensione vita mia durante eguale agli due altri Maestri di Capella, ma colla differenza che a me accorda la libertà d'ogni Estate onde poter esercitar il mio mestiere altrove: Questa condizione l'ho voluta ottenere per poter a un tempo stesso approffittare de' Comandi Rispettabili di Vostra Maestà. Perdoni se ho voluto umilmente rappresentarle una porzione de' miei affari, ma fin'ora non ho nulla celato a Vostra Maestà, e per me sarebbe stato un rossore, che l'avesse saputo da altra parte. – Sono contento, che a Vostra Maestà piaccia anche la 3.ᵃ parte della Cantata; qui siamo in grand'affari, e mio malgrado al solito mi resta poco tempo per scrivere, ma faccio, e farò tutto quel che potrò assolutamente.

Codesto Sig. Principe di Lobkovitz[53] si è fin'ora lusingato che Vostra Maestà sarebbe andata da Lui a Raudnitz[54]; chi lo avea lusingato era il Sig. Conte di Cottek; ma credo che la speranza vadasi a languire – Non così dal canto mio, che spero mettermi a Suoi Imp[crial]i Piedi in Praga, prima della mia partenza per Dresda.

Chieggo di nuovo scusa a Sua Maestà se troppo mi sono esteso colla presente, ma è necessario che V. Maestà sappia che un solo picciol suo desiderio è per me un ordine assoluto, e che non vivo se non per dirmi, ed ossequios[amen]te prottestarmi eternamente:

Di Vostra Imperiale Reale Maestà

Umili[issi]mo Dev[otissi]mo Obb[ligatissimo]
Servitore Ferd.ᵈ Pär

Eisenberg 18 Agosto 1804

---

[50] Baron Peter von Braun, manager of the court theaters from 1794 and of the Theater an der Wien from 1804.

[51] *Achille*, first performed on MT's birthday, 6 June 1801, was the last opera written by Paer for the public theaters of Vienna. He mentioned it here because, in asking De Gamerra to write the libretto, MT had played a role in its creation.

[52] Friedrich August, elector of Saxony.

[53] On Lobkowitz see chapter 10. Paer wrote this letter from Lobkowitz's summer palace at Eisenberg (Jezeří).

[54] Roudnice, another Bohemian residence of Prince Lobkowitz.

15. Rome, 3 November 1804. Source: HHStA, Fa, Sb., Kart. 63, fol. 390r–391r

Sacra Cesarea Real Maestà!

Più lontano, ch'io sono da Vostra Maestà e più a ragione mi do 'l coraggio di mettermi agl'Imperiali Suoi Piedi e prottestarmi sempre, e poi sempre uno de' Suoi Fedeli Credenti supplicandola a conservarmi l'Altissima Sua Prottezione, senza di cui sarei il più sfortunato fra tutti gli uomini. Sono Grazie a Dio arrivato felicemente in Roma ma ho avuto il viaggio il più penoso, che mai dire si possa: diffatti il traggitto non è indifferente. Mi sono fermato a Firenze; sono stato invitato a Poggio Cajano villeggiatura del Re di Etruria – Colà Sua Maestà la Regina[55] fece per due giorni consecutivi alla sera sempre musica, e mi accolse con somma bontà, e Clemenza – Essa canta, ed ha voce forte, e chiara, ma sinceramente non ha lo studio di musica, ne la prontezza del leggere di Vostra Maestà. – Sono arrivato in tempo di veder la partenza di Sua Santità il più bel colpa d'occhio che goder si potesse pel concorso del Popolo, e la magnificenza degli apparati. Ed ora sono tutto dedito alla scelta del libro, che deve coadiuvare alla riescita delle povere mie fattiche.

Spero, che la presente troverà La Maestà Vostra, e tutta l'Augusta Sua Famiglia in perfetto stato che Iddio la benedica per sempre, e in eterno.

Non dimentico le comissioni che S. Maestà ha voluto onorarmi – Intanto mi metto agl'Imperiali Reali Suoi Piedi le chieggo la Sua Grazia, e mi rassegno col più distinto Ossequio, ed alta Venerazione: Quale ho l'Alt'onore di ripetermi:

Di Vostra Sacra Cesarea Maestà

L'umili[ssi]mo Osseq[uiosissi]mo e Dev[otissi]mo Ser.ᵉ

Ferdinand Pär

Roma a dì 3 Nov[em]bre 1804

16. Rome, 1 December 1804. Source: HHStA, Fa, Sb, Kart. 63, fol. 392r–393r

Sacra Cesarea Imperiale Reale Maestà!

Mi metto agli Imperiali e Reali Suoi Piedi, e nel medesimo tempo riscontro il clementissimo Suo Scritto – Prima di tutto spero che La Maestà Sua averà ricevuto l'ultimo mio foglio umigliatoLe appena ch'io giunsi in Roma, e così anche il Sig. Simoni m'averà messo a Suoi Piedi, perchè di ciò lo

---

[55] Maria Luisa, queen of Etruria.

incaricai – Dissi in Salisburg, che il mio ritorno sarebbe stato alla fine di Gennaio, non per quella parte, ma per Vienna direttamente, e promisi dopo Vienna di passare a Salisburg (se averei potuto farlo). Onde su tal rapporto ho l'Alt'Onore di assicurare la Maestà Sua, ch'io avendo lasciato, e 'l contratto di Venezia, di Napoli, e di Milano per ademplire alla parola data a Sua Maestà, non è possibile ch'io mi trattenga, ne passi per Salisburgo fin a tanto che non abbia servito a miei Doveri con La Maestà Sua.

Non so cosa mai suggerire per la nota festa di contadini dell'Austria Superiore, poichè essendo in un *grannajo* non trovo nulla d'addattato al caso, ma se mi verrà un idea gliela comunicherò immediatamente e cred'io che saremo in tempo ai primi di Gennaio per fissarla (se Iddio vorra) La paura della *Febbre gialla* dominante in Livorno e cordoni tirati a tale oggetto per le vie della Toscana impediranno ch'io nel mio passaggio possa provvedere i Capelli che sua Maestà tanto desidera – Nulla ostante se le cose miglioreranno come diggià sono in miglior stato present[ament]e, io farò di tutto per ubbidirla; ma preveggo che non potrò passare per Firenze, altrimenti io, che sono grazie all'Altissimo sano, sanissimo, mi toccherebbe far due quarantene, ed arriverei *tre dì dopo la rotta* come si suol dire. – Provvederò bensì i guanti ma per averli buoni sono di Francia, e non del paese che sono ordinarissimi, e mal cuciti – Io non desidero altro che la Continuazione della Grazia, e Prottezionc di Sua Maestà: al mio arrivo accomodaremo la Cantata[56] in tutto, e per tutto: Non è neccessario un Teatro se non si fa il Finale come si era pensato, ma possiamo darla come Sua Maestà diede la Cantata di Veigl l'anno scorso tutti travestiti dal principio della Cantata sino al fine.

Intanto mi metto a Suoi Clementissimi Piedi, ed ho l'Alt'Onore di prottestarmi sempre qual sono:
Della Cesarea Imperiale Sacra Sua Maestà
L'umil[issi]mo Dev[otissi]mo Obb[ligatissimo] Ser[vitor]e
Ferdinando Pär
Roma a dì p[ri]mo 10bre 1804

17. Parma, 22 January 1805. Source: HHStA, Fa, Sb, Kart. 63, fol. 394r–395v

[Address:]
Alla Sacra Cesarea Imperiale

---

[56] *Il conte Clò*, which, unperformed on Franz's birthday, 12 February 1804, was now planned for performance on 12 February 1805.

E Reale Sua Maestà
Teresa II.^da Imperatrice Regina
di Boemia Ongheria &c &c &c

Sacra Cesarea Imperiale, e Reale Maestà!
Dietro al riscontro, che stando in Roma io rassegnai a Sua Maestà, ed
anche in forza della promessa rinnovatale di ritrovarmi costì pel giorno *12*
del prossimo Febb[rai]o^57 avevo con tutto il piacere rinunziato alle scritture
di Venezia, Milano, e stante la bontà con cui è stata sentita la mia musica
in Roma, ero pur anche stato invitato per comporre un Opera in Napoli.
    Tutto era superiore all'Alt'onore di mettermi agl'Imp[eria]li e R[eali]
Piedi di Sua Maestà, e già ripreso con tutta sollecitudine il cammino della
Lombardia pensavo di abbracciar di volo mia Madre in Parma, e ripartire
per costà – Prima d'arrivare a Bollogna si è fracassata la mia vettura; per
grazia di Dio non ho sofferto nella persona, ma ho dovuto far quasi una
posta a piedi con un freddo crudele, ed in una strada indiavolata, il che mi
ha proddotta un'ostinata costipazione, ed una febbre periodica, e tuttochè
da' Medici mi si dice, che non avrà conseguenze, sono però consigliato ad
avermi il maggiore riguardo – Sto in letto, e non si vuole in conto alcuno
ch'io azzardi il viaggio di Vienna massime, che da pochi giorni in qua la
stagione si è fatta assai peggiore. Egli è questo il solo rammarico cioè il
dover mancare alla promessa fatta a Sua Maestà, e solo mi consola il sapere
a prova che Sua Maestà ha sempre avuta una particolare bontà e clemenza
per me, e che anche senza la fede del medico, che averei potuto ricavare, la
Maestà Sua sarà persuasa pienamente della mia indisposizione, e che il solo
riflesso di non esporre mia vita mi trattiene sagrificato in Parma, e quel ch'è
peggio in ozio; Ma più di tutto ricolmo di dispiaceri per non poter essere
in Vienna.
    Supplico infine la Maestà Sua a voler accogliere colla Sua Connatu-
rale Bontà lo Spartito della mia opera di Roma^58 (che col mezzo della
Diligenza di Verona Le innoltrerò l'ordinario venturo) e continuarmi l'Alto
Suo Padrocinio, ed a credermi in ogn'incontro: Quale ho l'Alt'onore di
prottestarmi eternamente:
Della Sacra Cesarea R. Imp. Maestà Sua
            L'Umili[issi]mo Dev[otissi]mo Obbl[igatissimo] Ser[vitor]e
                                                Ferdinand Pär
Parma a dì 22 Gennaio 1805

---

57 Birthday of Emperor Franz.
58 *Una in bene e una in male.* Score and parts: Mus. Hs. 10054–5.

18. Parma, 5 March 1805. Source: HHStA, Fa, Sb, Kart. 63,
fol. 396r–397v

Sacra Cesarea Reale Maestà!

La benigna sua, e Clemente lettera m'ha tolto da un inquietudine, che
non mi lasciava vivere un momento tranquillo – Io sono stato fuor di me
dalla gioja di sapere, che anche senza la mia presenza la Cantata abbia
avuto luogo, ne dubito che la Sud[dett]a sia andata male.[59] Vostra Maestà
può ben esser certa, che il mio proffondo rispetto, e la venerazione, che
ho per V. M. è al superlativo grado, e l'amico Crescentini che passò per
Parma, e mi vidde averà testificato il dispiacere che provai non potendo
in Persona rinnovarle i miei più umili sentimenti – Siccome non tutto il
mondo poteva sapere ch'io mi ritrovai incommodato a Parma onde non
approffitare di una 2.^{d} Opera carnevalesca così per non essere screditato
nella proffessione essendomi capitata l'Opera Seria dell'Apertura del nuovo
Teatro di Bollogna, io l'ho accettata se non altro per poter presentare alla
Maestà Vostra un 2.do Spartito di genere diverso.[60]

Consegnai all'amico Crescentini l'Opera di Roma che sebbene picciola
musica ebbe il grand'effetto. E sebbene piovino le trattative pel tempo
successivo di Milano, di Venezia e di Napoli, io a tutto rinnunzio e alli
primi circa di Maggio sarò in Vienna agli Imperiali Piedi di Vostra Maestà.
Tengo già la prima parte della Cantata che ho costì fatto comporre a certo
Poeta Sig. Domenico Rossetti e che scrive come un angelo – Essa ha per
titolo La Passione, e la Risurrezione – Se il Teatro di Vienna abbisognasse
un Poeta alla piazza del Sig. Brividali codesto giovane di anni 30 sarebbe il
più atto e 'l più convenevole agli Imp[eria]li Teatri anzi lo metto umilmente
agli Imp[eria]li Piedi di Vostra Maestà, e glielo raccomando vivamente. Egli
ha lo stile Mettastasiano, ed è pieno di educazione, e talento.

Maestà, io vivo per l'onore, e per far onore a Quella che si degna prot-
teggermi, onde spero che La Maestà Vostra scuserà se ho accettata la scritta
di Bollogna, e perciò ritardato il mio arrivo in Vienna – Ora sto passabil-
mente bene, a riserva di una flussione che mi gira o al Capo, o alle spalle,
ma la buona stagione mi farà guerire perfettamente.

Com'io desidero la clemente sua Grazia, così Le auguro ogni celeste
Benedizione tanto a V. M. quanto a tutta l'Imperiale, e Reale Sua Famiglia –
Io non cesserò mai d'essere a costo della vita il Suo Fedele Credente 3.[61]
Della Cesarea Reale Imp[eria]le Maestà Vostra!

---

[59] *Il conte Clò.*
[60] *Sofonisba*, Bologna, 19 May 1805; score and parts: Mus. Hs. 9981–2.
[61] Possibly MT assigned a number to each of her closest musical collaborators.

Umil[issi]mo Dev[otissimo] ed Oss[equiosissi]mo
Servitore Ferdinand Pär

Parma adì 5 Marzo 1805

19. Bologna, 2 April [1805]. Source: HHStA, Fa, Sb, Kart. 63,
fol. 398r–399v

Sacra Cesarea Reale Imperiale Maestà!

Ieri soltanto ho ricevuto il preziosissimo Suo foglio, e sebbene io sono ingolfato nella piena del lavoro di codest'Opera,[62] io farò il mio possibile onde servirla, darle un picciolo contrassegno dell'alto mio Rispetto, e della conservazione del N.° 3.

Il mio amico Cinti ch'ebbe l'onore di scrivere per La Maestà Vostra la Cantata del Conte Clò; si applicò parimente con indeffessa fattica all'Opera *Le Mine di Polonia*, che Vostra Maestà ebbe la Bontà di trasmettermi a Dresda sino dell'anno scorso – Il suddetto siccome mi credè a Vienna (come pur troppo non potei proseguire quel viaggio) colà mi spedì quel libretto ridotto, e tradotto in lingua italiana ad uso di Dramma. Il libro ossia la lettera col pachetto andò in casa del Principe Lobkovitz, e quest'oggi dal sugger[itor]e dell'Opera Italiana di Vienna ricevo avviso che il Sud[dett]o Sig.^e abbia aperto il pacco, e ritenuto il libro sud[dett]o – Ciò non parmi credibile: ma se ciò fosse, è un evvidente segno che il Principe sud[dett]o (che altamente venero, e stimo) non sapeva essere il Dramma destinato ai serviggi della Maestà Vostra.

La supplica adunque, che faccio alla mia sola, ed adorata Padrona si è di volersi degnare di far ricerca da qualche sua persona seconda del detto libro senza comparire la Maestà Vostra, ma con maniera poter far comprendere, che il libro è della Maestà Vostra.

Il povero Cinti, che l'ha traddotto n'è desolatissimo e teme, che qualche cabala abbia a lui impedito di farsene merito. – La cantata è riescita dal Poeta ottima, e questa la faremo servire per un'altr'occasione ma sempre per gli ordini sacri della Maestà Vostra.

Più ampiamente ho scritto l'ordinario scorso all'amico Simoni intorno la pre[se]nte opera. Ma procurrerò di servire anche la Maestà Vostra dei tre pezzi ricercatimi, e con ogni silenzio.

Mi lusingo che non avendomi Vostra Maestà prefisso il tempo in cui abbisognan gli tre sud[dett]i pezzi non sarà la cosa all'eccesso pressante.

---

[62] *Sofonisba.*

Io non desidero altro, che la conservazione dell'Augusta Sua Imperial Famiglia, non che la continuazione del Potente e Valevol[issi]mo Suo Padrocinio – Mi metto a' Suoi Piedi: mi prostro, ed ossequiosamente, ed umilissimamente mi dico:

P. S. Umilmente la supplico (onorandomi di qualche riga) mettere la *data* in succinto acciò regolarmi possa per le care sue commissioni – Mille Perdoni –

Della Reale Imperiale Maestà Vostra

Umili[issi]mo Dev[otissi]mo Obb[ligatissimo] Ser[vitor]e

Ferdinand Pär

Bollogna a dì 2 Ap[ri]le

20. Bologna, 25 May 1805. Source: HHStA, Fa, Sb, Kart. 63, fol. 400r–v

Sacra Cesarea Reale Maestà!

Sono stato oltremodo mortifcato non potendo servire Vostra Maestà di ricercati pezzi di musica, che comporre dovevano le Sue accademie, ma la continua occupazione dell'Opera, che costì doveasi rappresentare e d'altronde la premura di terminarla fattami da codesta direzione mi hanno proprio impedito il vero mio genio che è quello di servirla indeffessamente. L'Opera è andata in scena Sabbato scorso.[63] La musica ha piaciuto general[men]te. La prima sera na[c]quero molt'inconvenienti soliti accadere nelle prime aperture d'un nuovo teatro, ma la 2.da e 3.^{za} recita fui chiamato sul palco; con grandi acclamazioni. Essendoci mancati i due soggetti principali la Banti e Crivelli,[64] che forzat[ament]e furon trattenuti a Milano per colà servire alle Feste &c io temevo moltissimo dell'esito.

Ho fatto copiarne lo spartito per Vostra Maestà, e lo porterò io stesso a Suoi Imp[eria]li Piedi.

Il Principe Lobkovitz vorebbe dar il Re Teodoro in Sua Casa con me al solito: Io le ho rispett[osament]e risposto che sono per anco in dubbio se passerò per Vienna, ma ancorchè io passi sono prevent[ivament]e impegnato per una Cantata[65] con Vostra Maestà anzi dovrò alloggiare in

---

[63] *Sofonisba*.

[64] The soprano Brigida Giorgi Banti and the tenor Gaetano Crivelli.

[65] Probably *I bisogni sollevati*, concerto drammatico, followed by a divertimento mimico (i.e. ballet) entitled *L'amore guerriero per riconoscenza*, of which the date of the printed libretto, 1805, suggests that MT performed it privately some time that year. MT owned two scores (the autograph and a copy) and a set of parts: Mus. Hs. 10136–9. On 9 August 1805 she rewarded Paer for an opera and ballet: "Augusty [1805] / Dem 15. Dem Kapellmeister Pär für eine Opera und Ballet / Eine Brilliantene Nadel wie [illegible word] von 300 fl. / 100 Ducaten in Gold / 50 d^{to} zur Reise" (HHStA, Fa, HKF, Kart. 24, diary, fol. 218r).

Vienna dove l'adorabile nostra Padrona mi averà prefisso – Tale è stata la mia risposta.

Il B. Braun fu qui di passaggio avanti che si aprisse il Teatro. Mi parlò di mettere in scena il Sargino in tedesco, io lo desidererei di tutto cuore quando anche ciò gradisce alla Maestà Vostra.

Nulla mi può più trattenere – Oggi a otto, cioè il primo del prossimo Giugno mi metto in Viaggio per Vienna.

Mi sono arrivati ieri i Capelli di Firenze per Vostra Maestà e spero saranno della Imp[eria]le e Reale sua approvazione.

Io non vedo l'ora di mettermi a Suoi Imp[eria]li e Reali Piedi e di dirmi con ogni ossequio, ed obbedienza –

Della Sacra Cesarea Reale Maestà Vostra

L'Umil[issi]mo Dev[otissi]mo Obbl[igatissimo] Ser[vitor]e

Ferdinand Pär

Bollogna il 25 Maggio 1805

21. No place, no date; but probably written shortly before 12 August 1805. Source: HHStA, Fa, Sb, Kart. 65, Private an Kaiserin Marie Therese, fol. 365r–366r

Sacra Imperiale, e Reale Maestà!

Non ho voluto incommodar direttamente la Maestà Vostra nella lettura di una mia lettera, ma ho scritto all'amico Simoni acciò mi mettesse a' Suoi Piedi, e la ringraziasse fervorosamente della Clemenza Sua e degli effetti ch'io tutt'ora godo, e che mi renderanno eternamente, ed immutabilmente pronto a' Suoi Veneratissimi cenni.

Giacchè la Maestà Vostra desidera le scene nella Soffonisba pel noto Tenore, io sono prontissimo a comporle, ma devo a tal'effetto supplicarla d'una Grazia: Avanti di partire da Vienna consegnai al poeta Brividali il libro di dett'Opera pregandolo a volermelo rendere più interessante conservando sempre però la stessa musica; ora non rimane, che una sola premura di Vostra Maestà da dimostrarsi al Sud[dett]o acciò sia effettuata subito, e così aggiungergli che faccia una bell'aria nell'atto primo pel Tenore, ed una scena con effetto, e con cori pel 2.do – Senza la poesia nuova vede V. M. ch'io non potrei comporre i ricercati due pezzi.

Basta che rimanghino le due arie di Massinissa le due di Soffonisba, le due di Scipione il Terzetto, ed il Quartetto del resto quanto egli mi prescriverà (basta che non si allunghi di troppo) io sono pronto a far tutto nuovo, e con dare a V. M. un opera che si possa *premieramente* dare ne' Suoi R[eali]

Imp[eria]li Appartamenti, e poi se V. M. lo comanderà anche in Teatro a Vienna.

Il Fine dee essere secondo l'istoria colla morte di Soffonisba, perché deesi in Germania stare attaccati alla storia, e non fare le solite incogruenze d'Italia.

Non dubito, che con un solo desiderio di V. M. la cosa sarà subitamente fatta per la parte del poeta, che m'avea già promesso.

Tanto in Ottobre, quanto in Febb[rai]o due volte non mi sarà possibile d'ottennere la licenza, ma Sua Maestà dee decidere in qual de' due tempi desidera ch'io venga, e allora mi preparerò fin d'adesso per ottenerla una sol volta.

Intanto starò in attenzione de' Suoi venera[tissi]mi Ordini. Anche costì tutto è tranquillo. Iddio benedisca la Sua Degn[evolissi]ma, e preziosissima famiglia – Mia Moglie si mette a' Suoi Piedi. Io le baccio devot[ament]e La Mano ed umilmente sono.

Di Vostra Maestà

Um[illissi]mo Dev[otissi]mo Obb[ligatissimo] Ser[vitor]e

Ferd. Pär

22. Dresden, 12 August [1805].[66] Source: HHStA, Fa, Sb, Kart. 63, fol. 384r–v

Sacra Maestà!

Non mancai di risponderle a tenore della onorevol[issi]ma Sua, e mettendomi come al solito a Suoi Imp[eria]li Piedi la supplicai risguardo l'Opera Soffonisba di ordinare al Poeta L. Brividali qualche salutare *arrangement*.[67]

Ma rifflettendo in appresso, che forse Sua Maestà averebbe desiderati i due pezzi per l'amico Simoni subito, aggiungo la pre[se]nte per dirle, che il Sud[dett]o Poeta potrebbe intanto farli sciolti cioè l'aria, e la gran scena anche avanti d'aver terminato il restante del libro.

La ringrazio dell'Opera l'Uniforme, che jer l'altro ho ricevuto unitamente all'opera Soffonisba. Appena copiato il Sud[dett]o Spartito lo rimanderò all'Impr[esari]o di Praga Sig. Guardasoni.[68]

---

[66] This letter can be assigned to 1805 because of its references to *Sofonisba* (first performed in May 1805) and Domenico Guardasoni, impresario of the Italian opera in Prague, who died on 14 June 1806.

[67] Paer evidently refers here to his undated letter beginning "Non ho voluto incommodar direttamente la Maestà Vostra."

[68] Weigl's *L'uniforme*, written for MT and performed at Schönbrunn in 1800 with MT in the role of Giannina, was later performed in German in the court theaters (premiere 15 February 1805). In

Attendevo riscontro se Sua Maestà forse averebbe più gradito ch'io fossi venuto in Ottobre, o in Febb[rai]o a Vienna, ma il debole mio parere sarebbe che attendessimo in Febb[rai]o perchè così potressimo far qualque cosa di bello, e di nuovo – E poi almeno avrò l'onore, che Sua Maestà sia fra gl'interlocutori.

Mi è sovvenuto, che Sua Maestà desiderò un catalogo dei libri, che di mano in mano sortono da codesto amplio negozio de' FF. Välter, e perciò mi prendo la libertà d'inviarglielo in questo stesso ordinario diretto alla Fraile Costanze.[69]

Desidero la Continuazione del suo Inpareggiabile Padrocinio l'alt'Onore de' Suoi Comandi per cui mi offro, e mi prottesto Eternamente: Di Sua Sacra Maestà Umil[issi]mo Dev[otissi]mo Obbl[igatissimo]

Ferd. Pär
Dresda

12 Agosto

23. Dresden, 23 September [1805?]. Source: HHStA, Fa, Sb, Kart 63, fol. 388r

Sacra Cesarea Reale Maestà!

Appena ebbi dal Sig. Simoni il catalogo de' libri ove piacque alla Maestà Sua marcare quelli, che desiderava, non ho mancato di farne fare un pacco, e spedirlo in quest'ordinario alla Direzione della Maestà Sua.

Io voglio sperare mediante l'assistenza divina, che Sua Maestà si sarà perfettamente ristabilita in salute, vivo con questa speranza, ma da gran tempo sono privo delle tanto sospirate sue nuove.

A Momenti spedirò alla Maestà Sua una Messa intera ch'ora si sta copiando per Lei: avendone promessa io una copia anche a S. A. R. L'adorato Gran Duca, Sua Maestà si degnerà quando Le aggradirà passargliene un esemplare.[70]

Intanto prostrato a' Sacri Suoi Piedi imploro la Grazia ch'Ella mi metta agli Imp[eria]li e R[eali] Piedi di Sua Maestà L'Imperatore giacchè mio malgrado per S. Fran[ces]co non posso venire a divertirlo, ma non dubito

---

thanking MT for the score but promising to return it to Guardasoni, Paer implied Guardasoni sent him the score at MT's request. The copy Paer says he is having made probably served as the basis for a production of *L'uniforme* in Dresden (in Italian) in 1805.

[69] Constanze Streffler, MT's chamber servant.

[70] Apparently the mass that Paer mentioned for the first time on 22 June 1804; despite the statement in the present letter that he would send it to MT "very shortly," he did not actually send it until February 1806 (letter of 3 February 1806).

che per Febb[rai]o Sua Maestà accorderammi tal grazia per cui umilmente mi rassegno ossequi[osament]e:

Di Sua Sacra Cesarea Maestà

L'umili[ssi]mo Dev[otissi]mo Obb[ligatissimo] Ser[vitor]ᵉ

Ferdinand Pär

Dresda 23 7ᵉ

24. Dresden, 28 October 1805. Source: HHStA, Fa, Sb, Kart. 64, Verschiedene Briefe an die Kaiserin, fol. 96r–v, 100r (enclosure, consisting of two theatrical sketches in Marie Therese's hand, not transcribed here)

Sacra Cesarea Reale Maestà!

Ho calcolato con quiete, e tempo le due commissioni di cui Sua Reale Imperiale Maestà si è degnata inviarmi il piano – Riguardo al piano della commedia, prosa, musica, e ballo tuttociò può riescire perfettamente, e spero che Sua Maestà si fiderà di me circa le aggiunte, che vi faremo per renderla interessante – Il Poeta del Conte *Clò* ne ha diggià preso l'incarico. Riguardo poi al piano dei Tableaux,[71] comprendo che potrà forse far buon effetto, ma non divertirà quanto la prima. Devo anche umilmente mettermi a' Suoi Reali ed Imp[eria]li Piedi e dirle che ho accomodate tutte le opere per codesto Ellett[oral]e Teatro, ho fatti tutti i Recit[ativ]i nuovi della *Soffonisba* colle due gran scene, che in seguito Le spedirò – Ho composta un intera *Messa* con fughe &c, che devo per lo più stare al Cembalo nelle Opere anche non mie – Che ora sto componendo le *Mine di Polonia* indi la *Cantata* sud[dett]a per Sua Imp[eria]le, e Reale Maestà, e se devo per la metà di Genn[ai]o ritrovarmi ai suoi Imp[eria]li Piedi a Vienna, devo con mio dispiacere dimostrale che l'azione dei Tableaux io non la potrò mettere in musica. Spero che La Somma Clemenza di Sua Maestà accetterà la mia costante servitù nel lavoro della prima cantata, ed attribuirà alle tante mie facende l'inesecuzione dell'altra – Anche per ottenere il dovuto permesso dall'Ellettore per Gennajo devo mantenere le mie promesse, e compiere i doveri assunti pel serviggio del suddetto. Allora tutto andrà a dovere, ed

---

[71] *La lanterna magica*, which, despite his initial reluctance, Paer did set to music (autograph score and parts: Mus. Hs. 10046–7), consists of a series of scenes in each of which a different group of characters presents a stage picture, or tableau, as if projected by a magic lantern. Since Paer wrote on 22 April 1806 that he might have to work on *La lanterna magica* until September 1806, MT probably planned for a performance on 4 October 1806; it may have been the last piece that he wrote for her. A copy of a privately printed libretto, *La lanterna magica* / Cantata comica / Musica del Sig. Mro. Pär (no publisher, no date), is in A-Wn.

io sospiro frattanto il momento onde renderla servita, onde mettermi alle Imp[eria]li e Reali Sue Piante.

Qui accluso Sua Maestà troverà i due piani uno de' quali cioè quello del Numero 2 ho copiato per mia norma, e quella del poeta.

Le auguro dall'altissimo ogni Celeste benedizione sopra l'Augusta Sua Figliolanza,[72] e sopra sì Degni Sovrani a Cui umilmente, e proffondamente mi metto a' Suoi I[mperiali] Piedi e mi dico eternamente:

Della Cesarea Reale Imperiale Maestà Sua

L'umili[ssi]mo Dev[otissi]mo Obbl[igatissimo] Ser[vitor]e

Ferdinand Pär

Dresda 28 Ottobre 1805

P. S. Mia moglie parimenti tutta la mia famiglia si prende la libertà di prostrarsi a' Suoi Piedi.

25. Dresden, 3 January 1806. Source: HHStA, Fa, Sb, Kart. 65, Private an Kaiserin Marie Therese, fol. 355r–356r

Sacra, Reale Maestà!

Credo, che niuno più di me ha sofferto nel sentire gli incomodi fisici, e morali della Maestà Sua: ne ho sofferto a un grado, che ho creduto impazzirne – Ho scritte più, e più lettere all'amico Simoni credendolo in Vienna, oppure supponendo, che la di lui famiglia gli avarebbe respinte le mie lettere ov'ei sarebbesi trovato. In quelle sempre ho richiesto nuove di Sua Maestà, e della preziosa Loro Salute, che più di tutto mi interessava, ed interesserà sempre l'onesta gente e sopratutto quelli, che hanno avuto la consolazione d'avvicinarsi alle L[oro] M[aestà] e conoscerli sì Adorabili, Giusti, e Clementi.

Qui parlasi della Pace: Iddio ha dunque esauditi i miei voti, come anche quelli che ha fatto porgere all'Altissimo da miei figli per la guariggione della Maestà Sua – Non ho mai tanto desiderato di essere vicino alla Maestà Sua, quanto nelle scorse settimane, allora sì, che ho potuto sentire sino a qual grado io sono attaccato alle L[oro] M[aestà].

Auguro di tutto cuore, che le pene siano oramai cessate col cessare dell'anno, e che il nuovo sia ripieno di felicità eterne come merita l'Augusto Loro Cuore.

Supplico proffondamente La Maestà Sua a continuarmi l'Altissima Sua Prottezione, e credermi constantemente a' Suoi Augusti Piedi:

Della Maestà Sua

---

[72] MT's eleventh child, Johann Nepomuk, was born on 29 August 1805.

L'umil[issi]mo Dev[otissi]mo Osseq[uiosissi]mo Serv[itor]e

Ferdinand Pär

Dresda il 3.ᶻᵒ 1806

26. Dresden, 3 February 1806. Source: I II IStA, Fa, Sb, Kart. 65, Private
an Kaiserin Marie Therese, fol. 357r–358v

Sacra Cesarea Reale Maestà

Col carro di diligenza ho l'onore di spedire alla Maestà Vostra La Messa, il
Credo, Sanctus & Agnus che da gran tempo Le devo.[73] La metto a Suoi Piedi
abbisognando la Sud[dett]a di tutto il magnanimo di Lei Compatimento
essendo anche d'un genere tutto diverso dal mio.

La Lanterna magica di cui ho spedito sono otto giorni a Simoni la metà
della poesia sta sul lavoro, ma per disgrazia mia non posso io travagliare
come vorrei avendo Chiesa, Teatro, prove, recite, e sopratutto pochissima
salute – Soffro vertigini orribili, e perciò m'hanno fatto salassare, e sto
piuttosto peggio. Qui unisco alla Maestà Vostra il resto della Poesia, ed ora
di questa non manca che il Finale – Ho immaginato per quest'ultimo vetro
La Casa del diavolo – Cioè la *Corte di Pluto* – Staffieri – Maggiordomi –
Ciambellani tutti diavoli con corna, e Zampe nude; e siccome parmi che
possano passare per lo meno a due a due restando sempre da un lato il Trono
di Pluto, e Proserpina questo può fare un buon effetto, perciò se la Maestà
Sua non è contenta abbia la clemenza di farnelo dire. Io sono privo di lettere,
e dopo quella dei 2 dello scorso Genn[ai]o non ho più avuto dall'amico
Simoni alcun riscontro. – Oh quanto m'è stato sensibile che costì m'abbian
rifiutato di poter venire a Vienna, ne sono restato veramente afflitto, e ciò
non mi farà durare longo tempo la mia residenza sarei anche stato meglio
di salute.

Siccome adunque Vostra Maestà averà saputo tutto ciò che mi ha impedito di prontamente servirla, così io spero che non le dispiacerà tanto il
ritardo del mio lavoro – Esso non potrà servire pel giorno 12 ecco tutta
la mia pena – Ma si degni l'innata Bontà della Maestà Vostra considerare
che il lavoro non è si picciolo come a prima vista m'è comparso (e ciò
lo considererà dalli squarci della poesia) che le loro lettere in data de' 2
mi arrivarono ne so perchè alli 18 o 19 dello scorso – altri dieci, o dodici
giorni si perdette per pensare al Poeta, aspettando sempre riscontro dal
Simoni sopra certe spiegazioni alla nostra poca intelligenza, che erano più

---

[73] This is presumably the Mass in D by Paer that MT owned, promised by the composer on 23
September [1805?] and mentioned again on 28 October 1805.

che neccessarie. Ora dunque chiedendo mille perdoni alla Maestà Vostra Le prometto di spedirle il tutto al più presto ch'io potrò – Intanto mi facci sapere se così è la Loro intenzione poichè non travaglio corragios[amen]te se non so che l'abbiamo a puntino interpretata – La ristrettezza del Tempo non mi permette di scrivere al Simoni – Mi dica Sua Maestà se desidera una Sinfonia annaloga.

Mi metto a Suoi Clement[issi]mi Piedi, e bacciandoli umilissimamente sono eternamente:
Della Sacra Cesarea Reale Sua Maestà

L'umil[issi]mo Dev[otissi]mo Obbl[igatissim]o Serv[itor]e
Ferdinand Pär

Dresda adi 3 Febb[rai]o 1806

27. [Dresden], 7 March 1806. Source: HHStA, Fa, Sb, Kart. 65, alt 271, fol. 359r–360r

Sacra Cesarea Reale Maestà!
A quest'ora spero che il mio amico (come lo pregai nell'ultima mia) m'averà messo a' Suoi Reali, ed Imperiali Piedi, e l'averà ringraziata per me in tanti modi quanto è possibile di farlo colla mia sola Padrona e Benefatrice.

La Soffonisba va in scena il giorno 15 del corr[ent]e – I molti pezzi parte nuovi, e parte rinovati hanno resa necessaria l'intera copia dello spartito che d'oggi a otto sarà trasmesso, ed umiliato a' Suoi Piedi.

Ho sentito, che l'Opera del M[aest]ro Cherubini ha avuto un esito felice, e di ciò niuno dubitarne poteva.[74]

Siccome l'occasione di farsi onore nel mestier nostro nasce dalla fortuna di aver trovato un buon libretto, così non posso negare che tal fortuna per l'Opera *Le mine di Pollonia* ch'io dovevo esserne il primo autore di musica, m'è stata tolta dal avverso destino... L'amico Sim[on]i mi ordina di spedire a V. M. il libro superbo d'*Androcle*,[75] ed ecco un'altra lusinga toltami per questo verso. Ubbidisco cecamente ma non posso impedirmi di supplicarla ricordarsi che sarei stato ben felice se avessi potuto io scriverlo pel primo, e produrlo come Cherubini le *Mines* – A tale oggetto avea chiesta la licenza per tutto l'estate, e volevo sopratutto passarne due mesi a Vienna – Poichè

---

[74] Cherubini's *Faniska* (score and parts: Mus. Hs. 10180–1), on an Italian libretto (probably the one that Cinti had prepared for Paer) based on Pixérécourt's *Les Mines de Pologne*, translated into German by Sonnleithner and first performed in the Kärntnertortheater on 25 February 1806.

[75] MT owned a manuscript of *Androcle o Il leone riconoscente*, an anonymous translation of Louis-Charles Caigniez, *Androcles, ou Le Lion reconnaissant*, *melodramme en 3 actes*, Paris, 1804 (HHStA, Fa, Sb, Kart. 66). The manuscript contains notes in MT's hand on how it was to be set to music.

ho rinunziato nelle presenti circostanze al viaggio di Roma nel vent[ur]o Carnevale – Mi rimetto in tutto alle saggie ed autorevoli detterminazioni della Maestà Vostra, ma però mi lusingo di molto nell'innata Sua Clemenza di cui io più d'ogn'altro mi glorio d'averne provati indegnamente i più efficaci effetti.

Mi metto di nuovo a' R[ea]li ed Imperiali Suoi Piedi ed umilmente, ossequiosamente, ed eternamente sono –
Della Sacra Cesarea Reale Imperiale Maestà Sua –
L'Umil[issi]mo Dev[otissi]mo Osseq[uiosissimo] Serv[itore]
Ferdinand Pär
7 Marzo 1806

28. Dresden, 24 March 1806.[76] Source: HHStA, Fa, Sb, Kart. 64, Verschiedene Briefe an die Kaiserin, fol. 94r–95r

Sacra Cesarea Reale Maestà!
Onor sommo, ed infinito piacere m'ha reccato il poter con fondamento leggere che la Maestà Sua non farà per ora scrivere ad altri il noto libretto *Androcle* poichè egli è tale che dato come si deve può far la riputazione d'un Compositore di musica – Io mi faccio un dovere di comporlo nell'autunno vent[ur]o come Sua Maestà lo comanderà. Riguardo all'Orsino,[77] se Vaigel lo scrive in Tedesco, e se non ha difficoltà che io pure lo metta in musica, potrebbe Sua Maestà accordar la grazia al povero vecchio Guardasoni ch'io le scriva tal libro? Egli è senza libretto, ed io gli ho data parola che pel mese di settembre le darò un Opera nuova: Se Sua Maestà le accorda tal libro, egli le presenterà la musica da me composta, e la cosa sarebbe fatta fra noi senza, che l'aria nemmen lo sapesse eccettuato il tempo in cui l'Opera anderebbe in scena in Praga – Se poi Sua Maestà non acconsente io già m'attengo al primo cioè al Androcle: Quello per Sua Maestà da certo.

Ho anche l'onore di trasmetterle l'atto 2.ᵈᵒ della Soffonisba – Le agilità cangiate possono per Sua Maestà essere rimpiazzate dalle vecchie come stanno nella vecchia partizione.

Iddio volesse, che potessi un giorno aver la sorte di fissarmi in Vienna sarei ben contento, come lo fui per cinque anni, che colà ho passati di Paradiso – Io qui ho troppo a travagliare per la chiesa, e pel Teatro, e poi sono soggetto ad un travaglio servile ch'è quello di battere in un' umida chiesa la musica

---

[76] Paer gives the year 1805, but the contents of the letter (in particular the reference to *Androcle*) and the fact that Paer was in Italy, not Dresden, in March 1805 suggest that he wrote it in 1806.

[77] Carpani's libretto *L'allievo dell'orsa*, of which MT owned a manuscript copy dated Vienna 1805 (HHStA, Fa, Sb, Kart. 65).

degli altri – onde non farò che continuare di benedire la mia Prottetrice, cui venendo l'occasione supplico umilmente di non dimenticarsi del suo:
Della Sacra Cesarea M[aest]à Sua

Umili[ssi]mo Dev[otissi]mo Ossequ[iosissimo] Serv[itor]e

Ferdinand Pär

Dresda il 24 Marzo 1805

29. Dresden, 21 April [1806]. Source: HHStA, Fa, Sb, Kart. 62, Verschiedene an Kaiserin Marie Therese 1803, fol. 140r–141r

Sacra Cesarea Reale Maestà!

Spero, che a quest'ora l'amico Si[mon]i le averà comunicata l'ultima mia, e m'averà messo agli Imperiali, e Reali Piedi Suoi, col farle noto, che la mia moglie verrà sola a Vienna per far godere un pajo di mesi dell'aria nativa al mio figlio Allessandro il quale felicemente vien per l'ottava volta di sottrarsi da una mortale malattia, che lo conduceva al sepolcro, se le infinite cure del medico e le nostre non l'avessero ajutato. La Sud[dett]a profitterà del cortese invito del Principe Lobkovitz ma sarà sempre agli ordini di Sua Maestà caso che per i poveri (come Sua Maestà ha la bontà di dirmi) fosse di qualche utile la sua persona. Essa conta anche di dare un Concerto al Pubblico.[78] Io non ho potuto venir con essa, poichè troppo m'interessava poter venirvi per la metà di Settembre, e restarvi un pajo di mesi agli ordini venerat[issi]mi della Maestà Sua.

La Lanterna sarà finita in breve. Ora sento che Sua Maestà desidererebbe il Pimmalione in travestimento. Su di ciò umilmente Le dico che farò tutto il mio possibile, ma non l'assicuro, poichè da qui al mese di Settembre devo finir la Lanterna – Finir l'opera per codesto Ell[etto]re e scriverne un'altra per Guardasoni come scrissi tempo fa all'amico. Però ho già data l'idea al Sig. Cinti autore del *Clò* – e potendo approfittar con usura del tempo mi lusingo di render contenta la Maestà Sua, acciò tutto sia spedito per tempo colle annotazioni neccessarie, acciò sia studiato, copiato, e pronto pel Giorno faustissimo ch'io di tutto cuore celebrerò, e benedirò mai sempre in pubblico, ed in privato.

Accludo la pre[se]nte lettera sperando che Sua Maestà lo permette, come S[imoni] me lo disse.

---

[78] Francesca Riccardi Paer was in Vienna during May 1806. On 20 May she gave a public concert in the Kleiner Redoutensaal; on 25 May she participated in a Wohlthätigkeits-Anstalten concert in the Grosser Redoutensaal, probably organized by MT, in which Paer's *Sofonisba* was performed (Morrow, *Concert Life*, 338).

A Suoi Clementissimi Piedi mi prostro, e fedelissima[ment]e ho l'altissim'onore di ripetermi
        L'umil[issi]mo Dev[otissi]mo Obbl[igatissimo] Servo F. Pär
Dresda 21 Ap[ri]le

30. Dresden, 6 June 1806. Source: HHStA, Fa, Sb, Kart. 65, Private an
        Kaiserin Marie Therese, fol. 361r–362r

Sacra Cesarea Reale Maestà!
Sono tanto penetrato dalla immensa bontà, e clemenza con cui s'è degnata accogliere a Suoi Piedi la mia moglie, e compatirla nel suo canto, e modo di recitare, ch'io non ho espressione bastante onde umilmente ringraziarla pel mio particolare e per quello della sud[dett]a mia moglie – Iddio doni a Sua Maestà tutte quelle grazie, di cui n'è veramente degna, e la faccia felicemente vivere in grembo dell'Adorabile Sua Reale Imperial Famiglia gl'anni di Nestore che ben lo merita. Ecco tutto ciò ch'io posso dirle in ringraziamento di tante, ed Eterne obbligazioni.
    Ho ricevuto il preziosissimo suo foglio e la spiegazione dei vetri che sono conformi alla cantata[79] all'eccezione dei n. 17. 18. 19. ove vi sono i diavoli &c questi non v'entrano, ed a mio parere diminuiscono poi l'effetto dell'ultimo vetro, ma quando piaccia a Sua Maestà si faranno anch'essi.
    M'ha divertito, e sorpreso a un tempo stesso il mattrimonio del nostro Ebler.[80] Non dubito che per la bontà d'ambedue forse si troveran felici (che glielo auguro di tutto cuore) ma all'aspetto loro pare che congiunti siansi la Quaresima, e la Carestia – Perdoni Sua Maestà questa mia idea.
    Io termino per non rendermi importuno – Mi metto agli Imp[eria]li, e Reali Suoi Piedi la supplico indefessam[ent]e a continuarmi la sovragrande Sua Prottezione, le baccio la Imp[eria]l e Real sua veste, e mi prottesto ossequios[ament]e
Della Cesarea Reale Sua Maestà
        Umil[issi]mo Dev[otissi]mo Obbl[igatissimo] Osseq[uiosissimo]
                                                    Ser[vitore]
                                                    Ferdinand Pär
Dresda il 6 Giugno 1806

---

[79] *La lanterna magica.*
[80] Eybler married Theresia Müller, one of MT's chamber servants, on 27 October 1806 (Robert Haas, "Josef Leopold Edler von Eybler," *Mozart-Jahrbuch* 1952, 64).

31. Dresden, 1 October [1806?]. Source: HHStA, Fa, Sb, Kart. 65,
     Private an Kaiserin Marie Therese 1807, fol. 21r.

Sua Maestà
Umilio a' suoi Piedi il Cantico, che Sua Maestà si è degnata comettermi,
ma così in fretta era moralmente impossibile il far qualche cosa di buono –
Qui non vi sono Poeti, o almeno non ne conosco – Di lingua Boema poi,
ne manchiamo affatto – Supplisca adunque l'innata bontà della Maestà
Sua, e quel zelo di far bene, e di servirla in tutto, e per quanto mai sempre
lo permetteran le mie deboli forze –
     Mi metto a Suoi R[eali] ed Imperiali Piedi, e mi prottesto osseq[uiosa-
men]te
Di Sua Maestà

L'Umili[ssi]mo e Dev[otissi]mo Ser[rvitore]
Osse[quiosissi]mo Ferd. Pär
Dresde 1 Ottobre

32. Dresden, 24 November 1806. Source: HHStA, Fa, Sb, Kart. 65,
     Private an Kaiserin Marie Therese, fol. 363r–364r

Sacra Cesarea Reale Maestà!
Siamo tutti nella massima agitazione essendoci arrivato in questo punto
l'ordine di dover subitamente partire per Berlino io, e mia moglie. Mi faccio
un dovere nel pormi agli Imp[eria]li Suoi Piedi, di farglielo sapere sperando,
che ci continuerà sempre l'efficcacissima Sua Prottezione. L'agitazione nostra è derivata *primo*: dal non sapere cosa andiamo a farvi, se per l'Opera
se per Accademie o per cosa…? Secondo perchè la mia moglie è debolis-
sima rinvenendosi appena da una pericolosa malattia. – Ecco il tenore
del biglietto che jer sera alle ore 9 mi fu conferito da codesto Sig. Conte
di Visthum Direttore degli Ellett[ora]li spettacoli.[81] Questo è scritto dal
Conte Marc[ol]ini[82] al Sud[dett]o Dirett[or]e:
     *Ayant S. M. L'Empereur Napoleon demandé Mons. e Mad.ᵉ de Pär, Mons.
L'Ellecteur lui ordonne de partir au plutot possible pour Berlin. Et vous Mr. Le
Comte Directeur est chargé de lui faire parvenir cette ordre &c* Io sono molto
angustiato non sapendo quanto tempo dovremo restarvi, ne potendo per
ora dire alla Maestà Vostra se posso venire pel mese di Gennajo. Ma non
mancherò appena giunto a Berlino di scrivere all'amico onde ragguagliarla

[81] Court Carl Alexander Nicolaus Vitzthum von Eckstädt, *Directeur des Plaisirs* at the court of Dresden.
[82] Count Camillo Marcolini, minister at the Saxon court.

di me, e della commissione dei Tableaux. Qui dovrà l'ellettore privarsi affatto dell'Opera italiana, giacchè noi partendo convien chiudere il Teatro dell'Opera sud[dett]a. Non c'è che il M[aest]ro Schuster[83] ammalato ed anche la chiesa ne soffrirà pel suo serviggio, ma ora tutto dee cedere a un mero desiderio del Conquistatore.

Spero, che Sua Maestà si troverà in ottima [salute?][84] glielo auguro di tutto cuore. Sarò sempre il [Fedele?] Credente del No. 3. – Frattanto mi metto [agli?] Imp[peria]li e R[eali] Piedi, e mi prottesto [umil?]mente, ed ossequiosamente:

L'umil[issi]mo Dev[otissi]mo Ossequiosissimo
Suo Servitore Ferd. Pär

D[resden] 24 1806 Nov.ᵉ

33. No place, no date, but probably written between 24 November 1806 and 14 January 1807. Source: HHStA, Fa, Sb, Kart. 63, fol. 402r–403v

Sacra Cesarea Reale Maestà!
Se non soffrissi quanto soffro, e pel freddo, e per la pena che mi costerà la fattica enorme d'un prossimo viaggio, direi che quanto m'accade, è un sogno, è una chimera.

Trovo un ottima occasione d'un galant'uomo mio amico che reccandosi a Praga metterà la presente in posta onde pervenga ai Piedi dalla Maestà Vostra, e quest' occasione ne è uno sfogo che mi vien reccato dal Cielo onde farle conoscere la situazione in cui mi trovo.

Come, ebbi l'onore di scriverle, (e come l'ho replicato a Simoni) quando l'Ellettore venne a Berlino; due giorni prima del di lui viaggio, mi ordinaron di portarmi costà con mia Moglie, perchè l'Imperatore Napoleone volea sentirla e conoscer me stesso. Le scuse furono inutili, m'accordarono cinque dì, acciò mia moglie si ristabilisse maggiormente, poi ci fecero partire. Io calcolai, che il mio soggiorno di Berlino non sarebbe stato di lunga durata, ed obbedii.

Tant'io quanto L'Ellettore giungemmo allorchè l'Imper[ator]e era partito per Bosen[85] – Io adunque mi preparai di ritornarmene a Dresda secondo l'esempio del mio Padrone; quando all'improvviso mi è dato l'ordine di portarmi immediat[ament]e sino a Bosen, e di prender meco anche il Sig.

---

[83] Joseph Schuster, composer and music director at the count of Dresden.
[84] The margin of this letter is damaged, making a few words illegible.
[85] Poznań in Poland, on the road from Berlin to Warsaw.

Brizzi – S'immagini Sua Maestà, che disordine per me, e che inbarazzo per i miei figli! La femmina l'ho lasciata in casa di Cinti a Dresda, e il maschio (calcolando un picciol viaggio da Dresda a Berlino, e facendogli bene il cangiar aria) l'ho preso meco. Ora mi tocca di lasciarlo anch'esso costì, e partire io solo, con mia Moglie. – Mio Dio! Con si pessime strade; chi sa cosa ci succede – ? Qui non sta tutto il male – Da più d'uno, sento che L'Imp[erator]e ci ha cercati ambedue all'Ellettore, che il Sud[dett]o ci abbia ceduti. Che si pensa di farci andare anche a Varsavia (se S. M. non è più in Bosen,) e che dovremmo ancora portarci a Parigi al Suo Serviggio quando tutte le cose saranno disposte in istato pacifico.

Può esser mai possibile, che l'Ellettore ci abbia (come si suol dire) venduti senza prima farmene parole? senza consultare la nostra volontà? Ecco cosa mi ha costato il partire da Vienna – Per dar in succinto una prova a V. M. del mio scontentamento si è, che avendo io proddotte varie ragioni per non andar attualmente in Pollonia, il Gent[ilissi?]mo Comand[ant]e Sr. de Clarc ha finito per dirmi *ch'egli dovea far eseguir l'ordine dattogli dal Maresch: Durok*,[86] e quando io *avessi insistito a non voler partire m'averebbe fatto accompagnar* dai *Giandarmi* – Eccomi a un bel momento per diventar sorbetto e forse per non aver più il contento di mettermi a suoi Imp[erial]i, e R[eali] Piedi. Io so di non poter ricevere per ora ala con riscontro allegorico alle mie, ne da Sua Maestà, ne dall'amico ma pazienza, io Le ho scritto tutto questo per dimostrarLe onestamente, e sinceramente, che non ne ho alcuna colpa: E che spero Vostra Maestà mi continuerà il suo altissimo Padrocinio, perchè non passerà gran tempo ch'io verrò a Vienna. (almeno farò tutto il mio possibile) Non posso però venire al tempo destinato, e ciò mi fa una pena, che non posso esprimerLe. Sua Maestà: si assuri che questa volta sono proprio ingannato, e che la prepotenza mi strasciva più oltre. Mi persuado, che S. M. non comunicherà ad altri questi miei sentimenti, poichè in occasioni simili farebbero un grave flagello, ed a me, ed alla mia famigliola che tutta rivverente si mette a Suoi Imp[erial]i e Reali Piedi.

Mi conservi la Sua Altissima Prottezione, e mi permetta di dirLe che sebben lontano conserverò sempre quei perpetui sentimenti di stima, ossequio, venerazione:
–Tutto sta come alli 20 d'ottobre–

L'Umil[issi]mo Dev[otissi]mo Obb[ligatissimo] Serv[itor]e
Ferd. Pär

---

[86] Géraud Christophe Duroc, Napoleon's grand marshal of the palace.

34. Warsaw, 14 January [1807]. Source: HHStA, Fa, Sb Kart. 63, fol.
361r–362v

Sacra Imperiale, e Reale Maestà!
Da Dresda a Berlino; da Berlino a Posen; e da Posen a Varsavia, ove mi trovo
colla mia moglie, la quale fa qualunque cosa per rendermi men sensibile
la lontananza di miei figli (uno lasciato in Berlino, l'altro a Dresda) ed
ambedue ci consoliamo reciprocamente nei momenti dispiacevoli.

Col mezzo dell'Impr[esari]o di Praga ragguagliai la Maestà Vostra di
quanto mi accadde, ora non manco del mio dovere col ripeterci i miei
costanti sentimenti di costante venerazione, obbligazione, ed umili[ssi]mo
rispetto, che non cesserà se non colla mia vita.

Arrivassimo a Posen dopo il viaggio più penoso, e più nojoso (esente
però grazie a Dio d'ogni disgrazia). Colà si cominciarono le musiche nelle
camere dell'Imp[erator]e un'ora per sera; Brizzi, mia Moglie, ed io col
solo Cembalo – Egli ne fu sì contento, che fece scrivere al Re di Sassonia,
che ci avrebbe tenuti volentieri al suo servizio, al che il sovrano chinò
volentieri la fronte, e quando men l'aspettai ricevetti la lettera dal Direttore
de' Spettacoli di Dresda, che mi prendo la libertà di umiliare alla Maestà
Vostra, e ne accludo la copia fedele qui dentro.

Dopo letta tal lettera, vedute le cose in quest'aspetto, mi son consigliato
colla mia moglie, ho consultato l'interesse della mia famiglia, la felicità fut-
tura de' miei figli, ed ho concluso infine di chiedere assai per mio onorario,
e per mia moglie cosiché o mi accorderanno tal somma considerabile o sarò
in libertà, e di Dresda, e di Parigi.

Ho chiesto adunque per me *18*-milla lire di Francia per tutto il tempo
di mia vita, la Carrozza, e l'alloggio per tutta mia famiglia (come avea
Paesiello;) E per mia Moglie *30*-milla lire annue per dodici anni dopo tal
tempo una retraite di *12* milla lire da godersi ovunque. Più: quattro mesi
ogn'anno di congedo ad ambedue per approffitarne, e mettermi a Piedi
Clement[issi]mi di Vostra Maestà, che spero mi accoglierà sempre con
quella benignità, ed amabilità propria alla Maestà Vostra, ed all'Augusto
Consorte a cui spero non mi si farà un aggravio se sarò eternamente memore
alla Clemenza Sua, ed all'amabile modo con cui mi ha sempre trattato. Se
non ci vien accordata tal somma ritorneremo.[87]

Scrivo quest'oggi anche al Conte Clò – Non ho più lettere da che son
partito da Vienna del mese di Novembre.[88]

---

[87] Paer's contract, dated 1 January 1807, is transcribed in Fleischman, *Napoléon et la musique*, 229–30.
[88] "Conte Clò" was presumably Simoni, who, in Paer's cantata of the same name, portrayed Conte
Clò in a duet that he sang with MT.

Supplico la Maestà Vostra se oso sperarlo di sole due righe nella lettera dell'amico, che mi assicurino della sua Prottezione, e Grazia.

Mia Moglie incinta di quasi tre mesi, col mezzo mio si mette ai Piedi di Sua Maestà, e meco si offre eternamente:
della Sacra Maesta Vostra

L'Umili[ssi]mo Devo[tissi]mo Ossequi[issim]o
Servit[or]e Ferdinand Pär –

Varsavia 14 Genn[ai]o

Enclosure (Fol. 404r):

Copie

Monsieur de Pär!

Sa Majesté l'Empereur des Francois, et Roi d'Italie, ayant ordonné à Mons. Thiard (N.B. comandant de la place de Dresde) de donner à connoitre a S. M. Le Roi de Saxe le plaisir qu'Elle auroit de vous retenir vous, & Mad.^e de Pär dans Son Service: Sa Majesté Royal[e] saisit avec empressement cette occasion pour prouver à Sa Majesté Imperial[e] e Royal[e]: combien il lui tient à coeur de prevenir ses desirs.

Sa Majesté le Roi mon Maitre m'ordonne donc de vous faire savoir incessament qu'Elle consent à vous d'egager dès à présent des obbligations que vous, et Mad. Pär aviez contractées pour Dresde, et qu'Elle vous accorde la permission d'entrer au Service de Sa Majeste Imperiale, et Royale.

Je vous prie d'agreer les assurances de la plus parfaite consideration avec &c.

20 December   M. de Pär

Signé par le Directeur de Plaisirs

Votre tres affectionè
Charles Conte Vitzthum

Correspondence between Paisiello and Marie Therese

These four letters are presented in English translation and discussed in chapter 8.

1. Marie Therese to Paisiello, Vienna, 18 July 1802. Source: Folchino Schizzi, *Della vita e degli studi di Giovanni Paisiello*, Milan, 1833, 85–6

Vienna, 18 Luglio 1802

Signor Paisiello

Ho troppa stima della vostra persona e del vostro singolar merito per non rivolgermi a voi perchè vogliate mettere in musica l'opera che troverete qui compiegata sotto il titolo: *La corona del merito* o sia *il Torquato Tasso*.[1] So bene che siete affollato da molte occupazioni, e che questo nuovo lavoro vi potrebbe per avventura giungere inopportuno; ciò non ostante mi compiaccio a lusingarmi che non ricuserete ad una vostra antica conoscenza la soddisfazione di questo suo desiderio.

Con questa speranza passo a comunicarvi alcune avvertenze, che dovete aver presenti nell'intraprendere questo lavoro. Prima di tutto dovete osservare che questa Opera deve servire per la camera, e non per il teatro.

Se vi piacesse di far entrare in qualche aria o altro pezzo un istrumento concertante, vi serva di regola, che noi abbiamo un buonissimo Violoncello, Oboè, e Clarinetto.

Il Basso che fa la parte di Gherardo canta perfettamente.[2] Gradirei di avere quest'Opera, se pure fosse possibile, per il mese di Gennajo dell'anno venturo; se ciò non può essere, sono anche disposta ad aspettare quanto vorrete, piuttosto, che affrettando il lavoro, questo non riuscisse così perfetto come desidero.

Le osservazioni che di più potessero occorrere vi saranno in appresso comunicate.

[1] Libretto by Giovanni de Gamerra of which MT owned a manuscript copy (HHStA, Fa, Sb, Kart. 66).
[2] Probably Carl Weinmüller

La premura, che non dubito vi darete a soddisfare alla mia richiesta, mentre sarà a me ben grata ed accetta, darà a voi un nuovo titolo alla mia stima e benevolenza, della quale mi compiaccio ora di assicurarvi.

Vostra affezionata

Teresa

2. Paisiello to Marie Therese, Paris, 4 August 1802. Source: Pierpont Morgan Library, Mary Flagler Cary Music Collection[3]

S[ua] M[aestà] I[mperiale] e R[eale]

Signora!

L'onore col quale la Maestà Vostra Imperiale, e Reale mi ha colmato, col'onorarmi de' suoi Imperiali, e Reali comandi, coi quali si è degnata ordinarmi da mettergli in musica *la Corona del Merito, o sia il Torquato Tasso*, sarà per me una gloria maggiore, potendo io sodisfarla a tenore delle brame della Maestà Vostra Imperiale, e Reale, che con tutto l'impegno procurerò di meritarla.

Il mio gran ringraziamento è solo quello da non poterla ubbidire sul momento, per appagare alli desiderj della Maestà Vostra Imperiale, e Reale, per essere io in questo punto occupato sopra di un Poema francese, datomi dal Primo Console, per farlo eseguire nel gran Teatro dell'Opera, il quale ha per titolo il *Ratto di Proserpina*, di cui ho il travaglio nelle mani da otto giorni a questa parte, e che a dir poco, mi terrà occupato per quattro mesi in circa.[4] Avendo perciò ben previsto la Maestà Vostra Imperiale, e Reale, che subito, che avrò terminato l'attuale travaglio, nel medesimo momento mi metterò ad occuparmi in mettere in musica il Torquato Tasso, con questa attenzione, premura, e zelo, per quanto comporta il mio debbole talento, per potermi meritare dalla Maestà Vostra Imperiale, e Reale un semplice compatimento non trascurando tutte le avvertenze, ed osservazioni datemi relative al soggetto.

Priego intanto umilmente la Maestà Vostra Imperiale, e Reale a volersi degnare a continuarmi la di Lei valevole Imperial Protezzione, e di umiliarmi ai piedi di Sua Maestà Imperiale, e Reale l'Imperatore, ed a tutta l'Imperial

---

[3] The Morgan Library acquired the letter from Otto Haas, London, in November 1968 (my thanks to Rigbie Turner, music curator at the Morgan Library, for this information). The inventory of HHStA, Fa, Sb, records the presence in Kart. 62 (formerly alt 250) of a letter written by Paisiello to MT in 1802. That letter, which must have been filed with Cobenzl's letter with which it was enclosed (see chapter 8) is no longer to be found in the archive. It is almost certainly the one now in New York.

[4] *Proserpine*, first performed in Paris on 29 March 1803.

Famiglia; mentre, che con tutto il profondo rispettoso ossequio, umilmente
mi professo

Di Vostra Maestà Imperiale, e Reale
Umilissimo, ubbidientissimo, devotissimo, ed
ossequiosissimo servitore, Giovanni Paisiello

Parigi li 4 Agosto
1802

3. Marie Therese to Paisiello, Vienna, 12 January 1805.
Source: Schizzi, 86–87

Vienna, 12 Gennajo 1805

Caro Sig. Paisiello

Nella lusinga che Ella non abbia potuto ancora mettere mano alla musica, che tempo fa la pregai di volere scrivere, o che il suo lavoro non sia
troppo inoltrato, io gradirei che al libretto, che gli mandai, e che a dire
il vero non è di tutto mio piacimento, potesse essere sostituito un altro
migliore.

Le mando pertanto qui compiegati due libretti francesi,[5] affinchè Ella
scelga quello che più le piacerà, pregandola, dopo di avere dal medesimo
preso il soggetto, di farne comporre uno in italiano, e di voler poi Ella stessa
scrivere la musica. L'altro libretto favorirà di mandarmelo.

Nel comporre questa musica La prego di avere presente per sua direzione
e regola, che l'Opera non deve essere più lunga di due ore e mezzo, che
per ogni prima parte non vi sia che un'aria sola, tutto al più due, ed anche
una cavatina: desiderando che il rimanente dell'Opera contenga molti cori,
pezzi concertati, finali, e pochi recitativi non istrumentati.

Le persone per le cui voci si desidera che vengano scritte le parti si trovano
notate in ciaschedun libretto, e le scale delle voci sono scritte in questa mia
lettera.

Non limito il tempo per il quale deve essere terminato questo suo lavoro,
lo lascio alla sua disposizione, desiderando che l'opera riesca degna del
valente professore.

---

[5] Later references to these "libretti" reveal that they were two *mélodrames*: Pixérécourt's *Les Maures
d'Espagne* and Caigniez's *Androcles, ou Le Lion reconnaissant*, both first performed in Paris in 1804.

I sentimenti, che Ella ha per me sempre dimostrati, e di cui mi ricordo con compiacenza, mi sono garanti, che Ella si vorrà di buona voglia prestare a questo mio desiderio, sicuro di acquistarsi un nuovo diritto alla riconoscenza e stima della sua

Affezionatissima
Teresa

4. Marie Therese to Paisiello, Baden, 6 July 1805. Source: Schizzi, 87–88

Baaden, 6 Luglio 1805

Caro Sig. Paisiello

Ho ricevuto la di Lei lettera in data 11 Maggio in replica della quale mi compiaccio prima di tutto di dimostrarle la mia particolare soddisfazione per la premura che Ella si dà per eseguire il da me commessole incarico. La traduzione del Melodramma, che Ella ha scelto in preferenza dell'altro i *Mori di Spagna*, ha incontrato molto il mio piacere: la bella musica, quale si ha il diritto di attendere dal classico e valente professore che la scrive, non può che far risaltare maggiormente il libro ed assicurare al medesimo una felice riuscita. Relativamente ai balli staccati dal canto si desiderano di una giusta durata di tempo: per la qualità della musica poi ne lascio la scelta al di lei gusto, non sapendosi ancora qual sarà il Maestro di ballo, che dovrà metterli in iscena; qualunque però egli sarà, dovrà sempre adattare le sue idee alla musica. Solamente Ella mi farà cosa grata di farmi sapere per quali voci avrà scritto le parti di *Settimio* e di *Pubblio*.[6]

Intanto assicurandolo, caro sig. Paisiello, della mia stima e speciale benevolenza, sono

Sua affezionatissima
Teresa

---

[6] Settimio and Pubblio are the names of two characters in an Italian translation of *Androcles* that MT owned (HHStA, Fa, Sb, Kart. 66).

Documents pertaining to the development and performance of Paer's Il conte Clò

A. Marie Therese's sketch for the cantata with Paer's response

Source: HHStA, Fa, Sb, Kart. 65, Schriften der Höchstsel. Kaiserin: Theatralische Gegenstände, fol. 143r–144v

Marie Therese's Sketch

805: 12 February

L'Idea che ho è di fare (come questo Anno cada il giorno di nascita dell'Imperatore in Carnevale) una piccola Accademia vocale ed istrumentale nel genere carnevalesco, cioè molto ridicola composta dei Pezzi seguenti.
1. Una gran Sinfonia difficilissima ad eseguire per i stromenti e specialmente per i violini sapend o che questo diverte l'Imperatore che anche suonarebbe.[1]
X [mark inserted by Paer]
2. Aria che cominciasse molto seria, e poi tutto d'un colpo diverebbe molto buffa, e così cambiasse tra il buffo e il serio colle parole o colla musica, questo come anche chi la canterà lascio alla vostra scelta.

Paer's Response

È stato fissato un Padre di fam[igli]a M[aest]ro di Capella che si diverte in una sera di Carnevale co' figli una Nipote e varj Parenti.

La Sinfonia Curiosa, e difficil[issim]a resta

L'aria colla correzione del Zio cioè del M[aest]ro è sostituita a questa: NB. per la Sig.ª A[ltamonte] Nipote siccome il 2ᵈᵒ piano.

---

[1] Emperor Franz was a violinist.

353

3. Terzetto ove i cantanti ed i stromenti si confondano e non possono più continuare.

Questo fingerà un Duetto e 'l Padre suggerirà così si forma Terzetto. Alla Metà v'è la Confusion dell'orchestra &c. V. M. – Sim[oni] ed il Buffo.

4. Aria di qualche opera cognita ma cantata in parodia, questa chi la canterà lascio anche alla scelta vostra.

L'aria segnata X resta qui a questo luogo – cantata da Sim. passerà dal gran serio ad una venezianata.

5. Un pezzo di Musica Istrumentale a gusto vostro solamente desidererei se è possibile che vi ci entrassero di quei piccoli Istrumenti che si chiamano Bertolsgadner.[2]

Resta come il piano 2do cioè qui il coro colle sortite dei Sig.^{i} notati X e pel N.° Sei qui appresso.

6. Un Coro con dei piccoli Soli Duetti da fare cantare da quelli segnati col X.

6. Il Pezzo di musica istrument.^{e}

7. Un Quartetto ove ognuno dei Cantanti si proporebbe, e cercarebbe d'imitare ma comicamente qualche cognito gran Cantante.

7. Quartetto resta coll'imitaz.^{e} di Guadagni[3] &c. V. M. L'Alt: Sim: e'l Buffo.
8. Aria di V. M. allusiva &c.

8. Aria seria coi Cori che starnutassero, tossissero, sbadigliassero, per renderla comica.

9. Aria del Buffo del Terz' atto di Giulietta, e Romeo; *Ombra adorata* in parrodia di musica, e accomp. dello sbadiglio &c degli altri.[4]

9. Duetto ove uno fosse tutto flemmatico e l'altro furioso con dei passagi comici.

10. Duetto del Lunatico, Sim.^{i} e V. M. che mostra l'umor diverso all'altro.

10. Finale tramischiato di Canto e di Suono chiassoso, e difficile ad eseguire per i violini.

11. Finale chiassoso &c. I pezzi sono sempre 10 – non contando La Sinfonia.

---

[2] Berchtesgadner Instrumente.
[3] Gaetano Guadagni, the *musico* who created the role of Orfeo in Gluck's *Orfeo ed Euridice*.
[4] "Ombra adorata" was the celebrated aria composed by Crescentini for Zingarelli's *Giulietta e Romeo* (Milan, 1796).

Se l'ordine di questi Pezzi non vi piace o non va bene o se avete migliori idee vi prego cambiatelo e rimandandomi questo foglio del quale ho bisogno di scrivere all'altra parte quel che cambiate e come dividete le parti.

Le Persone che canteranno in questa Bambinata son i fedeli credenti cioè

Io
Altamonte[6]
Simoni[7]
Voi se venite, o Brochi[8] o Vogel,[9]
Se venite Eibler desidererebbe cantare anche lui qualche piccola parte se poi non venite credo che lui sarebbe il migliore per diriggere per raggioni a voi note.

Quelli poi segnati X che cantarebbero nel Coro, e potrebbero anche suonare dei piccoli istrumenti sarebbero

Schosulan[10]
Constance[11]
Young[12]
Schmidmayer[13]
Altri i Coristi musicali

NB. Avanti la Sinfonia c'è qualche parola di Recit.° preceduto da una Tromba che annunzia ad uso del Banditor dell'Opera *Alceste*[5] indi segue l'Ovvertur &c

Chieggo mille perdoni a V. M. io faccio con tutto il cuore quanto posso, e mi metto frattanto prostrato a' Suoi Benef[icent]i e Clem[entissi]mi Piedi.

P. S.
Sono in una continua febbre per il Copista, e per il Poeta. Questo primo è bravissimo ma lento come una Lumaca.

[5] Gluck's *Alceste* (Vienna, 1767).   [6] Katherina Altamonte.
[7] Giuseppe Simoni   [8] Giambattista Brocchi, comic bass; see chapter 2, n. 11.
[9] Johann Michael Vogl.   [10] Ursula Schosulan, MT's lady-in-waiting.
[11] Constanze Streffler, one of MT's chamber servants.
[12] Thomas Peter Young, one of the emperor's private secretaries.
[13] Sebastian Schmidmayer, one of MT's chamber servants.

Le Parole come non devono essere
tutte in un senso ogni pezzo
essendo per sè vi pregherei di
pensarci anche perchè desidererei
che la cosa restasse segreta e qui
temo che non lo sarebbe
servendosi del solito Poeta.
Quantunque avrei molto piacere
di vedervi, desidererei che non
veniste temendo che ciò di nuovo
vi possi cagionare dei dispiaceri e
facendomene una vera coscienza,
ma se poi lo desiderate e credete
che la vostra presenza sia
necessaria per fare andare la cosa
bene, allora vi permetto di venire
ma per solo otto giorni per le
prove potendo ognuno
prima studiarsi la parte: vi prego
se avete un buono e sollecito
copista di farla anche copiare e
cavare le parti afinche resti più
segreta, e di mandarmela pezzo
per pezzo. Se non venite vi prego
nella mia parte di scrivermi e fare
tutto quello come desiderate che
la canti. Mi dispiace
d'incomodarvi con questa
Bambinata, ma sono sicura che
nelle vostre mani riuscirà bene, e
farà piacere a quello per cui si fa, e
poi i fedeli devono restare tuti
anche nell'Anno nuovo.

B. Plan for the cantata in Paer's hand

Source: HHStA, Fa, Sb, Kart. 63, fol. 364 r–v

I Dilettanti di Musica in Famiglia[14]

Le 4 prime parti saranno

Un Padre di familia	o per me, o per Brocchi
Una Figlia	V. M.
Un Figlio	Sim.
Una Nipote	L'Alt.

    Le altre parti saranno accessorie

Distribuzione

1. Sinfonia secondo il piano concert.°
2. Aria della Nipote
3. Terzetto fra il Padre, e i due Figli (Il Soggetto di questo Terzetto sarà il Padre che fa il Suggeritore ad un Duetto; l'idea sarà bizzarra.)
4. Aria del figlio (A me piacerebbe l'idea prima cioè Dal Gran Serio passare ad un vernacolo p.e. L'Arlechino.)
5. Coro co' concertanti segnati #
6. Il pezzo istrumentale col Cembalo, coll'arpa &c. Si desidera sapere in che tono sarà quella picciol arpa non avendo ne chiavi ne pedali – Per quanto ho studiato non posso comprendere cosa sia l'istrumento che mi è stato descritto nel primo piano, almeno supplico di sapere com'ei si scrive; ciò può farsi spedendomi subito una parte scritta in altra Cantata per tale stromento.
7. Quartetto dell'imitazione – Pachiarotti,[15] Guadagni, David,[16] e qualch'altro – Motivi delle conosciute arie di questi tali continuando il Quartetto &c.
8. Romanza villereccia della Figlia coi Cori.
9. Duetto fra i due Fratelli come il 2do piano.
10. Aria del Padre. Buffissima.
11. Finale intitolato L'incendio di Troia in parrodia.

N. B. Abbenchè siano 11 i pezzi sono soltanto 10 – perchè non s'entra la Sinfonia.

---

[14] A preliminary title, later discarded in favor of *Il conte Clò*.

[15] Gasparo Pacchierotti, one of the finest *musici* of the late eighteenth century.

[16] Giacomo David, a celebrated heroic tenor.

I Recit.[i] soli si diran a memoria. Il padre sarà maestro di capella.
Mi faccio un dovere di mettermi a Suoi Piedi e di restituirle i due Piani come me l'ha comandato.

C. Paer's instructions for the performance of *Il conte Clò*

Source: HHStA, Fa, Sb, Kart. 65, Private an Kaiserin Marie Therese, fol. 370r–v

Carta d'Istruzione per la Cantata

A piacere di chi comanda potrà recitarsi la pre[se]nte *Cantata* cioè o su d'un picciol Teatrino, o in camera – Travestiti tutti parmi indispensabile.

Il Principio è tal e quale l'Alceste di Kluk.

Il Buffo dispenserà le parti cantanti come lo accenna la Poesia – Soltanto saranno già al luogo loro quelle dei stromenti – Indi segue la Sinfonia difficilissima come è stata ordinata. V'è un certo passaggio nella Sinfonia il quale vien replicato nella Romanza, di tal replica lascio l'interpretazione a chi la sentirà.

Il primo pezzo dopo la Sinfonia è l'aria d'Enrichetta a mio parere il Sig. Ubaldo, che tratto tratto la corregge dev'esserle vicino, e così potrà guardare nella parte stessa se vuole, oppure nella propria ma la deve sapere quasi a mente – La Sig. Enrichetta procuri di eseguire a puntino il forte, il piano &c – tutto il resto anderà da se.

Il n.° 2 è il Terzetto – In cui Ambrogio, e Luigina devono cantarlo a memoria – Perciò è composto facilino – La Confusione dell'orchestra sarà rimarcabile se ognuno attenderà alla sua parte con marcar assai la misura eguale &c &c. Al *reffren* il Buffo con i suoi occhiali, oppure un sol occhialetto, anderà a cantarlo sulla partitura – N. B. *Miei signori riveriti* convien che lo dica a memoria.

Ambrogio, è un carattere d'uno che non è mai contento e Lunatico – La sua aria è il 3.° pezzo – Ei deve dirla in grande sul principio, e in buffo quando vengon le parole veneziane – Dopo l'aria deve mostrarsi offeso d'aver cantata quell'aria come nel libro – &c – Segue il N. 4 Coro.

A cadaun cantante ho scritto il proprio nome sulla parte – e mi son tenuto più facile che ho potuto – Raccomando che sia dal resto del coro cantato con energia e spirito senz'eccedere nel troppo presto del tempo come pur troppo spesso succede – I Parenti si avvanzeranno &c e gli stessi suonerano gli strumenti descritti – Al Sig. Brocchi toccherà di suonar il *Corno*, ma sono due sole note 𝄞 del corno in F.[ut] e basta che conti le battute; il restante divertirà – Il Zuffolino deve essere accordato in C acuto una sol nota s'intende. – Quando arriveranno le parti di questo nominato Concertone si prega di legarle alla parte di cadauno a chi appartiene acciò non nascon disordini.

Il Quartetto, che segue, dovrebbesi pure cantarlo a memoria così esiggendo le imitazioni dei Cant[an]ti &c – e la collera del Sr. Ubaldo nel fine.

La Romanza è in parte allusiva al giorno che si da la cantata – Sopratutto si raccomanda che essendo il principio un canto ameno, e campestre non sia preso ne troppo adagio, ne troppo presto.

L'aria, che viene in seguito e l'aria contrafatta di Giulietta, e Romeo col cor diviso &c.

Poi succede il Duetto fra Ambr.º e Luigina; il carattere di questi due è dipinto coi colori della Musica, ne abbisogna spiegazioni.

Il Finale è l'Incendio di Troja; in questo v'entrano quei Sig.ⁱ che hanno cantato il coro, ma è una cosa di niente.

Si raccomanda il *Buona notte a lor signor* – natural[ment]e con riverenze comiche &c. Finis

D. Paer's instructions for the performance of *Il conte Clò*

Source: HHStA, Fa, Sb. Kart. 66, Theatralische Gegenstände, fol. 101r–v (reproduced, in part, in Fig. 9.2)

Annotazioni

Ho marcato nel pezzo istrumentale le Campanelle, ma queste sono quei campanelli uniti in differenti toni che si suonano con una scossa di braccio nelle bande turche da una sola persona.[17] Ho cercato che il triangolo vada col zuffoletto perchè suonando il triangolo il Sig. Ebler[18] ossia Calassanzio così egli dirige il zuffoletto che sarà suonato dalla Mad. Constance e vanno unissono.

Desidero che l'Orchesta sia composta di 8 bravi Violini al solito, e due violoncelli, e Due Contrabassi &c. Mi raccomando il Sud[detto] pezzo istrumentale.

L'Ordine di non servirmi più dell'Arpa m'è arrivato troppo tardi, e non v'è più rimedio, ma è così facile e poco concertata che se l'istrumento (come mi fu scritto) non fa grand'effetto, non serve, essendomi molto appoggiato all'Oboe, Cembalo, Clarinetti, e Viola che raccomando al Orna[tissi?]mo Sig. Dottore de Stift[19] riverendolo distintamente.

---

[17] See Paer's illustration in Fig. 9.2.   [18] Joseph Eybler.
[19] Probably Baron Stifft, Emperor Franz's personal physician.

La Parte di Ascanio,[20] che non son che due parole è per un ragazzo corista – ma che vi sia, entro la parte al luogo che va prima di cominciar la Cantata.

Gli strumenti che dispenserà Ubaldo ossia Brocchi che sian tutti preparati avanti l'Accademia e a lui vicini.

Il Cembalino, ossia Tamburino desidero quello di Sua Maestà che si suona con una picciol mazza. Il Triangolo che sia d'argento se si può, e non quel del Teatro cattivo.

Ho inserito un mottivo conosciuto nel Duetto N. 9 – Sopra il conosc[iu]to *Nel cor più non mi sento*, ciò è per derider maggiormente il Conte Geloso come si vedrà. Adunque prego di prender lo stesso tempo come si prendeva al Teatro. I Fioretti di cadauno gli ho scritti nelle rispettive parti. Raccomando al Degno Direttor di Orchestra il Sig. Vraniski[21] l'esecuzione, ma più la correzione di qualche nota sbagliata se vi sarà occasione.

Il Nostro Sig. Junk[22] sarà Ulisse, ha poco, ed ha la carta in mano, cioè non deve cantar a memoria.

Raccomando il Recit.° del N. 7 – colle sordine p[ri]mo un tempo Andante come di Minuetto mosso – Indi il Pezzo, che segue essendo il mio favorito.

Il Finale siano eseguite dalli stessi del Coro le Parti delle tre Donne come ho marcato col *tocca lapis*.

Spero, che sebben tardi arriverà per fattalità la Cantata: sempre si potran fare due prove d'Orchestra, e poi si noti, che v'è pochissimo recitativo d'imparare a mente il più era quello che ho spedito – L'Aria del Buffo, il Duetto, e 'l Finale sono da cantarsi colla parte in mano.

Questa Cantata è fatta per servire la Padrona ma anche oltre il solito Zelo del mio dovere, l'ho scritta col genio e col desiderio che non resti al di sotto dell'Altre &c &c.

---

[20] Ascanio and (later in the *Annotazioni*) Ulisse are characters in the finale, a parodistic depiction of the fall of Troy.
[21] Paul Wranitzky.   [22] Young.

Bibliography

ARCHIVAL SOURCES

Florence, Archivio di Stato
  Imperiale e Reale Corte 5429, 5430 ("Catalogo delle Opere ridotte Sinfonie &^{ra}"; "Catalogo della Musica da chiesa")
Vienna, Gesellschaft der Musikfreunde
  Verzeichniss der mit Allerhöchster Genehmigung an das Archiv der Gesellschaft d. Musikfreunde in Wien abgegebenen Musikalien a. d. Sammlung weiland S. Mj. d. Kaisers Franz I
Vienna, Haus-, Hof- und Staatsarchiv, Familienarchiv
  Handarchiv Kaiser Franz, Kart. 1–5, 10, 24
  Sammelbände, Kart. 19, 30, 39, 53, 60–66a
Vienna, Österreichische Nationalbibliothek, Musiksammlung
  Catalogo alter Musickalien u. gehört in das privat Musikalien Archiv S. Maj. des Kaisers, INV. I / Kaisersammlung Graz I
  Erwerbungs-Nachweis, INV. III / Tabulae 2
Vienna, Österreichisches Theatermuseum
  Theaterzettel, Burgtheater and Kärntnertortheater, 1795–1807
Vienna, Universität für Musik
  Ignaz Ritter von Seyfried, *Scizze meines Lebens. Theilnehmenden Freunden zum Andenken geweiht*, manuscript I.N. 36561

PRIMARY SOURCES

Allgemeine musikalische Zeitung 4–7 (1801–5), 28 (1826)
Beethoven, Ludwig van, *The Letters of Beethoven*, translation by Emily Anderson, 3 vols., New York, 1961
Beethoven, Ludwig van, *Beethoven: A Documentary Study*, ed. H. C. Robbins Landon, New York, 1970
Beethoven, Ludwig van, *Ludwig van Beethoven: Die Werke im Spiegel seiner Zeit*, ed. Stefan Kunze, Laaber, 1987
Beethoven, Ludwig van, *Briefwechsel: Gesamtausgabe*, ed. Sieghard Brandenburg, 7 vols., Bonn, 1996–8

361

Beethoven, Ludwig van, *Letters to Beethoven and Other Correspondence*, ed. Theodore Albrecht, 3 vols., Lincoln, Neb., 1996

Beytrag zur Characteristik und Regierungs-Geschichte der Kaiser Josephs II. Leopolds II. und Franz II., Paris, 1799

Calvi, Girolamo, *Di Giovanni Simone Mayr*, ed. PierAngelo Pelucchi, Bergamo, 2000

Carpani, Giuseppe, *Le Haydine, ovvero Lettere sulla vita e le opere del celebre maestro Giuseppe Haydn*, Padua, 1823

De Gamerra, Giovanni, "Lettere di Giovanni De Gamerra," ed. Federico Marri, *Studi musicali* 29 (2000), 71–183, 293–452; 30 (2001), 59–127

Dittersdorf, Carl Ditters von, *Lebensbeschreibung*, ed. Norbert Miller, Munich, 1967

Du Montet, Alexandrine, *Souvenirs de la Baronne du Montet, 1785–1866*, Paris, 1904

Elisabeth, Archduchess, "Briefe an Erzherzog Franz (nachmals K. Franz II.) von seiner ersten Gemahlin Elisabeth, 1785–1789," ed. H. Weyda, *Archiv für Österreichische Geschichte* 44 (1870), 111–262

Griesinger, Georg August, *Biographische Notizen über Joseph Haydn*, Leipzig, 1810, repr. Leipzig, 1979; translation in Vernon Gotwals, *Haydn: Two Contemporary Portraits*, Madison, Wis., 1968

Griesinger, Georg August, *"Eben komme ich von Haydn...": Georg August Griesingers Korrespondenz mit Joseph Haydns Verleger Breitkopf & Härtel, 1799–1819*, ed. Otto Biba, Zurich, 1987

Gyrowetz, Adalbert, *Biographie*, ed. Alfred Einstein, Leipzig, 1915

Haydn, Joseph, *Joseph Haydn: Gesammelte Briefe und Aufzeichnungen*, ed. Dénes Bartha, Kassel, 1965

Hof- und Staats-Schematismus der röm. kaiserl. auch kaiserl. königl. und erzher-zoglichen Haupt- und Residenz-Stadt Wien, Vienna, 1796–1804

Maria Carolina, Queen, *Correspondance inédite de Marie-Caroline reine de Naples et de Sicile avec le Marquis de Gallo*, ed. M. H. Weil and C. di Somma Circello, 2 vols., Paris, 1911

Mozart: Briefe und Aufzeichnungen, ed. Wilhelm A. Bauer, Otto Erich Deutsch, and Joseph Heinz Eibl, 7 vols., Kassel, 1962–75

Musikalisches Taschenbuch auf das Jahr 1803, ed. Julius Werden and Adolph Werden, Penig, [1803]

Pressburger Zeitung, "Musik zur Zeit Haydns und Beethovens in der Pressburger Zeitung," ed. Marianne Pandi and Fritz Schmidt, *Haydn Jahrbuch* 8 (1971), 165–265; abridged translation, 267–93

Realis [pseudonym of Duetzele Gerhard Coeckelberghe], *Das k. k. Lustschloss Laxenburg*, Vienna, 1846

Reicha, Anton, *Notes sur Antoine Reicha*, ed. Jiří Vysloužil, Brno, 1970

Ritorni, Carlo, *Commentarii della vita e delle opere coredrammatiche di Salvatore Viganò e della coregrafia e de' corepei*, Milan, 1838

Rosenbaum, Joseph Carl, "Die Tagebücher von Joseph Carl Rosenbaum, 1770–1829," ed. Else Radant, *Haydn Jahrbuch* 5 (1968), whole issue;

translation, "The Diaries of Joseph Carl Rosenbaum, 1770–1829," *Haydn Yearbook* 5 (1968), whole issue

Schinn, Georg, and Franz Joseph Otter, *Biographische Skizze von Michael Haydn*, Salzburg, 1808

Schönfeld, Johann Ferdinand von, *Jahrbuch der Tonkunst in Wien und Prag*, Prague, 1796; ed. Otto Biba, Munich, 1976

Schönholz, Anton von, *Traditionen zur Charakteristik Oesterreichs*, ed. Gustav Gugitz, 2 vols., Munich, 1914

Thürheim, Countess Lulu, *Mein Leben*, ed. René von Rhyn, 2 vols., Munich, 1913

Weigl, Joseph, "Zwei Selbstbiographien von Joseph Weigl (1766–1846)," ed. Rudolph Angermüller, *Deutsches Jahrbuch der Musikwissenschaft* 16 (1971), 46–85

SECONDARY SOURCES

Acton, Harold, *The Bourbons of Naples (1734–1825)*, London, 1956

Albrecht, Theodore, "Beethoven's *Leonore*: A New Compositional Chronology Based on May–August, 1804 Entries in Sketchbook Mendelssohn 15," *Journal of Musicology* 7 (1989), 165–90

Albrecht, Theodore, "The Fortnight Fallacy: A Revised Chronology for Beethoven's *Christ on the Mount of Olives*, Op. 85, and Wielhorsky Sketchbook," *Journal of Musicological Research* 11 (1991), 263–84

Becker-Glauch, Irmgard, "Joseph Haydns Te Deum für die Kaiserin: Eine Quellenstudie," *Colloquium amicorum: Joseph Schmidt-Görg zum 70. Geburtstag*, ed. Siegfried Kross and Hans Schmidt, Bonn, 1967, 1–10

Biba, Otto, "Die private Musikpflege in der kaiserlichen Familie," *Musik am Hof Maria Theresias*, ed. Roswitha Vera Karpf, Munich, 1984, 83–92

Blümml, Emil Karl, and Gustav Gugitz, *Von Leuten und Zeiten im alten Wien*, Vienna, 1922

Bonds, Mark Evan, "Haydn, Laurence Sterne, and the Origins of Musical Irony," *Journal of the American Musicological Society* 44 (1991), 57–91

Bongiovanni, Carmela, "Le fonti della musica vocale da camera di Ferdinando Paër," *Fonti musicali italiane* 6 (2001), 21–104

Brandenburg, Sieghard, "Beethovens Streichquartette op. 18," *Beethoven und Böhmen*, ed. Sieghard Brandenburg and Martella Gutiérrez-Denhoff, Bonn, 1988, 259–309

Brock, Annedore, *Das Haus der Laune im Laxenburger Park bei Wien*, Frankfurt, 1996

Brosche, Günter, "Das Hofmusikarchiv," *Musica Imperialis: 500 Jahre Hofmusikkapelle in Wien, 1498–1998*, exhibition catalogue, Tutzing, 1998, 117–24

Brosche, Günter, "Besondere Neuerwerbungen der Musiksammlung der Österreichischen Nationalbibliothek in den Jahren 1998 und 1999," *Studien zur Musikwissenschaft* 48 (2002), 489–502

Brown, A. Peter, *Joseph Haydn's Keyboard Music*, Bloomington, Ind., 1986

Brown, A. Peter, *Performing Haydn's The Creation: Reconstructing the Earliest Renditions*, Bloomington, Ind., 1986

Carner, Mosco, *Major and Minor*, New York, 1980

Chew, Geoffrey, "The Night-Watchman's Song Quoted by Haydn and its Implications," *Haydn-Studien* 3 (1974), 106–24

Chroust, Anton, *Lebensläufe aus Franken*, 6 vols., Würzburg, 1930

Cole, Malcolm S., "Peter Winter's *Das unterbrochene Opferfest*: Fact, Fantasy, and Performance Practice in Post-Josephinian Vienna," *Music in Performance and Society: Essays in Honor of Roland Jackson*, ed. Malcolm S. Cole and John Koegel, Warren, Mich., 1997, 291–324

Cooper, Barry, *Beethoven*, Oxford, 2000

Corti, Egon Caesar, *Ich, eine Tochter Maria Theresias*, Munich, 1950

Croll, Gerhard, ed., *Musik mit Kinderinstrumenten aus dem Salzburger und Berchtesgadener Land* (Denkmäler der Musik in Salzburg, vol. 2), Munich, 1981

Croll, Gerhard, and Kurt Vössing, *Johann Michael Haydn: Sein Leben, sein Schaffen, seine Zeit*, Vienna, 1987

Dean, Winton, "Beethoven and Opera," *Essays on Opera*, Oxford, 1990, 123–63

DeNora, Tia, *Beethoven and the Construction of Genius: Musical Politics in Vienna, 1792–1803*, Berkeley, 1995

Dietz, Hanns-Bertold, "Instrumental Music at the Court of Ferdinand IV of Naples and Sicily and the Works of Vincenzo Orgitano," *International Journal of Musicology* 1 (1992), 99–126

Edge, Dexter, "Recent Discoveries in Viennese Copies of Mozart Concertos," *Mozart's Piano Concertos: Text, Context, Interpretation*, ed. Neal Zaslaw, Ann Arbor, Mich., 1996, 51–65

Edge, Dexter, *Mozart's Viennese Copyists*, Ph.D. dissertation, University of Southern California, 2001

Engländer, Richard, "Zur Musikgeschichte Dresdens gegen 1800," *Zeitschrift für Musikwissenschaft* 4 (1922), 199–241

Engländer, Richard, "Ferdinando Paër als sächsischer Hofkapellmeister," *Neues Archiv für sächsische Geschichte* 1 (1929), 204–24

Engländer, Richard, "Paërs 'Leonora' und Beethovens 'Fidelio,'" *Neues Beethoven-Jahrbuch* 4 (1930), 118

Enßlin, Wolfram, *Die Opern Ferdinando Paërs (1771–1839)*, dissertation, University of Saarbrücken, 2001

Feder, Georg, *Joseph Haydn: Die Schöpfung*, Kassel, 1999

Fleischman, Théo, *Napoléon et la musique*, Brussels, 1965

Floros, Constantin, *Beethovens Eroica und Prometheus-Musik: Sujet-Studien*, Wilhelmshaven, 1978

Fojtíková, Jana, and Tomislav Volek, "Die Beethoveniana der Lobkowitz-Musiksammlung und ihre Kopisten, *Beethoven und Böhmen*, ed. Sieghard Brandenburg and Martella Gutiérrez-Denhoff, Bonn, 1988, 219–58

Gandolfi, R., C. Cordara, and A. Bonaventura, *Catalogo delle opere musicali... Biblioteca del Conservatorio di Musica a Firenze*, Parma, 1929, repr. Bologna, 1977

Glossy, Karl, "Ein Gedenkblatt (Zur Erinnerung an die erste Aufführung von Beethovens 'Fidelio')," *Österreichische Rundschau* 5 (1905–6), 131–3

Goldschmidt, Harry, "Beethoven in neuen Brunsvik-Briefen," *Beethoven-Jahrbuch* 9 (1973–7), Bonn, 1977, 97–146

Green, Robert A., "Haydn's and Regnard's 'Il Distratto': A Re-examination," *Haydn Yearbook* 11 (1980), 183–95

Haas, Gerlinde, " 'Wunschtraum und Wirklichkeit': Korrigierende Notizen zu Leben und Werk der Josepha Müllner-Gollenhofer," *Studien zur Musikwissenschaft* 44 (1995), 289–302.

Haas, Robert, "Zur Wiener Ballettpantomime um den Prometheus," *Neues Beethoven-Jahrbuch* 2 (1925), 84–103

Haas, Robert, "Josef Leopold Edler von Eybler," *Mozart-Jahrbuch* 1952, 61–4

Hajós, Géza, *Romantische Gärten der Aufklärung: Englische Landschaftskultur des 18. Jahrhunderts in und um Wien*, Vienna, 1989

Heartz, Daniel, *Haydn, Mozart, and the Viennese School, 1740–1780*, New York, 1995

Herrmann, Hildegard, *Thematisches Verzeichnis der Werke von Joseph Eybler*, Munich, 1976

Holschneider, Andreas, "Die musikalische Bibliothek Gottfried van Swietens," *Bericht über den Internationalen musikwissenschaftlichen Kongress, Kassel, 1962*, ed. Georg Reichert and Martin Just, Kassel, 1963, 174–8

Jacobs, Helmut C., *Literatur, Musik und Gesellschaft in Italien und Österreich in der Epoche Napoleons und der Restauration: Studien zu Giuseppe Carpani (1751–1825)*, 2 vols., Frankfurt, 1988

Jancik, Hans, *Michael Haydn: Ein vergessener Meister*, Vienna, 1952

Joseph Haydn in seiner Zeit, exhibition catalogue, Eisenstadt, 1982

Kinderman, William, *Beethoven*, Berkeley, 1995

Kirkendale, Warren, "More Slow Introductions by W. A. Mozart to Fugues of J. S. Bach?" *Journal of the American Musicological Society* 17 (1964), 43–65

Kirkendale, Warren, *Fuge und Fugato in der Kammermusik des Rokoko und der Klassik*, Tutzing, 1966

Kirkendale, Warren, *Fugue and Fugato in Rococo and Classical Chamber Music*, 2nd ed., Durham, NC, 1979

Kobuch, Agatha, "Ferdinando Paer in Dresden," *Die Dresdner Oper im 19. Jahrhundert*, ed. Michael Heinemann and Hans John, Laaber, 1995, 35–41

Köchel, Ludwig, *Die kaiserliche Hof-Musikkapelle in Wien von 1543 bis 1867*, Vienna, 1869

Landon, H. C. Robbins, *Haydn: Chronicle and Works*, 5 vols., London, 1976–80

Langsam, Walter, *Francis the Good*, New York, 1949

LaRue, Jan, "A 'Hail and Farewell' Quodlibet Symphony," *Music & Letters* 37 (1956), 250–9

Longyear, R. M., "Ferdinand Kauer's Percussion Enterprises," *Galpin Society Journal* 27 (1974), 2–8

Lühning, Helga, "Florestans Kerker in Rampenlicht: Zur Tradition des Sotterraneo," *Beethoven zwischen Revolution und Restauration*, ed. Helga Lühning and Sieghard Brandenburg, Bonn, 1989, 137–204

Macek, Jaroslav, "Franz Joseph Maximilian Lobkowitz: Musikfreund und Kunstmäzen," *Beethoven und Böhmen*, ed. Sieghard Brandenburg and Martella Gutiérrez-Denhoff, Bonn, 1988, 147–201

Macek, Jaroslav, "Die Musik bei den Lobkowicz," *Ludwig van Beethoven im Herzen Europas*, ed. Oldřich Pulkert and Hans-Werner Küthen, Prague, 2000, 172–216

MacIntyre, Bruce C., *Haydn, The Creation*, New York, 1998

Maehder, Jürgen, "'Der Kerker eine Gruft': Zum Orchesterklang in den Kerkerszenen der *Leonore*-Opern," program book of the Salzburg Festival, 1996, 92–115

Mahling, Christoph-Hellmut, "Original und Parodie: Zu Georg Bendas *Medea und Jason* und Paul Wranitzkys *Medea*," *Untersuchungen zu Musikbeziehungen zwischen Mannheim, Böhmen und Mähren im späten 18. und frühen 19. Jahrhundert*, ed. Christine Heyter-Rauland and Christoph-Hellmut Mahling, Mainz, 1993, 244–95

McGrann, Jeremiah W., "Of Saints, Name Days, and Turks: Some Background on Haydn's Masses Written for Prince Nikolaus II Esterházy," *Journal of Musicological Research* 17 (1998), 195–210

Morrow, Mary Sue, *Concert Life in Haydn's Vienna: Aspects of a Developing Musical and Social Institution*, Stuyvesant, N.Y., 1989

Münster, Robert, "Wer ist der Komponist der 'Kindersinfonie'?" *Acta Mozartiana* 16 (1969), 76–82

Pesendorfer, Franz, *Ein Kampf um die Toskana: Großherzog Ferdinand III, 1790–1824*, Vienna, 1984

Pfannhauser, Karl, "Glossarien zu Haydns Kirchenmusik," *Joseph Haydn: Bericht über den Internationalen Joseph Haydn Kongress*, ed. Eva Badura-Skoda, Munich, 1985, 496–501

Pohl, Carl Ferdinand, *Denkschrift aus Anlass des hundertjährigen Bestehens der Tonkünstler-Societät*, Vienna, 1871

Poštolka, Milan, "Thematisches Verzeichnis der Sinfonien Pavel Vranickys," *Miscellanea musicologica* 20 (1967), 101–27

Quetin, Laurine, "*Die Entführung der Prinzessin Europa, oder So geht es im Olymp zu!*: Un Divertissement burlesque à Vienne en 1816," *D'Europe à l'Europe II: Mythe et identité du XIXe siècle à nos jours*, ed. Rémy Poignault *et al.*, Tours, 2000, 41–54

Reichenberger, Theresa, *Joseph Weigls italienische Opern*, dissertation, University of Vienna, 1983

Rice, John A., "Sense, Sensibility, and Opera Seria: An Epistolary Debate," *Studi musicali* 15 (1986), 101–38

Rice, John A., *Emperor and Impresario: Leopold II and the Transformation of Viennese Musical Theater, 1790–1792*, Ph.D. dissertation, University of California, Berkeley, 1987

Rice, John A., "Stein's 'Favorite Instrument': A Vis-à-vis Piano-Harpsichord in Naples," *Journal of the American Musical Instrument Society* 21 (1995), 30–64

Rice, John A., "The Musical Bee: References to Mozart and Cherubini in Hummel's 'New Year' Concerto," *Music and Letters* 77 (1996), 401–24

Rice, John A., *Antonio Salieri and Viennese Opera*, Chicago, 1998

Riehl, Wilhelm Heinrich, *Musikalische Charakterköpfe*, 7th ed., 2 vols., Stuttgart, 1899

Robinson, Michael F., *Giovanni Paisiello: A Thematic Catalogue of His Works*, 2 vols., Stuyvesant, NY, 1991

Rommel, Otto, *Die alt-Wiener Volkskomödie*, Vienna, 1952

Schaumberg, Uta, *Die opere serie Giovanni Simone Mayrs*, 2 vols., Munich, 2001

Schiedermair, Ludwig, *Beiträge zur Geschichte der Oper um die Wende des 18. und 19. Jahrh.*, 2 vols., Leipzig, 1907–10

Schmid, Ernst Fritz, "Die Privatmusikaliensammlung des Kaisers Franz II. und ihre Wiederentdeckung in Graz im Jahre 1933," *Österreichische Musikzeitschrift* 25 (1970), 596–9

Schmidt, August, *Denksteine*, Vienna, 1848

Schnürl, Karl, "Haydns 'Schöpfung' als Messe," *Studien zur Musikwissenschaft* 25 (1962), 463–74

Schröder, Dorothea, *Die geistlichen Vokalkompositionen Johann Georg Albrechtsbergers*, 2 vols., Hamburg, 1987

Senigl, Johanna, "Neues zu Joseph Eybler," *De editione musices: Festschrift Gerhard Croll zum 65. Geburtstag*, ed. Wolfgang Gratzer and Andrea Lindmayr, Laaber, 1992, 329–37

Shaheen, Ronald T., *Neoclassic Influences in the Two Versions of Giovanni Simone Mayr's Lodoiska*, Ph.D. dissertation, University of California, Los Angeles, 1996

Shaheen, Ronald T., "Mayr's Revised *Lodoiska* as an Example of Stylistic Transition," *Johann Simon Mayr und Venedig*, ed. Franz Hauk and Iris Winkler, Munich, 1999, 195–210

Sherman, Charles H., *The Masses of Johann Michael Haydn: A Critical Survey of Sources*, Ph.D. dissertation, University of Michigan, 1967

Sherman, Charles H., and T. Donley Thomas, *Johann Michael Haydn (1737–1806): A Chronological Thematic Catalogue of His Works*, Stuyvesant, NY, 1993

Sisman, Elaine R., "Haydn's Theater Symphonies," *Journal of the American Musicological Society* 43 (1990), 292–352

Smither, Howard E., *A History of the Oratorio*, 4 vols., Chapel Hill, NC, 1977–2000

Solomon, Maynard, *Beethoven*, New York, 1977

Somfai, László, "Albrechtsberger-Eigenschriften in der Nationalbibliothek Széchényi, Budapest," *Studia Musicologica Academiae Scientiarum Hungaricae* 1 (1961), 175–202, 4 (1963), 179–90, 9 (1967), 191–220

Thayer, Alexander Wheelock, *Life of Beethoven*, ed. Elliot Forbes, Princeton, NJ, 1967

Volek, Tomislav, and Jaroslav Macek, "Beethoven's Rehearsals at the Lobkowitz's," *Musical Times* 127 (1986), 75–80

Volek, Tomislav, and Jaroslav Macek, "Beethoven und Fürst Lobkowitz," *Beethoven und Böhmen*, ed. Sieghard Brandenburg and Martella Gutiérrez-Denhoff, Bonn, 1988, 203–17

Wangermann, Ernst, *From Joseph II to the Jacobin Trials*, Oxford, 1959

Will, Richard, *The Characteristic Symphony in the Age of Haydn and Beethoven*, Cambridge, 2002

Wertheimer, Eduard, *Die drei ersten Frauen des Kaisers Franz*, Leipzig, 1893

Wheelock, Gretchen, *Haydn's Ingenious Jesting with Art: Contexts of Musical Wit and Humor*, New York, 1992

Wolfsgruber, Cölestin, *Franz I. Kaiser von Oesterreich*, 2 vols., Vienna, 1899

Wurzbach, Constant, *Biographisches Lexikon des Kaiserthums Oesterreich*, 60 vols., Vienna, 1856–91

Zaubertöne: Mozart in Wien, 1781–1791, exhibition catalogue, Vienna, 1990

Index

369

ratchet, 146, 150
Rathmayer, Mathias, 62–63, 122, 236, 318
  in MT's private concerts, 63, 77, 93,
    171–172, 184, 207, 279–309, 315
Redoutensaal
  Grosser, 62, 171, 174, 175, 176, 178, 211,
    280, 319, 342
  Kleiner, 279, 342
Regnard, Jean-François, *Le distrait*, 244
rehearsal, 1, 115, 119, 168, 173, 214, 224,
  312
Reicha, Anton, 4, 59, 69, 234
  Argene regina di Granata, 234
  L'Ouragan, 234
requiem, 41, 98
rescue opera
  early articulation of the idea of, 194
  MT's interest in, 11, 254
Resik (two instrumentalists), 289
Rettensteiner, Werigand, 198, 270
Reutter, Georg, 41, 101
  "Tu de vita," 276, 303
  Mass in C, 262, 276, 293, 303
  Missa S. Ignatii, 303
  Requiem, 41, 276
  Te Deum, 101, 295
Riccardi Paer, Francesca, 176, 281, 311, 312,
  313, 315, 321, 335, 338, 342, 343, 344,
  345, 346, 347, 348
Richter, Joseph, 109, 155
  Eipeldauer Briefe, 109, 176
  Kinder sollen Kinder seyn, 143–145, 155
  as recipient of gifts from MT, 109
  Die travestirte Alceste, 154
  Das Urtheil des Paris travestirt, 154
Riffel (medical doctor), 312
Righini, Vincenzo, 18
  aria for bass, 171, 172
  L'incontro inaspettato, 18
  "Pensa," 300
  Mass, 276
Rispoli, Salvatore
  aria with horn obbligato, 174
  Nitteti, 60
Ritorni, Carlo, 249
Robinson, Michael F., 188
Rochlitz, Johann Friedrich, 100
Rodel, 146–147, 150
Romagnoli, Ettore, Psalms 45 and 46, 1,
  173–174
Rome, 322, 324, 325, 326, 328–330
  Teatro Valle, 322
Rong, Wilhelm, *Volks-Freude*, 22
Rosellini (secretary to Grand Duke Ferdinand),
  183

Rosenbaum, Joseph Carl, 62, 118, 122, 127,
  173
Rosenbaum, Therese (née Gassmann), 56, 62,
  118–119, 122, 172, 173, 174, 220
Rossetti, Domenico, 331
Rossi, Gaetano, *L'amor coniugale*, 256
Roudnice (Raudnitz), 327
Rudolph, Archduke, xviii, 48
Rummel, Sigismund, 18
Rusiczka, Joseph, 304
Russian dance, 124

Saal, Ignaz, 56, 57, 60, 168, 173, 178, 210, 236
Saal, Therese, 172
Sacchini, Antonio, *Il finto pazzo per amore*, 21
St. Stephan's Cathedral, 260
Sala, Emilio, 24
Salieri, Antonio, 2, 4, 54, 177, 203, 233, 252,
  316, 319
  as president of the *Tonkünstler-Sozietät*, 173,
    176, 318
  rewarded by MT, 206
  Works
  Annibale in Capua, 299; aria for soprano
    with chorus, 308; aria for tenor with
    chorus, 308; chorus, 308; duet, 71, 308;
    trio, 308
  Axur re d'Ormus, 20, 59, 207; "Dove andò
    quel maschio ardire," 207; "Non partir, la
    scelta è ingiusta," 283
  Il barone di Rocca Antica, 21
  Cesare in Farmacusa, "Disciolto qual pria,"
    286; finale of act 1, 286
  La cifra, 20
  La fiera di Venezia, 21
  Gesù al Limbo, 63, 206–209, 238, 308;
    "Dalla pietra del deserto," 207, 208; "Dio
    d'Abramo e di Giacobbe," 207; "Quando i
    beati istanti," 207; as sequel to *Die
    Schöpfung*, 206–207; "Sotto il giogo del
    peccato," 209
  La grotta di Trofonio, aria for bass, 293;
    melody varied by Brunner, 289; trio, 294
  La locandiera, 21
  Mass for double chorus, with gradual,
    offertory, and Te Deum, 52, 111
  Palmira regina di Persia, finale of act 1, 290;
    "Silenzio facciasi," 97, 104, 105, 138, 139,
    290
  Il pastor fido, 20
  Prima la musica e poi le parole, aria for
    soprano, 285
  Il ricco d'un giorno, 19
  La secchia rapita, 21
  Il talismano, 19